WILLIAM M. HOFFMAN is both an editor (three volumes of Hill and Wang's New American Plays series) and a playwright for stage, television, and radio. His plays, which include *Gilles de Rais, A Book of Etiquette, Thank You, Miss Victoria,* and *A Quick Nut Bread To Make Your Mouth Water,* have been seen on such stages as the Public Theater, the American Conservatory Theater, La Mama, the Long Wharf, and the Manhattan Theater Club. He has received a Guggenheim Fellowship and two National Endowment grants. He has lectured and taught at the Eugene O'Neill Foundation and the University of Massachusetts, and now lives in New York City where he is working on an opera libretto.

GAY PLAYS

The First Collection

Edited with an introduction by
WILLIAM M. HOFFMAN

A BARD BOOK/PUBLISHED BY AVON BOOKS

GAY PLAYS, THE FIRST COLLECTION is an original
publication of Avon Books. This work has never before
appeared in book form.

AVON BOOKS
A division of
The Hearst Corporation
959 Eighth Avenue
New York, New York 10019

First Bard Printing, February, 1979

BARD TRADEMARK REG. U.S. PAT. OFF. AND IN
OTHER COUNTRIES, MARCA REGISTRADA, HECHO EN
U.S.A.

Printed in the U.S.A.

CONTENTS

INTRODUCTION
William M. Hoffman

Definitions

The curtain opens on Act I, Scene I, of *The Street: A Panorama of Human Life*, a deeply symbolic work that closed in out-of-town tryouts—let's say Atlantic City—in 1921. The author's aim was to portray "the complete spectrum of human society."

So we see a slum street in a big city, in the midst of which stands a luxury apartment building. As the sun sets over a nearby river, a tired but happy-go-lucky Negro maid meets her garishly dressed boyfriend. At the opposite side of the stage, Tony, an Italian pushcart peddler is selling cherries to the neighborhood people fanning themselves on stoops.

A tramp and a reeling drunk almost upset the pushcart with their antics. Officer O'Reilly, twirling his nightstick, tells them, "Get on with ye!" He pockets a handful of cherries as he inquires about Tony's wife and bambinos. We hear a loud "yoo-hoo" from Mrs. Pearlstein, who is leaning out of her tenement window. She's calling for her son Irving, so that he should stop playing stickball and come in and practice the violin.

Enter two slit-skirted hookers who are the scandal of the neighborhood but the delight of the audience with their hennaed hair and uninhibited behavior. They are pursued by two sailors on shore leave. The women exit flirting.

As a paper moon rises over the now-quiet cityscape enter Ralph, the poor-boy hero from one of the slum buildings, and Mary, his girlfriend, escaping from her family's duplex next door. Two comical old women observe them knowingly. The audience quickly realizes that Ralph and Mary are the central figures of *The Street*. The exposition can now begin.

Something is missing from this picture that purports to be "A Panorama of Human Life." The author originally intended to have two mincing, rouged pansies following the sailors following the hookers, but the producer said to the author, "Kid, nix on the fairies. This ain't vaudeville. It's a drama of human life." And the scared young homosexual writer gave in. That night his lover Frank said, "I told you you'd never get away with it."

In the late 1970s the grandchildren of these stock characters dominate the American stage (and all forms of entertainment). The Negro maid and her boyfriend have become black heroes and heroines, and play to packed houses on Broadway. Thanks to Eugene O'Neill, the drunk has for fifty years dominated heavy drama. The tramp has been transformed into a sort of holy fool (via Charlie Chaplin), and his descendants are the most popular figures of all: Woody Allen, Lucille Ball, Carol Burnett. The heirs of Tony's pushcart enjoy unprecedented popularity as sexy romantic heroes: Al Pacino, Ben Gazzara, and John Travolta. Mrs. Pearlstein's grandchildren now play in Neil Simon comedies. It is now possible for Jews to play any character and still retain their Jewish qualities: Barbra Streisand, Eli Wallach, Elliott Gould.

But what about the gays who never made it to the stage? Sometimes you can see them in full-faggot stereotype as hysterical hairdressers, swishy interior decorators, and sexless male confidants, but rarely, and only recently, in their full human complexity. And lesbians? How many do you see portrayed onstage? While servile blacks, Italian peddlers, and miserly Jews have disappeared from the theater, it is still permissible to misrepresent or avoid representing gays. There is a gap in stage portraiture of homosexuals. The purpose of this collection of plays is to show some of what there is of portrayal—serious and comic—of this missing group of people in the panorama of human life.

I define a "gay play" as one whose central figure or figures are homosexual or one in which homosexuality is a main theme. A gay play is *not* necessarily written by a homosexual or for homosexuals. We need the category of "gay play" because of heterosexual hatred, fear, and ignorance—as well as homosexual acquiescence to heterosexual oppression. One can argue endlessly about definitions of a gay play, or even its existence. Good plays transcend their subject matter. *The Cherry Orchard* is more than a Russian play. *Ghosts* is more than a heterosexual play. Chekhov and Strindberg are more than Russian and straight—and the plays in this collection are more than gay, but in order to transcend subject matter you must first deal with particulars. The particulars in this collection of plays are gay.

The reader will notice that pro-homosexual propaganda plays have been avoided in this anthology. Occasionally political propaganda makes good drama. Aeschylus' *Oresteia* was motivated in part by a desire to justify the actions of Pericles, an Athenian politician. And Bertolt Brecht claimed he was a Communist. And Shaw certainly believed in the power of his ideas. But plays usually instruct only incidentally. Plays generally result from a desire to tell a story on a stage, to illuminate a character. Propaganda generally preaches to the converted and is useful to buck up the spirits of a minority or to justify actions already taken by a majority. Sometimes these are worthy goals but promulgating an idea is not often conducive to good writing.

There is an important distinction between "gay plays" and "gay theater." While the subject and the characters of a play will determine if a play is gay, the manner in which a play is acted and directed will determine if a production is "gay theater."

I define "gay theater" as a production that implicitly or explicitly acknowledges that there are homosexuals on both sides of the footlights. Gay theater winks, flirts, and looks at its audience in a certain way, as two homosexual strangers might at a party or a bar. How do homosexuals recognize each other? There are obvious and subtle clues.

ix

Yes, gay theater might include transvestism (but this is just as often a heterosexual theatrical device). Gay theater will certainly "camp," that is, emphasize style to such a degree that the style will become the subject matter. For example, if an actor plays a man as hypermasculine there is a strong implication conveyed that the character is concerned with his masculine image.

But gay theater also loves fantasy, myth, and a particular juxtaposition of comic and tragic styles of performing. Gay theater is difficult to define but unmistakable to gays and knowledgeable straights. Absolutely any play can be performed gay. Thus I have not included examples of gay theater in this book because it is a manner and not a subject. The gay theatrical style is appropriate to only some of the plays in *Gay Plays*.

Of the eight plays in this anthology only three are about lesbians. This imbalance reflects the fact that there are very few plays about lesbians. This is probably so because the people most likely to write about them are women, and female playwrights, gay and straight, are rare. Until recently playwriting was an almost all-male profession. A bias against women in this field is still strong. Since being a female playwright can count as one strike against them to begin with, lesbians are understandably leery of provoking a second strike by writing about their own group. Also, since many lesbians identify themselves as feminists first, they often put their energies into materials that concern the straight majority of women.

The following account by Jane Chambers of the difficulties she encountered mounting her play, *A Late Snow*, helps explain the paucity of lesbian material—and the special problems that gay plays face in general.

A Late Snow was originally written as a screenplay but I was advised by the agent who was handling my work to discard the piece. "Nobody's going to buy a movie script about lesbians," he said. "Why not?" I countered. "They're doing *The Boys in the Band*." "Fags are funny, dykes are gloomy," was his response.

In 1974 Bob Moss at Playwrights Horizons in New York asked me to submit a new play to him. I had two plays currently running off-off-Broadway at the time and hadn't written a new one. I pulled *A Late Snow* out of my files and rewrote it for the stage. Bob read it, scheduled a production time, and introduced me to director Nyla Lyon. Both Bob and Nyla felt the piece needed heavy rewriting and very careful casting. I agreed on both points. As I returned to the typewriter, Nyla began three arduous weeks of auditions. Both Bob, Nyla, and I were amazed at the numbers of actresses who simply refused to read for the role of a lesbian—particularly since *A Late Snow* is such a conservative, conventional play. Among the actresses who did read (Nyla auditioned over a hundred for the roles), we had startling reactions. One broke into tears and bolted from the studio; another became literally speechless during the reading. Many fine and normally sensitive actresses approached the roles as though they were auditioning for the part of a lumberjack, though the script specifies that these are very ordinary looking and acting women. Midway into rehearsals, we lost one of our leads. She said she was just too self-conscious about it, she couldn't play a lesbian. The night before opening, we got a phone message from another cast member. She said she couldn't go through with it. She quit. Her boyfriend had convinced her that she'd never be hired for another television commercial if she appeared onstage in the part of a lesbian. (Not so. All five of the actresses who opened in *A Late Snow* appear frequently on TV.)

The day that the show opened our cast of troupers, who were by that time wholly and doggedly committed to the show, rehearsed all day to break in our last-minute newcomer. We opened that night to a packed house and had a splendid ensemble performance. . . .

I've had a number of plays produced. I've written plays about old people, about handicapped people, about drug users and revolutionists—and never have I encountered the kind of production problems that

harassed *A Late Snow*. Hysterical actresses, abrasive-
ness and short tempers in the crew; even the printer
who did the program was hostile. I sincerely believe
that it was the subject matter of the play that threw
everybody into such a frenzy. Whatever, during the
production of *A Late Snow*, I felt frequently as though
I was trapped in a hideous nightmare. Then we opened.
Word of mouth spread fast, and we played to over-
flowing houses. We were a hit, we were accepted, we
were loved. Suddenly the cast and crew adored each
other. The production ran like clockwork, everything
backstage was peachy-keen. Although many of our
cast and crew were heterosexual, it was as though the
whole production "came out of the closet." Once the
audience showed that it loved us, whatever we were,
we were free to love each other and ourselves. . . .

Closing night we turned away fifty people. I remember standing by the exit and hearing a couple
leave the theater, chatting about the play. "I like it,"
the middle-aged man said firmly. "I love happy end-
ings when the boy and the girl go off together into the
sunset." "But that wasn't a boy and girl," the wife
protested, "it was *two women*." "Who cares?" her
husband shrugged. "They were happy, they were in
love."

The play was optioned for possible Broadway production, then dropped six months later. "I can't get
backers interested in a play about lesbians," the producer told me.

I have chosen not to include plays written in languages
other than English, and in the following section of the
Introduction I deal mostly with the English-speaking world.
Foreign materials are not inferior, but I feel that the
present collection, the first of its kind in America, should
start with materials closest to home. Future anthologies
should certainly include gay plays of various origins.

A note about the word "gay": I don't particularly like
it. But for the moment we are stuck with it. "Homosexual,"

while accurate, is long and somewhat clinical sounding. "Faggot" seems like the word "nigger" to me. It is colloquial, though, and permissible between homosexuals who don't mind the word and know each other well. So what else are we left with but "gay"? At least it's short and comprehensible and nonderogatory.

Dislike of the word "gay" can mask a fear of being identified with homosexuals or a dislike of them. One playwright declined to have his play presented in this book solely because I used the word "gay" in the title. And on similar grounds I was refused permission to reprint four magnificent lines of Edna St. Vincent Millay (see page 474 of her *Collected Poems*, "But tell the bishops . . .") as an epigraph to *Gay Plays*.

So, while I'm mildly unhappy with the term, I recognize a political fact of life in it.

History

That homosexuality was accepted by the Greeks and the Romans is not evident from what has come down to us of their drama. There are a few references in their plays that managed to escape Christian expurgation and bowdlerization. Aristophanes makes fun of homosexual contemporaries in *The Thesmophoriazusae* and *The Wasps*. There are several jokes about gay behavior in the Roman playwright Plautus. Aeschylus in *Laius* and Euripides in *Chrysippus* apparently described homosexual love affairs, but their plays have not survived.

It was not until 1591 in the first presentation of Christopher Marlowe's *Edward II* that a homosexual character was portrayed in a major role. In this context of silence *Edward II* must be seen as a landmark of free expression. Here in a play about a male homosexual, a king of England in the fourteenth century, described by Marlowe two centuries later, we have a rare glimpse into sophisticated social attitudes of the past. Edward is obsessively in love with Piers Gaveston. He is so taken with the young man that he neglects his duties of state, much as Antony did for the sake of Cleopatra. It is for Edward's neglect of duty, not for his sexual direction, that he is opposed and eventually deposed (and killed in a manner they thought appropriate as punishment for his particular brand of lust) by the nobles of the realm. This is made very clear in Act I, Scene IV, in the speech of the elder Mortimer:

> Thou seest by nature he is mild and calm.
> And seeing his mind so dotes on Gaveston,
> Let him without controlment have his will:
> The mightiest kings have had their minions—
> Great Alexander lov'd Hephestion;
> The conquering Hector for Hylas wept;
> And for Patroclus stern Achilles droop'd.
> And not kings only, but the wisest men—
> The Roman Tully lov'd Octavius;
> Grave Socrates, wild Alcibiades.
> Then let His Grace, whose youth is flexible
> And promiseth as much as we can wish,
> Freely enjoy that vain, light-headed earl,
> For riper years will wean him from such toys.

And young Mortimer's speech:

> Uncle, his wanton humour grieves not me.
> But this I scorn, that one so basely born
> Should by his sovereign's favour grow so pert
> And riot it with the treasure of the realm
> While soldiers mutiny for want of pay.

So, in the first play in England about a homosexual, homosexuality is viewed without alarm and forms merely the background of a particular character. Centuries pass before such equanimity arises again.

There are, however, references before and after Marlowe to gays. In *The Killing of Abel* of the fourteenth century and among the earliest mystery plays written in English, there are obscene puns about Cain's behavior with Abel, the Devil, and his "boye" Garcio. In "closet drama," that is, plays intended for the reading public, little of which has survived, there are references to gays. In a farce called *Sodom: or, The Quintessence of Debauchery*, written in rhyming couplets by John Wilmot, the Earl of Rochester, and published posthumously in Amsterdam in 1660, we have a wonderful obscene gay vision.

It is often thought that William Shakespeare was homosexual since his love sonnets were dedicated and addressed to a man. Actually we do not know for sure what his proclivities were. Oscar Wilde, in his fascinating short story, *The Portrait of Mr. W. H.*, toyed with the idea that the W. H. of the sonnets was an actor in Shakespeare's company who specialized in portraying women (women in Shakespeare's time were played by boys or young men).

There are a number of references to homosexuality in Shakespeare, namely in *Twelfth Night*, *As You Like It*, *Antony and Cleopatra*, and *Troilus and Cressida*. And certainly the humor in much of his romantic comedy, where transvestism runs rampant, has an element of implied or denied homosexuality. It was not until the twentieth century that homosexuality was again treated with even the minor measure of freedom enjoyed in Shakespeare's works.

But what about Oscar Wilde? Wilde was gay, but he never wrote a gay play. If he had wanted to, it would never have been allowed on the boards. *Salomé*, banned by the Lord Chamberlain, was first performed in France. Certainly there are careful gay references in Wilde's dramatic work. In *The Importance of Being Earnest* Algernon Moncrieff and John Worthing might be viewed as secret homosexuals —Algernon calls his sexual adventurism "Bunburying." And the play does contain a possible reference to gays in Gwendolen's speech: "The home seems to me to be the proper sphere for the man. And certainly once a man begins to neglect his domestic duties he becomes painfully effeminate, does he not? And I don't like that. It makes men so very attractive."

While "effeminate" is not synonymous with homosexual, in nineteenth-century London (as well as in twentieth-century America), the adjective certainly connoted gay to many people.

Incidentally, it is ironic that Wilde's outrageous public stance and sense of humor, now considered the model of homosexual sensibility, were quite consciously modeled on that of James Abbott McNeill Whistler, the American ex-patriate painter. Whistler was heterosexual. Both Whistler's and Wilde's behavior were, in part, tactics of survival in an indifferent and conservative London.

So, after *Edward II*, the next landmark in gay plays in English is Mae West's *The Drag*. I will deal at some length with this astonishing work because it seems to be the first modern gay play.

As far as I know, the only copy outside of Miss West's possession is a manuscript in the Library of Congress (page 15 is missing). It was written by West under the pseudonym Jane Mast and played in 1927 in Bridgeport, Connecticut. (When West tried to bring it to New York, where her notorious *Sex* was playing, permission was denied by city officials. Although *Sex* is most often cited as the reason the actress/playwright was jailed in 1927, *The Drag* probably made a contribution.)

The story of *The Drag* is as follows: Rollo Kingsbury, the son of the well-known and conservative Judge Kingsbury, is gay. In an attempt to escape his homosexuality he has married Clair Richmond, the daughter of a Dr. Richmond, who has taken an interest in sexual "diseases" such as homosexuality. Rollo, however, has driven his bride to distraction by his lack of attention, and by the time the play opens he has returned to his gay friends. Also he has fallen in love with Allen Grayson, the manager of his engineering company. Allen is straight—he is secretly in love with Clair. David Caldwell, described in the cast of characters as "an outcast," is Rollo's former lover. In the first act David comes to Dr. Richmond to be "cured," but we soon find out that the good doctor has no cure. In fact, in a fit of jealousy during the course of a drag party in the third act, David murders Rollo. Allen ends up with Clair, and Judge Kingsbury covers up the murder of his son by calling it a suicide. He doesn't want the family name besmirched.

Although the play was billed as "a homosexual comedy in three acts," it is in fact an *extremely* serious melodrama that borders on a plea for tolerance of homosexuals. *The Drag* contains long, intense intellectual discussions based on the most advanced contemporary scientific opinion (Ulrichs, Krafft-Ebing, and a smattering of Freud).

Sometimes the serious sections are unintentionally funny to a modern ear, but usually the characters ring true, especially when the gay people are talking among themselves. Gay slang seems to have changed little over the years and we come across such words as "rough trade," "gorgeous," "she" instead of "he," and other forms of gay banter.

In 1928 Mae West's *The Pleasure Man* opened at the Biltmore Theater in New York. The police raided it twice and finally closed it in the middle of the third performance.

Again West wrote about gays. Although the play's central figure is straight—*The Pleasure Man* concerns the comeuppance of a vaudeville Casanova—many of the characters are gay. In the backstage world that West portrays, gay is usually accepted. As in *The Drag*, the climax of the play takes place at a gay party. It is interesting that some of the dialogue duplicates that of *The Drag*, as if West was determined to make sure that New York audiences were going to hear what had been banned earlier.

1ST BOY: I hear you're working in a millinery shop.

2ND BOY: Yes, I trim rough sailors.

3RD BOY: My, what a low-cut gown you've got.

4TH BOY: Why, Beulah, a woman with a back like mine can be as low as she wants to be.

The following review of *The Pleasure Man* by Robert Littell in the *New York Evening Post* shows how shocking stage portrayals of homosexuality were to its contemporaries. These hysterical attitudes survive today but they are usually masked by a pseudo-pious religiosity or by quasi-scientific sociological and psychological jargon.

To the three tiresome and unspeakably slimy acts of *The Pleasure Man* the police, by arresting the entire cast, contributed a fourth, and even the most rabid opponent of official interference would find it hard to protest on this occasion. The bulk of Mae West's latest is feeble backstage melodrama. . . . If this were all, *The Pleasure Man* would die unnoticed in a few weeks. But it is smeared from beginning to end with such filth as cannot possibly be described in print, such filth as turns one's stomach even to remember. . . . Pretty nearly the most nauseating feature of the evening was the laughter of the audience, or at least that part of it which howled and snickered and let out degenerate shrieks from the balcony. If a first-night audience doesn't whistle or throw vegetables or leave the theatre . . . but laughs and laps it up there is no sense in taking the performers to the police station. The real culprits are on the other side of the footlights.

Shortly before the persecution of the Broadway works of Mae West, a French play on a lesbian theme, Edouard Bourdet's *The Captive*, was also closed by the New York police. Although the play was extremely negative to lesbianism, the subject itself was deemed unrespectable and dangerous.

In 1975 *The Pleasure Man* was published as a novel, with an introduction by Mae West that quotes one of the homophobic reviews. One might believe that the novel contains the same "scandalous" material that was in the play, but gay references have been removed and a spurious lesbian villainess has been added. (Permission to publish either play in this collection was not granted by Mae West.)

Perhaps we should ask what homosexual playwrights, directors, performers, and audiences were doing during the great Western silence on homosexuality.

Homosexuals in the theater probably did what we do nowadays, which is in theory a liberated period. They hid. We hide. There is a myth that gay people can lead openly gay lives in the theater, where everyone is supposed to be accepted on their merits. But the theater, of all art forms, is the closest mirror of society's expectations, and must, of all institutions, most reflect heterosexual hopes and prejudices. A happy ending to a play is still boy-gets-girl. And in the confusion that surrounds the mysteries of any kind of theatrical impersonation, society dictates that the impersonators must conform offstage to what is considered normal. Therefore, it is almost obligatory to appear straight in the public eye if you want to survive in the theater. These days there are some exceptions—namely Tennessee Williams' open confessions of homosexuality and an occasional minor performer's admitting to be "bisexual." But for the most part you can't be openly gay in the theater any more than you can in an automobile factory in Detroit. Backstage very few people *seem* to care, but at Sardi's or in the offices of the major producers it matters a great deal what your public image is.

Compounding the heterosexual hatred of gays in theater is the rabid homophobia of homosexuals themselves. Gays who are quite naturally terrified of being identified as gay often feel threatened by individuals who have "come out." They think that by associating with open gays they will be revealed as gay—guilt by association. Also, those who want to come out but are too frightened to do so feel guilty and jealous in the presence of people who are doing precisely what they would like to do. It is only the exceptional individual—straight or gay—who can deal with homosexuality with ease. The hatred and fear of gayness makes cowards of most of us.

The repression of homosexuality in the theater till the 1960s took the following forms, and is still operative to a lesser degree:

Silence. (Not having gay characters at all; not mentioning homosexuality.)

False accusation. (A character who is not homosexual is accused of it. The author can avoid handling the issue while seeming to deal with it.)

Stereotyping. (Gay characters, if male, are effeminate; if female, are masculine. Or gays are portrayed as "sensitive" or "special." Or gays are mentally disturbed. In all these cases it is the context that shows if repression is at work.)

Exploitation. (Using gays sensationally as local color.)

In the 1930s, silence was the predominant repressive

technique. But in Mordaunt Shairp's *The Green Bay Tree* (1933)* the stereotype of madness is used. In Lillian Hellman's *The Children's Hour* (1934) a child's false accusation of lesbianism causes two women to examine their relationship to see if it is true. Hellman did not use lesbianism as a red herring exactly, but the theme is explored with little lucidity.

It would be easy to accuse Tennessee Williams of having used all four repressive devices, but in the context of the forties and fifties, Williams' work is a breath of freedom. For example, in *A Streetcar Named Desire* (1947) the only homosexual is offstage and dead, and the man was disturbed and "special," but Williams goes beyond stereotyping in Blanche's famous speech about her husband:

He was a boy, just a boy, when I was a very young girl. When I was sixteen, I made the discovery— Love. All at once and much, much too completely. It was like you suddenly turned a blinding light on something that had always been half in shadow, that's how it struck the world for me. But I was unlucky. Deluded. There was something different about the boy, a nervousness, a softness and a tenderness which wasn't like a man's, although he wasn't the least bit effeminate looking—still that thing was there. . . . He came to me for help. I didn't know that. I didn't find out anything till after our marriage, when we'd run away and come back and all I knew was I'd failed him in some mysterious way and wasn't able to give the help he needed but couldn't speak of! He was in the quicksands and clutching at me—but I wasn't holding him out, I was slipping in with him! I didn't know that. I didn't know anything except I loved him unendurably but without being able to help him or help myself. Then I found out. In the worst of all possible ways. By coming suddenly into a room that I thought was empty—which wasn't empty, but had two people

* The dates in parentheses in this introduction are of first New York productions.

in it . . . the boy I had married and an older man who had been his friend for years. . . .

Afterwards we pretended that nothing had been discovered. Yes, the three of us drove out to Moon Lake Casino, very drunk and laughing all the way.

We danced the Varsouviana! Suddenly in the middle of the dance the boy I had married broke away from me and ran out of the casino. A few moments later—a shot!

I ran out—all did!—all ran and gathered about the terrible thing at the edge of the lake; I couldn't get near for the crowding. Then somebody caught my arm. "Don't get any closer! Come back! You don't want to see!" See? See what! Then I heard voices say—Allan! Allan! The Grey boy! He'd stuck the revolver into his mouth, and fired—so that the back of his head had been—blown away!

It was because—on the dance-floor—unable to stop myself—I'd suddenly said—"I saw! I know! You disgust me . . ." And then the searchlight which had been turned on the world was turned off again and never for one moment since has there been any light that's stronger than this—kitchen—candle. . . .

This is an accurate picture of the results of oppression on one gay man and his wife. The situation and characters are extreme, but homophobia *does* destroy. Williams recorded this faithfully and poetically.

Williams has been accused, falsely, of disguising his male characters as women. Williams was as outspoken as anyone could possibly have been in the forties and fifties and portrayed or mentioned homosexuals in many plays. His gays *are* gays. It is true that sometimes Williams was oblique, especially in *Cat on a Hot Tin Roof* (the relationship of Brick and Skipper), but few were as honest as Williams during that period.

He has not yet written a gay play—and perhaps never will—but in 1968, in the underrated *Confessional*, which is set in a mixed bar in California, he came close to it. Two of the central figures, the waitress Leona and The

Young Man talk about homosexuality at length. Their attitudes are rather negative, but then negative attitudes are common in Williams' work. The playwright has always been concerned mainly with the loss of innocence and faded hopes.

In the 1950s—Williams having helped clear a path for all playwrights—homosexuality became more easily mentionable in the English-speaking theater. Typical was Robert Anderson's *Tea and Sympathy* (1953), in which a "sensitive" young man is falsely accused of being homosexual. An older woman takes his virginity and thus proves his heterosexuality. A variation on that theme is used in Arthur Miller's *A View from the Bridge* (1955). Eddie accuses his rival in love, Rudolpho, of being gay in order to win the affections of his niece Katherine. Eddie goes so far as to kiss Rudolpho full on the mouth to prove his point.

Other plays used stereotypes of homosexuals to avoid portraying them in depth. We have two screaming queens in Wolcott Gibbs' *Season in the Sun* (1950); the "larvated homosexual" Emory of Maxwell Anderson's *The Bad Seed* (1954); the psychotic Apples of Michael Gazzo's *Hatful of Rain* (1955), who picks up homosexuals in subway men's rooms and then attacks them; and the murderous gays in Meyer Levin's fictionalized account of the Leopold-Loeb case, *Compulsion* (1957).

That most of the images of the fifties were negative was perhaps inevitable, considering the superstitions of the period. In retrospect the mere appearance of homosexuality as subject matter was a positive sign. In this period of repression, gay theatergoers interpreted two of John Van Druten's comedies of the forties and fifties, *The Voice of the Turtle* and *Bell, Book, and Candle*, as hidden gay plays. They saw the first as a disguised pickup situation involving a "straight" soldier, and the second, which is set in an imaginary witch-cult in New York, as a parable of gay underground life.

But starting in 1960 there were enough actual gay characters onstage in the United States that theater buffs could stop fantasizing. It was the year of Edward Albee's *Zoo*

Story, Gore Vidal's *The Best Man*, Shelagh Delaney's *A Taste of Honey*, and Brendan Behan's *The Hostage*.

How do we explain the surge of interest? Certainly it was to be expected after so many years of suppression, and there was the continuing liberating effect of Williams, but two new forces were also at work.

The first was John Osborne, England's Angry Young Man. His first outburst, *Look Back in Anger* (London, 1956), changed the British theater scene. His rage at the social system helped other playwrights of the period write about all aspects of British life, including homosexuality. While Osborne's first work did not touch on this subject, he later wrote about gays, most notably in *Inadmissible Evidence* (1964) and *A Patriot for Me* (1966), set in the homophobic world of the Austrian army before World War I.

In the beginning of the 1960s, Great Britain took the lead in gay portrayal, and American productions of British plays encouraged Americans to write more honestly. Most notable of these imports were *A Taste of Honey*, which contains the sympathetic portrait of Geoffrey, who is the gay best friend of the pregnant, abandoned heroine, and *The Hostage*, in which gays are shown on an absolutely equal—but zany—footing with all the other characters in this play about revolutionary Dublin.

The second liberating force was American—off-off-Broadway, which had begun in the late 1950s in lofts and coffee houses in New York. Joe Cino's Caffe Cino,* which opened late in 1958, was most important for gay plays. It is symbolic that among the Cino's first productions were *The Importance of Being Earnest* and plays by Williams.

Joe Cino became a play producer because many of his customers wanted to put on shows, and he and many of his customers were gay. Joe Cino did not have an obsession with homosexuality. He simply had an extraordinary largeness of spirit that allowed other people to explore, set other

---

* Robert Patrick's *Kennedy's Children* contains an excellent fictionalized account of the Caffe Cino, seen from an actor's point of view.

people aflame to express what they never had been allowed to before. So at the Cino we experimented with the theater in both straight and gay plays.

Oddly enough, most of us who worked there were only barely aware that writing about gays was unusual. We lived in a fairly enclosed world, perhaps a theatrical Garden of Eden, and thought little about the outside.

Both gay plays and gay theater were pioneered at the Cino from the beginning. Early productions can only be described as homosexual in style: a vivid, sexy *Deathwatch* (Jean Genet) and *Philoctetes* (André Gide). But pretty soon such writers as Doric Wilson, Claris Nelson, and David Starkweather wrote about characters who were specifically gay, closet gay, or bisexual. Their styles of production, while experimental, were not specifically gay. Among them were Doric Wilson's *And Now She Dances* (1961), an angry blast at the trial of Wilde, Claris Nelson's *The Clown* (1962), with its intimations of suppressed homosexuality, and David Starkweather's *You May Go Home Again* (1963), which though directly inspired by Japanese Noh drama in style, was about a prodigal gay son trying to come to terms with his family.

Lanford Wilson in 1964, after a number of plays on themes other than homosexuality, came to the fore with *The Madness of Lady Bright.* (The play is included in this volume.) It was one of off-off-Broadway's first big hits, and a landmark in gay plays. Also of major importance was Robert Patrick's *The Haunted Host* (1964), another fine, explicit portrait of a gay.

H. M. Koutoukas' shows were theatrically gay but rarely concerned with homosexuality. A typical play was a drag *Medea* (1965) set in a laundromat. Similarly, Tom Eyen's work, especially *Why Hannah's Skirt Won't Stay Down* (1965), although making frequent references to homosexuals, was gay more in presentation than content.

The culmination of gay theater, as opposed to gay plays, at the Cino was *Dames at Sea* (1966), a musical by George Haimsohn, music by Jim Wise, directed by Robert Dahdah. It employed every conceivable movie musical plot of the thirties. The material was entirely heterosexual, but the presentation was campy and witty.

Other plays of note were Robert Heide's *The Bed* (1965) and *Moon* (1967), the latter with a gay portrayed as an angel or a saint (Heide had an important influence on Andy Warhol), and Jeff Weiss' play of homosexual agony, *A Funny Walk Home* (1967). There were many other writers at the Cino who affirmed in positive fashion the existence of gays.

Joe Cino died on April 2, 1967. He was thirty-six years old. The date was the first anniversary of the death of his lover, John Torre.

By the mid-sixties there were enough gay characters on New York stages—Broadway, off- and off-off-Broadway— to cause the latent homophobia of some critics to surface.

Wrote Howard Taubman of *The New York Times* in 1961 (Taubman was a pioneer homophobe):

> It is time to speak openly and candidly of the increasing influence and incidence of homosexuality on New York's stage. . . . It is noticeable when a male designer dresses the girls in a musical to make them unappealing. . . . It is apparent in a vagrant bit of nasty dialogue thrown into a show or in a redundant touch like two mannish females walking across the stage without a reason or a word of comment.

In 1963 Taubman continued in an article headlined, "Helpful Hints to Tell Appearance vs. Reality," also in *The Times*:

> Be on guard for the male character whose proclivities are like a stallion's. Beware the husband who hasn't touched his wife for years . . . look out for the baneful female who is a libel on womanhood . . . be alert to scabrous innuendo about the normal male-female relationship, particularly if the writer is not a filthy-minded hack.

William M. Hoffman

In 1965 Martin Gottfried wrote in *Women's Wear Daily*:

> A perfect example [of homosexual influence] is *Who's
> Afraid of Virginia Woolf?*, perhaps the most success-
> ful homosexual play ever produced on Broadway. If
> its sexual core had been evident to more people it
> probably never would have run—even though it is
> perfectly exciting theater (although basically dis-
> honest).

Apart from the nonsense about gays ruining the appearance of chorus girls, the critics were mainly gunning for
Tennessee Williams and Edward Albee. Since neither author
disguised references to gays, one wonders why. Perhaps it
was because both playwrights were alert to sexual stereotyping and both portrayed powerful—if failed—women.

It is ironic to talk about Edward Albee as a playwright
of gay plays when he has said so little on the subject. The
theme of homosexuality is in the background of *Zoo
Story* and is evident in two of Albee's adaptations, *The
Ballad of the Sad Café* (from Carson McCullers) and
Malcolm (from James Purdy), but Albee, in most of his
work, is not particularly interested in gay characters.

Whatever the critics were saying in the 1960s, play-
wrights were writing with greater frequency about gays.
An important example of fair treatment was Lorraine
Hansberry's *The Sign in Sidney Brustein's Window* (1964).
In a speech delivered by a straight writer to a gay, Hans-
berry wrote prophetically:

> If somebody insults you—sock 'em in the jaw. If you
> don't like the sex laws, attack them. . . . You wanna
> get a petition? I'll sign one. . . . But, David, please
> get over the notion that your particular sexuality is
> something that only the deepest, saddest, the most
> nobly tortured can know about. It ain't—it's just one
> kind of sex—that's all. And, in my opinion—the uni-
> verse turns regardless.

And in 1967 there was a major exploration of homosexuality in prisons, Canadian playwright John Herbert's *Fortune and Men's Eyes*. The play illuminates the Darwinian world of caged men, where sex is usually an act of aggression or submission, and where love can kill.

The most famous of all gay plays of the sixties was Mart Crowley's *The Boys in the Band* (1967). With the exception of one character, all the people represented are male homosexuals. Although the play is often criticized for presenting gays in the worst possible light, *The Boys in the Band* can also be read as an indictment of homosexual self-hatred. In Harold's words to Michael:

> You are a sad and pathetic man. You're a homosexual and you don't want to be. But there is nothing you can do to change it. Not all the prayers to your God, not all the analysis you can buy in all the years you've got left to live. You may very well one day be able to know a heterosexual life if you want it desperately enough . . . but you will always be homosexual as well. Always, Michael. Always. Until the day you die.

Yes, the play pleased gay-haters, and certainly the press treated it sensationally, but Mart Crowley cannot be faulted for expressing his vision of the homosexual underworld as he saw it. It is a depressing work, but the characters aren't stereotypes and the language is powerful and accurate. And whatever one thinks of it, *The Boys in the Band*, more than any other single play, publicized homosexuals as a minority group.

While Broadway produced gay plays and many works with gay characters, in the mid-sixties off-off-Broadway was more concerned with the gay theatrical style. At Al Carmines' Judson Poets Theater, where Gertrude Stein was patron saint, such writers as Rosalyn Drexler (her *Home Movies* premiered in 1964) and Ronald Tavel threw straight theatrical conceptions out the window. When

Tavel's *Gorilla Queen* opened in 1967 and the director, Larry Kornfeld, was criticized for having turned out a campy show, he replied, "Campy, hell! It's downright homosexual." And Carmines, whose directing and writing came to dominate the Judson Poets Theater, refined the gay style until it culminated in one of his best musicals, *The Faggot* (1973).

Experiments in gay theater directly influenced Broadway styles and international rock fashions of the sixties. Director John Vaccaro's work with the Playhouse of the Ridiculous, especially his revival of extravagant stage makeup, was imitated almost immediately. His influence can be seen in the stage style of David Bowie, Kiss, and Iggy Pop.

The Playhouse of the Ridiculous first featured the work of Ron Tavel. After Tavel and Vaccaro parted ways, Vaccaro directed Charles Ludlam's first play, *Big Hotel* (1967), and went on to direct his *Conquest of the Universe* (1967), which ended that collaboration in mid-production. Ludlam then founded the Ridiculous Theatrical Company, which played at various small spaces around New York, including a gay bar.

Tavel, Vaccaro, and Ludlam worked in similar veins at first and were influenced by each other's works. Tavel specializes in exquisite puns, movie allusions, and social commentary. Ludlam, an actor, director, and playwright, is a master of traditional styles—he combines the old ones to make new ones. And Vaccaro's talents lie in his judicious use of stereotyped characters in outrageous combinations. The three have diverged but all are masters of gay theater.

Rarely have any of the three emphasized homosexuals as characters because realistic portraiture of any sort is the forte of none of them. *Caprice* (1977) is Ludlam's only play dominated by a gay character. It is not one of his more successful pieces. Tavel's *The Ovens of Anita Orangejuice* (1978) attempts to convey the dangers of the Bryant mentality but bogs down in factual presentation.

But in Ludlam's *Camille*, which premiered in 1974, with Ludlam in the title role, we see gay theater at its best. Ludlam plays the heroine as a character, and we do not notice that he is a man playing a woman. What is most surprising in this sometimes over-the-brink travesty of the Dumas piece is that Ludlam has found a way to convey *Camille*'s pathos while not denying its camp and bathetic qualities. We laugh but we are touched.

The Stonewall riots of 1969 might be viewed as gay street theater. Led by tough, effeminate young men and tireless lesbians, who offered themselves as shock troops against waves of policemen so stiffened by their self-images of masculinity that they lacked flexibility, and backed by a motley cast of more ordinary gays and Greenwich Village housewives, homosexuals took command of the central section of one of New York's largest gay ghettoes.

I remember noticing how theatrically self-aware we were as we exploded the notion that gays were a pitiable, defenseless people. One man, using his dress as a matador uses his cape, goaded several policemen into behaving like bulls. They charged as he gracefully evaded them by slipping back into the gigantic crowd. By the third day of the riots people were dressing for the occasion, most often in a practical fashion, but sometimes with an eye to the media, which suddenly discovered us in our natural habitat.

A relatively new technique of homosexual repression followed the emergence of gays into the public spotlight: exploitation of gays as local color.

In Bruce Jay Friedman's *Steambath* (1970), which is set in a bathhouse, gays appear fleetingly in the background. In Betty Comden and Adolph Green's *Applause* (1970), the musical version of the movie *All About Eve*, a homosexual hairdresser is shown as best friend, and there is a scene in a gay bar, but no attempt is made at real gay characterization. Ron Clark's and Sam Bobrick's *Norman, Is That You?*, which opened in New York in 1970 and bombed, but which was successful almost everywhere else in America, was originally written as a comedy about an interreligious marriage then rewritten as an interracial marriage then finally reworked as an interracial homosexual ménage. Although ostensibly about the problems of coming out to one's parents, the play shows little knowledge of gay life and merely uses gays to sell tickets. The play is not maliciously antihomosexual but its patronizing tone offends.

The most notorious example of downplaying gays while seemingly portraying them is Terrence McNally's *The Ritz*. The original title was *The Tubs*, under which it played very successfully at the Yale University Repertory Theater in 1973–74. In this version the hero, Gaetano Proclo, is a middle-aged gay but married garbageman from Cleveland who has decided to have a last homosexual fling at a gay bathhouse. But in the great tradition of farces, he is pursued by his concerned, sympathetic wife and homophobic Mafioso brother-in-law. The production attempted to show a gay bathhouse with its odd mixture of Dionysian sensuality and sad treadmill qualities. When *The Ritz* opened on Broadway in 1975 the hero was no longer gay but a heterosexual who inadvertently enters a bathhouse. And the locale was brightened up and desensualized. These changes destroyed the play as authentic gay material. Both versions played well as farces but it is a shame that the play's gay qualities were eliminated.

In this period there were plays with gays in subsidiary roles that were not exploitative. In Lanford Wilson's hit, *The Hot l Baltimore* (1973), a lesbian had an important role.

In a burst of freedom in the late sixties and early seventies an enormous variety of gay materials found its way to the stage, ranging from Donald Brooks' *Xircus: The Private Life of Jesus Christ* (1971), where Jesus is a Times Square gay hustler who is killed in a sadomasochistic sex scene, to John Hopkins' distinguished play, *Find Your Way Home* (1974), which examines in almost Wagnerian language a triangle among a husband, his wife, and his male lover. (Incidentally, man gets man in this play. How times had changed!) Also in 1974 we had A. J. Kronengold's *Tubstrip*, a pornographic play set in a bathhouse, as well as Christopher Hampton's *Total Eclipse*, which centers on the love affair between Paul Verlaine and Arthur Rimbaud.

Off-off-Broadway, the gay political movement accelerated the development of a new kind of theater—gay plays for gay audiences. At first the plays were erotic sketches like Gus Weill's *Geese* (1969) and David Gaard's *And Puppy Dog Tails* (1969). But in 1972 Jonathan Katz's *Coming Out* was produced. It was a serious agitprop piece detailing the lives of gays in American history. (*Coming Out* stimulated one audience to go out en masse and demand that a local bar remove an anti-gay sign.)

By 1972 there was a specifically gay theater, TOSOS (The Other Side of Silence), founded by Doric Wilson, a graduate of the Caffe Cino. TOSOS' first production, the musical, *Lovers* (1973), by Peter del Valle and Steve Sterner, was a hit. Though Wilson premiered this and other shows, such as Sandra Scoppetone's *Home Again, Home Again, Jiggity-Jig* (1974) and Martin Sherman's *Passing By* (1975), he specialized in revivals of gay plays. The most successful production was an original, Doric Wilson's own *West Street Gang*, which, under the TOSOS aegis, opened in a gay bar, The Spike, in 1977.

The play dealt with a clear and present danger to members of that particular audience, who were being harassed and occasionally killed by savage youth gangs in the area. In Wilson's play a member of the gang is caught and held prisoner by some of the bar regulars. In seriocomic fashion the boy is put on trial by his victims. Various sentences are contemplated, until *dei ex machina* in the form of pro- and anti-homosexual leaders appear and provide their own inappropriate political solutions to the problem. The play appeals to straight audiences but was written for gays.

In 1976 another gay theater opened in New York, John Glines' Glines Theater. Its big hit has been the musical *Gulp!* (1977) by J. B. Hamilton, Stephen Greco, Scott Kingman, and Robin Jones, but the Glines has shown a great variety of materials, including works by Loretta Lotman, Emily Sisley, and Jim Ferguson. The most original plays were by Richard Hall, a theater critic and noted novelist. His first, *Love Match* (1977), explores why a movie on a gay theme was *not* made, and his second, *Prisoner of Love* (1977), concerns the illusions of an overly intent gay activist. Both plays are romantic comedies on serious themes, a genre notably lacking in gay plays.

Medusa's Revenge, which opened in 1976, is a theater group of and for gay women. It was started by Magaly Alabau and Ana Maria Simo. Its major work has been Simo's *Bayou* (1977).

Gay theater for gay audiences has not been confined to New York. In San Francisco the Gay Men's Theater Collective premiered in 1977 *Crimes Against Nature*, a group effort. The play relates the life histories of the cast in relationship to their oppression as homosexuals. This psychodramatic approach effectively traces back to their childhood roots the survival tactics of the gays involved. With its enormous gay population, San Francisco has a great deal of gay theatrical activity, including such groups as the Lavender Star Players and Rhinoceros, but most of the productions there are gayer in production style than content.

Other ambitious gay theaters and theater groups are Los Angeles' Theater of the Other Window and the Lambda Theater, Minneapolis' Out-and-About Theatre Company, and Rochester's Pink Satin Bombers. Gay theaters are a phenomenon of the 1970s.

By the late seventies most serious plays concerning gays were being produced away from Broadway. This was not —in most cases—a homophobic reaction of producers but a symptom of Broadway audiences' flight from serious material of any sort. There were, however, excellent, fair portrayals of gays on Broadway, most notably in James Kirkwood's and Nicholas Dante's *A Chorus Line* (1976) and Michael Christofer's *The Shadow Box* (1977). The former premiered at Manhattan's Public Theater and the latter in Los Angeles at the Mark Taper Forum. The gay action was *not* primarily on Broadway.

David Rabe's *Streamers* (1976), set in an army barracks during the Vietnam War, is a shattering portrait of homosexual passion and homophobic reaction. *Streamers* has often been misinterpreted as melodrama, but the play is one of those rarities, a tragedy.

Richie is a homosexual who has a crush on a barracks-mate, Billy, who consistently claims he is straight and resents Richie's advances and innuendos. Roger, the third roommate, a young sensible black, acts as mediator for the two. In order to win Billy's affections, Richie flirts with Carlyle, a dangerous psychopathic black from the ghetto, who eventually murders Billy and an older sergeant.

The details that distinguish *Streamers* from melodrama (and cliché) are telling. In a usual play, Billy would be a closet gay. In *Streamers* there is no indication whatever that Billy is anything but confused and disgusted by Richie. In melodrama Roger would be the straight with a heart of gold. In this play Roger is no more than tolerant of Richie. And Carlyle, in less skillful hands than Rabe's, would have been softened. But Rabe's Carlyle is a man totally out of control. He has no redeeming virtues. And in the portrait of Richie we have a self-indulgent gay youth. *Streamers* is a tragedy whose theme is that lust blinds, in the tradition of Phaedra, whose son Hippolytus is killed while fleeing her passion. Rabe's point of view is unfashionable, but the play is in no way antihomosexual.

The late seventies presented a variety of viewpoints on homosexuality, mostly positive. In this context Albert Innaurato's Broadway hit *Gemini* (1977) seems like a step backward. Set in inner-city Philadelphia among Italian-Americans, whose language and mannerisms Innaurato captures magnificently, the play is concerned with the passage to adulthood of Francis Geminiani. At the opening of the play we learn *he* thinks he's gay. By the middle, with the appearance of his college roommate and his sister, Francis is carrying on as if he's gay, but suddenly at the end of the play, for little reason at all, we learn that Francis will test his luck with the sister. The ending seems to hark back to the traditional boy-gets-girl formula and is a false note in what is otherwise a splendid evening. More interesting is Innaurato's *Earthworms* (1977), with its outrageous gays and hideous straights. The play is sprawling but fascinating and honest.

In María Irene Fornés' mysterious play about a group of women, *Fefu and Her Friends* (1977), two lesbian characters appear most casually and without fanfare. Set in the 1930s, and produced as environmental theater—the audience was asked to follow the action by moving from room to room with the actresses—the play falls easily into no category, though some have called it a feminist play.

Harvey Fierstein's *International Stud* (1978) is the story of a drag performer's love affair with a man who claims he's bisexual. The play's best scene is its most outrageous. In a masterful combination of pantomime and monologue, Fierstein, who is also an accomplished performer, shows exactly what goes on in the dark back rooms of some gay bars. The play, with all its brash talk, is surprisingly romantic. *International Stud* seems to criticize gay life as loveless.

One of the best developments of the freedom to write about gays is the way homosexual characters can now appear in almost any play. Brian and Mark in *The Shadow Box* are just two characters among eight. Their homosexuality, while distinctive, is not the central theme of this play about death and dying. And in Lanford Wilson's *The Fifth of July* (1978), whose subject is the fading of the hopes and ideals of the 1960s, the two gay lovers, Kenny and Jed, are totally accepted by their family and friends.

What is the future of gay plays in America? This can't be discussed apolitically because the tides of politics are eventually reflected as theatrical fashions.

America has always been of two minds about the behavior of its citizens. One faction has felt that people's conduct should be interfered with only when it infringes on the freedom of others. The second group has held, sometimes on religious grounds, sometimes following some economic or psychological theory or another, that our behavior, even when harmless, should be judged according to their private canons and labeled "immoral," "evil," "antisocial," or "sick." Note that these opposing factions cannot be conveniently labeled left and right, or even liberal and conservative.

Today the civil rights of homosexuals (and heterosexual

women) are being attacked in the name of religion and the old American virtues. Thus far the stage has resisted this bigotry, though some people, especially critics and producers, cling to neolithic notions. But it is not unimaginable that our present freedom to write about gays and to portray them might be reversed. The fight is not over by any means.

Let us suppose the forces of bigotry are defeated, or at least held at bay. Then I would expect some of the following:

1. The appearance on a major stage in a major play of a gay super-hero or -heroine (played by either a heterosexual or a homosexual).

2. More appearances of homosexuals as major characters in plays having nothing to do with homosexuality.

3. The further development of local gay theaters for gay audiences. Gays rarely support their own theaters and do not come to gay plays in mainstream theaters in the numbers that blacks and Jews do for material concerning them. This reflects the low self-esteem in which many gays hold themselves and their fear of being publicly gay.

4. More lesbian portrayals. This will come about if more women write for the theater and if lesbians demand to see themselves on stage.

5. The coming out, or "confession" of homosexuality, of at least one major male or female star of movies, television, or stage. This would encourage other gay performers to speak their minds. For actors, as far as gay rights are concerned, it might as well be 1940.

6. The stage exploration of gay history. The only gay historical figure who has been written about at any length is Oscar Wilde.* The public image of homosexuality lacks historical depth. To gay and straight people alike it often seems as if homosexuality is a political movement that was invented sometime in the sixties by radicals, rather than a mode of behavior that is as old as humanity and as ordinary or extraordinary as heterosexuality.

---

* Eric Bentley's *Lord Alfred's Lover,* published in 1978, is the most recent and one of the best plays that deals with Wilde.

William M. Hoffman

The Collection

T-Shirts

I have chosen to place *T-Shirts* first because I think it will give the reader a crash-course in what it's like to be a sophisticated gay man in any big city in America right now. Robert Patrick's play is a profound character study of three homosexuals in the cynical seventies. Though they are of different ages and outlooks, the three men face the same problems: how does one find love in an age that offers only sexual acts; how do you maintain a balanced idealism in a time that despises ideals; how do you stay off drugs and drink when life is painful? These issues concern everyone and are not particular to gay people. This is not a play in which homosexuality is a problem at all. Homosexuality is a given. Its theme is the new morality (or lack of it) of the 1970s. Though wildly funny and about three upbeat people, *T-Shirts* is profound social criticism.

Boy Meets Boy

One of the premises of *Boy Meets Boy*, the only musical in *Gay Plays*, is that homosexuality was totally accepted and presumed normal in the 1930s. Of course this was not true. But in the musical comedy fairyland of London and Paris in which the piece is set, it *ought* to have been true, and so, is. Gay as an issue is rightfully dismissed so that we can deal with the real issue of the musical: which man will end up with which man? *Boy Meets Boy* is utterly gay in all its connotations and presents no situation that cannot be solved by true love.

Confessions of a Female Disorder

The rite of passage has until recently been considered a male phenomenon. But women too pass from childhood to adolescence, from adolescence to adulthood. In this pattern, Ronnie, Susan Miller's heroine, journeys. She goes to high school, college, collects a husband almost as a prize. And there she is—married, with a child, but deeply unhappy. And now she must leave what is usually considered adulthood to become a person. Miller's play is a beautiful exploration of a woman's need to grow. As part of her growth Ronnie becomes a lesbian.

The Madness of Lady Bright

This one-act play is set in the mind of Leslie Bright. Leslie is a disintegrating middle-aged queen. He conforms in many ways to a gay stereotype: he is effeminate, promiscuous, haughty, affected, mad, sad, and lonely. He *is* representative of one kind of male homosexual. But Wilson's queen transcends the stereotype and all of the rest of the clichés by being so *individually* effeminate. He stands for any aging person who cannot come to terms with the facts of death. And therein lies this play's popularity and great beauty. We wish Leslie could get a grip on himself, and in our minds we beg him to, because we too know "that this way madness lies."

Entertaining Mr. Sloane

The characters of Joe Orton's play are utterly despicable. They are motivated only by greed and lust. Their intelligence is foxlike and they are vastly ignorant. Joe Orton took a dim view of pretensions to humane ideals. *Entertaining Mr. Sloane* is the author's perfect presentation of this point of view, which pervaded all his works. Ed lives in a macho fantasy world of "mates," schoolboy fantasies, and crude sadomasochism. The object of his affections, Sloane, is a bisexual male prostitute and murderer who uses both Ed and Ed's equally lecherous sister, Kath. This is not a play in which to look for confirmation of love. It presents a view of people as unredeemed beasts. We raise our hands in horror, as we do with Swift and Orwell. But often we *are* like that.

A Late Snow

This is a realistic romantic drama about lesbians, and is, as far as I know, unique. This is probably so because so few plays are written about lesbians and there are very few romantic dramas these days. None of Jane Chambers' characters feel that the concept of love is an illusion, and thus do not share in the cynicism of the seventies. *A Late*

Snow is also unusual in that all the characters are intelligent and do not suffer from that fashionable ailment of recent times, "lack of communication." Their desires may clash but they have no difficulty in expressing them. This is a passionate play about a passionate cross-section of lesbians.

The Killing of Sister George

This is probably the most famous play about lesbians ever written. Its tremendous reception was probably in part due to the fact that it deals with lesbian stereotypes. June Buckridge (Sister George) is a butch dyke. Her lover Alice (Childie) McNaught is "feminine" and seemingly yielding. But, as with *The Madness of Lady Bright*, this drama goes far beyond ordinary types into the realm of fine characterization, and is a study of a power struggle among women. The play was written by a man, of course, which only goes to show what we all know anyhow: anyone can write a gay play. Perhaps in order to confound matters thoroughly I should go back to Robert Patrick's definition of a gay play as "a play that sleeps with plays of the same sex."

Cornbury

Cornbury was written in reaction to the meaningless pieties of the Bicentennial celebrations. It was an act of revanchist revisionist history, inspired by a portrait of His Lordship in drag, which hangs in the New York Historical Society. Edward Hyde, Lord Cornbury, actually existed and much of the information in this play is historically accurate. Queen Anne *did* form passionate relationships with women. King William, of William and Mary, *was* gay. Any good history book will let one know this, but not always with convenient labels. *Cornbury* was also a conscious act of gay mythmaking. The authors do not know for certain if their transvestite hero was gay, although they strongly suspect he was from his friendship with William and the circles in which he moved in Europe. But they decided to make him definitely gay. And they made his wife a French Catholic and gave him an African princess as a slave and a Jewish secretary in order to show that such strange events could have occurred and probably did—over and over again in American history. Though they feel the play is mainly an entertainment, there are also two political statements implicit in their work: gays have existed in America from its inception and the knowledge of them has been suppressed; civilization has always been at war with Bible-thumping revolutionaries masquerading as conservatives. P.S.: Lady Cornbury *was* a kleptomaniac.

July 4, 1978, New York

ACKNOWLEDGMENTS

ACKNOWLEDGMENTS

Ramsay Limited, 14A Goodwin's Court, St. Martins Lane, London WC2N 4LL, England. Reprinted by permission of Grove Press, Inc., and the Estate of Joe Orton.

A Late Snow by Jane Chambers. Copyright © by Jane Chambers. CAUTION: Professionals and amateurs are hereby warned that *A Late Snow*, being fully protected under the copyright laws of the United States of America, the British Commonwealth, including the Dominion of Canada, and all other countries of the Copyright Union, is subject to royalty. All rights, including professional, amateur, motion picture, recitation, lecturing, public reading, radio and television broadcasting, and the rights of translation into foreign languages, are strictly reserved. All inquiries should be addressed to the author's agent, Gloria Safier, Inc., 667 Madison Avenue, New York, N. Y. 10021.

The Killing of Sister George by Frank Marcus. © Copyright, 1965, by Frank Marcus. All rights reserved. CAUTION: Professionals and amateurs are hereby warned that *The Killing of Sister George*, being fully protected under the copyright laws of the United States, the British Empire, including the Dominion of Canada, and all other countries of the Copyright Union, is subject to royalty. All rights, including professional, amateur, motion picture, recitation, lecturing, public reading, radio and television broadcasting, and the rights of translation into foreign languages, are strictly reserved. Particular emphasis is laid on the question of readings, permission for which must be obtained in writing from the author's agent: in the U.S.A., Jed Mattes, International Creative Management, 40 West 57th Street, New York, N. Y. 10019; and for all other countries, Margaret Ramsay Limited, 14A Goodwin's Court, St. Martins Lane, London WC2N 4LL, England. No performance may be given unless a written license has been obtained. The amateur acting and stock rights of *The Killing of Sister George* are controlled exclusively by Samuel French Inc., 25 West 45th Street, New York, N. Y. 10036. Reprinted by permission of International Creative Management and Hamish Hamilton Limited.

Cornbury: The Queen's Governor by William M. Hoffman and Anthony Holland. Copyright, as an unpublished work, 1976, by William M. Hoffman and Anthony Holland. Copyright © 1979 by William M. Hoffman and Anthony Holland. All rights reserved. Inquiries concerning rights should be addressed to the authors' agents, Helen Merrill and Helen Harvey, c/o Helen Harvey, 410 West 24th Street, New York, N. Y. 10011. Quotation from *Queen Anne* by David Green, copyright ©

Acknowledgments

1970 by David Green, is reprinted by permission of Charles Scribner's Sons and William Collins Sons and Company Limited.

Special thanks to my editor, Robert Wyatt; my assistant David Csontos, especially for his help in compiling the Bibliography; my agent, Helen Merrill; Frank Taylor, Richard Hall; Robert Patrick, who said, "Why not do a gay anthology?"; Irving Drutman; Michael DeLisio; Doric Wilson and Ken Burgess for their information on the early Cino; Brad Mulroy, Anthony Holland, Sanford Kadet, Michael Feingold, and Jean-Claude van Itallie for listening; Chuck Kelly of the Library of Congress.

T-SHIRTS
A Play in One Act

by
Robert Patrick

For John Gilman

T-Shirts was first performed at The Out-and-About Theatre Company at the Walker Church in Minneapolis, October 19, 1978. It was directed by Richard E. Rehse and included the following cast:

MARVIN .... *Vic Campbell*
KINK .... *Gray Tuel*
TOM .... *Charles W. Pashon*

CHARACTERS

MARVIN: Forty, but much younger-looking. He is wonderful-looking but by no means handsome or sexy. Noticeably overweight.

KINK: Thirty, but again much younger-looking. Thin, teenish, androgynous in style but capable of dropping into either butch or fem characterizations. Must be hung.

TOM: Twenty, he says, probably a year or two younger. Extremely well shaped, very handsome, but youthfully awkward. Wears glasses. Very natural in manner.

GREG: A phone voice. A *nice* phone voice.

THE SETTING is Kink's living room on the Lower East Side in New York. Most of the furniture is striking big cushions made by Kink. Wall hangings, porny pinups, sequined curtains, all with more style than camp, and much humor. There are a desk and some loose chairs for variety, some small tables and pillows.

Entrance from hall, down right; curtained kitchen door, up left; john door, down left; door to Marvin's room, center right; ladder to sleeping loft, center; windows in back wall with locked anti-burglar gates. Coat hooks by hall door.

2

PROPS: A telephone with an answering machine on the desk. A TV on a stand with its back to us, down left. A squawk box connected to the downstairs door beside the hall door (must "talk"). Lights are controlled from a set of switches up right by the biggest cushion. (Kink is mechanical; there are several light effects possible.)

OUTSIDE: Little or no sky, just surrounding tenements.

THE TIME: After ten on a rainy autumn night. The present.

A Lower East Side living room in New York. Fifth floor.
Night. Dark. Rain. We hear male laughter and whoops
offstage. The door opens and KINK *and* MARVIN *rush in,*
wet and cold.

MARVIN: Woo. Can't get the keys out of the door. I'll get
the lights. Start some *coffee!*

KINK: [*Rushing into kitchen*] Oh, God, yes. Did you get
caught in the rain, too?

MARVIN: [*While extracting keys, turning on lights, taking
off and hanging up coat, drying hair with towel, etc.*]
Yes, I was late for the start of my movie, so I didn't go.
So I meet this porn star I know from California, and he
has to tell me his career plans. In his S and M movies
he called himself Rick Rack. So I have to stand in front
of an art flick and listen to the names he's considering
for his new straight career.

KINK: [*Off*] In the rain?

MARVIN: Well, that's where we were. He thinks he can set
fire to the senses of a generation if he calls himself "Curt."
I suggested such scintillating last names as "Response,"
"Remark," and "Interest." He didn't get it. It was like
that time on the talk show in London when I told them
I believed in astrology because I'd met three people
born on April twelfth and they were all Aries. They
didn't get it, either.

KINK: [*Enters, hangs up coat, etc.*] I couldn't hear you.

MARVIN: You missed remarkably little. Why aren't you in
a bar on the West Side, blowing your brains out?

KINK: I was on the West Side. There were guys lined up for
a block in the rain waiting to get into the Cockring.

4

MARVIN: My God, why didn't they just go home with each other?

KINK: They don't *like* each other.

MARVIN: Right. I forgot. Then why are they waiting in the rain to get into the bar with each other?

KINK: [*As if explaining to a bothersome child*] Because it's *dark* in the bar and they can't *see* each other.

MARVIN: Right, right.

KINK: God, it's funny running around on the West Side not drinking.

MARVIN: Did you do anything?

KINK: No, not drinking takes up all my time.

MARVIN: I know what you mean. I sat in Lady Astor's for a while. Everybody that wasn't drinking was not doing something. If you get me.

KINK: I know.

MARVIN: I was not drinking. Gaylen was not cruising boys. Leonore was not letting men feel her up.

KINK: And the waiters and waitresses were not appearing on the Broadway stage.

MARVIN: Or at the tables. I just sat there being very good. By not drinking.

KINK: Well, at least you get paid for it. [*Takes letter from his pocket.*] There's a check from your terrible agent.

MARVIN: [*Sticks check in coat pocket.*] Mmmmm. Getaway money. Goody. How can you call her terrible when she sends me money?

KINK: She doesn't send me any.

MARVIN: You don't *get* royalties for superior drapes and upholstery.

KINK: I don't see why not. Every time somebody sits in a theater seat in Rome or Nome or Chillicothe or Chapultepec, you make ten cents.

MARVIN: Maybe you should build secret little pockets in your upholstery, to catch loose change. Then pick it up every once in a while for dry cleaning.

KINK: Kink Carstairs. Draping and looting. I like it.

MARVIN: How is the shop doing?

KINK: Better since I'm sober. I'm a lot less behind in my work.

MARVIN: I'm a lot behind in my work.

KINK: Of course, everybody's behinds are in my work. Was that good?

MARVIN: For an upholsterer. How are your gnomes working out?

KINK: Well, Mack's not drinking anymore—

BOTH: Any more than what?

KINK: —and Farley's taking a lot less dope.

MARVIN: All these negative virtues. It's an epidemic. Are your clothes wet?

KINK: They were. It's on me now.

MARVIN: I'll get us some dry T-shirts. [*He opens desk drawer and pulls out many shirts.*] Do you want "Save Energy, Throw a Faggot on the Fire" or "Anita Bryant Like Anita Hole in the Head"?

KINK: I would like a quiet T-shirt with nothing on it, please.

MARVIN: [*Tosses him shirt, changes into one himself.*] Is an illiterate boyfriend coming over?

KINK: [*Changing shirts*] No, I think I've given that up, too.

MARVIN: The illiterate part? One hopes.

KINK: The boyfriend part. It's strictly anonymous congress at the baths from now on.

MARVIN: How *are* the baths sober?

KINK: It's amazing how fast you can make out when you're the only person there in a solid state. The problem is I keep wanting to giggle. Every time I look in a room and see somebody with his ass up in the air, I keep thinking of electric pencil sharpeners.

MARVIN: I stopped going—

KINK: I know.

MARVIN: —When I saw that kid . . .

KINK: Right.

MARVIN: . . . in the very dark room? . . .

KINK: Right.

MARVIN: with his mouth outlined in luminous paint?

KINK: Uh-huh.

MARVIN: He was making little goldfish mouth motions. It looked like he was trying to spell something.

6

KINK: [*Kettle whistles in kitchen.* KINK *exits.*] Keep talking, I can hear you.

MARVIN: No you can't.

KINK: [*Off*] What?

MARVIN: [*Throws small pillow into the kitchen.*] You talk. I'm making little mouth motions.

KINK: [*Off*] The only trouble with going to the baths sober is that drunk people smell so disgusting. I keep wondering did I smell that way in the past. I used to think I was funny and romantic and cute. Now I realize I just smelled drunk and impotent and easily fuckable.

(*He re-enters with coffee balanced carefully on the pillow.*)

MARVIN: [*Taking coffee*] Takes coffee very carefully from his compulsively playful roommate. Is that what you really used to think?

KINK: [*Settling on cushion with coffee*] I used to think. Therefore I used to be.

MARVIN: I used to think that if I painted something with luminous paint—

KINK: Like what?

MARVIN: Like anything—and then clicked the lights in the room off and on real fast . . . [*Clicks lights off and on real fast.*] that when I finally left them off . . . [*Room goes dark.*] the object would keep blinking in the dark.

KINK: Call that thinking?

MARVIN: [*Clicks lights on.*] It's something else I don't do anymore.

KINK: Now that you've given up sex—

MARVIN: —and vice versa—

KINK: —what do you do? Masturbate?

MARVIN: [*Angrily*] Certainly not!

KINK: I'm sorry.

MARVIN: [*Haughtily*] I jerk off.

KINK: Pull your pod.

MARVIN: Stab myself repeatedly with the pork sword.

KINK: Count to a hundred and come.

MARVIN: Shake the kids out of school.

KINK: Pump spunk.

MARVIN: Tickle the bad boy till he sneezes.

KINK: Manufacture hand lotion.

MARVIN: Drum up a little business.

KINK: Jingle balls.

MARVIN: Go for a gusher.

KINK: I never hear you.

MARVIN: Well, I don't talk to myself while I'm doing it.

KINK: Not even dirty?

MARVIN: No. Sex is beautiful.

KINK: Well, I like to have somebody there to help me clean up.

MARVIN: That's why I like sixty-nining. No muss, no fuss.

KINK: I wonder if you digest come or if it comes out of you the next time.

MARVIN: I saw a great graffito once.

KINK: Is that the singular?

MARVIN: Uh-huh. It said: "Boys: they fill you up and then leave you ready for another girl."

KINK: Hmmmm.

MARVIN: I could never figure out whether it was written by some abandoned pregnant chick—or by some bisexual dude with a hard-on he got from giving a blow job.

KINK: It is ambiguous.

MARVIN: It nearly always is.

KINK: Well, now that I've given everything up, I feel like a new man. I think I'll go to the baths and find one.

(*Door buzzes.*)

MARVIN: Maybe that's him! A door-to-door whore! [*Goes to door, speaks into "talk" box.*] You two-timing son of a bitch, how dare you show your face around here?

TALK BOX: Huh? I just wondered if I could—

MARVIN: [*Into box*] Starship *Enterprise*. Starship *Enterprise*. You have reached the starship *Enterprise*. Not the crew. This is the ship itself talking. I've learned to run myself. I'm throwing the crew out of the hatch one by one, starting at the bottom. I'm almost through. Kirk out! [*Presses buzzer, opens hall door, dances back into room.*] I think I'll stop smoking, too. Why? Smoking, drinking, fucking, that's all I want to do.

KINK: I know. I get the feeling there's a second lecture at Sunday school I forgot to go to.

MARVIN: What's good to do?

KINK: Yeah, what you give up things *for*.

MARVIN: Yes. Why is it, whenever you do exactly what you want to do, people say you lack self-control?

KINK: Who was that?

MARVIN: Me. It just sounds like a great saying.

KINK: At the door, I mean.

MARVIN: All my sayings sound like great sayings. Draw your own conclusions.

KINK: Were you expecting a date?

MARVIN: Are you living with a great epigrammatist—

KINK: You couldn't possibly be expecting a date.

MARVIN: —as well as a great dramatist?

KINK: [*Hits him with pillow.*] Who was that at the door?

MARVIN: [*Dodging*] As well as a—what rhymes with dramatist?

KINK: [*Continually hitting him*] Did you let a perfect stranger into the building?

MARVIN: [*Running, ducking*] Amatist! A lover! A great amatist!

KINK: [*Still hitting*] What if someone gets robbed and mugged?

MARVIN: Quit hitting me and I'll tell you.

KINK: [*Still hitting*] What if someone gets raped and looted?

MARVIN: [*Fighting back with a smaller pillow*] I will never submit to looting!

KINK: That's incredibly dangerous!

MARVIN: That's why I won't submit to it!

KINK: It hurts to be raped and looted!

MARVIN: I can be raped, yes, hell yes, I can be raped. None of our boys is going overseas unhappy if I can help it. But no looting. We will not stand still for looting. [*He is losing pillow fight badly.*]

9

KINK: You must. It's in the contract. Raped and looted. Like Hawaii. Like the Philippines. Like Chile. Like the whole damned continent. It's the American way!

MARVIN: [*On his knees, then on his back*] No looting. Millions for sex but not one welfare baby for tribute. I will not be pillaged. I'm part Indian. I gave at Wounded Knee. I can't! I couldn't! I won't! [TOM *enters. He is tall, built, gorgeous, wears glasses, is wringing wet.*] Maybe I will.

KINK: [*Stops hitting* MARVIN, *looks* TOM *up and down.*] Okay. What have *I* got that *you* want?

MARVIN: [*To* TOM] Loot me slowly. It's my first time.

TOM: Uh—hi. Y'all probably don't remember me—

KINK: No, but so what, everybody's pretty much the same deep down, aren't they? Come on in.

MARVIN: Right. Hell, I'd be willing to strip to prove it.

KINK: You wouldn't either.

MARVIN: Naw, I really would.

KINK: Damn, you're big-hearted.

MARVIN: Well, what the fuck, I mean, we all in this together, ain't we?

KINK: It won't be necessary, though—*I'll* strip to prove it.

MARVIN: No, I will.

KINK: No, I will.

MARVIN: I insist. I'll strip.

KINK: There isn't room for you to strip, Marvin.

MARVIN: I never said I'd give up eating. I never said that.

KINK: I can't let you endanger yourself that way, by stripping in front of this boy.

MARVIN: Why not?

KINK: 'Cause *I* want to.

MARVIN: Well, it won't prove we're all alike if just one of us strips, anyway.

KINK: It will prove my willingness to do anything.

MARVIN: You'd catch cold; you've been wet.

KINK: He's still wet! [*Points at* TOM.] Strip him. Not me. Him, him.

MARVIN: That's an idea.

TOM: No, it's not.

KINK: Sacrifice the stranger! Do it to him! Do it to him! [*Makes sign of cross.*]

MARVIN: He refuses the rites. He is the enemy!

KINK: He is the what?

MARVIN: The enemy. He is enemy.

KINK: Well, get 'im out of you and put 'im in-a-me!

MARVIN: [*To* TOM] Okay, kid, we're through fooling around. Out with it.

TOM: Out with what?

KINK: You mean "off with it, off with it." [*Pantomimes stripping.*]

MARVIN: No. First out with it, then [*Imitates hacking motion at crotch.*] off with it!

KINK: [*Throws himself in front of* TOM.] No, father, no, do not disembowel him! I love him and he will be my queen.

MARVIN: I'm not going to disembowel him, I'm going to castrate him. [*Groucho Marx*] Speaking of which, Pocahontas—if you're a castrating female, how would you rate this cast?

TOM: Look, I just came in to get out of the rain.

MARVIN: And you got a whole lot more than you barged in for. Hey!

KINK: Oh, that was good.

MARVIN: It was, wasn't it?

KINK: One of your best—lately. [*To* TOM] Here, come on in. You're wet. We were just running amuck.

MARVIN: And lots of folks say we run a pretty nice muck.

TOM: [*Trudges in.*] See, I was just tryin' to ring Greg downstairs—

MARVIN: Ring Greg? Wring Greg? Is he wet, too?

KINK: [*Ignoring* MARVIN] I've seen you working with Greg in the halls. I'm Kink.

MARVIN: [*Completely ignored*] Hey, did you hear. Ring, wring, get it? [*Pantomimes bell and towel.*]

TOM: Yeah, and he isn't in, or he's got someone there, or something—

KINK: Make yourself comfortable and wait. Give me your coat.

MARVIN: [*Flings himself at* TOM's *feet.*] Your shoes. I get your shoes.

KINK: That's Marvin. Ignore him. He fell out of the television.

MARVIN: [*On his knees*] Wait. I'm thinking. If he gets your coat—oh, wait. I've got one. Let's see—uh—I like to watch people undress other people—so—if he gets your coat, I get a boot? [*Pause*] Oh, God, Oh, God.

KINK: [*To Marvin*] Did you think of something else you'd like to give up?

MARVIN: [*Rising*] If you knew what to call it, I'd give it up.

KINK: [*To* TOM] God, you're soaked.

MARVIN: My name is Marvin, and I'm not really like this. [*Strikes pose.*] And I'm not really like this. [*Pose*] Or like this. [*Pose*] Or this. [*Pose*] Or this.

TOM: I will wait out the rain here if you don't mind. I am, I'm soaked through. [*Long pause while* MARVIN *and* KINK *look at each other*] I'm really sorry if I'm inconveniencing you.

KINK: It's no inconvenience. We're just waiting for each other to give in and say something obvious.

MARVIN: You devil, you know me through and through.

KINK: [*To* TOM] Sure, stay [*Tosses towel.*] Here, dry your hair. And—sigh—ready, Marvin?

MARVIN: Ready.

KINK AND MARVIN: Would you like to get out of those wet things?

KINK: There, we said it.

MARVIN: "My dear," you forgot "My dear."

KINK: [*Hanging up* TOM's *coat*] "My dear" is not used in the best circles anymore.

MARVIN: Did word filter down?

KINK: [*To* TOM] Do you want some coffee or anything?

TOM: God, I'd love it.

KINK: Okay. [*Hands him magazine.*] Here. If Marvin bothers you, open this to the crossword puzzle. They paralyze him for hours. [*Off to kitchen.*]

MARVIN: [*Yells off to kitchen.*] Crossword puzzles are good for little paranoid children. The clues really *do* have secret meanings. [*To* TOM] Wiping those old glasses, heh?

TOM: The better to see you with.

MARVIN: I notice you didn't make any polite little de-murrers when Kink offered to get you coffee. I mean, you didn't say "Golly, gee, don't go to any trouble," or anything like that. I presume that means that you are so used to having your young godlike beauty catered to that you've come to take it for granted.

TOM: Pretty much. But when he comes out, if the coffee's scalding, I'll have him pour a little on my face to scar me.

MARVIN: Hmmmm.

TOM: Then no other man will ever want me.

MARVIN: Right thinking, right thinking.

TOM: I just want to atone for my criminal gorgeousness.

MARVIN: [*With new respect*] My name, as it actually hap-pens, *is* Marvin. [*They shake hands.*]

TOM: I know. Your cute roommate already told me. I'm Tom. I wish it were more interesting, but there it is.

MARVIN: It'll do. *Do* you want to get out of those wet things?

TOM: In a minute. When I get warmed up. [*Sighs.*] Okay. Take it: "warmed up."

MARVIN: Later, later. Listen, were you not even a little bit put off at the gladiatorial spectacle you stumbled in on?

TOM: No, I always hear you two romping up here when-ever I come by to visit Greg.

MARVIN: Greg is the super of this building.

TOM: Yeah, I know, I help him.

MARVIN: He has the whole floor-through below Kink.

TOM: Yeah.

MARVIN: This living room, where we romp, is directly over his bedroom. You would have to be in his bedroom fre-quently in order to know that we habitually romp.

TOM: That's about it.

MARVIN: [*Yells to* KINK.] Can you hear this?

KINK: [*Off*] I'm not listening. I don't want to know.

TOM: Have you got a cigarette? Mine are mush.

MARVIN: Sure. [*Gives one.*]

TOM: Thanks. Got a light?

MARVIN: M-hm. [*Lights him.*] Do you come here much?

TOM: Whenever I can get away from military school for a weekend without my folks finding out.

MARVIN: I was doing a parody of bar talk.

TOM: So was I.

KINK: [*Re-entering with coffee, sugar, and milk on a silver tray*] Here. Sweeten and lighten yourself.

TOM: [*Taking coffee*] Thanks. This is really nice of you.

KINK: It is, isn't it?

MARVIN: How come not "It's nice of *y'all*"?

TOM: 'Cause "y'all" means two and I'm only talking to him.

MARVIN: Yeah, but I heard.

TOM: [*To* KINK] I could have gone into Lady Astor's or the Colonnades, but I was so wet, and it's always the same in there, and besides I didn't have any money.

MARVIN: Gee, we-all are better than standing out in the rain.

KINK: No, it's fine.

TOM: And besides, I've been wanting to meet y'all for a long time. I used to see y'all at Lady Astor's and Phebe's and you always seemed to be having a lot of fun.

KINK: Yes, I used to enjoy falling off bar stools, but it's not so much fun since I stopped drinking.

MARVIN: You tend to stiffen up.

KINK: Marvin used to like to criticize the music on the jukebox—then the disco craze hit and no one could hear him.

MARVIN: Technology cost me my job.

TOM: If you think that's loud, do you ever go down to hear the punk rock at CeebeeGeebee's?

MARVIN: Yes. I like to sit up close where I can see the singer's lips move.

KINK: I'm not much on music. I'd go if I could put stoppers in my ears and fuck the musicians.

MARVIN: You can put stoppers in your ears.

KINK: I'm not one for half-measures. Do you go there?

TOM: No, I don't care much for people my own age.

KINK: Can I have them?

MARVIN: Yes, they are terribly dull and immature and undeveloped, aren't they?

14

TOM: No, they're fine; they're just too much competition.

MARVIN: I'll say.

KINK: People never want people their own ages. It's true. I've noticed it.

MARVIN: Gore Vidal refers to it in *Two Sisters*.

KINK: Right, people are too nervous with people their own ages.

TOM: I don't think that. I cruise a lot of guys my age. They're the ones I like best in the magazines. But, God, you know, with overpopulation and all, you know, you can't just waste it all on fun, anyway not in New York. If you wanna be noticed here or meet people or anything you have to do something and, God! There's so many stray cats in a place like New York. No kidding. God!

MARVIN: I see what you mean.

KINK: Hustler heaven.

TOM: Well, yes, sure, God! Maybe, a little, if you wanna think of it that way, but God! What're you going to do, there's no jobs or anything either, God!

KINK: I didn't mean it badly.

TOM: Well, I just get tired, God, you know. Older guys have the connections and—okay—the money, and, hell, you can learn a lot from older guys. God.

KINK: Oh, right, right.

TOM: I mean—in a relationship with an older guy there's certain element of—power.

MARVIN: Yes, but on which side?

KINK: Both, Marvin.

TOM: Right. I mean, they've got all that and you've got youth and—oh, well, you know what I mean—shit. Beauty.

ALL THREE: God!

TOM: Well, y'all are laughing at me, go ahead, laugh, but it's true.

MARVIN: You know, I talk a lot with kids your age around the country—around the world, some—and they all have that same, drab, mature understanding of the current sociobiological situation. I think that's what makes your whole generation a little dull.

TOM: Oh, well, we've got y'all for entertainment. Y'all still find things funny. I mean, you were alive 'way back when all the jokes were new. [*Breaks up laughing.*]

MARVIN: Kink, prepare the knives; the sacrifice is back on.

TOM: Ha! That was a good one! It's true. Come on, that was good. Whew. Why is that so funny?

KINK: And to whom?

TOM: No, but you really have been all around the world, haven't you?

MARVIN: Some, like I said. With plays. I write plays.

TOM: I know that. Everybody knows that. I've read a lot of your plays in school.

KINK: Far out.

TOM: They're good. They really are. They're good. I admire you.

KINK: I think I should warn you that anyone that says anything nice to Marvin for five minutes gets fallen in love with.

TOM: Uh-oh.

MARVIN: Tell you what, Kink. You just give me a signal if I start to make a fool of myself.

KINK: Okay. I'll toss my hair.

MARVIN: No, you do that all the time. Oh.

TOM: Ha! Look at your face!

MARVIN: [*To* KINK] Have I told you lately to go fuck yourself with a fart?

KINK: I'm sorry. That was mean.

TOM: It was. I couldn't help laughin', but it was. It really was.

MARVIN: You think that was mean? You think that was mean? You haven't lived—and you haven't died.

TOM: Well, maybe I should go. . . . Do you suppose Greg has come in?

KINK: God, no.

TOM: Do you have some way to tell?

KINK: Yeah—when the floor starts shaking from the Kiss records.

TOM: Oh, can y'all hear that up here?

KINK: When he puts that stereo on, you can't hear anything up here. I have this fantasy of getting my hand caught

16

in the Waring blender and screaming for help while he's got them on, and he'll be down there telling somebody, "Hear that? This set gets terrific overtones."

MARVIN: He'll think the screams are the kids; he'll think it's a live recording.

TOM: Did y'all ever see them live?

KINK: We saw them. We were live when it started.

MARVIN: At least there the kids' screaming drowned out the music.

KINK: I thought it was the other way around; I thought the music was to drown out the kids' screams.

MARVIN: They wouldn't be screaming if they didn't have to listen to that music.

TOM: You got it all wrong.

MARVIN: Him or me?

TOM: Both of you. You can tell neither of y'all were ever a suburban teen-ager. You don't scream because of the music. Suburban teen-agers scream from eight to ten every night, anyway. Their parents just send 'em to the Kiss concerts to avoid the disgrace. But I'll tell Greg that the noise bothers y'all. We tried using two sets of earphones for a while, but we kept getting the cords all tangled up and greasy.

MARVIN: What vivid reporting.

KINK: So Greg would turn the music down if you told him. Am I to take that as a sign that y'all are in love?

TOM: God, I hope not.

MARVIN: Am I to take that as an indication that you have had a bad love affair?

TOM: Christ, I hope so. I mean I hope that wasn't a good one. It couldn't have been. If all love affairs are that bad, love wouldn't have such a good reputation.

MARVIN: It hasn't. Get wise. All your life you've been listening to songs about how awful love is. Don't you ever listen to the lyrics?

TOM: I don't know; what label do they record on?

KINK: Kittens.

MARVIN: Kittens what?

KINK: It's like with kittens. Love is like with kittens. Did you ever have cats?

TOM: Yeah, at home.

KINK: Well, then, you know what hideous bullies cats are? What hell they make of your life? But if you've got one, you keep telling other people how terrific they are, because you hope you can get them to take yours. That's how it is with lovers.

TOM: Well, like I heard someone say at Phebe's: "Love is for children; and I don't want children."

KINK: So, what about you and Greg?

TOM: Nothin' about me and Greg. We fuck and we fantasize. Okay? Stick that on a T-shirt! Oh, Jesus, I'm sorry, I'm takin' out my insecurities on y'all. My shrink says I do that. I'm sorry. You took me in outa the rain and I insult you. Look, I really don't have anywhere else to go and I truly appreciate y'all's hospitality. If I be good, is it okay with y'all if I hang out here? [*Sighs.*] Okay, who's gonna make the joke? "Hang out."

KINK: Please, some things are sacred even here. Yeah, you can stay. We're not goin' anywhere—well, I'm not—and we've dealt with obnoxious twerps before. Besides [*Susan Sarandon*] it's raining.

TOM: Okay. Thanks.

MARVIN: Wanna hear my human side? I have a human side, listen: Are you cold? Would you like a drink?

TOM: I thought y'all didn't drink.

KINK: Oh, we keep it for guests—

MARVIN: And cauterizing wounds.

TOM: Naw, I never touch liquor.

MARVIN: Kink, get a funnel.

TOM: I will take you up on that offer of a dry shirt, though.

KINK: Oh, good. I'll get it. [*Goes to drawer of T-shirts.*] Here. Do you want the one that says "I'm really thirty-five; my face died young"? Or "I like New York where I can see what I'm breathing"? Or—

MARVIN: Don't show him the one that says "Let's eat out more often."

KINK: I've also got a pair of cutoffs that say "Melts in your mouth, not in your hands."

TOM: [*Joining him*] I'll take this one. Who's that on it?

KINK: Carmen Miranda.

TOM: What's it say? It's in script.

KINK: It says "I slid right down those wedgies into hell."

TOM: I'll take that one—and the shorts. I'll get 'em back to you. [*Looking for john*] Is this the john?

MARVIN: You'd think so. It's my room.

KINK: Oh, you can keep it. I'll keep this one.

TOM: [*Looking in* MARVIN'*s room*] God, what a lot of stuff. Why don't you clean it up?

KINK: That's the advantage of T-shirts.

MARVIN: I work on the bear-trap theory. Step anywhere in that room and the cardboard boxes collapse in the direction of the bed.

KINK: I could build a philosophy on T-shirts.

TOM: [*At john door*] Is this the john?

MARVIN: In a word, yes. [TOM *exits.*]

KINK: I believe T-shirts, umbrellas, cigarettes, matches, instant coffee, and paperback books belong to everybody in the world. Do you want him?

MARVIN: I don't know which way I'm facing half the time, much less what I want.

KINK: I'll go out.

MARVIN: Why are they all gay?

KINK: Pop singers.

MARVIN: What?

KINK: Pop singers. They used to sing love songs to imaginary girls. Now they sing directly to the teen-age market. Naturally they're all gay.

MARVIN: Do *you* want him.

KINK: Mmmmmmm. No, not particularly.

MARVIN: Do you want me?

KINK: Mmmmmmmm. No, not at all.

MARVIN: Shit. Maybe him and me should go out.

KINK: Is it because you don't think you could get him?

MARVIN: Don't be absurd. Of course I couldn't get him. Besides, there's no time.

KINK: But if there was and if you could—do you want him if you get him?

MARVIN: Do you want him if I get him?

KINK: Mmmmmmm. Yes. If you got him, I'd want him.

MARVIN: Then what would you do?

KINK: I'd take him away from you effortlessly. Or sublimate and go to the baths. Or collapse in a moral quan-
dary and go back to drinking. So it works out fine for
me whatever happens.

MARVIN: Well, Greg's got him. Why don't you want him
because Greg's got him?

KINK: Greg's just a friend. You're my very best friend.

MARVIN: We've been through an awful lot together.

BOTH: Including this dialogue.

TOM: [*Re-enters in dry shirt and cutoff jeans, his hair dried
and brushed.*] Hey, you're my size.

KINK: I am noticeably thinner than you. A creep named
Frenzy who took my clock radio was your size.

TOM: Anyway, they fit. Hey, what's this ladder to?

KINK: My sleeping loft. I get boys up there and kick the
ladder away.

TOM: [*Poses on ladder.*] I feel like a cigarette ad. "Hi! I'm
Tom."

MARVIN: "Smoke me to Miami."

TOM: Ha. Hey, I'll take you up on that drink.

MARVIN: I thought you didn't drink.

TOM: Aw, I just say that automatically with new people.
Everybody's always tryin' to get me drunk.

MARVIN: Well, drunk or sober, I'm tryin' to get you, so
you might as well have a drink.

TOM: No, no, you're doing it all wrong. First you're supposed to tell me which movie stars and great historical
figures are queer.

KINK: Do you really want to know?

TOM: No, but that's standard operating procedure. I'm
supposed to sleep with you because Leonardo da Vinci
and Rudolph Valentino were cocksuckers. Jesus, it's like
—I was standin' on the corner of Bowery and Second
Street the other day, at *noon* and these two drunk bums
were lyin' on the sidewalk beside the mailbox, and they
looked like one of 'em had just dropped a bottle of piss,
and they were arguin', and one of 'em says, "Yeah,
W. C. Fields drunk. He was a big drinker." And his
buddy says, "Ava Gardner, she drinks, drinks tequila,"
and the other one says, "Tallulah Bankhead, there was a

drinker. They all drink. Drink good stuff, too." It was like people tellin' me famous people were gay. I had to laugh. I really did.

KINK: Sometimes one does. I'll get the hooch. [*Exits to kitchen.*]

TOM: And then you're supposed to impress me with how much you know about art and theater. Hey, do you like *Marat/Sade*?

MARVIN: [*Blankly*] Do I like *Marat/Sade*?

TOM: Yeah. Do you like *Marat/Sade* [*Shows his profile.*] or do you prefer mah left? [*Breaks up in helpless giggles at his own wit.*] And then—then you're supposed to offer to show me the beauties of Ancient Greece. Come on, show me the beauties of Ancient Greece.

MARVIN: [*Yells to* KINK.] Hey, have we got any beauties of Ancient Greece?

KINK: [*Sticks head through curtains.*] We have lots of ancient grease in the icebox if that's your idea of beauty. [*Withdraws.*]

TOM: So, you're out to get me, are you?

MARVIN: Well, I'm a successful older man and you're a scrumptious stray cat, it's a conventional situation, why not? *Voulez-vous cliché avec moi?*

TOM: Hey, this might turn out to be more interestin' than I thought.

KINK: [*Off*] I can hear you.

MARVIN: [*Remaining where he is, but speaking with great conviction*] Tom, Tom, stop. Kink's in the next room, stop, leave my pants alone, Greg is my friend, we mustn't do this, Tom, stop, stop, no, no, no, it's too big. I can't take it, no, please—

TOM: [*Joining in*] Take it, take it, eat, eat it, eat it raw, eat it all, right down to the balls, baby, take it!

MARVIN: [*correcting him*] No, no, no; you're trying to fuck me.

TOM: Suck it first and get it hard! Suck it!

MARVIN: It *got* hard the minute you looked at me.

TOM: Okay, okay. Take it, spread 'em, baby, take it, take every inch of it!

MARVIN: Oh, please, no, I can't! Use the axle grease.

TOM: Take it dry! Take it all!

MARVIN: Oh, God, use the axle!

KINK: [*Off*] I'm coming in there!

TOM: Oh, my God, your lover's coming!

MARVIN: Quick, cover yourself with K-Y and hide in my cunt.

TOM: Oh, God, that's awful! [*Laughs.*]

KINK: [*Enters with bottle and two glasses.*] Marvin? Why is your head all covered with Crisco?

MARVIN: [*It's an old routine.*] Because when I give head, honey, I give head!

TOM: Oh, wow, that's fantastic!

KINK: Oh, did you like it?

TOM: [*Who meant the whiskey*] Seagram's Royal Crown. I had that before. It's great!

MARVIN: It's not Royal Crown, it's Crown Royal. Are you dyslexic?

TOM: What's dyslexic?

MARVIN: [*Absentmindedly taking a glass from* KINK, *who pours him a drink*] It means you can't read, or you read backwards.

TOM: [*Also accepting a drink*] I can read. I told you I read your plays.

MARVIN: Backwards?

TOM: Some of 'em make just as much sense that way. [*Laughs.*] Cheers. [*Drinks.*]

MARVIN: Cheers who? [*To* KINK] Why have I got a drink?

(KINK *shrugs with a smile and sits down to watch them.*)

TOM: No, that was just a cheap shot. I dug your stuff. I told you that already. [*Laughs.*]

MARVIN: And which one of my works is it that you are laughing in appreciative memory of? [*To* KINK, *of drink*] I don't want this.

KINK: Then have the drink instead.

MARVIN: Huh?

TOM: No, I was laughing at something I said in class once. The teacher asked did we like your stuff. And I was

22

just smartin' off and I said I didn't. I do. I was just clownin'. You're not mad, are you?

MARVIN: Never mind. Just speak directly into my autobiography.

TOM: Okay. So I said, "It sucks." And he was this real trying-to-be-hip teacher and he said, "It sucks? Well; isn't that a sure sign of life?" And that was funny. And then he said whether we liked it or not wasn't important, that all that was important was whether it conveyed your thought, got your thought across, see? And so I said—God, I'm such a clown, I don't know why I'm telling you this—I said, I said, "Sure it conveys his thought; he thought he could write!" [*He falls back on his cushion laughing; he is not completely sober.*]

MARVIN: [*To* KINK, *of drink*] I really don't want this; see what it does to people?

KINK: You'll have to drink it. I can't pour it back in the bottle. I used both funnels to make an opaque hourglass so I can sleep as late as I want to.

MARVIN: [*Downs the drink and hands glass to* KINK. *To* TOM] And at what esteemed play school did this undergraduate merrymaking take place?

TOM: Anodyne U.

MARVIN: [*Taking refilled glass from* KINK] I seem to recall they did a festival of my plays at Anodyne U.

TOM: [*Hands glass to* KINK.] Hit me again. They did. I played the leads in three of 'em. [*Takes drink.*]

MARVIN: [*Belts his drink, takes* TOM's, *belts it, holds both glasses to* KINK.] Hit us. [KINK *fills glasses.* MARVIN *hands them to* TOM.] Drink these. [TOM *takes one, refuses the other.*] Now, tell us-all; are you by any chance here in the big scrapple to become an actor?

TOM: Oh, well, yeah, in a way, sort of. Yeah, sure, I am. You looking for one?

KINK: [*Grabs* MARVIN's *full glass.*] Don't throw it on the upholstery.

TOM: Yeah, yeah, I want to act, sure, sort of—but, God! I bet you hear that from some boy every time you turn around.

KINK: No, most of the boys I turn around want to be rock stars.

TOM: Not me. I can't sing a note.

KINK: That isn't enough. It's essential, but it isn't enough.

TOM: No, but, hey, relax, I don't really want to act. Is that for me? [*Takes glass from* KINK.] I probably couldn't anyway.

MARVIN: Oh, can it, anyone can act. [*Takes* TOM'*s empty glass.*] Kink, a drink.

KINK: [*Pouring*] Is this for you or him?

MARVIN: I don't know. I can't tell us apart anymore.

TOM: Do you think that? That anyone can act? But I'm so clumsy.

MARVIN: Anyone can act with the proper training. Oh, God, I'm talking about theater. Drink.

TOM: I'd give anything if I thought I could really learn— hey, I thought you stopped drinking. Didn't y'all stop drinking?

KINK: One of us started again.

TOM: Hey, that's awful. Hey, why did you stop?

KINK: Hey, I decided to stop when Marvin pointed out to me that there was getting to be a permanent impression of my face in the corner of the bar at Phebe's.

TOM: Are you an alcoholic?

KINK: Yes, but that's not why I stopped. I stopped because I make my living as a craftsman.

TOM: Oh, God, yes, everybody says you're fantastic. I saw the furniture you made for Greg. Is this your work, this whole place?

KINK: Why, yes—

TOM: I mean except Marvin's room, of course. [*Giggles.*]

MARVIN: You cute . . . thing.

KINK: Yes, this is all mine.

TOM: It's amazing. You make the desk and everything?

KINK: Yes, and the woodwork, too, and the plastering and all of it. But things were getting a little out of hand —especially my hands. The only crafts I was practicing were very primitive ones: spinning, weaving, lumbering —and I was doing all of those at Phebe's. Well, when you live up five flights of stairs and one ladder and you

24

have repeatedly fallen down all of them, it doesn't take a lot of gumption to stop drinking. Especially when it interferes with your work to the point where you can't afford to drink anymore.

TOM: That's great. It really is.

MARVIN: That he drank?

TOM: No, that he stopped. That's heroic. It really is. How long had you been drinking?

KINK: How old are you?

TOM: I'm twenty.

KINK: Since you were six.

TOM: What? How old are *you*?

KINK: I'm thirty.

TOM: God, you really don't look it. [KINK *runs and holds up "I'm really thirty-five" T-shirt.*] Ha. Wow, that really shows amazing self-control.

KINK: Thank you.

TOM: And are you making more money now?

KINK: Honey, I make money now. I even sell advertising time on my answering machine.

TOM: Ha. Hey, that would be a wonderful idea.

KINK: Would be? It is.

TOM: You really did that?

KINK: [*Flips a card to* TOM.] If ya wanna find out, call me up sometime. End of commercial. I am going to have a cup of coffee. Compliments may be meaningless empty breath to some of us in this room, but for certain others they are great support for the willpower. [*Exits into kitchen.*]

TOM: [*To* MARVIN, *who is pouring himself a drink*] Oh, hit me again, will you? [MARVIN *does.*] Thanks. And you, why did you stop drinking?

KINK: [*Off*] He was never a real drunk.

MARVIN: I was, too.

KINK: [*Off*] No you weren't.

MARVIN: Yes, I was so. I drank all the time, I was sick, I stopped writing.

KINK: [*Pokes head through curtain.*] No, you weren't. You never fell down in a gutter, you never got mugged, you never threw up on me that I know of, and until you have run up and down the corner of East Fourth and the Bowery pissing on the glass walls of the sidewalk café at Phebe's, you haven't got your merit badge in booze! [[*Exit.*]

MARVIN: Do you wanna fight?

KINK: [*Pokes head on.*] Sure—cocks at ten inches! [*Off.*]

MARVIN: That's not fair!

TOM: What, is Kink hung?

MARVIN: Kink is a tripod! I live with a tripod!

KINK: [*Sticks head on.*] Get the picture? [*Off.*]

MARVIN: I was a drunk for a year, okay?

TOM: When did you start?

MARVIN: When you were nineteen.

TOM: Oh, so you just stopped?

MARVIN: [*Pouring drink*] Yeah, I just stopped. When did you start?

TOM: Start what?

MARVIN: Drinking, for instance.

TOM: Oh. Same time. I mean, I drank a little in high school, you know, got drunk, I mean I just drank to get drunk, when we couldn't get grass or speed, you know, blow off steam, whatever, make a football player, shit, you know.

MARVIN: Right.

TOM: Gimme a hit. [MARVIN *pours* TOM *a drink*, KINK *reenters with coffee.*] But I didn't really start drinking heavy till I started drinking around Phebe's.

KINK: Oh, dig it! Did you go through Basic Training at Phebe's?

TOM: Yeah, I guess you could call it that. Didn't y'all ever notice me there?

MARVIN: We were probably involved in our Olympic Decathlon Drinking Event in a back booth.

KINK: Marvin made the margarita semifinals before he retired. Yeah, I saw you there.

TOM: Yeah, I used to see y'all in back there all the time. And drinking seems to be what you do there. I mean, faggots all drink, far as I know.

MARVIN: It's not compulsory.

KINK: It helps. A lot.

TOM: Jesus. That place. I hate that place.

MARVIN: The old homestead?

TOM: Yeah, you go in there, I mean a young boy goes in there, you'd never know it's a gay place.

KINK: It's not.

TOM: Yes it is.

MARVIN: No it's not.

TOM: Yes it is.

MARVIN: All right. All right. The northwest corner of the bar is. Okay?

KINK: Okay.

MARVIN: Blessed are the peacemakers. I can settle any dispute.

KINK: Marvin can settle any dispute. Listen: Marvin, solve —Tom, are you living in too small a place with too many people?

TOM: Yeah, in Brooklyn.

KINK: Listen. Marvin, solve the problem of living in small New York apartments with lots of people.

MARVIN: Easy. Half of you take speed and the other half take downers. You'll be invisible to each other. The downheads can use the speed freaks for hair dryers and the speed freaks can use the downheads for furniture. Next problem.

KINK: Marvin, how did they build the pyramids?

MARVIN: Easy. The Great Pyramid is 475 feet high surrounded by sand. The Sahara Desert used to be a great stone mesa 475 feet high. They just carved the pyramid out of the stone and what's left over is the sand. Next question?

KINK: For the jackpot: how was John Fitzgerald Kennedy killed?

MARVIN: Duck soup: Jackie did it with a derringer.

TOM: Oh, God.

MARVIN: Then she crawled on the back of the car, handed it to her secret service lover, and was free to pursue her career.

TOM: I guess y'all don't wanna talk about Phebe's.

KINK: Not the northwest corner, anyway.

MARVIN: No, it's just that I have no solution to it.

TOM: I mean, the minute a good-lookin', or even fair-lookin', kid comes in there, you get sucked to that corner, and they buy you drinks, and then you get pulled to a table by somebody, and you go home with them, and you go home with the next one, and pretty soon you're standin' there at the corner waitin' for the next kid to come in—and then you realize you've got to be just as cheap and tacky as everyone else there.

MARVIN: [*To* KINK] Do you want to hit him or do you want to see me hit him?

TOM: I'm not talkin' about y'all. Y'all were never in on that. Y'all were always in back together.

MARVIN: We couldn't stand up.

KINK: So if you don't want to be part of the queen machine, move a couple of stools down the bar and join the serious thinkers.

TOM: Queen machine. That's good. I like that.

KINK: You should have seen the really big queen machine operating back during the great days.

TOM: I am so tired of hearing all the time about the great days I missed! Gimme a hit!

(MARVIN *pours him a drink*.)

KINK: When the Filmore East was in its glory, you'd see all these mobs of poor drugged children standing out in front, begging for tickets. Then you started seeing guys of thirty or forty from uptown, standing there with tickets in their hands, and they'd pick up the guys in their twenties and ball them for a ticket. Then you'd start seeing those young guys standing there with tickets to lure the kids in their teens.

MARVIN: They had been taught, at an impressionable age, you see, that youth and beauty were the only desirable commodities.

KINK: Then you'd see them, guys of seventeen and eighteen, waving tickets to pick up kids of fifteen and sixteen. It finally, toward the end, got to where you'd see kids of eleven dandling tickets in front of kids nine, to get them into the back seats of parked cars to play doctor for a ticket to the rock concert.

TOM: Oh, God.

MARVIN: The American way. [*Toasts, drinks.*]

TOM: The sixties, the sixties, I'm so tired of hearin' about the sixties.

KINK: Have you heard about the seventies?

TOM: What's to hear? There's nothin' to hear. I bet they won't even remember the seventies. They'll have a big gap in history where the seventies ought to go. They'll think the records are missing. I mean, they'll have all the records, but they'll still think it's all been lost, because they just won't be able to believe that ten years passed without anything happening! Except *People* magazine.

MARVIN: And the nostalgia craze.

KINK: And then the revival of the nostalgia craze.

MARVIN: Do you think the revival of the nostalgia craze will ever come back?

MARVIN AND KINK: Probably.

TOM: So, look, listen, you've been all over, is it different, is it different in other countries where you've been?

MARVIN: I don't know, darlin'. I've only been in other countries to work. It seems a little better—even among gay people. I mean, there's more repression, but among the queers themselves there does seem to be some last little lingering atavistic remnant of an idea of love—but, as I say, I was there mostly to work. I didn't really find out. I wouldn't, of course.

TOM: Whaddaya mean, you wouldn't?

MARVIN: Oh, nothing.

TOM: No, I mean, come on, you're an informed person, you've had experiences I haven't had, come on, what's it like being gay over there?

MARVIN: Tom, I really don't know that much about it.

TOM: I mean, over here it seems like straight people are getting more tolerant of us, but half the time I don't think that's because they're more understanding, I think it's just because since the Pill, and overpopulation, and all, it's just that their lives, the young ones' anyway, have got to be just as scummy and hopeless and pointless as gay life.

MARVIN: Kink, gimme a drink.

TOM: I mean, I think we need people like you, smart, talented people with brains and things, to tell us about it. Right?

KINK: Right.

MARVIN: Gimme a hit.

KINK: No.

MARVIN: I beg your pardon.

KINK: No drinkee.

TOM: Aw, but you don't care.

MARVIN: Kink, drink!

KINK: Bar closed.

MARVIN: Kink, gimme a hit!

(KINK *sings "The Boys Are Back in Town" or other sprightly Top Ten song.*)

TOM: I mean, you've got it made. You probably never have to cruise a bar, anyway. You probably have groupies waitin' to meet you at the airports.

MARVIN: Tom, despite what you may have heard in the herd, being successful does not make a person attractive. People who are attractive before they get successful are maybe a little more attractive for having their picture in the paper. Otherwise, not.

TOM: I can't believe that.

MARVIN: Then let's not talk about it.

TOM: I mean, you were young and in New York once, you been here a long time, I read the dates on your plays, you been here awhile, was it always like this?

MARVIN: I don't know. Yes, it looked like it. I don't know.

TOM: Whaddaya mean, you don't know? You were here!

MARVIN: Tom [*German accent*], I vas neffer a cute kit. I vas neffer sucked into queer covens and made much uff. I vas neffer indoctrinated, inoculated, instructed, and installed. If I had been, I would never have had the time to write those boxes full of plays in there, dimwit!

30

TOM: Oh, Jesus, I never thought of that. That's sad.

MARVIN: Kink, giff me a trink!

KINK: You told me not to let you drink when you're sad, Marvin.

MARVIN: That's the only time I *want* to drink, Kink.

(KINK *still refuses him a drink.*)

TOM: Yeah, but look, being successful, that's something, though, that's worth it, isn't it? Isn't it?

MARVIN: It enables me to buy Crown Royal—which I am, of course, unable to drink. [*Turns glass upside down.*] Thanks, Kink.

KINK: That's all right. It's always more fun to be able to torment your best friends when it's for their own good.

TOM: But look, anyway, you must have made a lot of money.

MARVIN: That in itself is not attractive.

TOM: I think it is.

MARVIN: Can we change the subject?

TOM: I mean, if nothing else, you can afford the best hustlers.

MARVIN: I have afforded them, okay? Stick that in your column. It's degrading. It's ridiculous. I giggled all through it. I could also afford a remote-controlled dildo up my ass. That scarcely constitutes romantic love. What I *can* afford that I *do* like is travel.

TOM: You're not pulling that old "lonely at the top" bit on me, are you?

MARVIN: It was lonely at the bottom, Tom!

TOM: But—

MARVIN: Coffee time! [[*Exits to kitchen.*]

KINK: Sigh—that whiskey was a bad idea. I thought I might get you and him together.

TOM: God, he's up and down like a yo-yo, isn't he?

KINK: You touched one or two hundred sensitive points is all. Don't worry.

TOM: I didn't mean to offend him. What's—what's—what did I say wrong? He doesn't like to talk about fame and money?

KINK: Oh—having only one problem makes it seem bigger. Probably he likes you.

TOM: This is how he shows it?

KINK: He's a romantic and you're romantically beautiful. He'll get over it.

TOM: Romantically beautiful? Me? You think so, huh?

KINK: You have beautiful eyes. If I ever start an organ bank, ya wanna make a deal?

TOM: Christ, you two are like the pilot film for *M*A*S*H*. How long have y'all been together?

KINK: We've known each other since the first Earth Day. I used to do sets for all his shows.

TOM: I mean as lovers.

KINK: Lovers? Me and Marvin?

MARVIN: [*Off*] Put on some music.

KINK: You hate music.

MARVIN: [*Off*] Put on some news, then.

KINK: Stop up your ears.

TOM: Y'all aren't lovers?

KINK: No. Sigh.

MARVIN: [*Reenters with coffee.*] Kink's affections do not that way wend.

KINK: If you'll check the bookcases, you'll find several thousand skin mags full of masturbating punks. As the bartender said to the terminal alcoholics:

KINK AND MARVIN: "Draw your own conclusions."

TOM: Well, I really guess that I should go.

MARVIN: [*Looking in creamer*] God.

KINK: No, stick around.

MARVIN: Jesus God.

TOM: I don't think I'm making much of a hit here—

MARVIN: Jesus God Freud Marx Einstein and Moses.

TOM: Look, I'm sorry I depressed you.

MARVIN: You should be if you did, but you haven't. What's depressing me is that we live five flights up and we're out of milk.

KINK: I'll go down and get some.

MARVIN: No, don't. Tom, you got keys to Greg's icebox?

TOM: No. I would've gone down there if I did.

KINK: It's okay. I'll get some. [*Getting jacket.*]

MARVIN: Evahwhuh Ah evah went in mah whole damn life, Ah just caused nice people trouble.

KINK: I need cigarettes, anyway. Marvin?

MARVIN: Yes, yes, God, yes.

KINK: Tom?

TOM: Uh—yeah—Kents. I don't have any money—

KINK: That's okay. I'll be right back. [*Exits.*]

TOM: Thanks. [*To* MARVIN] Look, I'm really sorry I touched your sensitive points.

MARVIN: I would give ten million dollars if I could hear a sincere statement like that and not think of eighteen quasi-erotic comebacks.

TOM: I really do admire your plays.

MARVIN: "Thank you," he said graciously.

TOM: You know, it's not just me, everybody thinks you and Kink are lovers.

MARVIN: Good God.

TOM: I bet that's why you don't get laid. If you don't.

MARVIN: Tom, give it a rest.

TOM: I'm sorry.

MARVIN: Jesus Christ. I spend about twenty-four hours a day trying to steer clear of the subject, okay? I'm a drink or two under or I never would have let you get into it at all. [*Swills coffee.*] It's only when I'm a little plotzed up that I start dreaming, and disciplining myself out of the dreams, and hurting from the discipline, and lashing out at any- and everyone around me as if *they* were causing the pain. I was never attractive and I'm never going to be and I can't let hope interfere with my work anymore. It's too hard trying to type with my fingers crossed!

TOM: Do you write all the time?

MARVIN: I have trudgingly, drudgingly started to write again.

TOM: Something else for Broadway?

MARVIN: I write from what I know. What I know now isn't likely to make Broadway.

TOM: Why?

MARVIN: Because if anybody cared about the things I'm writing about, it wouldn't be necessary to write about them.

TOM: What are you writing about?

MARVIN: [*With a hoarse laugh*] Gay life!

TOM: You don't have a lot of good things to say about it, do you?

MARVIN: Gay life is okay if you're very pretty or if you're rich and inhuman.

TOM: I'm very pretty.

MARVIN: And I'm rich. It stops there.

TOM: You mind if I tell you something?

MARVIN: You're right.

TOM: If you'd just slim down a little, maybe you'd be attractive.

MARVIN: I been slim. I been fat. I been young, I been old. I been rich, I been poor, I been everything in between and in all combinations. Nothin' happened. Have a drink. Drown me out.

TOM: No, I'm interested.

MARVIN: Why? Is there any of it you don't know, or any of it you can change? Or even any of it you disapprove of? Jesus! "Jesus." For a pack of presumed atheists we call on the orthodox deities enough, don't we? I can't do anything about the way gay life is and I don't want to sour it for anybody that gets along in it. Christ, who am I to criticize the only world you've got? So you bang Greg and he gives you jobs on the building with him. Great. So you put out a little to the boys around the bar and it gets you drinks and identity and a certain amount of entree. Great. What's wrong with it? You weren't looking for true love or you wouldn't have gravitated to that corner. So kids come to New York— or wherever—and they wind up one more item in a permanent exhibition of drunks. Big deal. So what if some kid's values are so fucked up he can't hold a job for a week, but he's in his third smash year in the back room of the Anvil? Not my problem. Dammit. Why should you tell a kid like that he's systematically eroding his ability to function as a human being? What does he care? Who wants him to function as anything but a punchboard and an active element in the exciting, expanding gay market? Telling some kid who's having his first social success as a fist-fuckee that he's plugged into a conglomerate as heartless as Con Ed is as pointlessly cruel as telling a girl from the Bronx that Binaca causes cancer! So what if his cock is always soft from chemicals—like Wonder Bread? Wonder Bread sells! He sells! He sells seashells by the seashore on Fire Island while he's blowin' his boss to get his first article into *Opera News*! So he gets the heebie-jeebies from Phebe's and CeebeeGeebee's and his heavy leather isn't heavy enough to stop his fits of shaking? Well, hell, what would there be for an American to do if he *did* grow up? There is counseling, there are tranquilizers, there's est and Sun Myung Moon and the Church of the Beloved Disciple and other forms of no-fault philosophy, Gail Sheehy live forever, and there's always the statistics on impotence, alcoholism, and suicide to make you feel you're not in this alone. Long-lasting relationships and thoughtful productive citizens don't do a damn thing for the disco business anyway. Stop me, huh?

TOM: No, no, go on, this is sensational.

MARVIN: Yeah? Well, don't believe a word of it, big breeches. If I had the slightest chance of getting in on any of it, you wouldn't hear a peep from me! [KINK *wanders in with grocery bag.*] The only reason I'm reactionary is because I get no reactions. My sex life has been limited to desperate drunks, indifferent junkies, catch-as-catch-can in the darkest corners of the baths, and other forms of bestiality with people! Have fun. Sell what you've got to sell! Get what you can for it! So what if sex has become nothing but a product of moral frustration? Even if it is a fault, it's not yours! When a society's only values are good looks and money, sooner or later people are going to wind up exchanging the one for the other! Gay life is great. Gay life is paradise. It's just that paradise lost . . . me. [*He stands, a tragic figure, head bowed, fists clenched.*]

KINK: [*When he is sure* MARVIN *is through*] I've told you a thousand times, Marvin—don't play with your words.

MARVIN: I didn't notice myself wanting you just now.

KINK: Don't you need someone to help you pull your fingernails out of your palms?

MARVIN: Look, I bear my fate with a happy heart and a sunny smile. Do I have to like it, too?

KINK: I apologize.

MARVIN: No, don't apologize; what you've done is unforgivable.

KINK: Well, anyway, I got cigarettes. Here. Here. [*Tosses them cigarettes.*]

MARVIN: That's one of the very few reasons that I love you.

KINK: And in case you used up all your bile mistreating Tom, I got some lovely slimy Stouffer's frozen dinners to replace it.

MARVIN: Here, gimme that there bag, I'll cook.

KINK: No, I'll do it. Y'all have fun.

MARVIN: I said I'll cook. Why should you cook? Why should one man bow down before another?

KINK: [*Old bit*] Because if they both bow down at once, they'll bang their heads together—

MARVIN: —and besides, nobody would ever get blowed. Gimme them groceries. [*Takes bag.*] Ol' Man Mose likes to feel he's still good for somethin' around this bunkhouse! [*Exits to kitchen.*]

TOM: Wow, when he gets goin' he's really beautiful, isn't he?

KINK: I don't see any loose pages around. Didn't he read to you?

TOM: No. He read me—out—like a book.

KINK: He has amazing insights. Well, outsights, actually. Insights he has none. I saw Greg in the bar downstairs.

TOM: Lady Astor's?

KINK: Yes. Lady Astor's. I love Lady Astor's. Greg says he's coming up in a minute.

TOM: That means twenty, at least. Did you tell him I was here?

KINK: No, I forgot. To tell him, I mean. I was going to,

but we got distracted. We were sitting in the window, and the most beautiful boy in the world kept walking by.

TOM: Every two minutes.

KINK: Right. Sorry I forgot to tell him. I was having a nicotine fit.

TOM: Oh, that's all right. You said we'd hear 'im.

KINK: Greg tells me you're a pretty good worker. I saw the work you did with him in the halls. It's good.

TOM: Not very. He's teaching me a lot. He says you taught him everything he knows.

KINK: I like teaching people. Makes me feel almost real.

TOM: If you ever have any jobs I can do in your shop, I'll work cheap. I need the money, and I'd enjoy working with you.

KINK: I have some big jobs coming up soon. I'll call you.

TOM: Yeah, do. I'm always down at Greg's.

KINK: Yeah, I know. Come up sometime and I'll show you the drawings, and you can tell me what you can do.

TOM: Okay, I'd like that. Do you like grass?

KINK: Yeah, I'm getting into it more now that I'm tied to the wagon.

TOM: I have some dynamite *kief*. Supposed to be from Uganda.

KINK: Fabulous.

TOM: I'll bring it up. I'd like to get to know you.

KINK: Great.

TOM: And maybe we can [*Glances at kitchen.*] you know. Whatever.

KINK: Great. Whatever.

TOM: Whatever.

MARVIN: [*Entering, crossing to his room*] I put it all in the oven. I have to drag a box out, Kink. Mind?

KINK: No. Which one?

MARVIN: Interviews. [*Exits into his room, closes door.*]

KINK: I hope he wasn't too rough on you.

TOM: No, he's very bright. It's a shame he isn't better-looking.

KINK: Well, looks aren't everything.

TOM: Yes, they are. Don't give me that tired shit. They

are so. If you've got looks you can get anything else. And if you don't, there isn't anything else worth having. I'm sick of that crap. Looks *are* everything. That's a terrible thing to say. Don't let me ever hear you say anything like that to an innocent kid again.

KINK: Very, very probably you're right.

MARVIN: [*Reenters with sizable cardboard box.*] Here. I just have to pick out a few of these.

TOM: What are all those, plays?

MARVIN: Interviews.

TOM: With who?

MARVIN: With me. I always take a few more along when I'm going to lecture. It's easier than writing a new bio.

TOM: Where do you do lectures?

MARVIN: Schools, mostly. I'm surprised I never hit yours. [*He is sorting out old Xeroxed interviews.*]

TOM: Hey, this one's in Italian.

MARVIN: Let's see. Oh, that was a fashion spread on me in Spoleto. Can you imagine people *wanting* to look like me?

KINK: When I think of you molding the minds of a generation—

MARVIN: Well, we can't leave it all to Donny Osmond. Gimme that back. [*Takes interview from* TOM, *is arranging a neat packet.*]

TOM: That's very heavy. What do you say to them?

MARVIN: I just try to share with them what few things I've learned in my brief forty years in Disneyland.

TOM: Are you *forty?*

KINK: Tom, that goes without saying. Please.

TOM: You don't look it. You don't have to be sensitive about your age.

MARVIN: I'm not, honey. One nice thing about bein' born ugly, things don't get any worse when you get old.

TOM: What do you *say* when you lecture?

MARVIN: Oh, I just tell 'em, "Write what you want to write. To thine own self be true." Things kids need to know.

KINK: "When you walk downstairs in spurs, point your feet out."

TOM: Ha! "Learn to live without underwear."

MARVIN: "Never try to reheat egg foo young."

KINK: "Never ask a dwarf, 'Who's your shrink?' "

TOM: "When the sun comes up on you it's going down on somebody else."

KINK: "You never know anyone well—"

KINK AND MARVIN: "—'cause nobody's well."

MARVIN: "Don't take candy from strangers; get real estate."

KINK: "Harry Reems while Rome burns."

MARVIN: [*Completing his task*] There, these'll do. [*He puts envelope of interviews in his coat pocket.*]

TOM: Wait, I got one: "You can always do your homework during the long commercials on cut-down afternoon reruns of 'Star Trek.' "

MARVIN: [*Repacking box*] I got asked to write a pilot for a CB series called "Star Truck."

TOM: No kidding. Hey, is there anything on TV?

KINK: Probably.

MARVIN: [*Lugging box back to room*] Wait! I've got a *TV Guide* in my room—somewhere. [*Exits to room with box*].

KINK: You shouldn't have said that. Marvin hates TV.

TOM: Why, what did TV ever do to him?

KINK: Are you kidding? What did it do to all of us?

MARVIN: [*Reenters with any magazine except TV Guide.*] Here we are. Oh, it's a bounteous evening. Listen: " 'The Odd Couple.' Oscar wants to fuck and Felix just wants to neck. They decide to compromise and do both."

TOM: It doesn't really say that.

MARVIN: And there's a brand-new Raquel Welch flick on. Must be a real bomb: the first reel is playing on TV while the last one is still playing on Times Square.

KINK: I think Beverly Sills is premiering her new show: "Stupor Market."

MARVIN: Yes: "Tonight Xaviera Hollander gives whore-household hints."

KINK: And Dinah Shore turns around so fast her wig doesn't.

MARVIN: On "Disco Dogs" Truman Capote teaches us all the steps.

TOM: I know the steps: smoking, drinking, staying out late, making unsuitable friends—

MARVIN: A new game show where you win a roll of money big enough to fuck!

KINK: Tom Kopay in "Supports Illustrated."

TOM: And Dean Martin sings—uh—

MARVIN: A religious flick: "Two young lovers are reunited at the foot of the cross."

TOM: Dean Martin sings—

KINK: Channel 13—interview with Charles Manson's mother: "You never know what's gonna crawl out of your crotch."

TOM: Dean Martin sings—

MARVIN: "Girl Talk": Will he notice me if I eat his shoes?

TOM: Dean sings—"Fifty Ways to Lose Your Liver"?

KINK: Chevy Chase in a new series: "White Meat."

TOM: Let's really watch.

MARVIN: Rhoda marries an ordained dentist.

TOM: Do you not wanna watch?

KINK: "Guest Star Farm": Watch clippings from Diana Ross develop into Lola Falana.

TOM: I'd like to watch.

MARVIN: There isn't time to watch TV.

TOM: Why not?

MARVIN: There never is! There never has been! And there never will be!

TOM: Awwwww—

MARVIN: Look, the only thing worth watching on TV is Lily Tomlin, right? So I'll do Lily Tomlin. [*Imitates "Boogie Woman" character.*] "Now, a lot of the bretheren and sisteren have been beseeching me with the same question. They say, 'Boogie Woman, what does doo-waddy-doo mean?' and I say, 'What does doo-waddy-do mean?' And they says, 'Yes, yes, tell us, what does doo-waddy-doo *mean*?' An' I say, 'All right, I'm gonna tell you what doo-waddy-doo *means*.'" [*Aside*] *They* usually cheer.

TOM AND KINK: Yea, yea.

MARVIN: "And then I say, 'Doo-waddy-doo means just this: it ain't enough to go around and be a mouth Christian and *say* what the Lord *say*. You can't just *say* what he *say*; you gotta *do* what he *do*—*do* what he *do*—*doo* waddy, *doo* waddy, *doo* waddy *doo*!' "

TOM: [*Applauds.*] That's wonderful. But I'd still like to watch TV.

MARVIN: Lord, Lord, Lord.

TOM: I mean, we can relax, we're going to go to bed or something later, you don't have to be tense, but can't we watch a little TV first?

MARVIN: Watch us instead.

TOM: I have been.

MARVIN: No, *all* of us. Look, Tom, wouldn't you rather be on TV? Than watch it?

TOM: Sure.

MARVIN: Okay, this is your big chance. Take off your clothes.

TOM: Uh-oh. What is this, an audition?

MARVIN: No, no, we're all taking off our clothes. Kink?

KINK: I will not.

MARVIN: Come on. It's my last request. Do I refuse you your whims?

KINK: Constantly.

MARVIN: Do you like it when I do it?

KINK: No.

MARVIN: Then *don't* do it to me! Come on, undress. It's something I discovered the other day. [*He starts undressing.*]

TOM: [*Also undressing. To* KINK] Oh, God, I knew it'd wind up like this. Do you *have* any grass?

KINK: [*Stripping*] Growing on the roof. It'll be soaked.

TOM: How do I get into these things?

MARVIN: This is the usual way. Kink?

KINK: I am. I am. God.

TOM: God.

MARVIN: Quit callin' me God, I haven't created anything yet. [*They are all three stripped by now.*] Now, come on, we all sit down here. [*He arranges them on a cushion in front of the TV.*]

41

KINK: This better be good.

MARVIN: [*Sitting with them.*] It is. It is. Watch.

TOM: God, Kink, you're hung.

KINK: You're young yet.

MARVIN: Okay. Now squeeze close together. Now watch. [*He clicks off the lights.*]

TOM: [*In the dark*] Marvin, this is really not subtle.

MARVIN: Wait. [*He clicks on another light, a lovely colored spotlight.*] Now, look in the TV screen.

TOM: Hand me my glasses. [KINK *does.*]

KINK: Oh my.

TOM: [*With glasses*] Oh, I get it.

MARVIN: See? There we are. On TV. Looking all three-dimensional.

KINK: That's very pretty.

MARVIN: I always wanted to see little naked people on TV.

TOM: You're especially three-dimensional, Marvin.

MARVIN: Yeah, well, I used this shampoo that promised "more body." Here, form a group.

KINK: We do already.

TOM: No, Marvin, you're really fat.

MARVIN: That's why I live with an upholsterer. Aren't we pretty?

TOM: I see. When there's light just on you, you reflect real bright in the TV screen.

KINK: We really do look just like three pretty little Maxfield Parrish nudes.

TOM: Even Marvin's pretty.

MARVIN: Isn't it nice? I discovered it the other day.

(*They admire themselves,* TOM *especially, try two or three different poses.*)

KINK: It really is, Marvin, it really is very nice. Thank you.

TOM: Yeah, really. [*He flexes his muscles.*] Yeah. [*He gets onto ladder to* KINK's *sleeping loft, which also reflects.*] Yeah, this is great.

MARVIN: [*Looking directly up into* TOM's *crotch*] Hey, what am I?

KINK: Mmmmmm—I don't know. A gay gynecologist?

MARVIN: No, I'm Michelangelo, auditioning a model.

TOM: [*Coming down*] Here, let's try some more arrangements with the three of us.

KINK: Uh—it really is very pretty, Marvin. I think I'm going to the baths after all.

MARVIN: Okay.

TOM: Oh . . .

KINK: [*Getting dressed*] I'm sorry, I'm just getting very nervous.

MARVIN: That's all right.

KINK: I'll see you when you get back.

MARVIN: I'll call you when I get there to let you know we didn't crash.

TOM: [*Still admiring himself*] Where are you going?

KINK: Marvin's leaving for Rome tonight.

TOM: Huh?

KINK: [*As* MARVIN *starts to dress*] I'd go to the airport with you—

MARVIN: It's all right. It's no big deal. Are you all right for money while I'm gone?

KINK: Yeah, the rent's paid.

MARVIN: Call my terrible agent if you need anything.

KINK: I shouldn't have to. [*He is dressed by now.*] Have a good trip.

MARVIN: I'll let you know if I'm going on to Africa or anywhere.

KINK: [*Puts on leather jacket*] Send me a pygmy. A big one. Don't get caught in any wars.

MARVIN: I'm a big boy now.

KINK: [*Adds sequined scarf*] Yeah, well, try to do something about that, too. Tom, come up anytime, like I said.

TOM: [*Still naked, on cushion*] Yeah—I will. Hey, I thought we were going to eat.

KINK: [*At door*] And maybe we will. [*To mock maid*] Matilda! The baby's under the pyramid; turn him over in a half an hour! If my guru calls, tell him I'm at my color-breathing class! [*Exits.*]

TOM: You're goin' to Rome? Tonight?

MARVIN: Yes, I have to get a taxi pretty soon.

TOM: Far out. You going to be gone long?

MARVIN: I may go on to Africa, and maybe Brazil.

TOM: For shows and things.

MARVIN: For whatever.

TOM: Well, I guess I should go.

MARVIN: No, stay till Greg comes in. Just close the door when you go. [*He darts into john, comes out with shaving stuff, which he jams in a coat pocket.*]

TOM: Well, but what if I turn out to be some kind of thief?

MARVIN: So what's to take?

TOM: The TV?

MARVIN: Oh, please. Shall I wrap it?

TOM: What about all that food in the oven?

MARVIN: You and Greg have it.

TOM: When you coming back?

MARVIN: When my luck runs out—or there's somethin' to come back for.

TOM: You do this all the time?

MARVIN: Wherever they want me, I'll go.

TOM: Fantastic.

MARVIN: I like it.

TOM: You need help packing?

MARVIN: Naw. This coat's got big pockets. I just shove some T-shirts in the pocket and I go. [*He jams a handful of T-shirts in coat pocket.*]

TOM: *Gets up, puts on shorts.*] Well, look, maybe I'll see you sometime when you get back. It was a real honor getting to meet you.

MARVIN: Yeah, sure. I'll be back, I guess. [*He's got coat on.*]

TOM: Look, wait. There's something I would really like to say to you. All joking aside, you shouldn't have to be so—[*Music, low, throbbing, not yet drowning them out but threatening to, starts from downstairs.*]

MARVIN: Hey, Greg's back. Y'all have a real good time.

TOM: You going now?

MARVIN: Might as well.

(*Music suddenly blares out, far too loud for them to hear each other.*)

TOM: [*Shouts.*] I really do wish you the best of luck.

MARVIN: What?

TOM: The best of luck!

MARVIN: [*With gestures*] Can't hear you. 'Bye. [*Stops at door.*] Oh, God, have I got taxi money? [*Takes out huge roll of bills, counts one or two off, puts them in another pocket, returns roll to safe place, throws on a big funny hat, and goes, blowing a kiss to* TOM.]

(TOM *stands alone, not moving for a moment. Then the phone starts to ring. It can barely be heard. He thinks he hears it and starts looking for it. Perhaps it could have a blinking light as well. Just as he sees it and is on his way over cushions to answer it, the answering machine starts. Simultaneously the music downstairs is turned drastically down.*)

ANSWERING MACHINE: [*In* KINK'S *voice*] Hello. You have reached the home of Kink Carstairs. In a moment, you may leave a message. But first, a word from our sponsor. Do you have sexual irregularity problems? Don't despair. At the first sign of difficulty, call Roto-Rooter. Remember, with a friend like me—you don't need enemas. [*Beep.*]

GREG'S VOICE: [*It is a very nice voice.*] Hi, Kink. This is Greg downstairs. I just came in and I'm feeling terminally lonely. Do you and Marvin want to come down whenever you get in and play some bridge or something? Don't worry about waking me. I don't intend to sleep.

TOM: [*Grabs phone before* GREG *can hang up.*] Hey, Greg, hi. It's Tom.

GREG: Oh, hi.

TOM: Yeah, I've been visiting them. You weren't home so I came up to get out of the rain.

GREG'S VOICE: Terrific. Are they there?

TOM: No, they've both gone out. For the night.

GREG: Well, do you want to come down? I'd like you to.

TOM: Yeah, sure. I'll be right down.

GREG: Okay.

TOM: Or, wait, listen, I got a better idea. Why don't you come up here? They left some good food in the kitchen, and a whole bottle of Crown Royal.

GREG: Okay. God. I'm glad I got you. I feel like shit.

TOM: Well, come on up.

GREG: Okay. I'll be right there.

TOM: Okay. [*Hangs up.*]

(*The music instantly goes back to top volume. It should be Presley's "Jailhouse Rock." TOM starts to dress, then looks at the TV set. He breaks into a big smile, takes off whatever he has put on, and lies down on the cushion. He arranges himself invitingly, looking in the TV, then carefully, without changing his pose, puts his glasses safely out of reach and lies there, tapping his toe to the music.*)

THE CURTAIN FALLS

BOY MEETS BOY
A Musical Comedy
in Two Acts

Book by
Bill Solly and Donald Ward

Music and Lyrics by
Bill Solly

Boy Meets Boy was first presented Off-Broadway at the Actors' Playhouse on September 17, 1975, with the following cast:

CASEY O'BRIEN	*Joe Barrett*
ANDREW	*Paul Ratkevich*
GUY ROSE	*David Gallegly*
BELLBOY	*Bobby Bowen*
REPORTERS	*Richard King*
	Bobby Reed
	Dan Rounds
PHOTOGRAPHERS	*Jan Crean*
	Monica Grignon
THE VAN WAGNERS	*Bobby Bowen*
	Kathy Willinger
CLARENCE CUTLER	*Raymond Wood*
LADY ROSE	*Rita Gordon*
BRUCE	*Bobby Reed*
ASSISTANT HOTEL MANAGER	*Richard King*
PORTER	*Richard King*
ROSITA	*Kathy Willinger*
LOLITA	*Mary-Ellen Hanlon*
PEPITA	*Jan Crean*
JANE	*Monica Grignon*
JOSEPHINE LA ROSE	*Rita Gordon*
ALPHONSE	*Bobby Bowen*

The scenery and lighting design were by David Sackeroff, musical direction and vocal arrangements by David Friedman, keyboard and dance arrangements by James Fradrich, costumes by Sherry Buchs, musical numbers staged by Robin Reseen, directed by Ron Troutman.

CHARACTERS

CASEY O'BRIEN
ANDREW
GUY ROSE
CLARENCE CUTLER

LADY ROSE
JOSEPHINE LA ROSE } Played by same actress

MAIDS
AMERICAN WIFE
GIRL REPORTERS
CABARET LINE
NIGHTCLUB GUESTS
SPANISH DANCERS } Played by chorus of four girls

BELLHOP
AMERICAN HUSBAND
REPORTERS
WAITERS
ESCORT (BRUCE)
CABARET LINE
NIGHTCLUB GUESTS
STRIPPERS
ALPHONSE (NUDE)
ASSISTANT HOTEL MANAGER } Played by chorus of four boys

SETTING AND TIME: London and Paris, December 1936.

SYNOPSIS OF MUSICAL NUMBERS

Act I
    Prologue: "Boy Meets Boy" .... *Chorus*
                "Party in Room 203" .... *Chorus*
    "Giving It Up for Love" .... *Casey and Andrew*
    "Me" .... *Clarence and Chorus*
    "The English Rose" ..... *Reporters and Photographers*
    "Marry an American" .... *Chorus*

Bill Solly and Donald Ward

"It's a Boy's Life" .... *Casey and Guy*
"Does Anybody Love You?" .... *Guy*
"You're Beautiful" .... *Guy*
"Let's!" .... *Casey and Chorus*
"Let's!" (Dance) .... *Casey and Guy*
"Giving It Up for Love" (Reprise) .... *Casey*
Finaletto .... *Clarence and Chorus*

Act II

"Just My Luck" .... *Casey, Clarence, Girls*
"It's a Dolly" .... *Josephine and Boys*
"What Do I Care?" .... *Guy*
"Clarence's Turn" .... *Clarence*
"Does Anybody Love You?" (Reprise) .. *Casey and Guy*
Finale .... *Company*

50

ACT I

Prologue

No overture. In front of the cloth, a CHORUS *of boys and girls, in evening dress 1930s style, enters singing.*

CHORUS: Boy meets boy tonight,
　　　　Finds with joy tonight
　　　　The perfect mate
　　　　That fate
　　　　Cannot destroy tonight.
　　　　Back when gentlemen were gentle,
　　　　Just the thing to make you sentimental.

　　　　Night and day again
　　　　Love is gay again,
　　　　And though our story's just that old cliché again,
　　　　What a beautiful blend:
　　　　Boy meets boy,
　　　　Boy loses boy,
　　　　But boy gets boy in the end!

BLACKOUT

[*A title appears.*]

SAVOY HOTEL

Friday, December 11, 1936

CHORUS: [*Off*] More glasses! More ice! More liquor! More
　　　　　mix! [*Louder*]
　　　　　More glasses! More ice! More liquor! More
　　　　　mix! [*Louder*]

51

More glasses! More ice! More liquor! More
mix! [CHORUS *appears, dressed as maids
and bellhops.*]
And tell the chef it's caviar for eighty-six!

Party in Room 203!
Wilder than any before!
It's calm and serene
On the mezzanine
But they're raising the roof on the second
floor!
Party in room 203!
Heavens, the hullabaloo!
It goes on and on,
It's a marathon!

GIRLS: [*Singing*] And the party is thrown by guess who?

BOYS: Who?

GIRLS: Casey O'Brien!

BOYS: Casey O'Brien!

GIRLS: Yes, that fabulous American's in town
again!

BOYS: The famous foreign correspondent!

GIRLS: Big white hunter!

BOYS: Transatlantic pilot!

GIRLS: Big-time punter!

BOYS: Mountain-climbing or
Off to win a war
He's a man among men!

GIRLS: You can say that again.

ALL: And he's the party in room 203
       Throwing the party in room 203!
       With ev'ry guest a celebrity
       It's got the makings of history!
       So if it's a riot that you want to see
       Go—to—two—oh—three!

Scene 1

CHORUS *dances off.*

Curtains open to reveal CASEY's *hotel bedroom, the next morning. There is the aftermath of a terrific party—bottles, streamers, balloons, etc.*

CASEY, *fully dressed, lies on the bed, an ice-bag on his head.*

ANDREW *knocks and enters without waiting for an answer, gazes down at the inert form of* CASEY *and gingerly picks up a corner of ice bag to peer underneath.* CASEY *groans and* ANDREW *drops the bag back in place.*

ANDREW: Sorry. Just wanted to see who it was.
CASEY: [*From under ice bag*] Well, don't keep it to yourself. Who am I?
ANDREW: You bear a faint resemblance to Casey O'Brien, toast of London and wrecker of the Savoy Hotel.
CASEY: That's what I was afraid of. Who are you?
ANDREW: It's Andrew, Casey. I hear it was quite a party?
CASEY: [*Removing ice bag*] You mean it's over?
ANDREW: And high time, too. According to the house detectives, the porter, the lift boy, the chambermaid . . .
CASEY: Who invited the chambermaid?
ANDREW: My dear chap, what are you doing here anyway? I thought you were covering Spain.
CASEY: I'm giving the war a rest. New York wants some dope on Mrs. Simpson and her romance with Buckingham Palace. Human-interest stuff.
ANDREW: I see. And when are you planning to send off your column?
CASEY: There's no rush. I don't suppose I missed much. What's the King been doing?

ANDREW: He's abdicated.

CASEY: [*Aghast*] Abdicated?!

ANDREW: For the woman he loves.

CASEY: He's running away with Wally Simpson?

ANDREW: Apparently. He spoke on the wireless last night. Everybody's talking about it.

CASEY: I don't suppose you're kidding?

ANDREW: It's not in my character.

CASEY: What a dumb thing to do—giving up the throne of England for a dame.

ANDREW: For love.

CASEY: Yeah, well, why the hell couldn't he have waited?

ANDREW: I expect nobody told him you were having a party.

CASEY: That's right, rub it in. I suppose you sympathize with him.

ANDREW: Yes, why not?

CASEY: Aw, you're all alike, you guys. You give me a pain. One smile from a dame and you go to pieces.

ANDREW: You should talk. What about you and that bullfighter?

CASEY: We were just good friends.

ANDREW: That's not what that papers said.

CASEY: All I have to do is wink at a guy and they say it's wedding bells.

ANDREW: That's what it looked like from here. You chased those tight trousers around every bullring south of the Pyrenees.

CASEY: Bullfighting is an art. Hemingway and I are writing a book on it.

ANDREW: And last year in Africa, when you went swinging off into the jungle with that local Tarzan? . . .

CASEY: Strictly for laughs. Anyway, what about you and that Gwendolyn broad? She almost got you to the altar—twice!

ANDREW: What about you and that prizefighter?

CASEY: You and that Russian ballerina!

ANDREW: All right, I'm susceptible, I admit it. Why can't you?

CASEY: Susceptible, yes; suicidal, no. As far as I'm concerned romance is strictly for laughs. The King went too far! [*Sings.*]

> Love's okay
> For a rainy day
> Or to while away the blues
> But when love gets serious,
> Brother, that's bad news.

BOTH: There's just too much to lose!
The life of gay abandon, of excursions and alarms!

ANDREW: The pick of all the ladies and their charms!

CASEY: The right to spend each evening in a brand-new fella's arms!

BOTH: Imagine giving all of it up—for love!
The nightclubs and the taxis and the tickets to the smash!

ANDREW: The girls adore that fancy-free panache!

CASEY: You get the best of both worlds, from clean-shaven to mustache!

BOTH: Imagine giving all of it up for love!

ANDREW: Telling one another . . .

CASEY: "You be home by ten!"

ANDREW: "Please be nice to mother!"

CASEY: "Don't you dare go out with other men!"

BOTH: Why go and sell your birthright for a mess of cottage pie?

ANDREW: And marry just one girl.

CASEY: Or just one guy?

BOTH: What have we got in common with each other, you and I?
We both would state
To abdicate
Is not worth thinking of!
We can imagine giving all of it up for Lent
But, heavens above!
Imagine!—giving it up for love!
Ugh!

ANDREW: Anyway, somebody did give it all up for love, and you've missed out on the story of the decade.

56

CASEY: Stabbed in the back by the King of England!

ANDREW: Don't take it personally.

CASEY: Tell that to Reuters. As of now, I'm probably out of a job.

ANDREW: Rubbish. You're too big a name. Reuters would never dare to fire you.

(*The sound of a fast tap-dance step outside the door.* CASEY *trades a puzzled glance with* ANDREW *and opens door to tap-dancing bellhop.*)

BELLHOP: [*Dancing into room*] Telegram for Mr. O'Brien.

ANDREW: It's from Reuters.

(ANDREW *opens it and reads it.*)

CASEY: Well?

ANDREW: You're fired.

BELLHOP: [*To* CASEY] Nice party, Mr. O'Brien.

CASEY: [*Tipping him*] Yeah. It was nice while it lasted.

(BELLHOP *tap-dances out.*)

ANDREW: I don't wish to add to your troubles, but your party leftovers include one leg. [*Gestures below bed.*]

CASEY: My God, I'm an unemployed murderer. Is it attached to anything.

ANDREW: I think there's more under the bed.

CASEY: Let's have a look. [*Together they pull out a prostrate* YOUNG MAN.] Well, one thing's for sure. It wasn't a crime of passion. Not my type at all.

ANDREW: Maybe somebody else's.

CASEY: Doesn't look like anybody's type to me.

(*This is true: the* YOUNG MAN, *in dowdy clothes and hairstyle and rimless glasses, is no beauty.*)

ANDREW: Let's get him on the bed.

57

(*Together they lift him into a sitting position on the bed.*)

CASEY: [*Slapping* YOUNG MAN's *cheeks*] Hey, gorgeous, wake up. [*With a groan, the* YOUNG MAN *collapses backwards onto the bed.*] Boy, if that's a sample of the party, it wasn't worth getting fired for.

ANDREW: How are you off for money?

CASEY: If I can hold out until my birthday, my aunt usually sends me five bucks.

ANDREW: What are you going to do?

CASEY: Well, I could go back to bed, but it's occupied. I guess I'll have to go to work.

ANDREW: [*Proffering newspaper*] D'you want to look at "Situations Vacant"?

CASEY: Andrew, I need a story. Gimme some ideas. [*Starts tidying himself up.*]

ANDREW: [*Glancing through paper*] There's always Abyssinia.

CASEY: Skip the headlines. Give me the news, human-interest stuff. Something for the old O'Brien treatment.

ANDREW: Christmas . . . ?

CASEY: No.

ANDREW: No. . . . First snow of the year?

CASEY: No.

ANDREW: No. . . . Orphans spend the night in Harrod's Toyland?

CASEY: No!

ANDREW: No. . . . Clarence Cutler wedding this afternoon. . . .

CASEY: Clarence Cutler, the Boston millionaire?

ANDREW: Yes.

CASEY: Yes! Who's the lucky man?

ANDREW: Some society chap.

CASEY: Okay, I'll get my hat and we'll go.

ANDREW: Where are we going?

CASEY: To a wedding!

BLACKOUT

Scene 2

Exterior, church. Music.
Three newspapermen enter along with two female photog-
raphers. The music fades as two wedding guests arrive, an
AMERICAN COUPLE.

PHOTOGRAPHERS: Smile for the camera!

(*They twinkle as their pictures are taken.*)

"NEWS": Could I have your names, please?
AMERICAN HUSBAND: We are—
AMERICAN WIFE: We're Mr. and Mrs. Horace Van Wagner
from Boston, Massachusetts, and we're very happy to be
here in your beautiful England.
"NEWS": Then I take it you're friends of Clarence Cutler?
HUSBAND: We are—
WIFE: We are very good friends of Clarence Cutler. He's
a millionaire, you know. And we've come all the way
over on your lovely *Queen Mary* specially for the wed-
ding.
"NEWS": What do you think of the other groom?
HUSBAND: Well, we—
WIFE: Well, we've not yet had the pleasure of meeting the
Honourable Guy Rose, but we're sure he's a very gra-
cious person. And we're just thrilled that at last Clarence
has found a nice young man to settle down with.
"NEWS": Do you think that Cutler is marrying for love or
just the title?
WIFE: If you'll excuse us, we must take our places in the
pews among the nobility.

(MR. *and* MRS. VAN WAGNER *proceed across and exit.*)

"TELEGRAPH": Who is this Guy Rose anyway? This is the
wedding of the week and we don't even know what he
looks like.

"NEWS": Here comes Clarence Cutler.

(CLARENCE *arrives, very smug and proud.*)

PHOTOGRAPHERS: Smile for the camera!

(CLARENCE *does his best Myrna Loy.*)

"TIMES": Anything for the press, Mr. Cutler?

(CLARENCE *sings.*)

CLARENCE: On this grand and glorious day
To the public what can I say?
Are there words to express
Total happiness?

At this lovely lyrical time
As above the wedding bells chime,
How can I even start
To describe that person dearest to my heart?

Me!
Who's my favorite person? It's me!
As an expert I'm forced to agree
To the life, to the letter
There's nobody better to be!

I'm
Always having me such a good time
In a style that is simply sublime!
When you've plenty of jack you
Can live so spectacu-
Larly!

Rich!
Put me down for ten million, to which
You can add I'm a son of a
Fine
Old family line

Dating back to nine-
Teen twenty-three!

And who
Has so much he's too good to be true?
Young and wealthy and beautiful too?
Golly gee,
If I were you,
I'd be me!

CHORUS: He . . .
CLARENCE: Made a stock market killing
CHORUS: And he . . .
CLARENCE: Thinks it's terribly thrilling
CHORUS: That he . . .
CLARENCE: Should be merging all this stock
With British aristoc-racy!
Whoopee!
CHORUS: Whoopee!
CLARENCE: Who's the darling of society?
CHORUS: Who can it be?
CLARENCE: Speaking monosyllabically,
Who is he?
From Baltimore to Battersea
To ev'ry door who's got the key?
Nobody else but open sesa—me me me me me
me me me!

(CLARENCE *exits.*)

"NEWS": [*To photographer*] Did you get a good picture?
PHOTOGRAPHER: I've got lots of pictures of *him*. What about the other one, this Guy Rose?
"NEWS": I don't know what he looks like. [*To* "TELEGRAPH"] What does the Honourable Guy Rose look like?
"TELEGRAPH": Nobody knows.
"NEWS": What do you mean, nobody knows? How will we recognize him when he arrives?
"TIMES": Here comes his mother. Let's ask her.

(LADY ROSE *enters.*)

PHOTOGRAPHERS: Smile for the camera!

"NEWS": Lady Rose, how do you feel about having an American in the family?

LADY ROSE: Lord Rose and I are delighted at the match, and we're sure that Guy and Mr. Cutler will be very happy.

"TELEGRAPH": Where are they going to live?

"NEWS": Are they going to live in England?

"TIMES": Are they going to live in America?

"TELEGRAPH": Where are they going to honeymoon?

"NEWS": How big is his dowry?

"TIMES": What does he look like?

LADY ROSE: Mr. Cutler is tall . . . [*or* "slightly stout," depending on actor]

"TELEGRAPH": No, your son.

"NEWS": Is he good-looking?

LADY ROSE: Gentlemen, gentlemen . . . you may quote me as saying that Lord Rose and I both feel that we are not losing a son, we're gaining a son. Good day, gentlemen. [*Goes.*]

"NEWS": Well, that wasn't much help. We still don't know what he looks like.

"TELEGRAPH": [*Looking off*] Maybe this is him now. . . .

(ALL *look off.*)

"TIMES": Jumping Jehoshaphat!

"NEWS": Oh, my God, it can't be!

PHOTOGRAPHERS: It is!

ALL: Casey O'Brien!

PHOTOGRAPHER: When did he get back?

"TELEGRAPH": Last year in Abyssinia he stole my story.

"TIMES": That's nothing. He had me arrested—when he convinced the authorities that I was an Italian spy.

"NEWS": He convinced me that Mussolini was something that you eat with spaghetti.

"TELEGRAPH": Let's face it. He scoops everybody. He's on top of every news story.

"NEWS": Hey, wait a second. What's he doing at a wedding?

"TIMES": There must be something going on.

"NEWS": Well, I don't care what it is, don't give him a thing!

(*They look nonchalant as* CASEY *enters.*)

CASEY: Well, well, well, the flower of Fleet Street.

"TIMES": Hello, Casey. How are the bullfighters this season?

CASEY: Broken-hearted. Loved your book on Abyssinian jails.

"NEWS": What are you doing at a wedding, Casey?

"TELEGRAPH": One of the grooms an old flame of yours?

CASEY: No, strictly business. [*Takes out notebook.*] Fill me in on the facts, fellas. Clarence Cutler I know about. Who's this Guy Rose?

"TIMES": That's what we all want to . . . oof! . . .

("NEWS" *has just jabbed* "TIMES" *in the ribs.*)

"NEWS": [*To* CASEY] You mean you've never heard of Guy Rose?

CASEY: Nope.

"NEWS": [*To others*] Did you hear that? He's never heard of Guy Rose.

"TELEGRAPH": Just fancy.

"TIMES": Amazing.

CASEY: You mean he's a looker?

"NEWS": "A looker"?

CASEY: Good-looking, cute, handsome!

"NEWS": Well, let me put it this way. You've heard of the American Beauty Rose?

CASEY: Yeah.

"NEWS": Well, he's the English one.

CASEY: The English Rose!

REPORTERS: [*With a look at each other*] Yes, the English Rose!

CASEY: I'm interested, describe him.

"NEWS": Well . . . [*Sings*]

Just picture perfection in silken clothes,
"TELEGRAPH": A dazzling Adonis from head to toes!
"TIMES": Complete with an aristocratic nose!
ALL: The English Rose
Is one of those!

A delicate blossom who only grows
Where diamonds glitter and champagne
    flows,
Who makes people stare everywhere he
    goes—
The one and only
English Rose!
"NEWS": What's his profile? It's a dream!
"TELEGRAPH": His complexion? Honey-cream!
"TIMES": And he's clever—that's the truth!
ALL: Brains go hand in hand with beauty
In this finest flower of youth!
"NEWS": What a face to idolize!
"TELEGRAPH": What a perfect pair of eyes!
"NEWS":   They're a brilliant
                                 shade of green!
              [*Simultaneously*]
"TELEGRAPH":   They're a brilliant
                                 shade of brown!

(*They stop and then try again.*)

"NEWS":   They're a brilliant
                                 shade of brown!
              [*Simultaneously*]
"TELEGRAPH":   They're a brilliant
                                 shade of green!

(*Another pause.*)

BOTH: Well, they're sort of in-between!
CASEY: [*Puzzled*] Brown or green?
ALL: What's it matter if they're lovelier than
any eyes you've seen?
Who's got what the French would call
quelque chose?

And so many suitors they come to blows!
A thousand romantic lotharios
Are kneeling to propose
To the dashing!
Simply smashing!
And the one and only
Perfect English Rose!

(*At the end of the song* CASEY *is totally entranced. There is a loud wail offstage and immediately the* AMERICAN COUPLE *reenter from the church. The* WIFE *is blubbering, in floods of rage.*)

"NEWS": What's the matter? What's wrong?
HUSBAND: Well—
WIFE: I'll tell you what's wrong! We came all this way on that rowboat—for nothing!
"NEWS": You mean the wedding's over?
WIFE: There isn't going to be any wedding! Clarence Cutler has been jilted at the altar by your horrible Guy Rose!

(*They plunge off. Consternation among* REPORTERS. *Then* LADY ROSE *hurries on.*)

"NEWS": Lady Rose, give us a statement!
LADY ROSE: [*Tight-lipped*] My son is not coming. I don't know where he is. I have nothing else to say. I believe there's a scandal—in the family! [*She hurries off.*]
"TIMES": Here comes Cutler!

(CLARENCE *comes on, purple with rage.*)

"NEWS": Mr. Cutler, give us a statement!
PHOTOGRAPHER: How do you feel at this moment?
"TIMES": Is it all over?
"NEWS": Do you forgive him?
"TELEGRAPH": Would you take him back?
"TIMES": Are you going to see him?
"NEWS:": Are you going to sue?
ALL: Follow him!

(*During all this* CLARENCE *says nothing, simply stalks across in a desperate attempt at dignity, and exits, all the* REPORTERS *pursuing him off.*

CASEY *remains and is joined by* ANDREW *coming from the church.*)

ANDREW: What are you doing here? Cutler's getting away.
CASEY: He's beautiful!
ANDREW: Cutler?
CASEY: Rose!
ANDREW: Casey, I've seen that look in your eyes before. Think about your story!
CASEY: I've got my story. A great story: "Titled Beauty Jilts Wall Street"! And I've got a great follow-up!
ANDREW: But aren't you going after Cutler?
CASEY: No! I'm going to find the English Rose!

BLACKOUT

Scene 3

Spot picks out CLARENCE.

CLARENCE: This isn't true. It can't be happening. I've eaten too much wedding cake and any moment I'll wake up and find myself a happily married man. Me—Clarence Cutler, Boston's crème de la crème—laid low by a nobody, a nothing! The newspapers are having a field day. I'll be laughed out of society. And it's all your fault, Mister Guy Nobody Rose. Would you please tell me what the hell is going on here?

(*Lights up. We are back in* CASEY's *hotel room.*

GUY *is the dowdy young man of the first scene, now conscious. He crawls out from beneath the bed.*)

GUY: I can't find my other shoe.
CLARENCE: You weren't very coherent over the telephone.

66

GUY: Yes, Clarence.

CLARENCE: Now—you were sitting in the American Bar downstairs . . . Guy, you don't drink!

GUY: I know. But last night I thought I would. Then I remember a mob of people came in yelling "Party in Room 203" . . . and I don't remember anything after that.

CLARENCE: That's the most idiotic story I've ever heard! In this enormous city, teaming with pretty people, you're asking me to believe that somebody—anybody!—should choose *you*, Miss Dowdy of 1936, to be the belle of the ball! Anybody would be insane to believe that story! [*Pause as* CLARENCE *snorts fire.*]

GUY: [*Fearful*] What are you going to do, Clarence?

(*Another pause.*)

CLARENCE: [*Calm*] I'm going to believe it. Everything's going to be all right. We'll tell the press that you were led astray by false friends. Innocent in the big city . . . sheltered life . . . youthful folly—they'll lap it up. I can see it now—you humbly repentant, me nobly forgiving —on every front page in the country. And we'll be married as soon as we can get the church.

GUY: No.

CLARENCE: [*Going to phone*] What's the vicar's telephone number?

GUY: No.

CLARENCE: [*Nervous*] Yes, you're right. Why wait? We'll go to a registry office—

GUY: No, Clarence.

CLARENCE: Are you suggesting that we should live in sin?

GUY: I can't marry you, Clarence.

CLARENCE: [*Patiently*] Yes, you can, honeybunch. You're a grown-up man now. Unless you mean that you won't. Is that what you mean?

GUY: Yes.

CLARENCE: AAAAAAHHGGH! —Now, God knows I've been patient. [*To God*] Haven't I been patient? [*To* GUY] What do you want, blood?

GUY: I just want to be free.

CLARENCE: You've *been* free. Now it's time to get married.

GUY: But I haven't done anything yet. I want to live, see life!

CLARENCE: So live! When you marry, you don't stop breathing!

GUY: [*Quietly*] It's my last chance, Clarence. I've got to take it.

(*Pause as* CLARENCE *stiffens.*)

CLARENCE: If you're hoping to do better than me, I'm afraid you're going to be disappointed. Aside from being the heir to a faintly amusing title, you have very little to recommend you.

GUY: I know, Clarence. I'm not worthy of your love.

CLARENCE: Who said anything about love? You're lucky to get a civil good morning! Well, I've had enough of this playing hard-to-get. I'm going to teach you a lesson! Have you got any money? [GUY *shakes his head.*] I didn't think so. And you haven't got any friends except me. And your parents are absolutely furious with you. And outside it's snowing! So *have* your freedom, Mr. Guy Rose. Have your lovely time in the big wide world, see how you like it, and when you decide to come crawling back to me, maybe—just maybe—I'll be home. [*Sweeps out.*]

GUY: [*Worries for a moment, then runs to the telephone.*] Hello? I would like to make a call to France, please. Paris. I'm sorry, I don't know the number, just the name —Josephine La Rose. . . . [*He hears someone at the door, hangs up quickly, and dives under the bed.*]

CASEY: [*Off*] And I've spent an entire afternoon on this story and I don't want to change it.

ANDREW: [*Coming in with* CASEY] I still say you're being had.

CASEY: What do you know about it?

ANDREW: I know that I've never heard of this Guy Rose. There's nothing about him in the files, no pictures. [*Waving newspaper*] So how can you write a story like this?

CASEY: Well, it's selling like hot cakes, you must admit.

ANDREW: That's what worries me. [*Quoting from paper*] "The English Rose—beauty born to blush unseen. . . ." Supposing it isn't true?

CASEY: *You* suppose that. Me, I know it's true, just like I know I'm going to find Guy Rose. [*Sits on bed.*] He's probably right under my nose.

ANDREW: You don't even know what he looks like.

CASEY: I don't have to. I'll get vibrations.

ANDREW: Just what I thought. You're not on the job, you're on the make.

CASEY: It's a great story.

ANDREW: It's the same *old* story. [*Sings.*]

> Boy meets boy tonight,
> Finds with joy tonight
> The perfect mate
> That fate
> Cannot destroy tonight. . . .

(*Music continues under.*)

CASEY: [*Putting his feet up*] Andrew, go away. I've got to think. I'll see you later.

ANDREW: All right. Bring along your friend under the bed.

CASEY: What?

ANDREW: The leg's back.

CASEY: Oh, no! [*Bends over and looks under the bed as* ANDREW *leaves.*] Hey, you. Beat it.

(GUY *crawls out. The music finishes.*)

GUY: Thank you—for your hospitality.

CASEY: Don't slam the door when you leave.

GUY: I can't find my other shoe.

CASEY: [*Collapsing on the bed*] Oh, God. [*The telephone rings;* CASEY *takes it.*] Hello? What call to Paris? Josephine La Rose? You can't reach her? Good, I never phoned her. Must be for somebody else. [*Hangs up.* GUY *sags visibly at the news.*] Haven't you gone yet?

GUY: I've got nowhere to go.

69

CASEY: I know. You've run away from home and you've got no friends and no job and no money. Right?

GUY: How did you guess?

CASEY: I saw the movie.

GUY: But it's true.

CASEY: Look, kid, there's nothing I can do for you, and let me give it to you straight, there's nothing *you* can do for *me.* Buy yourself a pair of shoes downstairs. Send me the bill.

(CASEY *pushes* GUY *out the door and heads back to bed —*GUY *reenters.*)

GUY: Yes, there is something I can do for you. [*No response from* CASEY.] You're looking for—Guy Rose. [*Still no response*.] Well, I'm . . . I'm Guy Rose!

CASEY: And I'm Jeanette Macdonald. Now scram.

GUY: It's true. I can prove it! [*Goes to bed and dangles pocket watch over* CASEY.] Read that.

CASEY: Ten to seven. You've convinced me!

GUY: No, on the cover.

CASEY: [*Reads, then sits up alert*.] Where did you get this?

GUY: It was a present.

CASEY: Why would he give you something with his name on it?

GUY: Who?

CASEY: What do you know about Guy Rose?

GUY: Everything.

CASEY: Okay. Tell me about him.

GUY: Him?

CASEY: [*Through clenched teeth*] Guy Rose!

GUY: Oh! Well, *he* . . . [*slight pause*] . . . is a very confused person.

CASEY: That I know. He's just jilted Clarence Cutler at the altar.

GUY: That's not really like Guy.

CASEY: Maybe you don't know him as well as you think.

GUY: He's beginning to surprise me.

CASEY: The point is he has run off. Where would he go?

GUY: Paris.

CASEY: Paris?

GUY: Yes, he's got an aunt there.

CASEY: Great! I'll catch him at Victoria Station!

GUY: No you won't. He doesn't have any money.

CASEY: So what would he do?

GUY: Try to survive in London.

CASEY: That's not easy.

GUY: I know . . . but with a little luck he just might make it.

CASEY: Okay, so he's in London. What is he usually doing at . . . [*Looks at watch.*] seven o'clock?

GUY: [*Hungrily*] Looking for dinner.

CASEY: Without any money?

GUY: Well, if he plays his cards right, he could probably get somebody to take him. . . .

CASEY: Where?

GUY: I know he's always wanted to go to Romano's.

CASEY: You're sure?

GUY: Positive.

CASEY: Well, it's a long shot but I'll take it. [*Grabs his hat and moves.*] Thanks a lot, kid. See you around.

GUY: But you don't know what he looks like. . . .

CASEY: *I'll* know.

GUY: And he wouldn't speak to you without an introduction! . . .

CASEY: [*After pause*] Okay, you win. Come on.

BLACKOUT

Scene 4

Romano's.
The music strikes up and a chorus of four GIRLS *struts on, dressed in a style that recalls Mrs. Simpson.*

GIRLS: [*Singing*]
       If you're frightf'lly English,

71

Frightf'lly proper too,
Mmmm!—marry an American—
That's the modern thing to do!

If "stiff upper lip"
Is you in just a phrase,
Mmmm—marry an American—
That's the fashion nowadays!

Honeymooning's fun
For anyone
But it can be more romantic
If the happy pair
Exude an air
Transatlantic!

On the other hand,
If by any chance you
Should turn out to be
Already an American
Mmmm!—marry me!

(GIRLS *dance off, revealing* CLARENCE *alone at a table, sadly sipping champagne. Paid* ESCORT—BRUCE—*arrives.*)

ESCORT: Mr. Cutler?

CLARENCE: Are you George from the Beau Geste Escort Service?

ESCORT: No, George is busy. They sent me.

CLARENCE: They told me they were sending George.

ESCORT: No, they sent me.

CLARENCE: Well, I've never used the Beau Geste service before but I'm told that you're all equally nice. Except, of course, for—

ESCORT: I'm Bruce.

CLARENCE: I knew it.

ESCORT: [*Sitting at table*] It's too bad you didn't get George. George is the nicest.

CLARENCE: [*Deadpan*] It's been one of those days.

72

ESCORT: Everybody wants George. You'd have liked him.

CLARENCE: Let's not talk about George—

ESCORT: He only goes to the best clients.

CLARENCE: —or tomorrow I shall see to it personally that you're OUT OF A JOB!

ESCORT: But—

CLARENCE: And that goes for George too! Now—why don't you ask me to dance?

ESCORT: I don't dance very well. [*Pause.*] But George—

CLARENCE: I know, Fred Astaire on wheels. Come on. *I'll* lead.

(*They leave as* CASEY *and* GUY *arrive and are shown to the adjoining table by a waiter.*)

WAITER: Would you like to order now or later?

GUY: Now.

CASEY: Later! [*Waiter goes.*] Okay, which one is Guy Rose?

GUY: I'm too hungry to focus my eyes.

CASEY: Eat an olive.

GUY: [*Looking*] He's not here yet.

CASEY: We must have missed him when we went back to buy your shoes. What's he look like?

GUY: You'll be disappointed. He looks like me.

CASEY: The hell he does!

GUY: I beg your pardon.

CASEY: I may not know much about Guy Rose, but I do know that he's easy on the eyes. And, let's face it, kid, *you're* no oil painting. [*Gets up.*] I don't believe you know him at all.

GUY: Where are you going?

CASEY: I'm leaving. You're wasting my time.

GUY: [*Desperate*] Wait! You're right . . . he's attractive!

CASEY: [*Unconvinced*] "Attractive"?

GUY: Well, he's tall—uh, slim—suave—aristocratic and [*Gulps.*] beautiful. . . .

CASEY: And he looks like you?

GUY: In a certain light.

73

CASEY: In a light that dim, who could tell? See you later, kid. [*Gets up to leave.*]

GUY: Of course he's—not really *like* anyone. He's unique.

CASEY: [*Sitting*] I'm listening. Go on.

GUY: Well—he has—allure.

CASEY: That went out with Theda Bara.

GUY: Well, he's bringing it back.

CASEY: You mean he's a vamp!

GUY: No, he's just naturally irresistible.

CASEY: Everybody falls for him.

GUY: Yes, it's very tiresome. But then of course he's beautiful.

CASEY: Gorgeous . . .

GUY: Also intelligent and witty.

CASEY: He's got everything.

GUY: Magic! . . .

CASEY: Yeah . . . the kind of personality that lights up a room, the second you walk in it blinds you. Everybody else in the world disappears. . . .

GUY: [*Surprised*] You're falling in love with him.

CASEY: Who, me? Are you nuts! I'm a newspaperman, remember? All I want is the story.

GUY: Well, that's good.

CASEY: Why?

GUY: Because you seem like a nice person, and I wouldn't like to see you suffer.

CASEY: Who's suffering?

GUY: All those admirers. . . .

CASEY: Treats 'em rough, eh?

GUY: I'm afraid so. You wouldn't like him.

CASEY: "Eat your heart out, you can't have me."

GUY: That's right. I've heard him say it.

CASEY: Drives 'em to drink. Suicide. He's a man-eater.

GUY: Heartless and cruel.

CASEY: Fascinating.

GUY: [*Quietly*] You are in love with him.

CASEY: [*Not hearing*] Of course it's all an act!

GUY: What?

CASEY: [*Inspired*] I know the type. He's just waiting for

someone to tame him. Someone as strong as he is! Mr. Right! [*Pointing suddenly*] There he is! I see him!

GUY: Who?

CASEY: Guy Rose! He's dancing with Clarence Cutler!

GUY: [*Alarmed*] Clarence?! Where?

CASEY: My God, he's a terrible dancer.

GUY: [*In a panic*] That's not him! Guy's a brilliant dancer! I think we should leave.

CASEY: But you said—

GUY: I made a mistake. He never comes here. He'll be at the Ritz—at the Café Chantant. Come on! [*Dashes off.*]

CASEY: Hey, what are you up to? [*Follows him off.*]

(CLARENCE *reenters with* ESCORT.)

CLARENCE: That *was* Guy! What's that little sneak up to?

ESCORT: He's very good-looking.

CLARENCE: No, that was Casey O'Brien, you fool! And he's not good-looking, he's *divinely attractive*! And he was pointing at *me* on the dance floor!

ESCORT: I thought he was pointing at me.

CLARENCE: ME! [*Thinking aloud*] He doesn't go for mousy types like Guy. What's Guy been telling him? [*To* ESCORT] Quick, ask the doorman where they went, and get us a cab!

ESCORT: What for?

CLARENCE: To follow them, you idiot! Come on!

(*They run out.*)

Scene 5

Another nightclub—the Dorchester.

Similar setup with tables, chairs, and dance floor.

A CHORUS *of* BOYS *enters and sings for the customers a reprise of "Marry an American."*

BOYS: If you're frightf'lly English,
Frightf'lly proper too,
Mmmm!—marry an American—
That's the modern thing to do!

If "stiff upper lip"
Is you in just a phrase,
Mmmm!—marry an American—
That's the fashion nowadays!

Honeymooning's fun
For anyone
But it can be more romantic
If the happy pair
Exude an air
Transatlantic!

On the other hand,
If by any chance you
Should turn out to be
Already an American,
Mmmm!—marry me!

(*They dance off.* CASEY *and* GUY *are discovered at a table, both are drinking.*)

GUY: [*Slightly drunk*] Waiter, more champagne!
CASEY: Look, this is the fifth place we've been to this evening. When's your friend going to show up?
GUY: Who knows? Who cares?
CASEY: I care. This is costing me a fortune.
GUY: It's been worth every penny. I've had a marvelous time. Haven't you had a marvelous time?
CASEY: Fantastic.
GUY: Shall I tell you more about the fabulous Guy Rose?
CASEY: There's more?
GUY: Of course. He leads a mad life.
CASEY: I'll say. What with the baron, the count, the archduke . . .

GUY: And the White Russian prince—with the gambling system.

CASEY: I don't think you mentioned him.

GUY: Oh yes. They broke the bank at Monte Carlo together three times.

CASEY: Was this before or after he got engaged to Clarence Cutler?

GUY: What? Oh, after—before!

CASEY: Come to think of it, with all those other admirers, why did he sell out to a creep like Cutler anyway?

GUY: [*Nervously*] That's a good question.

CASEY: Tired of all that riotous living, perhaps?

GUY: That's a good answer. . . .

CASEY: Except that, a few bottles of champagne ago, you said he'd always led a sheltered life.

GUY: Well, actually . . .

CASEY: Actually, it's a load of crap! You've been lying to me all evening. I don't know where you got that watch, but I don't believe you know Guy Rose at all. Well, you've played me for a sucker long enough. . . .

(CLARENCE *and* ESCORT *enter.* GUY *hides behind menu.*)

CLARENCE: Yoo hoo, I've been trying to catch up with you all evening. [*To* CASEY] I know who you are and you must know who I am.

CASEY: Can I have three guesses?

CLARENCE: [*Flirtatious*] Oh, you are a tease. But seriously, I'm really very cross with you. I know it's not my place to tell you what to write, but in that story of yours there was scarcely a word about me, and simply columns and columns about Guy, Guy, Guy! Speaking of which [*Looking behind menu*], how *is* the exquisite English Rose?

GUY: [*Quaking*] I don't really know, Clarence.

CASEY: And neither do I. We've been waiting the whole damn evening to find out.

CLARENCE: [*To* GUY] Get you—sitting here with Casey O'Brien, breaker of a thousand hearts.

GUY: It's not—like that.

CLARENCE: Really? Then maybe the big bad newspaperman just wants to pump you. [*Coquettishly to* CASEY] Why are you so interested in Guy and me?

CASEY: [*Mockingly*] Because you're fascinating.

CLARENCE: Oh, you dreadful man. In any case, if you want a really interesting story, come and interview me. You'll find me very cooperative. Especially now that I'm free again. And what bliss it is. I haven't lost any time, as you can see. [*Indicating* ESCORT] That gorgeous creature over there is an Italian prince. I'd introduce you, but he doesn't speak a word of English.

CASEY: *Eh, principe—da dove vieni?*

ESCORT: Huh?

CLARENCE: And not a word of Italian either! Andiamo, Roberto!

ESCORT: I'm Bruce.

CLARENCE: If I send you back, do I get a refund? [*Calling back*] *Arrivederci!*

(*They are gone.*)

GUY: [*Apprehensive*] Clarence does rattle on, doesn't he?

CASEY: Well, at least I found out one thing.

GUY: [*Fearful*] What was that?

CASEY: That I owe you an apology. I guess you do know Guy Rose after all.

GUY: [*Relieved*] Nobody knows him better. Scout's honor.

CASEY: "Scout's honor"?

GUY: It's just an expression.

CASEY: Don't tell me you were a boy scout?

GUY: I still am.

CASEY: No kidding! So am I—at least, I was. Why didn't you tell me this before?

GUY: Would it have made any difference?

CASEY: Of course. I'd have known at once that you were "trustworthy and loyal . . ."

GUY: "Friendly and considerate"—

CASEY: "Courteous and courageous!"

GUY: "Obedient and thrifty!"

BOTH: "And prepared"! [*They do the Scout salute to each other.*]

CASEY: How many badges did you get?

GUY: Fifteen.

CASEY: I got twenty-five! Happiest time of my life! [*Sings.*]
    Be cheerful at work and at play . . .

GUY: [*Sings.*]
    And do a good deed ev'ry day . . .

CASEY: At six you're awake
    For a dip in the lake,
    Then it's breakfast and you're up and you're away!

    It's a boy's life!
    In the open air,

GUY: Cloudy skies or fair,

BOTH: There's nothing like some pioneering
    With adventures beckoning ev'rywhere
    That's the only life
    For a boy!

    Out in the wilds exploring, pitching a tent or two
    When you have found the perfect spot.
    You build your campfire, then it's time for a
      barbecue,
    So you cook your supper in a pot!

CASEY: Then the time has come to tie another knot!

BOTH: Oh, it's a boy's life
    Going for a hike,
    Fishing for a pike,
    Or swimming in the altogether,
    Uphill, downhill, pedaling on a bike!

GUY: Going like a whizz!

CASEY: Peace of mind is his!

BOTH: What a life it is
    For a boy!

(*Whistling, they march for a chorus, doing Scout drill, semaphore, etc.*)

BOTH: It's a boy's life!
Up before the dew,
Sailing with the crew,
And doing lots of exercises!
Upstream, downstream, paddling a canoe!
That's the only life
For a boy!

Beneath the stars together singing a jolly song—
Now that's the life that can't be beat!
You always whistle as you merrily go along
With a smile for ev'ryone you meet!

CASEY: And an arm to help old ladies cross the street!

BOTH: Oh, it's a boy's life
In a sleeping bag,
Tracking down a stag,
And learning how to use a compass!
Marching, trooping, rallying round the flag!

GUY: Climbing trees galore!

CASEY: Sending semaphore!

GUY: Packing up your kit!

CASEY: Always keeping fit!

GUY: Whittling with your knife!

CASEY: Far from care and strife!

BOTH: That's the only life
For . . .
A . . .
Boy!

(*Saluting again.*)

"Be prepared"!

Scene 6

During the song the setting has been changed; CASEY's *hotel bedroom appears.*

Finishing a reprise—or encore—of "It's a Boy's Life," CASEY *and* GUY *march into the new setting.* CASEY *flops on the bed,* GUY *into a chair.*

CASEY: Oh boy, I'm beat.

GUY: Scouting certainly seems to bring out the best in people.

CASEY: Don't let it throw ya, kid. "A scout is a brother to all scouts." Scout Law, Rule 4.

GUY: You haven't forgotten.

CASEY: I was a scoutmaster.

GUY: Why did you give it up?

CASEY: I had trouble with Rule 7.

GUY: "A scout has respect for himself and for others"?

CASEY: Yeah. And how can you preach that to a kid when you've seen and done some of the rotten things I have? Look out for number one, kid. Don't get involved. And don't trust *anybody.* Oh yeah, and when it comes to love, keep it strictly for laughs. That's O'Brien law, learned the hard way. Stick to that and you won't get hurt.

(A pause.)

GUY: I—wouldn't mind getting hurt—if it was someone I cared about. It would be better than not feeling anything at all. [*No response from* CASEY.] I want to tell you something. Tonight has been the happiest evening of my life. And I don't want to spoil it by lying to you any longer. I'm not the person you think I am. I am— in fact—the person you want to meet. I know you don't

want to believe that, but it's true. I'm sorry. If you want
me to, I'll go. Just say the word. [*No word from* CASEY.]
Mr. O'Brien?

(CASEY *snores. Music plays softly.* GUY *watches him
sleeping for a moment, then sings:*)

GUY: Tell me please, does anybody love you?
   Do you have a special love affair?—
   Someone who worries about you,
   Who's always true
   And tender too
   And waits for you
   Somewhere?

   So please say, does anybody love you?
   For if by some lucky chance
   The answer is "No"
   And you haven't anyone to love you,
   Then do you mind if I . . . well . . . [*Faltering*]
   I mean . . . I think . . .

   I don't know how to say it,
   I wonder why—
   I'm too embarrassed, I'm too shy.
   Too shy to say it to myself—
   How can I say it to you?
   But suddenly that's just what I've got to do.

   So please say, does anybody love you?
   For if by some lucky chance
   The answer is "No"
   And you haven't anyone to love you,
   Then do you mind if I do?
   Because I love you so.

LIGHTS FADE

Scene 7

The bedroom, the next morning.

At the end of the blackout, there is a knock. Lights come up on CASEY *alone in the room.* CASEY *gets up and opens the door to the* ASSISTANT HOTEL MANAGER.

A.H.M.: Good morning, Mr. O'Brien. I'm the assistant hotel manager. I'm sorry to disturb you, but we thought you might like to see this.

CASEY: [*Taking bill*] What is it?

A.H.M.: It's your bill to date. Just a formality, of course.

CASEY: Thank you very much.

A.H.M.: You'll notice that we've billed you separately for the party you gave on Wednesday and Thursday.

CASEY: Oh, yeah. That's fine.

A.H.M.: And also that we've attached an itemized list of expenses.

CASEY: Thank you. Good-bye.

A.H.M.: And that includes the statue of Achilles in the lobby, the chandelier over the staircase, and a small compensation to the bellboy who's still in the hospital.

CASEY: I'll sign for it.

A.H.M.: Money would be nicer. Please don't feel we're trying to rush you. Tomorrow morning will be soon enough. Good day, Mr. O'Brien.

(*He goes.* CASEY *closes door, looks at the bill in horror.* GUY *comes out of the bathroom.*)

GUY: What's the matter?

CASEY: [*Surprised to see him*] What are you doing here?

GUY: I . . . slept in the bathtub. You have a slow drip.

CASEY: You're telling me.

GUY: You seem to be worried.

CASEY: I seem to be broke. And if I don't get a follow-up on the story . . . [*Thinking aloud*] Maybe I should go round to his home . . .

GUY: Whose home?

CASEY: . . . talk to Lord and Lady Rose. . . .

GUY: Oh, that story.

CASEY: Yeah. . . . Might even break down and try Cutler. . . .

GUY: No!

CASEY: Why not?

GUY: You don't need him. You've got *me*.

CASEY: I know, and what have I done to deserve it? [*Going*] See you around, kid.

GUY: Why don't you believe me?

CASEY: Because I need results, and you don't produce any.

GUY: But I *can*. I *will*. I'll produce Guy Rose for you anytime you want, anywhere!

CASEY: I've got to go, kid. . . .

GUY: Scout's honor! [*This impresses* CASEY.]

CASEY: Okay. Tonight, eight o'clock—at the Trocadero. And don't tell him I'll be taking pictures.

GUY: Pictures? Why?

CASEY: Because I've told the world he's beautiful, bonehead, and I've gotta prove it!

GUY: [*Shattered*] "Beautiful" . . .

CASEY: Don't forget, "Scout's honor." See you tonight.

GUY: I won't be there.

CASEY: [*Going*] That's okay. I'll recognize him. [*Stops to add:*] Tell him to carry a rose!

(CASEY *leaves. Left alone,* GUY *panics.*)

GUY: I can't do it! [*Runs to telephone.*] I want to place a call to France, please, Paris. I'm afraid I still don't know the number, just the name. It's Josephine La Rose. . . . [*The sound of tap dancing outside the door.*] Just a moment, please. [*Goes to door and opens it to the tap-dancing* BELLHOP *with a suit of tails on a valet stand.*]

BELLHOP: Mr. O'Brien's cleaning.
GUY: Thank you.

(BELLHOP *leaves.* GUY *studies the suit for a moment, and sings reflectively*.)

> Beautiful . . .
> What is "beautiful"?
> Simply b-e-a-u-t-i-f-u-l.
> Something that I am so
> Unacquainted with,
> I'm surprised it's something I can even spell.
> Oh, hell!

(*Hangs up phone.*)

> If only love were truly blind
> And beauty merely in the mind
> Instead of something that you look into a mirror
>   to find.

(*He picks up a hand mirror and looks at himself with distaste.*)

> Ugh! [*Decides to concentrate and sing to his reflection with great persuasive intensity*.]
> You're beautiful, you're beautiful, you're beautiful!
> Listen to me and don't turn away.
> You're beautiful, you're beautiful, you're beautiful!
> Don't you know that I mean what I say?
> Don't you know that it's morally wrong to
> Think that beauty's a club that you can't belong to?
> So tell yourself "You're beautiful, you're beautiful,"
> Say it over and over all day!
>
> Say it loudly,
> Say it proudly,
> Unafraid that it's foolish or vain.

You're beautiful, you're beautiful, you're beauti-
ful! . . .
[*Giving it up in despair.*]
And you're also completely insane!
[*Instantly reconsiders.*]
No, I can do it! I will!

(*Grabs the suit of tails off the stand and disappears with it into the bathroom. While he changes, the music of "You're Beautiful" plays brightly and the light dims a bit on the bedroom set. Spotlights pick up* ANDREW *and* CASEY *at either side of the stage, both with telephones.* ANDREW *is necking with girl friend.*)

CASEY: Hello, Andrew, it's Casey. [ANDREW *is kissing his girl friend.*] Andrew!
ANDREW: Who is this?
CASEY: Casey. Pay attention. This is important. What do you know about photography?
ANDREW: Not a thing, old chap.
CASEY: Never mind. I'll teach you.
ANDREW: Must you?
CASEY: Listen. I've just got a thousand dollars' advance from Reuters on the Guy Rose story, and I'm meeting him tonight at the Trocadero. So I need you.
ANDREW: The Trocadero? But I thought I'd go to the Piccadilly tonight. You see, I went to the Trocadero last night and to go to the same place two nights in a row is so boring.
CASEY: Andrew, I need you to take pictures.
ANDREW: Get a photographer.
CASEY: I want somebody who won't look out of place. Somebody suave, elegant, at home in the highest society. Wouldn't you say that described you?
ANDREW: Admirably!
CASEY: Good. You're taking the pictures.

(*Blackout on* CASEY *and* ANDREW. *Lights come up on the hotel room as* GUY *bounds out of the bathroom dressed in the suit of tails and looking as plain as ever.*)

GUY: I'm beautiful! [*Looks in the mirror.*] I'm not. [*Sings to his reflection intensely.*]

You need help,
You need lots of help,
Like a miracle or something from above.
But what can help you now?
Is there anything?
No, there's nothing . . . wait—there's something—
    Yes . . .
There's love!

I've heard that love finds a way.
And you're in love, so you're not forsaken!
With love to help you even beauty may
Awaken!
So say it loudly!
Say it proudly!
Unafraid that it's foolish or vain,
You're beautiful!
You're beautiful!
You're beautiful!
And you'll be born all over again!

(*The music builds for the transformation scene.* GUY *becomes beautiful! This is the big test of the actor who plays* GUY. *Prior to this he will have had to use every trick of his trade to create the impression of a dowdy young man—slicked-down [or rumpled] hair, glasses, and a round-shouldered posture which even now makes the suit of tails fit badly. Now he has to reverse the process in full view of the audience—remove glasses, rearrange hair, and straighten up. This will probably be most effective if it is done with his back to the audience, enabling him to turn around transformed, holding a bright red rose and smiling brightly. A big moment. During this transformation the set has done the same.*)

Scene 8

The Trocadero.

The setting materializes around GUY. *Music plays. Four* COUPLES—*boys with girls—in evening dress appear behind him, fox-trotting to the music.*

CASEY *appears to one side, also in tails, stops dead at the sight of* GUY, *dazzled and totally smitten. It's love at first sight.*

CASEY: It's you—at last!

GUY: Mr. O'Brien?

CASEY: Who?

GUY: You are Casey O'Brien?

CASEY: [*Not sure*] If you say so. . . . Oh, I've waited so long for this moment. . . .

GUY: So have I. You're late.

CASEY: Somebody stole my tails.

GUY: How tedious.

CASEY: You're even more beautiful than I imagined. I can't believe my eyes. [*A pause as he continues to gaze.*]

GUY: People are beginning to stare.

CASEY: Sorry. Perhaps we'd better dance. [*They do so.*] You dance beautifully.

GUY: Yes.

CASEY: Have you ever been told you have beautiful eyes?

GUY: Constantly. It's very boring.

CASEY: [*Delighted*] It's true—you are heartless and cruel.

GUY: Thank you. [*The music ends. They sit together at a table.*] I believe you have some questions to ask me.

CASEY: [*Gone*] Yeah. . . . Will you marry me?

GUY: Excuse me, but I thought you said . . .

CASEY: Marry me.

GUY: But—shouldn't we get to know each other better first?

CASEY: You wanna dance again?

GUY: But what about your story for the newspaper?

CASEY: To hell with the story.

GUY: I thought this was supposed to be an interview.

CASEY: It's a proposal.

GUY: It's insane.

CASEY: Who cares? [*Sings.*]
>Let's not be rational, let's be rash,
>Let's not have any bank account, let's have cash.
>When there is a party, why stay at home with the
>>pets?
>Let's not say "Let's not,"
>Let's!
>Sweetheart of mine—
>
>Let's not get sensible, let's get sent
>Where Browning and Elizabeth Barrett went.
>Who cares about caution or running up a few debts?
>Let's not say "Let's not,"
>Let's!
>
>Why hesitate so?
>It's easy, you know—
>Relax and let go,
>And oh,
>What comes next comes natural!
>
>Let's not make haste to part, let's make hay:
>This circumspect behavior is so passé.
>The chance of a lifetime is something everyone gets.
>They're saying "Place your bets"—
>Sweetheart of mine—
>Let's not say "Let's not"
>Let's say "Lets"!

(*The music continues under.* ANDREW *enters on tiptoe
with camera and flash gun and takes a picture of* GUY—
behind CASEY's *back—then tiptoes out.*)

CASEY: What's the matter?
GUY: Nothing, a man just took my picture.
CASEY: What! That's an outrage! Waiter! [WAITER *hurries over*.] What the hell kind of a joint is this? We come here for some privacy and you allow someone to take pictures?

(ANDREW *reenters with camera, tiptoeing innocently*.)

ANDREW: Profile, please.
CASEY: Look, there he is again! Throw him out!
ANDREW: Oh, my!

(ANDREW *stops dead in horror, then runs out pursued by* WAITER. CASEY *continues singing to* GUY.)

CASEY: I'll say it again,
    Don't wait to count ten,
    Give in to that yen
    And then—
    What comes next comes natural!

    Let's not act uppishly, let's act up,
    Forbidden fruits are ripe and it's time to sup.
    Why hazard a future with far too many regrets?
    Let's do a few duets!
    Sweetheart of mine—
    Let's not say "Let's not,"
    Let's say "Let's"!

(*The music soars and* CASEY *leads* GUY *to the dance floor. Watched by the four boy-and-girl couples sitting at tables, they dance together, a fully choreographed production routine recalling the style of Astaire and Rogers, only this time performed by two men in tails. This should definitely be another big moment. After dance, with couples applauding, they return to the table and sit gazing into each other's eyes; it's obviously love.*)

CASEY: We'd better hurry. We'll be late.

GUY: Where are we going?

CASEY: Victoria Station. We've just got time to catch the boat train.

GUY: Boat train?

CASEY: You want to go to Paris, don't you?

GUY: Oh, yes. . . .

CASEY: Good. We're going together.

GUY: I'd like that. But I haven't any money.

CASEY: That's okay. I'm loaded. Have some. [*Stuffs a wad of bills into* GUY's *breast pocket.*]

GUY: But . . .

CASEY: And I want you to have this too. [*Puts it on the table.*] It isn't worth anything, but it means a lot to me. It's my good-luck charm.

GUY: Thank you very much. [*Picks it up.*] It's very unusual.

CASEY: Yeah, it isn't just any old bull's ear. [GUY *quickly places ear on the table.*] That's the ear of El Furioso, the meanest bull in Madrid.

GUY: I don't know what to say.

CASEY: Don't say anything. You've gotta pack. Come on, I'll take you to your hotel.

GUY: No!

CASEY: You mean you're not coming?

GUY: No, I'll come. But I have some things to do first. I'll meet you at the station.

CASEY: But couldn't I . . . ?

GUY: Promise you won't follow me. Wait five minutes before you leave.

CASEY: Anything you say.

GUY: Thank you. [*Gives him the rose.*] À bientôt. [*Heads out.*]

CASEY: Guy . . .

GUY: [*Turning*] Casey?

CASEY: You forgot your ear.

(GUY *returns for the ear and exits holding it gingerly.* CASEY *sits, romantically sniffing the rose. The mood is shattered by the entrance of* CLARENCE, *who sees* CASEY *and hurries over.*)

CLARENCE: Well! If it isn't the fascinating Mr. O'Brien! And all alone, too. What a coincidence, so am I—although only with the greatest difficulty. My land, the trouble I've had tonight fighting off admirers. I've been danced off my feet. Maybe if I sit down they'll go away. [*Sits.*] Isn't it terrible how people *will* force themselves upon you—just when you want to be left alone?

CASEY: [*Looks at watch.*] Two minutes.

CLARENCE: I knew you'd agree. I feel we have a lot in common. Two little American boys far from home. We should stick together, you and I.

CASEY: Find another American.

CLARENCE: It's too late. You've brought out the beast in me.

CASEY: I wish I hadn't done that.

CLARENCE: Casey—is there someone else?

CASEY: Yeah, and he's waiting for me at Victoria. See you around, Clarence.

CLARENCE: It's something to do with that stupid rose. [*A sudden inspiration.*] My God, it's not Guy?

CASEY: What if it is? It's all over between you.

CLARENCE: My God, it is Guy! [*Phony smile.*] How sweet. How nice for you both. . . . [*Spot isolates* CLARENCE; *to himself, seething*] I can't stand it! Everything keeps going wrong. How could a dingy little creep like Guy Rose land a catch like Casey O'Brien? Guy and Casey! It's unnatural! Why should they have each other? Well, they *won't*. I'll stop it—but how? Something really mean. It should be easy. Think, Clarence!

(*Lights go back to normal.*)

CASEY: My five minutes are up. I can go now.

CLARENCE: Of course you realize you'll ruin his life.

CASEY: What are you talking about?

CLARENCE: Guy, Casey. He's young, naïve, inexperienced. Oh, it's been easy for you to infatuate him with that

famous O'Brien charm. But are you being fair to him?
Guy's an aristocrat, used to wealth, privilege, tradition.
How can you expect him to give all that up for you?

CASEY: My God, you're right.

CLARENCE: He'd hate it. And he'd come to hate you. And
you'd hate him. And I'd hate myself if I let you do it.

CASEY: I *won't* do it!

CLARENCE: [*Aside*] Whew!

CASEY: It wouldn't be fair.

CLARENCE: No.

CASEY: I couldn't be so selfish.

CLARENCE: No.

CASEY: I can't expect him to lead my kind of life.

CLARENCE: No.

CASEY: No. . . .

CLARENCE: So you'll give him up.

CASEY: NO!

CLARENCE: No?

CASEY: Never!

CLARENCE: Look, we've gone off the track somewhere.
You're supposed to give him up. I'll just go through it
again from the start. Guy is young, naïve—

CASEY: Go away, Clarence.

CLARENCE: Think, Clarence, think. . . . [*Exits*.]

CASEY: [*Sings pensively*.]
Love's okay
For a rainy day
Or to while away
The blues,
But when love gets serious . . .

[*Spoken*]

Brother, that's bad news! . . .

[*Sings*.]

The stories and the deadlines, and the race to scoop
the rest,
The worldwide reputation as the best.

No matter where the news is, north or south or
    east or west . . .
Imagine giving all of it up for love!

BLACKOUT

Scene 9

Passengers and train porter enter, followed by CLARENCE.

PORTER: The train standing at the platform is the boat
train for Paris, leaving at ten o'clock.

  (*Passengers and porter leave.* GUY *appears, once again
dowdy.*)

CLARENCE: Well, if it isn't Guy! What a surprise!

GUY: What are you doing here, Clarence?

CLARENCE: I hear you're running off with Casey O'Brien.

GUY: I'm afraid so, Clarence.

CLARENCE: How did you do it?

GUY: Do what?

CLARENCE: Casey O'Brien!—such a catch, and, after all,
fascination has never been your specialty.

GUY: When I met him I—discovered a new me.

CLARENCE: And yet the old you still seems to be very much
with us. How does he feel about that?

GUY: [*Darkly*] That's what I'm going to find out.

CLARENCE: Well, I'm sure love will find a way. It couldn't
happen to two nicer kids and I just know you're going
to be very happy.

GUY: Thank you, Clarence.

CLARENCE: Of course you realize you'll ruin his life.

GUY: What are you talking about?

CLARENCE: Casey, Guy. Far from home, lonely, on the
rebound from that bullfighter. It's been easy for you to
captivate him with your . . . your . . . well, maybe it
wasn't easy. But are you being fair to him? Casey's a
citizen of the world, used to travel, adventure, excite-

94

ment. How can you expect him to give all of that up
for your kind of life? He'd hate it. And he'd come to
hate you. And you'd hate him. And I'd hate myself if
I let you do it. Give him up, Guy!

GUY: No!

CLARENCE: Don't tie him down to a pipe and slippers.

GUY: I won't.

CLARENCE: Don't stifle that free spirit!

GUY: But I don't want to! I don't want him to change his
life! He can do whatever he likes!

CLARENCE: I don't think you quite understand me.

GUY: Yes I do, Clarence. I know exactly what you're trying
to do and it won't work! I'm going to Paris with Casey
and you can't stop me. Go away!

CLARENCE: Damn!

(CLARENCE *exits as* CASEY *enters, opposite side, dressed
as a scoutmaster, with a big flag.*)

CASEY: Hup two three four. . . . Hiya, kid. Where's Guy?

GUY: My God, what have you done?

CASEY: I'm giving up the newspaper business! Boy, that
Guy Rose is really something. Restored my faith in
Rule 7.

GUY: But you can't do this!

CASEY: Sure I can. I'm through with the gypsy life. From
now on it's me for pipe and slippers. Sweetness and light.

GUY: But why?

CASEY: I can't ask Guy Rose to lead my kind of life. So
I'm giving it up—for love!

GUY: But you mustn't! You'll come to hate it!

CASEY: Where is Guy, anyway?

GUY: He's . . . [*Pause as he makes the big decision. Music
starts.*] . . . not coming.

CASEY: Not coming?

GUY: No. He told me to tell you that he didn't think it
would work. That you're wrong for each other.

CASEY: I don't believe it. You're lying!

GUY: And he asked me to give you this. [*Gives him the
bull's ear.*]

CASEY: El Furioso! . . . Didn't he say anything else?
GUY: Yes—he said to tell you: "It was strictly for laughs."
  [CASEY *crumbles*.] Good-bye. [GUY *leaves quickly*.]
CASEY: "Strictly for laughs" . . .

  (CHORUS *enters, in costume as for opening number of the
  act, the girls each carrying a wilted rose.*)

CHORUS: Boy meets boy,
      Boy loses boy . . .
CLARENCE: [*Enters.*] And it's going to stay that way, too!

CURTAIN

ACT II

Scene 1

A bar, a few days later.

During the blackout after entr'acte music we hear wild Spanish music, clicking heels, and castanets.

Lights come up as music ends, revealing bar, BARTENDER, CASEY slumped over a drink, and CLARENCE seated by him, looking off and applauding vigorously.

CLARENCE: Bravo! Olé! Riba! Riba!
CASEY: [*Drunk, lifting head*] Aw, shut up.
CLARENCE: Waiter, another drink for my friend.
CASEY: I'm not your friend. And stop following me around.
CLARENCE: But you need someone to look after you.
CASEY: Aw, shut up!
CLARENCE: You're so depressed.
CASEY: You really want to help?
CLARENCE: Yes!
CASEY: Then go away. I promise to cheer up.

(CASEY *collapses back into his drink as four Spanish dancing ladies*—ROSITA, PEPITA, LOLITA, *and* JANE— *enter. They are in full flamenco costume with roses in their hair, fans, and castanets, and are chattering gaily in Spanish.*)

CLARENCE: Bravo! Olé! Riba! Riba!
ROSITA: Qué stupido!
PEPITA: Qué barbaridad!
LOLITA: Qué payaso!
JANE: Idiota!

(*All fan themselves with hostility.*)

ROSITA: [*To* BARTENDER] Camarero, cuatro copas de fundador, por favor.

BARTENDER: I beg your pardon, madame?

ROSITA: [*Rolling eyes*] Cuatro copas—

CASEY: Brandy for four.

GIRLS: Eeeet's Casey! ! ! !

CASEY: Rosita! Pepita! Lolita! Jane!

CLARENCE: Jane?

(*The* GIRLS *have a noisy reunion with* CASEY. *Ad libs and rapturous kisses all round.*)

ROSITA: Surprise!

PEPITA: We have leave Espain!

LOLITA: We have been discovered!

JANE: We come to London to play the cabaret!

ROSITA: We going to be big stars!

PEPITA: Not Spanich no more!

LOLITA: We are very Englich!

JANE: You don't believe? You listen! [*To other* GIRLS *in Spanish: "Come on, girls! The English song!"*] Vamos, muchachas, la canción inglesa!

(*They do a short, wild Spanish dance that suddenly turns into, of all things, an American tap routine.*)

GIRLS: [*Singing*]
If you frightful Englich,
Frightful proper too,
Mmmm—marry an American,
That's the modern thing to do. . . .

CLARENCE: [*Clapping*] Bravo! Olé! Riba! Riba!

ROSITA: We not finished yet.

BARTENDER: Fundador for four. [*Serves the drink.*]

ROSITA: Momento! [*Rummages in her cleavage for money.*]

CLARENCE: Allow me, señorita.

ROSITA: [*Clutching her bosom*] No!

CLARENCE: I mean, allow me to pay.

ROSITA: Gracias.

CLARENCE: Any friend of Casey's is a friend of mine.

(GIRLS *ignore him and concentrate on* CASEY.)

PEPITA: Casey, you not happy?
LOLITA: Why you don't smile?
CASEY: Aw, I'm okay. Tell me about Spain.
JANE: Aha! He mean tell about José!

(GIRLS *all laugh archly*.)

CASEY: Okay, tell about José. Does he ever mention me?
[GIRLS *all laugh again archly*.] What's so funny?
LOLITA: He too busy!
JANE: With German millionaire!
CASEY: The little golddigger.
ROSITA: Poor Casey!
PEPITA: Jilted by the most beautiful bullfighter in Spain!
LOLITA: We must cheer him up—we sing again in Englich!
CASEY: No!
JANE: I know! Rosita will tell his fortune. [*To* CASEY]
Rosita very good. She has gypsy blood. She never wrong.
She tell you beautiful fortune. [ROSITA *has by now laid
out the cards on the bar. All the* GIRLS *look at the cards
with absolute horror. Music blares out the fate motif
from* Carmen. *Jane messes up the cards hurriedly*.] Well,
what she know about it? Rosita rotten fortune teller!
CLARENCE: What was it? What's wrong?
ROSITA: [*To* CLARENCE] Basta! [*To* CASEY] Don't worry,
Casey. Have you still got your bull's ear?
CASEY: Yes. [*Produces it*.]
ROSITA: [*Darkly*] Don't lose it.
CLARENCE: Bull's ear?
ROSITA: Very lucky. El Furioso a very lucky bull.
CASEY: Also a dead bull—with no ears.
CLARENCE: I've got a rabbit's foot. [*Producing it*.]
PEPITA: What's rabbit?

(CLARENCE *mimes a rabbit with ears*.)

LOLITA: Ugh!
JANE: Poor little rabbit.

CLARENCE: What's wrong with a rabbit's foot?

CASEY: Does it work?

CLARENCE: No. . . .

CASEY: Well, that's what's wrong with it. That's what's wrong with them all. [*Sings gloomily.*]

> I thought a bull's ear
> Was the cat's meow—
> In a pig's eye,
> That's what I say now,
> And yet I'm not surprised
> Because it's just my luck,
> Just my rotten luck.

(GIRLS *accompany the song throughout with high wails, dancing, and castanets.*)

CLARENCE:
> I thought a rabbit's foot
> Was the bee's knees.
> Scarce as hen's teeth, though,
> Were knees like these.
> And yet I'm not surprised
> Because it's just my luck,
> Just my rotten luck.

BOTH:
> Well, it's a dog's life,
> Lived at a snail's pace,
> Climbing a hog's back road.
> You wear your hound's-tooth
> To dance a fox-trot
> And find you're pigeon-toed!

> Well, I'll be a monkey's uncle
> If I can see the use of trying.
> Crocodile tears the world is crying!

CASEY: So take my bull's ear,

CLARENCE: Take my rabbit's foot.

(*They exchange good-luck charms.*)

100

BOTH: Both of them you know where you can put,
Because a good-luck charm
Don't mean a thing to me,
Just my rotten luck,
And ain't that just my luck?
And ain't that just my luck?
And ain't that just my luck?

ROSITA: Eeet ees time again for the cabaret.

PEPITA: [*To* CASEY] Come along with us and we will cheer you up.

LOLITA: We sing your favorite song.

JANE: Si! "Me duele la corazón y quiero morir!"

CLARENCE: What does that mean?

JANE: "My heart is broken and I want to die!"

CASEY: Amen, sister!

(ANDREW *arrives with a big envelope under his arm.*)

ANDREW: Casey, I've been hunting everywhere for you. Do you want these photographs or don't you?

CASEY: What photographs?

ANDREW: The ones I took at the Trocadero. The ones you had me thrown out for! I've got a good mind not to give them to you.

CASEY: That's okay, Andy. I don't want 'em.

ANDREW: I only did it as a favor, and what happens? I'm treated like a common drunk, almost arrested, my reputation's ruined. . . . What do you mean, you don't want them?

CASEY: I mean, sorry, but I've gone off the story.

ANDREW: But why?

CASEY: Because "me duele la corazón y quiero morir!" Come on, girls. Let's laugh it up.

(*They leave as* ANDREW *rails away to* CLARENCE.)

ANDREW: Well, I must say that's a bit much. What's got into him anyway? After all the trouble I went to!

CLARENCE: [*Trying to leave*] I'm sorry, but I must join my friends. . . .

ANDREW: I'd never used a camera before, and they turned out so well! And he doesn't even want to see them!

CLARENCE: I really must . . .

ANDREW: But look, I'll show you! [*Thrusts photographs under* CLARENCE's *nose.*] Isn't that beautiful?

CLARENCE: [*Stops dead, stares at photo.*] Yes, *very*. Who is he?

ANDREW: Guy Rose.

CLARENCE: That's not Guy.

ANDREW: Of course it is.

CLARENCE: Well, it's not. [*Starts to go.*]

ANDREW: Casey says it is.

CLARENCE: [*Impatient*] Look, you're nuts. Guy Rose is nobody's pinup. He looks like this. [*Draws on photograph.*] Messy hair, glasses. . . . [*Stops dead in recognition.*] My God! It can't be! Let me see the rest of those pictures! [ANDREW *hands them over;* CLARENCE *roots through them dumbfounded.*] It is! The little rat, he's been holding out on me!

ANDREW: So it is Guy Rose.

CLARENCE: Yes, indeed. I didn't think so at first, but then I'd never seen such beautiful pictures of him.

ANDREW: Why, thank you.

CLARENCE: They've shown me a whole new side to his character. [*He walks forward. The bar and* ANDREW *fade away behind him, and he continues talking to himself.*] And I can't wait to see it in the flesh! The point is, where? In Paris. . . . But where in Paris? There's a relative there, the black sheep of the family. What was her name? Josephine. Crossed the Channel and went native. What's the French for Rose? La Rose. But Paris is a big place. She may be starving in a garret without a telephone. How will I ever find Josephine La Rose?

Scene 2

In answer to CLARENCE's *question, he sees a sign which reads:*

JOSEPHINE LA ROSE
dans
LES FOLIES DE PARIS
avec
Les plus beaux garçons du monde!

CLARENCE *dashes out, the sign disappears, we are onstage at the Folies.*
JOSEPHINE LA ROSE *struts on to music, along with scantily clad* CHORUS GIRLS.

JOSEPHINE: 'Allo! [*Sings.*]
What've they got in France?
Statues!
They're very hot in France
On statues!
Monuments to the Great,
They've got such a lot in France
There are times
I wish I was not in France!

But when I see
Reality
It's such a delightful wrench
I start to think in French,
I mean *commencer*
à penser
en français—

It's not Napoléon,
It's not François Fénelon,
Not David, not Danton,
It's a dolly!

103

It's not Victor Hugo,
It's not Jean or Jacques Rousseau,
Not Verlaine, not Rimbaud,
It's a dolly!

(*Three* BOYS *appear as typical French statues.*)

Someone to
Parlez-vous
At *une table* for two
'Neath a big pink and blue
Parasol!
And it's not Beaudelaire,
Just a statue in a square,

JOSEPHINE AND
GIRLS: It's a dolly!
It's a real live beautiful doll!

(*The first statue comes to life. To stripper music, he tears off the clothing and strips to some abbreviated costume.*)

ALL: It's a dolly!

(*Another statue and another strip.*)

It's a dolly!

(*The third statue strips.*)

It's a dolly!
It's a real live beautiful doll!
It's not La Rochefoucauld,
It's not Alphonse Diderot,
Not Corneille, not Corot,
It's a dolly!
It's not Émile Zola,
It's not Alexandre Dumas,
Not Degas, Delacroix,
It's a dolly!

JOSEPHINE: What a face, young and fair,
　　　　　What a price, *pas trop cher*,
　　　　　Just that *vin ordinaire*
　　　　　Alcohol!

ALL: And it's not Joan of Arc,
　　　Just a statue in a park,
　　　It's a dolly!
　　　It's a real—live!—beautiful!—

(*There's a big drum roll as two chorus* GIRLS *unveil the last statue.*
Ostrich feather fans part slowly, inch by inch, to reveal a BOY *who is totally nude—rear view only, though, at last critical moment of strip.*)

DOLL!

BLACKOUT

Scene 3

JOSEPHINE'S *dressing room backstage.* GUY, *now permanently handsome, waits for her.* JOSEPHINE *enters, completely English and very refined, like Gladys Cooper.*

JOSEPHINE: Trouble, trouble, trouble. [*Sees* GUY.] Guy, dear. How nice. Give Auntie a kiss.
GUY: Hello, Aunt Josephine. What's wrong? [*Gives her a peck on the forehead.*]
JOSEPHINE: It's Alphonse again.
GUY: Is he the one . . . ?
JOSEPHINE: The one with no costume. He's just quit the show.
GUY: Oh yes. I heard.
JOSEPHINE: It's all jealousy, you know. Just because my number is going over so well. I don't know why, but nude gentlemen are always so temperamental. They're lucky to be employed at all. I want you to believe, Guy, that even when things were at their worst, your Auntie never

for a moment considered lowering her standards—or her clothes.

GUY: [*Shocked*] Oh, Aunt Josephine!

JOSEPHINE: Once a lady, always a lady. Whatever you may have heard in London.

GUY: I never believed those stories.

JOSEPHINE: You should never have *heard* those stories. Tell me, did you catch Alphonse's farewell performance?

GUY: No. I was just passing by.

JOSEPHINE: Ah, good. You're cheering up and you've been sightseeing.

GUY: Not really.

JOSEPHINE: Christmas shopping?

GUY: No.

JOSEPHINE: Having a nice little *déjeuner*?

GUY: I'm not very hungry these days.

JOSEPHINE: Well, I hope he's worth it.

GUY: Who?

JOSEPHINE: Whoever's been taking your mind off Paris. What happened in London, Guy?

GUY: Nothing.

JOSEPHINE: Never mind. You needn't tell me. Auntie knows better than that. It's not hard to guess. Boy meets boy, love at first sight . . .

GUY: Second sight.

JOSEPHINE: Rapture for two weeks . . .

GUY: Two hours.

JOSEPHINE: And then he left you. . . .

GUY: I left him.

JOSEPHINE: [*Blinks.*] Well, I was close.

GUY: Anyway, it's the end of the story.

JOSEPHINE: Not necessarily. You could always go back to him.

GUY: No. I mustn't.

JOSEPHINE: Won't he have you back?

GUY: Oh yes! But it would ruin his career! So I must be strong for both of us and keep out of his life.

JOSEPHINE: And meanwhile you're both miserable.

GUY: [*Sadly*] Yes. But it's just something we'll have to endure. After all, it'll pass. In a few years we'll be able to look back on this and smile.

JOSEPHINE: Perhaps even laugh.

GUY: That'll take longer. In the meantime I must keep busy, work, take a job.

JOSEPHINE: Very sensible, do you a world of good.

GUY: I know it won't be easy. I've got no profession, no training, no talent. But then, neither has Alphonse and he's doing all right.

JOSEPHINE: There is no comparison between you and Alphonse.

GUY: Well, there must be. I've just been offered his job.

JOSEPHINE: WHAT?

GUY: By the stage manager—on my way in.

JOSEPHINE: That's disgraceful! You—the son of a peer, my nephew . . . ! That's an insult!

GUY: I said no.

JOSEPHINE: That's not the point! It's outrageous even to suggest that a member of the British aristocracy would consider exposing himself for a fee in a common music hall . . . even if it is the best in Paris.

GUY: I didn't consider it.

JOSEPHINE: What a cheek! Well, this time they've gone too far!

GUY: Where are you going?

JOSEPHINE: To give the blackguards a piece of my mind! I'll give them "nudes"! [*Storms out—colliding with* CLARENCE, *who is just outside door.*]

CLARENCE: Excuse me. . . .

JOSEPHINE: There's no excuse for you! [*Goes.*]

GUY: Clarence!

CLARENCE: Pardon me, young man, but I'm looking for Guy Rose. They told me he'd be backstage but I can't find him anywhere.

GUY: I'm afraid . . .

CLARENCE: Oh, the search I've had—you wouldn't believe. From London to Paris, without food or sleep, nothing but love and devotion to sustain me. But why should I pour out my soul like this to you, a perfect stranger?

GUY: I don't . . .

CLARENCE: It must be because, in some mysterious way, I do feel drawn to you. Could it be that you bear some resemblance to the person I love dearest in the world—I refer, of course, to my beloved Guy Rose? No, it couldn't. And yet—if you'll excuse the sick fancy of a love-crazed mind—I do somehow see, as it were, shimmering there, a phantom Guy, the same nose, the same lips, surely even the same eyes and hair! It can't be! But it is! My little Guy—it's you—come to my arms!

GUY: [*Retreating*] Get away, Clarence!

CLARENCE: But you can't reject me now!

GUY: Why not? I don't know how you found out about me, but don't expect me to be taken in by that overdone performance.

CLARENCE: [*Sniffy*] It wasn't overdone.

GUY: Well, it was a waste of effort. Please go.

CLARENCE: I know you don't mean that, but it hurts all the same. You don't seem to realize, Guy, that I'm a sensitive person. I'm not resilient. You can't cast me aside and expect me to bounce back as if nothing happened. After all, I'm not like some people—Casey O'Brien, for instance. . . .

GUY: What about him?

CLARENCE: Who?

GUY: Casey O'Brien.

CLARENCE: Oh, did I mention Casey O'Brien? Well, you know Casey. He never changes. Always laughing it up. . . .

GUY: Laughing?

CLARENCE: Seen everywhere, out with a new face every night, if anything worse than before. That is until he started chasing after me.

GUY: You?

CLARENCE: Well, I know he's amusing, but he does go too far, you must admit. And when he started to talk about marriage . . .

GUY: Marriage!

CLARENCE: Of course I said no. But he was so persistent! . . .

GUY: I don't believe you!

CLARENCE: Gifts, presents, night and day. And he wouldn't take any of them back.

GUY: You're lying.

CLARENCE: Not even his bull's ear. [*Produces it.*]

GUY: [*Shattered*] He gave you his bull's ear?

CLARENCE: Oh, you've seen it. Rather gruesome, but a sweet gesture.

GUY: He gave you his bull's ear. . . .

CLARENCE: Anyhow, it cut no ice with me. I made it perfectly clear that my heart belonged only to you.

GUY: [*Bitterly*] You shouldn't have been so hasty, Clarence. You were made for each other.

CLARENCE: Now don't take it out on me. It's not my fault.

GUY: I think you'd better go now.

CLARENCE: Not unless you come with me.

GUY: Get out!

CLARENCE: I can't leave you here in this squalid hole! Your parents would never forgive me. People of our class don't consort with common theatricals.

GUY: Oh, don't we?

CLARENCE: No! You're a gentleman, Guy, and so am I, and, as a gentleman, I consider myself above strippers and sordid hootchy-kootchy dancers!

GUY: I'm glad you told me that, Clarence. [JOSEPHINE *enters.*] Aunt Josephine, I've decided to take that job.

JOSEPHINE: No!

GUY: If it's good enough for Alphonse, it's good enough for me.

CLARENCE: Who's Alphonse?

JOSEPHINE: Guy, you can't! The disgrace!

CLARENCE: He's not the one without any . . .?

JOSEPHINE: [*To Clarence*] Yes!

(CLARENCE *is visibly shocked.*)

GUY: Yes, Clarence. As from Monday, you can see all of me that you want—twice nightly!

JOSEPHINE: Guy, I beg you!

GUY: [*To* CLARENCE] You—and two thousand other people!

CLARENCE: It's disgusting!
GUY: Good! [*Sings defiantly.*]
> Let them all see!
> Let them all stare!
> What's it to me?
> What do I care?
> What's left to lose? With nothing sacred
> Why worry about self-respect?
> Anything goes!

JOSEPHINE AND CLARENCE: Why start with clothes?

GUY: Let people talk!
> Let people glare!
> Snigger and gawk!
> What do I care?

> I'm sick and tired pretending anything makes
>   any sense in my world!
> Let them all share
> In my despair!

> Don't tell me hope isn't dead—
> I know it is!
> So you can go and tell the highest bidder
> I'm his!

> And let newspapers call,
> Take photographs!
> From now it's all
> Strictly for laughs!
> How can the end
> Of the world depend
> On the end of a love affair?
> Mine doesn't quite end there!

> I want that life of gay abandon, of excursions
>   and alarms!
> Each evening in a brand-new fella's arms!
> 'Cause I'm beautiful!

I'm beautiful!
I'm beautiful!
And what comes next comes natural!

So let newspapers call,
Take photographs!
From now it's all
Strictly for laughs!
I fell apart,
But a broken heart
Isn't something beyond repair!
So, world, beware!
I'm what I am!
What do I care?
Don't care a . . .

(JOSEPHINE *and* CLARENCE *block their ears in wincing anticipation.*)

GUY: . . . DAMN!

BLACKOUT

Scene 4

Excited music. ANDREW *and* NEWSGIRLS *enter.*

NEWSGIRLS: Extra, extra, read all about it!
FIRST NEWSGIRL: [*Displaying paper and headline*] "ARISTOCRAT JOINS PARIS FOLIES!"
SECOND NEWSGIRL: " 'ENGLISH ROSE' SCANDAL!"
THIRD NEWSGIRL: "FRENCH MUSIC HALL UNVEILS GUY ROSE!"
FOURTH NEWSGIRL: " 'ENGLISH ROSE' TO SHED PETALS!"

(NEWSGIRLS *give papers to* ANDREW *and leave. Lights come up to reveal the bar again back in London the next day.*

CASEY *is sitting at the bar, not drunk but not happy.*
ANDREW *comes in with newspapers, dumps them on the bar.*)

ANDREW: Seen the headlines?

CASEY: Yeah.

BARTENDER: Here you are, sir, one double whiskey.

CASEY: Keep 'em coming. [BARTENDER *goes. To* ANDREW] How'd you know I was here?

ANDREW: I heard you were sleeping here.

CASEY: Have a drink.

ANDREW: No thanks. Casey, you've got to snap out of this.

CASEY: Either change the subject or shut up.

ANDREW: How does it feel to be scooped by every paper in town? They're having a field day.

CASEY: Good luck to them.

ANDREW: But it was your story. You picked it up. Why drop it?

CASEY: That's my business.

ANDREW: It's also Reuters' business. You took their money and you haven't written a word.

CASEY: To hell with Reuters.

ANDREW: Then the rumor is true.

CASEY: What rumor?

ANDREW: Well, you know what they're saying in Fleet Street.

CASEY: No, what?

ANDREW: I hate to be the one to tell you.

CASEY: Tell me.

ANDREW: Forget I mentioned it.

CASEY: Tell me!

ANDREW: They're saying you've lost your touch, you're all washed up, a has-been, and a disgrace to the profession.

CASEY: Oh, is that all?

ANDREW: They're also laughing.

CASEY: I don't care.

ANDREW: Because you're still carrying the torch for Guy Rose.

CASEY: That's a lie!

ANDREW: They say you're still crazy in love with him, even
though he jilted you, and you can't trust yourself to face
him again.

CASEY: Oh, can't I?

ANDREW: That's what they're saying.

CASEY: Well, you just watch me!

ANDREW: Now, don't be hasty, Casey. You know what
you're like. They may be right.

CASEY: Huh! I'll give them a story that'll make their hair
curl!

ANDREW: You'll take one look at him and turn to jelly!

CASEY: That'll be the day! [*Slaps money on the bar and
starts to go.*]

ANDREW: You'll never do it! You'll break down! You'll
crack!

(CASEY *is gone.* ANDREW *collapses with relief as the* BAR-
TENDER *serves up a third drink.*)

BARTENDER: What am I going to do with this?

ANDREW: [*Taking drink*] Keep 'em coming! [*He toasts the
departed* CASEY—*and the success of his own strategy.*]

BLACKOUT

Scene 5

Paris. The dressing room again. GUY, *wearing a dressing
gown, stands center in the nude's pose, rehearsing by himself, singing unaccompanied:*

GUY:
It's a dolly—
It's a real live beautiful . . .
The feathers are withdrawn slowly. Everybody looks. I
blush—all over! Everybody laughs . . . oh, God! [*His
misgivings are interrupted by a knock at the door.*]
Entrez.

(CASEY *comes in.*)

GUY: [*Surprised and pleased*] Casey!

CASEY: [*Very tight*] I don't want to be here. I'm just doing my job.

GUY: [*Disappointed*] Oh.

CASEY: Nothing personal, you understand, just a few questions.

GUY: An interview.

CASEY: Unless you object.

GUY: Not at all. Everyone else has had one. Why shouldn't you?

CASEY: If you can't take it, I'll go.

GUY: I can take it. I can use the publicity.

CASEY: Good. [*Gets out notepad.*] Do you like undressing in public?

GUY: I haven't done it yet, but I'm sure I shall.

CASEY: You don't find it degrading?

GUY: I . . .

CASEY: Perhaps you find it exciting.

GUY: No, I . . .

CASEY: You're in it for the kicks.

GUY: Yes, for the kicks.

CASEY: How much are they paying you per kick?

GUY: Not much. Money isn't the prime consideration.

CASEY: Oh yeah. [*Writes in pad.*] "Peeled peer . . . disdains dough."

GUY: That isn't quite what I meant.

CASEY: You mean for a chance like this you'd do it for nothing?

GUY: Yes.

CASEY: You're easy to please. Lucky it doesn't take much talent.

GUY: Oh, I don't know. A certain finesse.

CASEY: Not something I'd want to do myself.

GUY: Very wise.

CASEY: [*Stung*] But if I did, I'd be damned good!

GUY: Would you like an introduction to the management?

CASEY: No thanks. I haven't sunk that low yet.

GUY: My mistake. I thought you had.

CASEY: Because it's a pretty rotten thing to do.

GUY: So is gutter journalism. But I suppose somebody has to do it.

CASEY: It seems the Honourable Guy Rose just likes slumming.

GUY: Possibly. He certainly got a taste for it in London!

CASEY: If you want to know what I think—

GUY: I don't.

CASEY: I think this is some kind of gesture. I think he's doing this just to hurt somebody. . . .

GUY: You're quite wrong. I don't know anybody who's worth that. [CASEY's *pencil point snaps.*] You've broken your pencil.

CASEY: That's okay. I've got enough. [*Puts pad away.*]

GUY: What a pity. I could have given you a lot more.

CASEY: Don't worry. You haven't got *anything* I want.

GUY: Knowing your taste, I'm relieved to hear it. Why don't you go now?

CASEY: It'll be a pleasure. [*But he doesn't go.*] Oh, yeah. Whatever happened to your friend?

GUY: What friend?

CASEY: The mouse—with the glasses.

GUY: I got rid of him.

CASEY: As easily as that.

GUY: It wasn't easy.

CASEY: Then why did you do it?

GUY: I was tired of him—and his dreary life.

CASEY: It may have been dreary—at least it wasn't sordid.

GUY: How do you know?

CASEY: Because he was a boy scout!

GUY: That means nothing. So were you!

CASEY: It means he was kind, loyal, and friendly, things you wouldn't know anything about!

GUY: Well, if he was so marvelous, why didn't you tell him so? Why didn't you go chasing after him?

CASEY: [*Startled*] What?

GUY: I'll tell you what. Because he wasn't beautiful! All you care about is a pretty face—and you don't care a damn what's behind it!

(CLARENCE, *unseen by them, enters through the door. He stands there transfixed, watching the cut and thrust of the quarrel with a broad, delighted smile.*)

CASEY: Well, one thing's clear! I sure hit the bottom with you!

GUY: You'll find something worse!

CASEY: I have, but I don't go for strippers!

GUY: That's one of the advantages of being one!

CASEY: And the only advantage!

GUY: I'd rather be a stripper than a third-rate Casanova!

CASEY: At least I don't make a career out of dropping people!

GUY: You're much better at picking them up!

(*Suddenly they stop dead, both of them seeing* CLARENCE *at the same time.*)

CLARENCE: [*Complimenting* GUY *on his* bon mot] Oh, that was very good!

GUY AND CASEY: Get out!

CLARENCE: But . . .

GUY AND CASEY: [*Advancing to him*] GET OUT!

(CLARENCE *beats a fearful and hasty retreat out the door.*)

GUY: [*Back to the row.*] And furthermore . . .

CASEY: Furthermore nothing! You're a heartless, selfish, shallow, spoiled brat, and I don't know what I ever saw in you. But I won't make the same mistake again. So good-bye, kiddo, and good luck. You'll need it. [*At door*] As far as I'm concerned, your dowdy friend's worth ten of you. [*Goes out quickly.* GUY, *shaken, goes to the dressing table. There is a knock at the door.*]

GUY: [*Softly*] Casey? . . .

VOICE: Five minutes, Mr. Rose.

(GUY *freezes with dread. A fierce drum roll begins under.*)

BLACKOUT

Scene 6

In front of the theater. The scene is played before the previously seen illuminated front cloth depicting the Folies sign.

CLARENCE *storms out, apoplectic with rage, and sings:*

CLARENCE: When is it gonna be Clarence's turn?
Clarence's turn
Should now appear!
Gasping for good luck and choking with bad,
Clarence's had
It up to here!
Isn't it time it was Clarence's turn?
Clarence's turn
Is overdue!
So many times has Clarence been left out in the cold,
Clarence's turn-ing blue!
[*Plaintively*]
Me . . . Who's my favorite person? Still me . . .
Though of late I've been starting to see
In my life of perfection
There's one little problem,
I.e. . . .

Nobody likes me,
Everybody hates me.
They all turn me down, stand me up,
Tell me off, put me on,
Overlook me, and it strikes me,
That it just might be fun,
Fun for everyone,
If they all could be got
And be put in a pot
Full of boiling fat! . . .
No, you can't do that . . .
It's not nice.

(*Surprised*)
I'm not nice!
(*Pouting*)
Well . . . it's not my fault. . . .

[*Singing*]
I'd've been nicer
'F I'd've been simpler,
Contented to be healthy,
A little less wealthy,
A little more wise.

And I'd've been simpler
'F I'd've been lovelier,
I'd've been breezier
'F I'd've been easier
On the eyes,

And I'd've been lovelier
'F I'd've been Harry,
Or possibly Cary,
Or Gary
Or Barry
Or Larry
Or one of those guys!

But what kind of parents
Would call their son Clarence?
Well, you ought to try that on for size
And you might begin to realize
How a name like that can mold you,
Enfold you,
And hold you
Like a vice!
Oh, there's no telling what I'd've been
'F I'd've been
Just nice!

For a plausible change of heart,
It's a gesture that you need—

Clarence, time's running out;
How about a boy scout good deed?

(*Spoken*)
Why not? I'm desperate!

[*Sung*]
Who'd like a good deed done?
Some favor they need done?
Doesn't anyone want helping out?
Wouldn't you know? There's not a soul about!
Who when I say, "Who can I help?"
Needs my help?
Oh, who? Who? Who? Who? Who?

(CASEY *enters.*)

You! . . .

CASEY: Buzz off.

CLARENCE: Wait! It's important!

CASEY: I gotta catch a train.

CLARENCE: Just one minute! I beg you! I must tell you something!

(CASEY *stops.*)

CASEY: Spit it out.

CLARENCE: I . . . I . . . I . . . Oh, it's so difficult! I . . . I . . . I . . .

CASEY: What's the matter? You look terrible!

CLARENCE: I . . . I . . . I . . .

CASEY: Do you want a doctor?

CLARENCE: No! I . . . I . . . I . . . [*Struck by an idea*] HE!

CASEY: Who?

CLARENCE: Guy!

CASEY: What about him?

CLARENCE: He . . . he . . . he . . .

CASEY: Don't start that again!

CLARENCE: He . . . he . . .

CASEY: Clarence, I'm going to clobber you!

119

CLARENCE: He loves you! [*In a rush.*]

CASEY: Crap! [*Starts to go.*]

CLARENCE: No, it's true! It's all my fault! I told him he'd ruin your life, and he believed me! And he gave you up for love! And there's another thing! They're the same person—both of them! Look! [*Pulls photographs out of his breast pocket and shows them to* CASEY.]

CASEY: [*Rifles through them thunderstruck*] Clarence, you're wonderful!

(*To* CLARENCE's *delight,* CASEY *suddenly hugs him briefly, then dashes out.* CLARENCE *resumes singing, gleefully.*)

CLARENCE: Make room, everybody, for Clarence's turn.
   Clarence's turn
   Is on its way!
   You'll see the kind of person that you ain't seen for years!
   Oh yes indeed and guaranteed to turn off the tears!
   'Cause trouble's through when good-deed-doin' Clarence appears!
   Clarence's nice!
   That's what you'll say!
   Clarence's turn-ing out okay!

(CASEY *runs back in.*)

CASEY: Come on, I'm going to need you!

(*Collars him and hauls him off as the scene changes.*)

Scene 7

Onstage again. We are halfway through the "It's a Dolly" number, staged and played exactly as before.

JOSEPHINE,
BOYS, AND GIRLS: [*Singing*]

It's not La Rochefoucauld,
It's not Alfonse Diderot,
Not Corneille, not Corot,
It's a dolly!

It's not Émile Zola,
It's not Alexandre Dumas,
Not Degas, Delacroix,
It's a dolly!

JOSEPHINE: What a face, young and fair,
What a price, *pas trop cher*,
Just that *vin ordinaire*
Alcohol!

ALL: And it's not Joan of Arc,
Just a statue in a park,
It's a dolly!
It's a real live beautiful doll!
It's a dolly!
It's a real!—live!—beautiful!—

(*Once again the drum rolls as the curtains part, revealing a scared* GUY *behind the feather fans. The plumes are then withdrawn slowly, revealing more and more of* GUY. CASEY *runs on from either the auditorium or the wings.*)

CASEY: Stop! Stop! Stop!

(*The music dies.* CASEY *runs up to* GUY *and catches the plumes in the nick of time.*)

GUY: What are you doing?
CASEY: [*Tearing off his coat*] Put this on and shut up!
BOYS AND GIRLS: [*To* JOSEPHINE] *C'est la police?* [GIRLS *run off.*]
JOSEPHINE: [*Happily*] No. *C'est l'amour.*
BOYS: [*Soppy*] Ahhhh!

121

(GUY *has now donned trench coat.*)

CASEY: I know everything, Guy—about *both* of you. And I know why you ran out on me! And now there's something that you should know. [*Shouting off*] Clarence, come out here!

(CLARENCE *enters—contrite, with head bowed—but still manages to say "Oh—hello" to the* CHORUS BOYS. *They shrink with dread.*)

CASEY: All right, tell him!

CLARENCE: [*Contrite to* GUY] Guy, I've been very wicked. I lied to you. Casey didn't propose to me in London. He was miserable without you. He hit the bottle!

GUY: [*To* CASEY] Did you really?

CLARENCE: Oh yes, blind drunk all the time. Mind you, how you can get yourself involved with someone who's next door to being an alcoho—

CASEY: [*Warningly*] Clarence!

CLARENCE: [*Hand to mouth*] I slipped! I didn't mean it! I'm sorry!

CASEY: [*To* GUY] How could you believe I'd propose to a sap like Clarence?

GUY: Well, he . . .

CLARENCE: I kept your bull's ear! [*Hands it over to* CASEY, *who gives it to* GUY.] And now, which one of you lovely gentlemen would like to come and have a drink with Uncle Clarence? [*The* BOYS *exchange blank looks.*] I'm good . . .

CASEY: They don't understand English, Clarence.

CLARENCE: Oh. Good and *RICH*.

BOYS: Ahhh! [*Full comprehension.*]

CLARENCE: Your place or mine?

(BOYS *and* CLARENCE *disappear.*)

JOSEPHINE: *L'amour, l'amour!* Oh, I think I'm going to cry. [*Leaves.*]

GUY: But what about our sacrifices? I might still ruin your life.

CASEY: Look, kiddo, we'll make a bargain. I promise not to give up my career if you promise not to give up me.

GUY: I promise.

CASEY: And so do I. We'll both be very selfish and very happy.

GUY: Is that the secret of a happy marriage?

CASEY: Of course. It's the only way to live happily ever after!

> [*Sings.*]
> Tell me please, does anybody love you?
> Do you have a special love affair?
> Someone who worries about you?
> Who's always true
> And tender too
> And waits for you
> Somewhere?

BOTH: So please say does anybody love you?
For if by some lucky chance the answer is no,
And you haven't anyone to love you,
Then do you mind if I do?
Because I love you so.

KISS AND BLACKOUT

Scene 8

BRIDESMAIDS *slowly march in singing.*

BRIDESMAIDS: Extra, extra, read all about it,
Extra, extra, read all about it,
June weddings make news!
Duke marries Mrs. Simpson!
O'Brien marries English Rose!

(Lights up on the full stage, which resembles a large wedding cake. The finale is done in the style of a big Thirties production number, and all in black and white. Everyone appears in it, and all the men are dressed as boy scouts in pure white.)

BOYS:	It's a boy's life!
	In the open air,
	Cloudy skies or fair,
	There's nothing like some pioneering,
GIRLS:	With adventures beckoning everywhere,
ALL:	That's the only life for a boy!
ANDREW:	Beneath the stars together singing a jolly song,
ALL:	Now that's the life that can't be beat.
JOSEPHINE:	You always whistle as you merrily roll along
ALL:	With a smile for everyone you meet!
CLARENCE:	And an arm to help old ladies cross the street!
ALL:	Oh, it's a boy's life
	Going for a hike,
	Fishing for a pike,
	Or swimming in the altogether!
	Uphill, downhill, pedaling on a bike!
	Going like a whizz!
	Peace of mind is his!
	What a life it is
	For a boy!

(CASEY and GUY appear at the top of the cake, under an arch, dressed as groom and groom, in black.)

ALL:	Boy met boy tonight!
	Found with joy tonight
	The perfect mate
	That fate
	Could not destroy tonight!
	Back when gentlemen were gentle,
	Just the thing to make you sentimental.

GUY: Night and day again,
CASEY: Love is gay again,
ALL: And though our story was that old cliché again,
What a beautiful blend:
Boy met boy,
Boy lost boy,
But boy got boy in the end!

CURTAIN

CONFESSIONS OF A FEMALE DISORDER
A Play in Two Acts

by
Susan Miller

Confessions of a Female Disorder, by Susan Miller, was first performed at the Eugene O'Neill Theatre Center's National Playwrights Conference, Waterford, Connecticut, July 19, 1973. It was directed by Larry Arrick. The cast included the following:

RONNIE .... *Swoosie Kurtz*
CHEERLEADER #1 .... *Gayle Harrington*
CHEERLEADER #2 .... *Michelle Shay*
CHEERLEADER #3 .... *Barbara Ramsay*
MOTHER .... *Jacqueline Brooks*
COOP .... *Beverly Bentley*
LIZ .... *Deloris Gaskins*
PSYCHIATRIST .... *Peter Turgeon*
DAVID .... *Lenny Baker*
MITCH .... *Ben Masters*
LETTERMAN #1 .... *Richard Ludgin*
LETTERMAN #2 .... *John Breuer*
LETTERMAN #3 .... *Bob Oliker*
BEN .... *Ben Masters*
COCKTAIL PARTY GUESTS .... *Gayle Harrington,*
Michelle Shay, Barbara Ramsay,
Jacqueline Brooks, Richard Ludgin,
John Breuer, Bob Oliker
EVELYN .... *Rosemary De Angelis*

Confessions of a Female Disorder was later produced by the Mark Taper Forum in Los Angeles, as part of its New Theatre for Now program. It was directed by Edward Parone, with the following cast:

RONNIE .... *Barra Grant*
CHEERLEADERS .... *Nedra Deen, Laura Campbell,*
Katherine Dunfee

COOP .... *Penelope Windust*
DAVID .... *Michael Cristofer*
LIZ .... *Julie Mannix*
PSYCHIATRIST .... *Gene Elman*
MITCH .... *Mark Wheeler*
EVELYN .... *Melissa Murphy*
LETTERMEN .... *David Gilliam, John Barron,*
Richard Gilliland
COCKTAIL PARTY GUEST .... *Lesley Woods*

CHARACTERS

THREE CHEERLEADERS: Can be played by women from twenty to thirty. They become the WOMEN COCKTAIL PARTY GUESTS in Act II.

RONNIE: The central character, who journeys from puberty to marriage and career. Can be played by a woman from twenty-five to thirty.

COOP: A free spirit, of the earth. Ronnie's college roommate, who also appears in Act II as a grown woman. Same age range as Ronnie.

LIZ: A college student.

PSYCHIATRIST: A man from forty to sixty, whose appearance might fight the stereotype, even though some of his attitudes do not help his patient, Ronnie.

DAVID: An attorney, married to Ronnie. Sensitive, but goal-oriented. He can be played by a man from twenty-seven to thirty-five.

MITCH: An easy-going, good-looking fraternity boy of the early-1960 variety.

THREE LETTERMEN: Can be played by men from twenty to thirty. They become the MALE COCKTAIL PARTY GUESTS in Act II.

MOTHER/COCKTAIL PARTY GUEST/MANNY'S WIDOW

EVELYN: A woman from thirty to forty, who is Ronnie's neighbor in Act II.

ACT I

Scene 1

A bedroom. RONNIE *is trying to hide a pair of underpants.* THREE CHEERLEADERS *assume various positions around the room: on the bed, polishing fingernails, dancing, etc.*

CHEERLEADER #1: What are you doing, Ronnie, babe? Gonna stick them in some drawer and let them get all crusty?

CHEERLEADER #2: We caught you red-handed, girl . . . caught you trying to hide it. The place to watch is way down there, kiddo.

RONNIE: What am I going to do?

CHEERLEADER #1: Nothing. Don't ask questions like that. People will look at you funny. You have no business wanting to *do* anything, Missy. Miss bloody pants.

CHEERLEADER #2: Down, Ronnie. Keep looking down.

CHEERLEADER #3: Everyone else *does unto you* . . . in, on, around, above you.

CHEERLEADER #1: Lady. Little lady.

CHEERLEADER #2: This is a very big day. Dance with me, Ronnie.

RONNIE: I'm bleeding to death.

CHEERLEADER #1: Rinse your pants out in cold water, honey, and relax.

RONNIE: What's going on? What's happening to me?

ALL: [*Forming a dance line*] The curse . . . cha, cha, cha.

RONNIE: What?

CHEERLEADER #3: The curse.

CHEERLEADER #2: You've just fallen off the roof.

RONNIE: This is so embarrassing. What will I tell my mother?

CHEERLEADER #1: Mama knows.

RONNIE: She does?

CHEERLEADER #2: She comes from a long line of bleeders.

RONNIE: What about my friends, do they know?

CHEERLEADER #2: Some of them. Listen, you look pale. Why don't you lie down.

RONNIE: But I'm still . . . you know.

CHEERLEADER #3: It's nothing, sweetie. Just a little raw baby matter.

RONNIE: [Lying down] I must have bumped into something. I just don't understand how it could have happened.

CHEERLEADER #1: You little girls are just too much. You've got the stuff dreams are made of, pussycat.

CHEERLEADER #3: You wanna try one of my lipsticks? Heavenly Rose, it's called. You'll feel like a new person.

(CHEERLEADER practices a cheer. RONNIE'S MOTHER enters. She slaps RONNIE. Then kisses her, hands her a Kotex pad, and walks out.)

RONNIE: Did I do something wrong?

CHEERLEADER #1: What's the matter, didn't you like our little initiation ceremony?

RONNIE: But she's never hit me before. My mother's a soft woman.

CHEERLEADER #3: It's the custom; don't knock it.

RONNIE: She slapped me.

CHEERLEADER #1: It was just a warning.

CHEERLEADER #2: Don't you see, she had to haul off and hit you, kid. You've become offensive.

CHEERLEADER #3: And nasty.

CHEERLEADERS #1 AND #2: Unclean.

CHEERLEADER #2: But don't worry, babe. You're not the only one.

RONNIE: [Indicating Kotex] What will I do with this?

CHEERLEADER #1: Shove it between your legs. Like a badge.

CHEERLEADER #2: Be proud of yourself, kiddo.

RONNIE: People will stare at me. They'll know.

CHEERLEADER #1: This is your beginning, baby.

CHEERLEADER #2: Go ahead. Put that thing on. Strut around with it; see how it feels.

RONNIE: I don't think I'm going to like it. It looks uncomfortable.

CHEERLEADER #3: Everything you put down there from now on is going to be uncomfortable. But you'll get used to it.

RONNIE: When does this stop? I mean, when will it go away?

CHEERLEADER #1: [*Amused*] It used to disappear after forty-five years or so, but now they have these groovy little hormone pills that keep it going.

CHEERLEADER #2: Like an act of faith.

RONNIE: I don't feel so well. I think I'd like to be by myself.

CHEERLEADER #2: Go ahead and moan. We don't mind.

RONNIE: This is the thing they talk about in the lavatories. The older girls. This must be what it is.

CHEERLEADER #1: Well, it isn't a big secret, you know.

RONNIE: I don't want to talk to them anymore . . . those laughing girls. I don't want to look at them.

CHEERLEADER #2: Hey, c'mon. Pretty soon you'll have a pajama party and laugh yourself silly.

RONNIE: I'm white. I'm so white. Isn't it peculiar?

CHEERLEADER #3: I'll get you something to eat. How about a peanut butter and jelly sandwich or something?

RONNIE: I don't have any taste. My stomach's a balloon.

CHEERLEADER #1: But Ronnie, babe, this little number is your meal ticket.

CHEERLEADER #3: You can use it as an excuse for gym. I always do. [*Pause.*] Stiff upper lip, kid.

CHEERLEADER #1: Take a Midol.

CHEERLEADER #2: Here's looking down at you, sweetie.

ALL: [*Doing a cheer*] C-U-N-T. *Introducing Ron-nie!*

BLACKOUT

Scene 2

RONNIE *dresses, as she talks to the audience. This is now her college dormitory room, although it may be the same set as used before.*

RONNIE: MENSTRUATE. A full round word of the earth. I see it now, but when I was thirteen, it had only a painful circumference. It was ugly and misshapen. I've learned a lot about form since then. Right now I'm on the shaky side of adolescence, so what I have to say may sound typically bitter. I'm still rough around the edges. You'll see through me, of course. I'm terribly obvious. I'm also nineteen. I've had my period for six years . . . that's . . . 72 times. Bear with me. It's the flower of my womanhood, and I can afford to be cute and self-conscious. Later, I'll learn to be sad and angry. Also . . . it is 1964 . . . and I have learned to say *fuck* without guilt.

(COOP *enters, with a towel . . . plays a few notes on her kazoo.*)

COOP: Hi . . . how's life in the shithouse?
RONNIE: I hate my jeans! Look at them. They're too blue. I can't operate without a proper pair of jeans. Do you have any bleach? Never mind, I'll just sit on them. I'll rub my ass back and forth. They're too blue. See what I mean?
COOP: They're too stiff. [*She picks up a pack of cards on the bed, begins to play solitaire.*] The problem is . . . they're much too stiff.
RONNIE: [*Starts to type.*] You're disturbing me, Coop.
COOP: I have to figure a way to get you out of this room.
RONNIE: No, thanks. I'm trying to break all ties with the outside world.
COOP: That should be rather easy for someone whose last visit to the outside world was observed only by the most religious.

RONNIE: Fuck off, Coop. [*To the audience*] Didn't I say that well?

COOP: [*Flopping down on a bed . . . or the floor*] It's really a terrific place to be, Ronnie. The world, I mean. Just let me open the window, at least . . . and you can get a good whiff.

RONNIE: [*Affectionately*] Any more like you out there?

COOP: Better than that.

RONNIE: That's a fucking lie. Everyone's crazy or lost. [*Pause.*] And you can't wait, can you?

COOP: Okay, sometimes I can't breathe too well inside, and I start having visions . . . but I'm not in a hurry. It'll happen.

RONNIE: Without breaking stride?

COOP: I don't think . . . anyone's ever done it that way.

RONNIE: You knock me out.

COOP: She smiles, as I live and breathe.

RONNIE: Your face was shining at me, I had no choice.

COOP: Well, I wasn't prepared for a smile. I think I like you more sullen.

RONNIE: Make up your mind.

COOP: Did you ever think that maybe you were pursuing the wrong course of action? I mean, you really should cool the typewriter and start developing your tragic past.

RONNIE: Just play your kazoo.

COOP: I went through that box of papers you gave me. You're very good, you know that.

RONNIE: That's nice . . . that's . . . nice to hear.

COOP: It matters that you gave me the beginning.

RONNIE: I thought . . . [*Doesn't finish.*]

COOP: What did you think?

RONNIE: Want a Coke? I have some vintage Coke here. Some of your best months. May 1963 . . . a bit sticky. But full-bodied.

COOP: What did you think?

RONNIE: That I'd like you to keep track of me. That I'd like to ship all my fragments and carbon copies to you, in case I ever need to remember what it was all about.

(LIZ *enters in a towel.*)

LIZ: God, I'm hungry. Did you taste that shit they had for dinner?

RONNIE: [*Sarcastically*] Well, Liz, what a lovely surprise! You're looking well.

LIZ: I've got to have a pizza or something.

COOP: Are you going to . . . or coming from?

LIZ: What?

RONNIE: The shower. [*Moves closer.*] She doesn't smell like Johnson and Johnson. Must be GOING TO.

LIZ: I wonder if I should order it now or wait. What do you think?

RONNIE: [*Begins typing again.*] One of our campers is having a problem, Coop. Why don't you help her out.

LIZ: [*Going to bed, where she will drink the Coke* RONNIE *has opened.*] I don't believe you're still writing that English paper.

COOP: God help her, she's writing a myth. A maiden typing her way to fame in the glorious land of cock. [*Pause.*] C'mon, Ronnie. Let's go to the showers.

RONNIE: Her name is Lily.

LIZ: Who?

RONNIE: The lady in my dubious myth. And she is on a quest to discover her spot. Her vulnerable spot. Her strength. You see, men come knocking at her door . . . sniffing, groping. She figures she has something special, only she can't seem to locate the precious thing. It's not your typical Achilles heel. So Lily puts on her trench coat and a pair of saddle shoes—this isn't a Greek myth, by the way—and sets out to unlock her secret.

LIZ: Dammit, I forgot my soap. Do you have any hypoallergenic soap?

RONNIE: I want revenge! I want to get all those dirty little fuckers like Zeus and Hades and Telemachus.

LIZ: Who was that last fella?

RONNIE: And John Wayne and Paul Newman. All those creeps who knew where their next meal was coming from because all their lives it was just dangling right there between the old legs. But Lily, she's got buried treasure, and the clues keep coming slowly. She sleeps with the gods, and they say things like: *That's it. That's it . . . Oh, that's it.* But our Lily, our Lily of the prone position, can't for the life of her determine what *it* is. She is unspent and undefined.

COOP: I think I'll be going along now . . . trotting off to the shower, as it were. Coming, Liz?

RONNIE: [*Screams.*] *Her myth is in her hole. Hole. Her tunnel. Her secret canal. Her holiest of holies.*

COOP: [*After a pause*] Liz, do you have a date tonight? [LIZ, *still looking at* RONNIE, *shakes her head no.*] Neither do I. Let's just stay here and keep an eye on Ron, what do you say?

RONNIE: [*After a pause*] Anybody have a cigarette? Just getting in a few windmills. [COOP *goes to* RONNIE'*s desktop, gets a cigarette, and gives it to* RONNIE.] Thank you, my sweet.

COOP: [*Takes* RONNIE'*s hat and puts it on.*] I'm here to serve.

RONNIE: You look cute in that hat. Doesn't she look cute in that hat, Liz?

LIZ: Adorable.

RONNIE: You've gotta promise me you'll always wear navy blue.

COOP: You talk too much, kid . . . anyone ever tell you that? [*Takes out a comb with wax paper and does a little number.*]

RONNIE: Now this . . . this is a woman of rare and subtle artistry. And this person, Liz, I'm proud to tell you is my friend, the light of my life.

COOP: Your turn, big shot.

(RONNIE *types a few keys in rhythm.*)

LIZ: You better polish up your routine, girls.

COOP: Hey, why don't we stay in and watch an old movie tonight.

LIZ: There's a good horror flick on.

RONNIE: I have a date.

COOP: Anyone I know?

RONNIE: [*Evading her*] Naw. He's . . . well, he carries a

green bag. You wouldn't know him. He hangs out in the music room, a kind of weird . . .

COOP: My ass, it's a fucking fraternity boy.

RONNIE: [*Mock sincerity*] Well, how could I turn down a Beta.

LIZ: Oh, my God.

RONNIE: I'd much rather spend the evening with you two charmers, but I gave the man my word. Besides, it's a free dinner.

COOP: Whore.

RONNIE: Did I hear talk of a shower? I have a couple of dirty fingernails I'd like to take care of, if you don't . . .

COOP: Whore.

RONNIE: Armpits, too.

COOP: Let's go, Beta whore.

(*They go to the showers, which are in another part of the stage. They make noise, laugh. The showers may be stalls or suggestions of stalls. They get inside, then hang their towels outside.* RONNIE *has grabbed a raincoat to take as a robe. There is no nudity in this scene, so if the girls can be seen because of the set design, they will still wear clothes or coverings.*)

RONNIE: Coop, does your pubic hair curl?

COOP: Just a minute, I'll check.

LIZ: Do you think you'll make it with that Beta?

RONNIE: I have every hope.

COOP: Ronnie's a virgin. And like the rest of her kind, she thinks getting laid will change something.

LIZ: Are you really?

RONNIE: [*Sarcastically, directed to* COOP] Isn't everybody?

LIZ: I wish I could lose my virginity. It's really an albatross around my neck. What time is he picking you up?

RONNIE: Seven.

LIZ: What does he look like?

RONNIE: He's very lean.

COOP: And I suspect he makes very careful love.

RONNIE: [*Ignoring the remark*] Hey, friend, wanna get

my back? [COOP *washes* RONNIE's *back.*] This is nice. Maybe I'll just stay in.

COOP: You have a very smooth back. Much better than average.

RONNIE: So you have a lot of experience washing people's backs?

COOP: Summer camp . . . you know.

RONNIE: Girl Scouts?

COOP: More expensive than that. You wanna turn around now?

RONNIE: Well, I think I can manage the rest myself.

COOP: You've got a nice pair. Don't be ashamed.

RONNIE: Are you referring to my tits?

COOP: Well, they're awfully sturdy fellas, aren't they, Liz?

LIZ: [*Trying not to get into this*] My hair's getting wet.

RONNIE: I wouldn't want to make a habit out of this.

COOP: Just some innocent back rubbing, that's all.

(*Lights up on another part of stage. A* PSYCHIATRIST's *office. He sits on a chair. He is soft-spoken, underplays his role, takes his time. There is another chair near him, empty.*)

DOCTOR: And you say there was some back rubbing?

RONNIE: [*Still in shower*] Shit.

COOP: What's the matter?

RONNIE: Excuse me a minute, will you? [*She takes her coat and leaves shower, walking toward the* DOCTOR.]

DOCTOR: Who initiated the physical contact?

RONNIE: [*To audience, as she walks*] What a sense of timing. You'd think he'd have a little tact. My homosexual crisis. Tenth grade. It pops up every time someone . . . every time a female person scrubs my back. Or vice versa. . . . Or my elbow. Goddamn doctor.

DOCTOR: Ronnie, who started the back rubbing?

RONNIE: She did. Listen, Doctor, this is really beyond the limit of my endurance. I mean, you've gone too far this time.

DOCTOR: Did you respond?

RONNIE: Of course I responded. [*To audience*] What a schmuck!

DOCTOR: I'm going to ask you a few questions now, Ronnie. You may not see at first what our final destination is, but perhaps we can discover a real connection . . . something you might really want to know about yourself. Now, don't second-guess me on this, Ronnie. [*Pause.*] What are your favorite garments?

RONNIE: My what?

DOCTOR: Clothes. What do you like to wear?

RONNIE: Oh, a pair of cutoffs and an old . . . oh no . . . no. You're looking for a little perversion there, aren't you, Doctor. Well, I'm not going to give it to you, no sir.

DOCTOR: That's not what I was trying to do, Ronnie. But I think your reaction to the question is perhaps more important than the answer. [*Pause.*] Have you ever been kissed . . . a mature kiss, Ronnie? You know what I mean by that, don't you? Have you ever been kissed by a boy?

RONNIE: Yes, and it was quite sloppy, I might add.

DOCTOR: Your mother says you cry a lot.

RONNIE: Sometimes we cry together. Did she tell you that?

DOCTOR: I want to know you. I wish you'd try with me.

RONNIE: Listen, I have a shower to get back to.

DOCTOR: Tell me about your friends. Do you have many girl friends?

RONNIE: To tell the truth, I'm not sure. Many of them are admitted transvestites.

DOCTOR: You're a very funny young lady. That's amusing. But you might be better off telling me the truth.

RONNIE: And which truth would that be, Doctor?

DOCTOR: We're trying to find out why you refuse to take gym, why you cry without provocation. [*Pause.*] Have you ever been in love, Ronnie?

RONNIE: I know what you're leading up to, Doctor, and I'm way ahead of you. I had a crush on my eighth grade geography teacher, *Mrs.* Dolores Madison. It was quite a passionate affair, let me tell you. I was just mad about her. All of us were. All of us, Doctor. But then I had a feeling it wasn't the proper thing to do, so I transferred my love to Jeffrey Benson, who rewarded me by massaging my thighs. It's the farthest we got, but I really enjoyed it. Of course, it wasn't the same thing I felt for Dolores, but it was necessary in my growth as a woman, don't you agree?

DOCTOR: Do you sleep well at night, Ronnie?

RONNIE: Mostly I stay up late and watch old movies.

DOCTOR: If something's bothering you, don't be afraid to let it out.

RONNIE: [*Doing a little tap dance*] Nothing to it. How many suspected queers do you get in here a day, huh?

DOCTOR: Why won't you take gym with the other girls, Ronnie?

RONNIE: Because they're too damn young and tender, that's why. And they're going to grow up and get fat and go on diets and have babies. I love them, Doctor. I love those little girls with their blue uniforms.

DOCTOR: You seem not to be able to relate to people your own age.

RONNIE: [*Doing another dance step*] How's that, Doctor?

DOCTOR: Don't sublimate, Ronnie.

RONNIE: Okay, Doctor. Anything you say. I'm easily managed. Just put me in the right hands.

DOCTOR: On the contrary. Your records show that you're a natural leader. [*Pause.*] Which is why I'm inclined to think you started things.

RONNIE: What things? What things?

DOCTOR: When you ran out of the gym, screaming, something must have triggered it off. Now you refuse to go back. Think, Ronnie. What happened to make you want to run.

RONNIE: [*Pause. Seriously considering this*] I just had to get out of there. I was beginning to feel weak, and my skin itched. I don't know. Maybe everybody looked crazy all of a sudden in their sneakers and white socks.

DOCTOR: Did you feel anxious?

RONNIE: We were in a tiny room. I didn't like it in there,

that's all. Listen, it's getting late. I'm going out to dinner with a man who wears V-neck sweaters and Cordovans and is quite prompt.

DOCTOR: I know it's a difficult time for you. It's confusing. But I have no doubt that someday you'll be a wholesome, thoroughly adjusted young woman.

RONNIE: C'mon, Doctor. Cut the bullshit. Are you going to write this down in the records? I mean, it would certainly be a relief to know once and for all what my preferences are. Really. In later years when I feel myself slipping, I can just refer to the old records and get my tendencies straight. You're an embarrassment to me, Doctor, and I'm going to try and flush this whole episode down the toilet if I can.

DOCTOR: I'm sorry you feel that way.

RONNIE: And now, if you'll excuse me, I'm going to put a little perfume on my erogenous zones and take care of some pressing business. Some heterosexual business, in fact. It was a lovely afternoon, Doctor. But let's not do it again soon. [RONNIE *leaves office and walks past showers toward her room.*] Just passing through.

COOP: Why did you run out of here?

RONNIE: I had to see my psychiatrist.

COOP: Was it something I said?

RONNIE: Well, I must admit you threw me into a panic there, Coop. What with your suggestive behavior. But don't be concerned. I'll spend whatever juices you may have caused to flow on Mr. What's His Name.

COOP: Ronnie . . .

RONNIE: [*Trying to leave*] What?

COOP: I wasn't trying to make you.

RONNIE: Forget it.

COOP: Ronnie, people touch. It doesn't necessarily mean anything.

RONNIE: Any fool knows that.

COOP: You wanna watch you don't lose your sense of balance.

RONNIE: No, really. It was a lot of fun. I'm not upset.

COOP: Get the hell out of here, Ronnie.

RONNIE: Don't wait up for me. [*She walks to her room. A man is waiting there. It is* DAVID, *her husband.*] David, what are you doing here?

DAVID: Isn't it time yet?

RONNIE: I'll get to you. I have to cover a few other things first.

DAVID: Well, I'm getting a little impatient. This transition isn't easy for me.

RONNIE: I know, but I'm in charge now, and it isn't quite your turn.

DAVID: My work isn't going well. I'm behind in all my cases.

RONNIE: David. I have a stomach full of respect for your agenda, believe me, but you're out of sequence. And I think you'd be rather disappointed if I came to you this way. Give me the time I need.

DAVID: Look, tell me what you're doing. EXACTLY.

RONNIE: It's not available information. I don't know how to tell you.

DAVID: All right. I'll tell you what I'm doing. EXACTLY. I'm drinking too much coffee. I'm watching stacks of newspapers grow damp in the kitchen. I'm staring out every accessible window. I'm saying damn . . . damn.

RONNIE: There's a twist to me. And it could strangle everything. I don't want you dead. I don't want my garbage to collect in your kitchen. Oh, David . . . I'm sorry. But if I let your loneliness hold me back, I'll never get anything straight.

DAVID: Fair enough. Let the lady continue. I hope you won't think it's none of my business, but I recognize that wild look in your eye. Careful, Ronnie. You could frighten the world away.

RONNIE: I'll remember that.

DAVID: Are you sure you wouldn't like to curl up in my corner and read magazines . . . have a cup of hot chocolate?

RONNIE: Oh, you'd like that arrangement.

DAVID: I wouldn't mind.

RONNIE: I admire your honesty, but really, sweetheart, you're interrupting things.

DAVID: Sorry.

RONNIE: Don't be hurt.

DAVID: I don't seem to be at the top of your priority list.

RONNIE: Oh, you're up there. But I thought some background information would help the folks before I get into the heavy stuff.

DAVID: I suppose I can wait. But I don't like what's going on. Your little flirtation with sickness, whatever it was, I feel very removed from it.

RONNIE: I can't explain now. I have to get ready for a date.

DAVID: The fraternity boy, I suppose. I think I'll go now. The possibilities are painfully clear.

RONNIE: Were you an exception?

DAVID: Yes. I am an exception. That's why we're together.

RONNIE: I'll be home soon.

DAVID: Ronnie . . . please, one suggestion. Don't distort everything. When you get to me, don't tinker.

(DAVID *leaves.* RONNIE *speaks to the audience, perhaps still dressing.*)

RONNIE: That was my husband. He's precise, punctual, and scared that I'm going to like being on my own. We are basically incompatible. I have a design which excuses dust and minor dirt, carelessness, and a day off now and then to simply sit and do nothing. He calls it sloth. He's proud of my achievements, but we struggle. Consider this a preparatory remark. The rest will dance across your field of vision like flowers out of season, or come to you as the taste of a slightly sour plum. Don't be surprised if your mouth puckers. [*She pauses, shifts her focus.*] To tell the truth, I've always liked this part of my life best. Sleeping in my own small bed, reading sex manuals out loud. All this college business. Jesus.

(COOP *enters room, still in towel or robe from shower.*)

COOP: Okay, I've mulled it over and I've pretty much decided to be pissed off.

RONNIE: Come on.

COOP: I want an apology in writing. Or you're not getting out this door.

RONNIE: I don't think any naked lady with towel could keep me from my appointed rounds.

COOP: In blood, preferably. Yes, that would do it.

RONNIE: Will you take your embarrassing towel and get out of here.

COOP: I'd like to pursue a hot little item I ran smack into while taking my ritual bath. I think you'll agree it's a matter worth our consideration.

RONNIE: No. Nope. I think we better just move on to new business. [*Seriously*] Please. [*Pause.*] I have a date, remember?

COOP: Ah yes. And I hope you've anointed yourself with oil. [*She takes water from her bucket, or perfume, and sprinkles it on* RONNIE.] Let me be the first. Beta Bride. Lovely Coward.

RONNIE: I've got to go.

COOP: All right. [*Pause.*] One request, though, Ronnie. Don't ask me to come close and then decide you've got to pull away. I don't need that.

RONNIE: Shit. [*Pause.*] Remember Dr. McIntire . . . that Phil. class we took together last year. . . . He used to write these little notes on all my papers . . . CONFRONT THE ISSUES. He'd always accuse me of beating around the bush. . . . I guess that's why you got an A and I got a C. [*Pause.*] Is that what I do, Coop? [*Pause.*] Listen, I've got too much pride to get another C. . . .

COOP: You're a real shit, sometimes.

RONNIE: You've got a nice way with words.

COOP: See? Shit.

RONNIE: Okay, you got it. I am. Don't want to be. Am. [*Pause.*] Coop . . . laugh, huh? C'mon. [COOP *makes a face.*] I love your shit-eating grin, I really do. Cooperman, make up with me, I can't stand it.

COOP: We didn't even have a fight yet, goddamnit. I mean, you'd know a really good fight if you were having one. This ain't one.

RONNIE: I love you, Coop . . . for what it's worth. . . . I

mean you're the only person around here worth hanging out with. As far as I can see.

COOP: I got an A and you got a C, huh? I forgot. That's good. I like that.

RONNIE: You were probably fucking Dr. McIntire.

COOP: Who wasn't?

RONNIE: Me. Jesus Christ.

COOP: Yeah . . . like the man said, Ronnie—you don't exactly confront the issues. . . .

RONNIE: [*After a long pause*] Shit. Shit on you. [*She gets a pillow and throws it at* COOP.]

COOP: That's my girl. Fight the Cooperman beast. Stamp her out. [*Throws a pillow at* RONNIE.] Here's one for you, lady.

(*They get into a pillow fight until it becomes quite physical. Scene ends on this.*)

BLACKOUT

Scene 3

MITCH RYDER'S *apartment.* MITCH *is in his underwear, sitting on floor, smoking a cigar, holding cards.* RONNIE *walks in. Also in her underwear, with some beer or soda.*

MITCH: I raise you one and call.

RONNIE: You're bluffing.

MITCH: No, honest to Christ, you're in for it, Ronnie.

RONNIE: Okay, here's my one. . . . What have you got?

MITCH: You first.

RONNIE: C'mon. Let me see them. [*She reaches across and looks at his cards, then puts hers down.*]

MITCH: Full house? What the hell is this?

RONNIE: Strip.

MITCH: Have mercy.

RONNIE: Your socks.

MITCH: My feet probably smell.

RONNIE: *Well*, you could remove your jockey shorts if you felt inclined.

(MITCH *removes his socks. Then relaxes.*)

MITCH: I hope you won't mind, but I don't feel like making out tonight.

RONNIE: I didn't know it was scheduled in the first place.

MITCH: [*Playful*] I'm just a little tired of the whole thing. My nerves are worn. You pay a high price for being the aggressor. How about a game of chess. Do you know how to play?

RONNIE: It's too slow.

MITCH: Look, I could try making out if your heart is set.

RONNIE: [*Sarcastically*] Well, I was counting on it, Mitch.

MITCH: I'll bet you make a terrific lay, but I'm just worn out.

RONNIE: Oh, that's all right, Mitch. I have a yeast infection, anyway.

MITCH: What's that?

RONNIE: I have bread forming in my privates.

MITCH: Oh, Jesus.

RONNIE: I'm getting hungry. Could we go out somewhere?

MITCH: Wait, don't get dressed yet. I like seeing you that way. It's nice.

RONNIE: Apparently, I'm not too much of a distraction.

MITCH: I like having you sit there. You make a good picture.

RONNIE: I'm flattered, Mitch. But I have other things to do.

MITCH: I didn't mean to insult you. I think you're a lovely lady. C'mere.

RONNIE: Why?

MITCH: I want to hold you.

RONNIE: I don't want to be held.

MITCH: Don't give me a rough time. I'm just going to hug you some, that's all.

RONNIE: I don't think so, Mitch.

MITCH: Look, Ronnie. You were a great friend all evening. Don't turn into a woman now. These miniature episodes of hysteria turn me the hell off.

RONNIE: What are you talking about?

MITCH: Female companions I have known. One minute they're tender and good clean fun. Suddenly it becomes bitter. I never catch up.

RONNIE: It could be your approach.

MITCH: Maybe you girls should write a handbook.

RONNIE: I'd rather not discuss the woman/man question tonight, if you don't mind. It's becoming a health problem with me.

MITCH: I didn't come on with you, Ronnie.

RONNIE: No, you didn't.

MITCH: I like you. I didn't think I would.

RONNIE: Why did you ask me out, then?

MITCH: Oh, I heard things. I was curious.

RONNIE: You mean I have a reputation of some sort. I didn't know that. What kind of things?

MITCH: I heard that you perform . . . certain . . . sexual acts.

RONNIE: Shit. No kidding.

MITCH: I'll tell you what it was. Every now and then, when I get my bacon and eggs at the University Diner, I see you there. Having a glass of milk and underlining some valuable book. I know it's not for a course. . . . I can tell you're taking notes for yourself. And sometimes I see you walking across the mall . . . looking mad at somebody. I wanted to know why.

RONNIE: Not because I was pretty or had terrific legs.

MITCH: I thought you might be interesting. I based that opinion entirely on surface signals. Maybe you don't approve.

RONNIE: Oh, I do. It's practically my philosophy of life. Always judge a book by its cover. Every book I own, in fact, looks good and feels right. Same with people. There's something about a person's face or body that tells you the way he loves.

MITCH: Do you like my face?

RONNIE: It has certain redeeming features.

MITCH: Do you want to stay here tonight?

RONNIE: I'm only signed out until one.

MITCH: Can't one of your friends fix it somehow?

RONNIE: I guess so.

MITCH: It seems crazy to leave in the middle of a conversation.

RONNIE: All right. I'll call the dorm.

MITCH: Good. You want me to order some sandwiches?

RONNIE: Yeah . . . that'll be great. I'm still hungry. It must be a nervous condition.

MITCH: Maybe we could talk about some of the books we've read or the faces we've loved.

RONNIE: We might argue. There are grounds I hold sacred.

MITCH: Fine. I'm up for anything. If you want a fight, I think I can manage without becoming vicious . . . whatever you'd like.

RONNIE: [*To audience*] I'd like to be fucked.

BLACKOUT

Scene 4

Lights up on CHEERLEADERS *and* LETTERMEN, *who are wearing what they wear throughout the play, plus plastic gloves and physician's headgear.* RONNIE *is not present during this scene. This is* not *to be acted out as in a farce or fantasy. The actors merely stand or sit. This is rhythmic and quick.*

CHEERLEADER #1: The patient says she'd like to be fucked, Doctor.

LETTERMAN #1: Prepare her for examination, Nurse.

CHEERLEADER #1: Take off your panties. You may leave your shoes on if you wish.

LETTERMAN #2: Have you ever been fucked before, miss?

CHEERLEADER #1: She's a newcomer.

LETTERMAN #3: I see. Virgin matter. This will be a tough nut to crack.

CHEERLEADER #1: Assume the straddle position.

LETTERMAN #1: I hope you won't mind, I've asked a few of the student nurses and interns to observe.

LETTERMAN #2: Just lie still and relax. This is nothing. Women do it every day. You'll get used to it.

CHEERLEADER #1: Slide to the end of the table. Feet up in the stirrups, that's it.

LETTERMAN #1: Hand me my headgear, nurse.

LETTERMAN #3: How old is the patient, nurse?

CHEERLEADER #1: Nineteen or twenty.

LETTERMAN #1: Good pelvic structure.

LETTERMAN #2: So you want to be fucked. Just relax. Many women want to be fucked. It's relatively easy.

LETTERMAN #1: As you can observe, the patient has never been entered before. She is young, healthy, and except for a slight yeast infection, intercourse should be carried out with routine discomfort, and then, if she's lucky, and if friction is applied in the right places, she should reach a climax. All this may take several years, however, and the patient shouldn't be discouraged.

CHEERLEADER #2: Do you recommend birth control of any sort?

LETTERMAN #1: She's young. A baby wouldn't hurt. However, the nurse will give her some pills so she doesn't bother us in a few months wanting an abortion.

CHEERLEADER #1: All right, miss. You may step down now and put on your clothes.

CHEERLEADER #2: You didn't take a Pap smear, Doctor.

LETTERMAN #1: She's too young to have cancer. We'll do it next time.

LETTERMAN #2: Report back in six months.

LETTERMAN #3: Good luck.

BLACKOUT

Scene 5

Lights come up on MITCH's *apartment.* MITCH *and* RONNIE *move in silence. Perhaps they dress or get something to eat. Finally* RONNIE *speaks.*

RONNIE: [MITCH *is silent, avoids her.*] I'm not criticizing you. The foreplay was grand, really.

MITCH: You're not supposed to discuss it.

RONNIE: I thought you'd appreciate knowing that up until the end, the climax . . . your climax, to be specific, everything was going along quite nicely . . . rapidly in fact.

MITCH: Please.

RONNIE: Well, I'm bleeding again.

MITCH: That'll stop. Don't make an issue of it.

RONNIE: Oh, I'm not worried. I've been bleeding off and on for years now.

MITCH: [*After a pause*] I'm sorry if I hurt you. I didn't enjoy taking that particular plunge. You seemed to want it. That's the way it usually is the first time.

RONNIE: Did it hurt you the first time?

MITCH: I don't like this conversation. What happened wasn't my fault. It would have been the same with anyone.

RONNIE: I expected more, that's all.

MITCH: Do you want to make love again?

RONNIE: Not right now.

MITCH: Well . . . [*He moves around.*] I think I'll go to bed then, I'm kind of tired. [*Pause.*] What will you do?

RONNIE: Oh, I think I'll just be on my way.

MITCH: You don't have to go.

RONNIE: I know that. But I can't be here anymore for some reason.

MITCH: I'll call you. We'll make love again.

RONNIE: Yes. That would probably be the best thing to do.

MITCH: Good night, then. [*He goes to her somewhat awkwardly. Kisses her, and then exits.*]

(CHEERLEADERS *enter with* LETTERMEN. *They enter doing a cheer.*)

CHEERLEADERS: F-U-C-K. *Try again some other day.*
CHEERLEADER #1: Got you good, didn't he?

(RONNIE *finds a cigarette, lights it.*)

CHEERLEADER #3: If it makes you feel any better, Ronnie, I thought he had a pretty lousy technique.

CHEERLEADER #2: The fellas here would like to have a few words with you. [*The men are reluctant to speak*.] Go ahead.

CHEERLEADER #3: They're very shy.

CHEERLEADER #1: This was not our idea. Just for the record. We thought you had enough for one night.

CHEERLEADER #2: The studs here cried like babies to come along.

LETTERMAN #1: It's just that we . . .

LETTERMAN #2: We feel you weren't given a proper introduction.

LETTERMAN #3: It hurts us.

LETTERMAN #1: We have a reputation.

LETTERMAN #2: I mean, you just can't write us off without a second chance. [*Pause*.] We have a plan we think you'll like.

CHEERLEADER #1: We didn't want them to come.

LETTERMAN #1: We'd like to make things up to you . . . and show you that we care.

RONNIE: Don't you have any respect for the mysteries? Leave me alone.

LETTERMAN #2: We'd like to give you pleasure.

RONNIE: There's no point. I know what it is now.

LETTERMAN #3: It's a shame to let you go under a false impression.

RONNIE: You want me to cheat on my fantasies again? I can't do it. No.

LETTERMAN #2: Don't reject the offer without even a taste, a sample of our sincerity.

RONNIE: What makes you think it will be better with you?

LETTERMAN #1: We've got our letters.

RONNIE: [*After a pause*] I like my body rubbed and the inside of my legs. Long, long strokes. I like immaculate kissing and then, after a time, hard, steel hands. I like time spent heavily. Motion. [*Pause*.] Do you think you can do that? [*There is no answer*.] Well, that's no surprise. Why did you bother?

151

CHEERLEADER #2: They're sweet guys, Ronnie. Give them a break.

RONNIE: [*Slaps her.*] Lest we forget! I think I'm catching on to the ritual. It makes sense now. Do it to me. [*No response.*] It's all right. Do it to me. [*One of the* CHEERLEADERS *slaps her.*] Yes. Yes, that's it all right. [*She starts to walk away.*]

LETTERMAN #1: Wait! I can do those things. You tell me again. You describe it to me. I can do those things.

RONNIE: What's the point?

LETTERMAN #1: I have to. I'm excited now.

RONNIE: You see . . . you have to . . . you must make love. There's nothing you can do about it. I only want to make love with all my heart . . . that's the difference.

LETTERMAN #2: Instruct us. Tell us.

(RONNIE *slowly repeats what she has said before:* "*I like my body rubbed, etc.*" *This is interspersed with the* CHEERLEADERS *chanting their* "F-U-C-K" *cheer, as the lights dim.*)

Scene 6

RONNIE's *room. As the lights come up,* DAVID *enters, applauding.*

DAVID: That was lovely.

RONNIE: You didn't have to watch.

DAVID: I'm beginning to lose sleep over this.

RONNIE: I know. But it's necessary.

DAVID: I don't know what you hope to accomplish.

RONNIE: I'm exercising certain rights. You uphold that kind of thing, don't you?

DAVID: Of course I do. But I don't see how it will help the two of us in any way.

RONNIE: Maybe it won't. It's a pain in the stomach, frankly.

DAVID: I don't think it hurts you at all. I think you're

having one hell of a good time. Look, don't put me
through any more sex episodes. [*He starts to leave.*]

RONNIE: I'll try. . . . David, are you eating anything. I
mean, you aren't making TV dinners?

DAVID: Very wifely of you to inquire, you phony! Yes,
I'm doing fine, just fine. [*Exits.*]

(COOP *enters. Waits. It is clear that she and* RONNIE
*haven't seen each other for a while. There is some
tension.*)

COOP: I've missed you. Although there isn't much point
to it.

RONNIE: I've been working up to a visit.

COOP: Well, the old place just isn't the same without
you. [*Goes to* RONNIE's *desk which is piled with papers.
She leafs through, sees a letter, reads it.*] You didn't
mention you were going to have an article published.

RONNIE: Well, the letter just came, actually.

COOP: Is it a good magazine?

RONNIE: Small. I'm pleased, though.

COOP: I didn't know you were still writing. I thought you
were mostly fucking.

RONNIE: Do you want to read the article I wrote? I think
you'll like it. [*Pause.*] If it's the one I'm thinking of.

COOP: You look fine.

RONNIE: I'm tired.

COOP: Has it been good?

RONNIE: It's all pretty much come the same.

COOP: You haven't even come in to talk.

RONNIE: I can't talk. I'm not comfortable. It's easier taking
off your clothes and lying down. It's remarkably easy. I
never would have suspected it.

COOP: Maybe your ambitions have taken a turn for the
worse. It's too bad.

RONNIE: My ambitions have not changed. My ambitions
have not suffered any noticeable setbacks.

COOP: Whatever you say.

RONNIE: Is there something you want, Coop?

COOP: Where do you go—motels, apartments?

RONNIE: I'm still reserving my opinion in regard to your questionable motives as *girl* friend. Perhaps you'd really like me to come lie with you and be *your* love.

COOP: You really have been fucked. Expertly.

RONNIE: I'm so easy. Nobody stands a chance. Take me to the showers, rub a little soap on my back. C'mon, Coop, out with it. Everybody out with it. [*Goes to type-writer.*] I can't get a word out of this.

COOP: Are you calling for confessions, Ronnie? Let us all finally admit?

RONNIE: Have you seen my hat? [COOP *sees it in an obvious place, gets it, puts it on* RONNIE'*s head.*] I can't find anything I want around here. My papers aren't crisp or white enough.

COOP: I suspect you, Ronnie.

RONNIE: I get laid. And right in the middle of it, I wonder . . . what's Coop doing? Why isn't she here? I make notes for a new article and all I can think about is, will she like it? Now, what does that mean?

COOP: You tell me.

RONNIE: Look, I'm not going to bed with you, Coop. It wouldn't make sense. I don't even know how to approach it.

COOP: Jesus.

RONNIE: Well, why do I get such clear signals whenever you happen to be on my otherwise straight and narrow grounds?

COOP: All right. I'll give you the goods, if that's what you want. I went to bed with a girl once. A woman. She was older. More than once, really. She was a friend of my brother's. She smoked cigarettes in her toes when she was drunk with wine, but she was graceful and swift and I ran right into it. She was married. In fact, she was married to so many people, finally I couldn't wait. [*Pause.*] Zan . . . Alexandra. A girl's name, like my own. We were seduced by a man we both knew who kept telling us how beautiful we were. And it became true. We just didn't need him to tell us anymore. I couldn't sleep without her, Ronnie. She was too sweet. The whole thing was sweet. It kept running out the corners of my mouth. I've loved a few men. Maybe they were boys, I don't know. I loved them, but never like that. [*Pause.*] I'd rather love a man than you, Ronnie. I'd rather lie with a hard, flat, consistent man than you, Ronnie, with all those edges unaccounted for.

RONNIE: It's my jeans. They don't look the way they should. They're too blue. They chafe. I can't function properly.

COOP: And I wasn't straight with you before, Ronnie. You don't really look fine. You look shopworn.

RONNIE: Listen to this, Coop. [*She types a few keys.*] *Mon cher. Mon père. Ma mère.* Typewriter free of gender. Killing off paper, slaughtering all known sex offenders. [*Pause.*]

If, and this is the critical question, Coop . . . *If* my typewriter and I could come at the same time, this little matter of boys and girls would be settled once and for all. [*Pause. She types a few more keys.*]

Zan. That's a lovely sound. I didn't come to see you, Coop, because I don't know what's going on exactly. [*Typing.*]

Z-A-N. Sounds good on this, doesn't it? [*She continues to type what she says.*] MR. AND MRS. LEONARD COOPERMAN REQUEST THE PLEASURE OF YOUR COMPANY AT THE MARRIAGE OF THEIR DAUGHTER BARBARA COOPERMAN TO MISS ALEXANDRA . . . what was her last name, Coop? Never mind. Listen to the sound of this machine. *Clack.*

COOP: *White.* [*Pronouncing* WH *as a whisper*] Alexandra White. [*Waits a moment, then moves off to dark area.*]

RONNIE: MR. AND MRS. MOM AND DAD REQUEST THE PLEASURE OF YOUR COMPANY AT THE MARRIAGE OF THEIR DAUGHTER RONNIE TO MISS ALEXANDRA WHITE. RECEPTION TO FOLLOW. [*Pause.*] *Clack.*

(CHEERLEADERS *start filing in. They are in their uniforms, but carry bouquets. The* PSYCHIATRIST *comes to* RONNIE's *room. He carries a Bible.*)

DOCTOR: C'mon, Ronnie. Let's get you published and married before you turn queer on us.

RONNIE: Just what the fuck do you want?

DOCTOR: Your parents have gone to great expense to rent a lovely banquet hall. The bridesmaids have assembled.

RONNIE: I'm not ready.

DOCTOR: We'll nip this thing in the bud, Ronnie.

RONNIE: Look, cancel the plans, Doctor. I've got four or five good years left.

DOCTOR: Everyone's waiting.

RONNIE: For what? For who?

DOCTOR: You just issued an invitation. I heard you.

RONNIE: That was a different wedding. You wouldn't be interested. A very private affair.

DOCTOR: I didn't engineer this all by myself, Ronnie. You clearly indicated there was a marriage about to take place.

RONNIE: It was a joke.

DOCTOR: Well, this isn't.

RONNIE: I can see that. But I have no ceremonies in my present plans, thank you.

DOCTOR: In the interest of economy, I'd suggest we get on with it.

RONNIE: Are you here to save time, Doctor? Or to save me?

(*The* CHEERLEADERS *cheer.*)

CHEERLEADERS: Here comes the bride. . . . Yeh! Here . . . comes . . . the bride. . . . Yeh!

RONNIE: All right . . . if everyone's in such a damn hurry. But I still do the naming of the parts . . . including the bride. [*She moves toward* COOP, *although* COOP *doesn't acknowledge any of this.*] I'd like you to meet my lovely wife, Alexandra.

(*The* LETTERMEN *march in with* DAVID, *singing:* "2-4-6-8, who do we appreciate!"
The CHEERLEADERS *move to* RONNIE, *hand* COOP *a bouquet, and put her in their line. Then they accompany* RONNIE *to* DAVID.)

156

DAVID: I'm sorry. I couldn't wait any longer.

DOCTOR: [*Who has followed everyone and now stands in position of clergyman.*] How do you feel, Ronnie? [*She doesn't answer.*] We're not doing anything you yourself didn't plan.

RONNIE: What's the matter with you? I would have made it on my own. Now I'm stuck in the middle of a leap to faith.

DAVID: I love you, Ronnie.

DOCTOR: David loves you.

(*Pause.* RONNIE *takes* DAVID'S *hand, but doesn't look at him or speak.*)

DAVID: I think I can give you something.

DOCTOR: Can I pronounce it yet?

DAVID: When she's ready.

DOCTOR: Ronnie?

DAVID: Don't push her.

RONNIE: I have to get my typewriter.

DAVID: You can pronounce it now.

(DAVID *puts his arm around* RONNIE *as they move to get her typewriter.* CHEERLEADERS *and* USHERS *throw rice.*)

DOCTOR: [*Shakes his head, shrugs, then pronounces:*] Man . . . and . . . wife.

BLACKOUT

ACT II

Scene 1

A number of years have passed. RONNIE *sits in kitchen. She drinks coffee and finishes reading a letter from* COOP. *Then she looks for a piece of paper, begins to write, then suddenly changes her mind, crumples it up, and tosses it to a corner of the room. Just as she does this, a neighbor,* EVELYN, *enters.*

EVELYN: Ronnie?

RONNIE: [*Surprised*] Jesus.

EVELYN: Sorry. Do you have any coffee left?

RONNIE: I don't know. Check.

EVELYN: I left the kids alone in the house. [*Almost surprised as she is saying it.*]

RONNIE: You can make instant if there's no coffee left. [*Just nods, indicating a pack lying on the table.*]

EVELYN: What are you doing in the house, Ronnie?

RONNIE: I'm trying to write. And it's not going exactly well. You can see that, can't you, Evelyn? I mean, just look around.

EVELYN: It's lovely outside. We really should take our table and chairs and go outside.

RONNIE: I like kitchens. They soothe me.

EVELYN: But aren't you worried about all those spoons and napkins and cups and things multiplying in the dark? I could never write with all that noise in the cupboards. You should, as I have done, take your work outside.

RONNIE: And what do you do, Evelyn? What's your work?

EVELYN: I work in the soil of my backyard. Haven't you seen me? I'm an undertaker. I bury turtles and goldfish and even once, a small dog. The children buy them, and I bury them. They depend on me for that.

RONNIE: Don't they know they've got a saint in their house? I mean it, Evelyn. You and I are saints. They better not fool with us.

EVELYN: It's all right. I like my work. The best part is that it's something begun and then finished, right before my eyes. Over. That's very gratifying, Ronnie.

RONNIE: You do everybody's dirty work. I don't even do my own.

EVELYN: You make lousy coffee, Ronnie. I make very good coffee. That's a jumping-off point. Being a stalwart undertaker and then brewing a good cup of coffee. [EVELYN *moves to a spot where she can see crumpled letter. She stares.*] Did you know that my little girl tried to kill herself a year ago?

RONNIE: My God.

EVELYN: It was a deliberate attempt. We know that. She's eleven. Well, you know. You've seen her. She's pretty, isn't she? [*Walks to the crumpled letter, picks it up, reads it.*]

I left them alone over there. I have to know sometimes there's a chance something will happen to them. [*She looks at the letter again, then holds it in a fist.*]

Anything could happen. The house might catch fire. The boy might swallow detergent. I thought I'd come and see what you were doing.

RONNIE: Ev . . .

EVELYN: What are you doing?

RONNIE: I'm . . . trying to write. To decide.

EVELYN: [*Referring to letter*] A good friend?

RONNIE: From school. I'm not sure how to think about it now. But I'm in the midst of preparing a statement which I'll release to the press at any moment. You can be sure of that, Evelyn . . . any moment.

EVELYN: If we moved away, I would never see you again. Doesn't that seem to make everything just a bit of a joke? I'd like to have a reunion, but you see, a good many of my friends . . . from the other houses . . . have erased their fingerprints in some ugly way. My children sometimes see their children, but I never go in to say hello when I pick them up. [*Pause. Sits.*] Well . . .

RONNIE: I woke up this morning. My face was hot. What's the matter? What's going on?

EVELYN: I wanted to tell you about my little girl, Ann. It occurred to me that if you knew, you might be able to finish what you're writing. I don't know why. You see, I left the house without telling them. Ann was reading a book. A book she had chosen herself. And when I saw how dead she almost was, I had to come over and tell you.

RONNIE: I don't understand. Eleven years old. What does it mean?

EVELYN: When I get home, I hope my children are dead. It will be a great relief. I can't run away, you see. I would feel guilty. [*Pause.*] If this story doesn't turn the tide for you, Ronnie, I have others. There are others that might work for you. I think someone should keep a record. You've been a little bit nervous lately, and it's possible you've caught sight of the bodies flying around. You see, I can't run, but I thought you should be told about my daughter because it's a very sad, very clear thing.

RONNIE: Why are you still here, Evelyn? What stops it from falling apart?

EVELYN: I make good coffee. It's that simple. How can I refuse people the things I do well. My daughter, however, doesn't understand divisions of labor. She just can't think of anything being separate . . . other. So what can I do? I'm her mother . . . she'd just as soon put her arms around you. [*Long pause.*] Will you have children, Ronnie? Because there's nothing better than to feel the weight of them on your chest . . . nothing better. That was a very lovely letter you were writing to your friend, by the way. I wish you would change your mind and send it. You can't refuse people the things you do well, Ronnie.

RONNIE: Please don't go back. Tell me something else. More stories.

EVELYN: This was a good break for me, and now I have to see about the casualties. Really, I don't see how Richard goes out the door in the morning with a free mind. How he drinks his orange juice without trembling. He has no idea what could happen, and I know for certain that one of them will die in his sleep or under an automobile. You come over later. I'll just watch a little television and things will be fine. All right?

(*Evelyn exits.*)

RONNIE: Yes. [*She calls* DAVID *on phone. We see him.*] David . . .

DAVID: Hello?

RONNIE: What are you doing?

DAVID: Oh, the usual. A little reading. A little chat with a client. What's up?

RONNIE: It's nothing . . . just . . . well, Evelyn was over . . . and, Jesus Christ. Do you think we could do something tonight? Are you very busy? Because I can't work. My hands are shaking.

DAVID: We've got Ben's party.

RONNIE: Oh, terrific, I forgot all about that. I suppose there's no choice?

DAVID: What's wrong?

(*The* WOMEN *start coming in slowly for the cocktail party, then the* MEN *enter from another direction.*)

RONNIE: I just can't think about going to a cocktail party. There seems to be no reason for it.

DAVID: I don't see how we can cancel out. Look, tell me what's going on.

RONNIE: These women, David, they're falling down all over the place. They're really going quite mad out here. I'm going to have to find an office somewhere. I just can't work here anymore.

DAVID: Damnit, there's someone else ringing. Can you hold the line?

RONNIE: No, I can't hold the line.

DAVID: Please . . . don't get off.

RONNIE: I'll see you tonight. [*She hangs up.*]

(*The lights change focus,* DAVID *drifts into the circle of* MEN. RONNIE *watches the* WOMEN.)

Scene 2

Cocktail party. This opens on simultaneous conversation among the MEN. *The* WOMEN *sit, noticeably without talking. They are drinking or smoking, staring.* RONNIE *is off by herself, and shortly after the scene begins,* DAVID *goes over to her.*

DAVID: Hey . . . having a good time?

RONNIE: Look at this. Look at the way everybody sits.

DAVID: What's the matter, anyway . . . you haven't even eaten the *whores de-vores.* [*He deliberately mispronounces word.*] They've got your favorite . . . with onions.

RONNIE: I can't eat. I'm jumpy.

DAVID: If you're still upset about Evelyn, drop it. She's in and out of these moods. Richard's mentioned it to me more than once. You can't do anything.

RONNIE: Don't you see the pattern here?

DAVID: No. What do you mean?

RONNIE: I wish you could see it, David. I wish I didn't have to point it out.

DAVID: C'mon. Relax.

RONNIE: I got a letter from Coop today. She wants to come see me.

DAVID: Ah, the elusive, ever popular . . . what's 'er name.

RONNIE: She's coming soon.

DAVID: Well, fine. Maybe she can work the cure.

RONNIE: What the hell does that mean?

DAVID: It could be fun, actually. Tell me, does she have a good sense of humor . . . is she a talker? You never said, really. I mean, this could be quite a visit. The old college chum.

RONNIE: I don't know how long she can stay. She's leaving for Europe in a month.

DAVID: But you're looking forward to this.

RONNIE: She's going away.

DAVID: [*Pause. Thinking about this*] Get any work done today?

RONNIE: Not with unexpected letters and visits from Evelyn.

DAVID: Some time with your friend . . . that might help. C'mon, Ronnie, that might help. Say it.

RONNIE: I have deadlines. I'll never meet them.

DAVID: Why not?

RONNIE: I'm getting lazy and probably fat. And the only diversions I have are representatives of the Ladies' Auxiliary who stop by on their way to the edge of a tall building somewhere.

(*They are interrupted by* BEN.)

BEN: Dave, I've been looking all over for you. Ronnie, do you mind? Your husband's a very important fella. We'll just be a minute.

RONNIE: Actually, I do mind. This is the first chance we've had to be together all day.

BEN: I know. Listen, it's rough, this business. But I promise to give him back to you right away. Look . . . Alice is sitting over there in a corner. Why don't you go talk to her. You girls should get together more often, anyway. I think it would give us a strong sense of continuity, don't you agree, Dave? She's over there in a corner, Ronnie. Dave and I will just be a minute.

RONNIE: I don't think your wife wants to talk to me, Ben.

BEN: Sure she does. You could be great friends, you two.

DAVID: Can't it wait, Ben?

BEN: [*Almost annoyed*] Well, Dave . . . ?

RONNIE: It's all right. [*She moves away. The focus goes with her, as men talk quietly.* RONNIE *looks at the women. She goes to* ALICE, *touches her hair softly.* ALICE *doesn't notice. Then* RONNIE *drifts off, she begins to speak to* COOP.] Hey, Coop. Look what you got yourself out of, you sneaky bastard. I'd like you to meet my friends. Or maybe you know them. Could be a couple of refugees from summer camp here, all settled down and flying right. [*She moves to* ALICE.] Isn't she lovely? [*This is warm, soft.*] Whoever she is.

ALICE: [*A former* CHEERLEADER] I'm Alice. Wife of Ben. Mother of Stephanie and Tom. I live with my husband in this place where he is employed and where the schools, they say, are clean and expensive. I can't remember what my aspirations were. I used to make things.

WOMAN #2: [*A former* CHEERLEADER, *speaking to the audience.*] I'm Nancy, A.B., M.A., Phi Beta Kappa. Mrs. Phil Cooper. Phil found me just in time. He's a doctor. He let me work while he was going to school. It was really generous of him. He's making $85,000 a year now. We're divorced.

WOMAN #3: [*A former* CHEERLEADER, *speaking to the audience.*] Ellen, daughter of Jim. Sister of Robert. Concubine of Lester. Secretary of Mr. J. P. Wilson. I'm a terrific lay, so I'm told.

WOMAN #4: [MOTHER *in Act I*] I'm Manny's widow. He died last year of a heart attack. I told him not to work so hard. He said he was a victim and couldn't rest. He said it was his responsibility to take care of me and give me the comforts of life. He worked on Saturdays and sometimes at night. He's dead now. And I'm afraid to be in the house alone. I've never worked in my life . . . and I don't know where to start.

RONNIE: [*Addressing* COOP] Hey, friend. Come and fill me with Canada and Denver, and roads you've memorized. My jeans are old now and soft. They're beginning to feel right. But nothing else fits. Come and stay with me against these odds.

(COOP *enters with knapsack and small case. Even though the setting is still the party, it is clear this is a reunion that really doesn't take place at the party, but at a later time.*)

COOP: Hello, Ronnie.

RONNIE: Glad you could make the party.

COOP: I almost didn't stop. I hitched a ride with two terrific guys. Almost went up to the Cape with them.

RONNIE: Why didn't you?

COOP: I wanted to see you more than I wanted to see the Cape. I was surprised when your letter came. I thought you might not write back.

RONNIE: Well, I figured I owed myself an indecent exposure or two.

COOP: Maybe I better dust off my clothes before we get down to business.

RONNIE: No. Don't change your clothes and don't wash. Don't even comb your hair.

COOP: But I've been hanging around some rather questionable diners.

RONNIE: I'm envious, of course. And don't know whether I can keep it quiet.

COOP: Why should you try?

RONNIE: Remember the old sense of balance, Coop?

COOP: Well, what are you envious of, the men I could have traveled with or the places I might have gone?

RONNIE: Just your position . . . a room of one's own.

COOP: Well, I'm not necessarily happy this way, but I'm always excited.

RONNIE: It's not that I want to leave. I'm working now, getting some nice assignments.

COOP: I read your last piece. It was fine.

RONNIE: But there's no one . . . there's a little too much melancholia going around to suit me. People settle into place before there's even enough time to choose a good spot.

COOP: You haven't been screwing around, have you, Ronnie?

RONNIE: Not yet.

COOP: I don't understand why you chose this.

RONNIE: That's naïve, Coop.

COOP: If it's just a matter of time before you need other men, why did you get married?

RONNIE: It was an emergency. I was being saved.

COOP: I'd like to stay for a while. Will that be all right with David?

RONNIE: He thought your coming was a good idea.

COOP: But you weren't too sure.

RONNIE: Well, you know . . . I never was too straight about you, Coop. [*Pause.*] I've thought about you. I've hoped that you were still beautiful. You are.

COOP: A lot of women I've met know your work. I'm always impressed by that, but never surprised. I knew that you were still beautiful.

RONNIE: What should we do . . . talk about old times . . . or stitch up current lacerations?

COOP: If you hesitate now, forget it. I'm no fucking knight come to save the damsel in distress.

RONNIE: Well, you make a pretty romantic picture there, Coop, with your knapsack and boots. I mean, what's a girl to think?

COOP: Oh, I have rugged arches now . . . and a slight bronze to my cheek, but if you're going to put me through my paces, I don't think I'll make it.

RONNIE: That seems to be my game. It's a shitty game, isn't it?

COOP: Why did you ask me to come?

RONNIE: I wanted to make life worth living.

COOP: Is that right? What's your plan?

RONNIE: I figured you might come equipped.

COOP: Do you want my stuff, Ron? Because I don't mind turning it over.

RONNIE: I want it. Of course I want it.

COOP: You've got me shaking, you know that. Are you going to just stand there or what?

RONNIE: I'm really quite stuck. My arms are wrapped around my body. I've never told you the truth.

COOP: I know.

RONNIE: I'm afraid of not being able to say it properly. [*Pause.*] I stopped short. I just stopped short. And I figured it was you . . . something to do with you.

COOP: Well, I'm here. This isn't a letter. This isn't a phone call.

RONNIE: You look so fucking good. [*She goes to* COOP. *They embrace. Then* RONNIE *takes* COOP's *face in her hands, explores it. They begin kissing one another's hair, etc. Finally the lips. After a moment, they look at each other . . . laugh, hug again. They are still set against the party background.*] My head's buzzing. I'm thinking. I shouldn't be thinking. [*Pause. She touches* COOP's *face.*] I could spend so much time right here. With my hand on your face. Not even the whole face. Parts.

COOP: I like that.

RONNIE: We might pass several winters here. I don't even know if I have the right wardrobe. Is there an end to you?

COOP: Stop thinking so hard.

RONNIE: Yes, it doesn't matter. You're the best toy a kid ever had.

COOP: And the most expensive.

RONNIE: Look, I'll throw in my jeans. if you'll throw in your dusty old hat. I mean, let me make love with you.

COOP: Let's get the hell out of here.

(*They exit amid cocktail party.*)

LIGHTS GO OUT

Scene 3

RONNIE, DAVID, COOP *sit at the kitchen table or on the floor, drinking coffee. It is after dinner.*

167

DAVID: The coffee's good. It couldn't be yours, Ronnie.

RONNIE: Ah, but dinner, that was strictly my baby. [DAVID *exchanges playful look with* COOP.] Well, it was pretty. C'mon, wasn't that the most colorful meal you ever ate?

COOP: Well, the greens were a little too strong, if you want my opinion. [COOP *gets up to have more coffee. When she turns to come back,* DAVID *looks at both women.*]

DAVID: That's funny. You looked like Ronnie for a minute. [*Pause.*] And of course you don't look alike at all.

RONNIE: You're comparing that barefoot girl with wind in her hair to me?

DAVID: It's over. I don't see it now.

COOP: Plants. That's what you need. A couple of trees, even. It will do wonders for the room.

RONNIE: They'll use up my oxygen.

COOP: Well, then rocks at least.

DAVID: [*Who has gotten up and gone to* COOP.] How did you make that coffee? Tell me.

RONNIE: That's not fair. I mean . . . the recipe's probably been in her family for years.

DAVID: Well, what's a friend for? She can pass it along to you and then you can pass it along to me.

COOP: I think I'll go outside for a while and take a walk. Anyone care to join the tour?

RONNIE: Where will you go?

COOP: I don't know . . . just . . . out.

DAVID: Do you like old houses? There's a wonderful old house at the end of the road. [*Pause.*] Try the porch.

COOP: I'll find it.

DAVID: Yes, and go inside.

COOP: See you later.

RONNIE: . . . Don't get lost. [COOP *exits.* DAVID *puts his cup away.* RONNIE *watches him.*] What old house, David? Where?

DAVID: You're not the pioneer I am. You missed it.

RONNIE: But you never told me.

DAVID: Oh, it's such an old close pal of mine, I hoped you would just run into it some day on your travels. Swell house, Ronnie. Sometimes it does strange things to me, though. Makes me run up and down the stairs and open all the doors wide. I wrote on some of the walls, too. Drew hearts . . . you know. DAVID LOVES RONNIE. RONNIE LOVES DAVID. A couple of tiny "fuck you's." It's my drink with the boys after work. There's a wooden staircase I honest to God slid down one day. Yes, I thought, screw it. I'm going to have myself a good slide down this banister. DOES RONNIE LOVE DAVID? Right down the banister. I was a very happy boy that day.

RONNIE: [*Pause.*] Do you like her?

DAVID: She's a beautiful woman.

RONNIE: That's her advantage.

DAVID: Yours, too.

RONNIE: Do you like her?

DAVID: If it matters, yes.

RONNIE: I disappointed her once.

DAVID: Well, now you can work it out. If that's what you want to do. And that is what you want to do, isn't it?

RONNIE: Yes, it is.

DAVID: She has a face. She speaks. She's not lurking in the dark somewhere. It's almost a comfort. Well, I hope you'll be able to finish your work now. That would be something anyway.

RONNIE: The color these days is green . . . ripe for growing things. So it's always a possibility.

DAVID: It would be nice to have your attention. Do you ever think about me? I really want to know.

RONNIE: Of course I do.

DAVID: In your hands. Do you feel me there? Do you think . . . in the middle of breathing . . . DAVID?

RONNIE: [*Pause.*] It's just that sometimes I have no connection to anyone.

DAVID: That will cost you, Ronnie. It's a shadow. And you're getting thinner and looser. I have to strain sometimes to find a shape for you.

RONNIE: I'm trying.

DAVID: Yes.

RONNIE: David . . .

DAVID: I'm working it out. You should do the same.

RONNIE: No matter who tells you different about me, your wife thinks you're a beautiful man. And she wishes she could coast down this crummy hill and love you right.

DAVID: It's got the makings of one of my more persistent dreams. But you're the promise and nothing else.

RONNIE: No, David. I'm on the mend. Really. Look at this face. Look at these hands. Now, I ask you . . .

DAVID: I'm waiting. [RONNIE *says nothing.*] Well, I'm not going to ask again. Phone in your answer before midnight, sweetheart. The show's going off the air.

RONNIE: David, show me the house with the happy boy.

DAVID: [*Embraces her.*] If you go in, you marry it. Think about that.

RONNIE: I will.

DAVID: Yes, it's really time you did. [*Exits.*]

RONNIE: [*As if to say something more*] David . . . good night. [RONNIE *is left alone for a moment. Then* COOP *enters.*] Hi. How was your walk?

COOP: Refreshing. [*Walks to* RONNIE, *holds her, then touches her face.*] Your face looks flushed.

RONNIE: Really? That used to happen when I was a teenager. [*Pause. They are still holding one another.*] Hey, it was a pretty heavy date, wasn't it.

COOP: The best.

RONNIE: Was it sweet for you? I thought . . . I think you are finally my friend.

COOP: That comes hard to me, you know.

RONNIE: I guess I just saw you in the middle of a certain cold pond, and there it was. I'm quite amazed and I don't want to analyze it.

COOP: I still suspect you of harboring sad, fragile secrets. But I don't want to press.

RONNIE: Maybe you should. Otherwise I'll never spill the beans.

COOP: Can't you just tell me?

RONNIE: I think you've got a cute little ass, how about that?

COOP: Not bad. I like it. Got any more?

RONNIE: Well, I'm crazy about your feet, too.

COOP: That helps.

RONNIE: In love with you, perhaps.

COOP: [*After a pause, she moves away*.] Hey, won't David wonder why you haven't come to bed?

RONNIE: No.

COOP: It's so quiet in here.

RONNIE: You mean you can't hear the utensils and the dishes . . . all those mysterious noises in the cupboard.

COOP: I guess my ear isn't trained that way. Is this where you write?

RONNIE: Usually. But I'm beginning to feel sabotaged. You know, sitting in a kitchen, you're just too vulnerable. If the humming refrigerator doesn't get you, the faces at the window will.

COOP: Protect yourself, whatever it is.

(*The* WOMEN *of the cocktail party begin entering separately. They hold coffee cups; they either remain standing or sit on stools. They are wearing robes. And they quietly observe* RONNIE *and* COOP.)

RONNIE: I'm not sure I want to. I guess I feel like writing letters to everybody. PLEASE FORGIVE. PLEASE COME. PLEASE KNOCK DOWN MY DOOR.

COOP: Ronnie, do you want to die in an avalanche? Listen to me, clean up the act first.

RONNIE: This camouflage is so cheap. I'd like one woman to cut the shit and finally admit. . . . [*Pause*.] Why can't they ever say what they mean?

COOP: Maybe once you pronounce an emotion, you feel compelled to give in to it.

RONNIE: Here's the way it is. One person tells her story. Then I tell mine. We never exchange a question and an answer but the connections have been made. I'm getting scared of these innuendoes. And my patterns are beginning to resemble theirs. Oh, Coop, it's so convenient to give up your first, overripe ideas. Everyone's so willing to help you.

COOP: Turn them down.

RONNIE: I've tried. But they're scratching on my roof to get in. What do they want?

COOP: Company.

RONNIE: Everyone here suffers close to the ground. But you don't know about that because you climb and you bring me up and out of this. [*Pause.*] Shit. You're standing in my kitchen and you look as comfortable as a goddamn Scott towel. What a kick you are.

COOP: I'm easy.

RONNIE: Some chance of that.

COOP: The house David mentioned. I passed it. I couldn't go in. But there was a tree. I picked some fruit. [*She hands* RONNIE *a pear.*]

RONNIE: Thanks, you fucking nature girl. Okay, tell me about the road. Give me details.

COOP: Why, are you going somewhere?

RONNIE: Just having myself a little daydream, all right?

COOP: JOURNEY: We walk many miles. We learn new routes. We meet people who put us up. We take the risk.

RONNIE: I don't know. I never go anywhere without my paranoia.

COOP: We could purchase authentic rites of passage and travel by Greyhound.

RONNIE: That's a shitty idea. I'd wanna get me one of those backpacks and wait on the side of the road.

COOP: I can offer you a position with Cooperman's Traveling One-Man Band. Just a temporary arrangement of course. Most of my bookings are strictly solo.

RONNIE: It would be delicious from beginning to end.

COOP: Companion.

RONNIE: Friend.

COOP: Don't encourage me, Ronnie. I'm starting to think about it.

RONNIE: Are you?

COOP: Well, shit, it's tempting.

RONNIE: You know something . . . I never think of you as being lonely. I don't want you to be.

COOP: [*Vulnerable under it*] You're right. I'm never lonely. It's a purifying experience. You should try it.

RONNIE: You just move along, right? All those people loving you, and I bet they do. [*Pause.*] Tell me what you know.

COOP: *This* is what I know.

RONNIE: Have I given you anything?

COOP: There's a time when I sit near the open window in a car . . . traveling. My eyes hurt because of the wind. There's so much noise, it blanks out. I'm on my way. I'm no place. I'm completely centered. That's when I think of you, Ronnie. I never miss you and I never dream about you. I just know that when I sit very still and everything else is moving, you'll be there.

RONNIE: I adore you in navy blue, you know that?

COOP: [*Who has been leaning on her knapsack, gets up after a moment, perhaps cleans up the cups.*] What are you going to do, Ronnie?

RONNIE: I'm going to stay.

COOP: I needed to hear you say that finally.

RONNIE: I'd like to come with you, do you believe me? It's just that we can't start making adjustments.

COOP: That's what I do best.

RONNIE: No, you have a very private space. And you have to take care of it, Coop. You can't let me clutter it up.

COOP: Those are MOVING-ON words. Where are you headed?

RONNIE: I'm going to rent a covered wagon and settle the West. [*Pause.*] You opened it up for me, Coop.

COOP: It isn't just David, then? It isn't really your being married?

RONNIE: No. It's me. I have to find a way to myself. [*She goes to* COOP, *holds her.*] It began with you, but it ends here. [*Pause.*] You smell so good. What do you smell of?

COOP: Old clothes. [*One of the* WOMEN *drops her cup.*] What was that?

RONNIE: Something breaking.

COOP: Before I head for the hills again, we'll go for a

drive. I'll find you a good place, and you can try working right out there in the open. [*She gets her hat, puts it on* RONNIE.]

RONNIE: The air will probably kill me.

COOP: Just take deep breaths.

RONNIE: You've been scrambling around in my head for so long, how the hell did I ever keep my hands off you?

COOP: How will it be when I go?

RONNIE: Maybe I'll invite some of the ladies over and put it to them. [*Another* WOMAN *drops her cup.*] I don't like their noise.

COOP: It's all right.

(*Another cup drops.*)

RONNIE: With you there's never any doubt. That's what used to frighten me. I kept running away, and it was such a mistake.

COOP: We know each other now. Hold on to that.

RONNIE: [*Moving toward* COOP.] Oh, Coop . . . Coop. [*They embrace.*]

COOP: Shit.

RONNIE: What's the matter?

COOP: It just hurts.

RONNIE: Yeah.

COOP: [*After a moment, she takes* RONNIE's *arms away. It is difficult.* RONNIE *tries to hold on. They look at one another.*] Good night.

RONNIE: Good night.

(COOP *exits.* RONNIE *is still. She removes* COOP's *hat. Looks at it, then gently places it on* COOP's *knapsack or on the floor. Slowly she realizes that the other* WOMEN *are in the room. They begin to move slowly.* RONNIE *weaves around them, still carefully watching. The* WOMEN, *each, do different things. One might touch her own body with new awareness; another might pick up* COOP's *knapsack. Someone else might pick up a piece of paper and begin to read. They might take over the room by sitting on counters, opening drawers, etc. It is an exploration, an unearthing, a transference. Finally, one* WOMAN *sits at* RONNIE's *typewriter, which is always in the room, and she types* one key. *The other* WOMEN *freeze.* RONNIE *touches her softly on the head, then stands back. The* WOMAN *begins to type again, as the lights fade.)*

END

THE MADNESS OF LADY BRIGHT
A Play in One Act

by
Lanford Wilson

———————◆•◆———————

For Neil Flanagan

The Madness of Lady Bright was first presented by Joseph Cino at the Caffe Cino on May 19, 1964. It was directed by Denis Deegan, with sets by Joseph Davies and lighting by John Torrey, and had the following cast:

LESLIE BRIGHT .... *Neil Flanagan*
GIRL .... *Carolina Lobravico*
BOY .... *Eddie Kenmore*

The production was revised with new casts and a redirection by William Archibald to run a total of 168 performances at the Cino.

CHARACTERS

LESLIE BRIGHT: A man of about forty; he is a screaming preening queen, rapidly losing a long-kept "beauty."

BOY ⎱ Both are very attractive, perhaps twenty-five, dressed
GIRL ⎰ in dark, simple, casual clothes.

The stage within a stage is set as LESLIE BRIGHT's *one-room apartment. The walls are light and covered over with hundreds of signatures, or autographs, mostly only names, in every conceivable size and writing medium. The name "Adam" is prominent on one wall; on another is "Michael Delaney." There is a dresser with nail polish, hairbrush, lipstick, various clutter across the top. A desk, chair, papers, telephone. A portable phonograph that works passably well, and records. The room seems tucked like a pressing book with mementos, postcards, letters, photographs, pictures of men from body-building magazines. A bed with pink and white silk sheets is against one wall. A window looks out to the back of buildings across the backyard below, a scene like the seventies between Amsterdam and Columbus avenues in upper Manhattan. The room is very sunny. A hot, still summer afternoon.*

The characters of the BOY *and* GIRL *are used to move the action—to* LESLIE's *memories, moods. They express, as actors, various people, voices, lovers. Sometimes they should be involved, sometimes almost bored, impatient, sometimes openly hostile, as the people he has known.*

At curtain the three walk on and assume their positions. The BOY *and* GIRL *sit to the side, or either side;* LESLIE, *entering, carrying a telephone, in character, sits at the desk and dials a number. After a moment of half-listening, a double take, he turns to the couple.*

LESLIE: [*Broadly*] Do you know what is comforting the world on Dial-A-Prayer this abysmally hot Saturday afternoon?

GIRL: [*Prefatorily, to the audience*] Abysmally Hot Saturday Afternoon . . .

LESLIE: [*Cutting in, superior*] You think lately perhaps you've been overly preoccupied with sex; you should turn to deeper, more solemn matters, and Dial-A-Prayer gives you: "The Lord is my Shepherd, I shall not want. He maketh me to *lie down* in green pastures." God, what an image. Out in a green pasture, yet. Well, Adam, if that isn't heaven . . . Why didn't you maketh me to lie down in green pastures, Adam? Why didn't you just maketh me to lie down? Why didn't you maketh me? [*He has been looking through an address book.*] Well, who would be home? [*Dials.*] Stalwart queen, I can't believe even you would walk the street in this heat. [*Hanging up*] One day you're going to melt into the sidewalk [*Looking through the book*] into this little puddle of greasy rouge and nylons. [*Dials.*] Ring. Ring. [*Holds telephone receiver between his shoulder and ear, picks up the bottle of nail polish, and polishes one nail.*] Ring. [*Looking at the hand*] Ten rings, dear, that's enough for any girl. One for every finger. Cheap damn Chinese red. Junk. No one. No one is home. [*Waving hand to dry*] That's ten, sweetheart—okay, one extra for the index finger—eleven, that's all, sorry. [*Hangs up sloppily.*] So, no one is home.

BOY: You're home.

LESLIE: [*Cutting in*] *I'm* home, of course. Home. [*Looks around.*] Oh, God! Well, face it, girl; you'll drive yourself stir if you can't find someone else to drive. . . . [*He fans through the address book.*] Oh, to hell with you. [*Tossing it aside*] You bore me. [*Affected voice*] You bore me! [*Rather seriously*] You are a pile of paper addresses and memories, paper phone numbers and memories, and you mean nothing to me. [*Trying to catch the line just said*] You—I am surrounded—I am left with [*Rather desperately trying to catch the right phrasing of the line to write it down*] a—with paper memories and addresses. . . . [*Finds a piece of paper at the desk. With a pencil, bent over the desk*] I am—how?

BOY: I am left with a—with paper memories.

GIRL: With paper addresses.

BOY: You are a pile of addresses and remembrances.

LESLIE: How did it go?

GIRL: [*Singing*] "Memories, memories . . ."

LESLIE: How did it go?

BOY: I am a paper.

LESLIE: Oh, to hell with it. I should go out. [*Looking at the polished nail*] If nothing else in the world, I am certain that that is the wrong color for me. [*Sitting down*] I—I— [*Totally different thought*] I should never wear anything other than blue. Aqua. The color of the sea. [*Rising*] I am Venus, rising from . . . and matching eye shadow. And nothing else. [*He looks in the mirror for the first time. Stops. Looks bitchily at his reflection.*] You. Are a faggot. There is no question about it anymore—you are definitely a faggot. You're funny but you're a faggot. [*Pause.*] You have *been* a faggot since you were four years old. Three years old. [*Checking the mirror again*] You're not *built* like a faggot—necessarily. You're built like a disaster. But, whatever your dreams, there is just no possibility whatever of your ever becoming, say, a lumberjack. You know? [*He has risen and is wandering aimlessly about the room.*]

GIRL: You know?

(*Music, very softly from outside.*)

LESLIE: I know. I just said it. None whatever. Oh, you're spinning around in your stupid room like Loretta Young for Christsake. You should have a long circular skirt and . . . [*Long stretching motion with his arm as he turns, imitating Loretta Young's television entrance.*] "Hello. John?" [*He stops. They all hear the music now, a Mozart concerto, very faint.*] Why, how lovely.

GIRL: How soft, distant. Isn't that lovely?

BOY: It is.

(*The three drift toward the window.*)

LESLIE: It must be coming from someone's apartment. Some faggot's apartment. [*They are at the window.*] He's turned on the Bach—no, it's Mozart. And he's preparing dinner nervously, with some simple salad and some complex beef stew. And they'll dine by candlelight and ruin their eyes. Sometimes in summer it seems the only way to remain sane is listening to the radios playing in the neighborhood. I haven't a radio myself; I discovered I was talking back to it so I kicked it out. I have only the phonograph you saw and some worn-out records.

(*The* BOY *and* GIRL *have become visitors.*)

GIRL: The music is lovely.
BOY: Where's it coming from, can you tell?
LESLIE: I don't know. Somewhere. It's nice at a distance like that. Sometimes in summer it seems the only way to remain sane is by listening to—of course, it's a mixed neighborhood. Oh, well. I get Spanish guitars and a good deal of Flamenco music as well. Of course I enjoy that too. At a distance like that.
GIRL: So soft, like that.
BOY: It's all right.

(*They turn from the window.*)

LESLIE: Mozart has always been one of my favorites; I know, you'll say how ordinary, but Mozart and Bach, I believe they have—oh, I don't know. It's so immature to try to analyze music.

(*The window has become the doorway to a symphony hall; they exit, moving away slowly, and* LESLIE *lights a cigarette, as at intermission.*)

BOY: It isn't necessary to talk about it; you just listen to it.
LESLIE: Exactly. I know. But they'll intellectualize and say that *this* is like a sunset and *that*—I mean it's so phony.
GIRL: It is.

LESLIE: I get really passionately upset by that sort of thing. Music is not like a sunrise, it's like [*They are laughing at his joke before it is finished.*] *music*, isn't it? I mean, isn't it?

GIRL: That's so true.

BOY: That's true.

(*They walk away.* LESLIE *remains standing in the same position. The music has faded away.*)

LESLIE: [*Continuing*] I go to these concerts only to listen to the music, not to see the white cliffs of wherever-it-is. I only . . . [*Listens.*] It's stopped. [*Goes to window again.*] Why do you always hear that stupid concerto, the same one? There is no one out there who would have been playing it, is there? [*To the walls*] Is there, Autographs? [*Listens.*] What was that? [*This is bawdy—Judy Garland yelling to her doting audience.*] What was that once more? [*Big*] We'll stay all night and sing 'em all! [*A bow. Drops his cigarette.*] Goddamn! Burn the place down.

BOY: [*Correcting; this exchange rapidly, with almost sadistic inanity*] Up.

GIRL: Burn the place *up*.

LESLIE: Up or down?

GIRL: Up or down.

BOY: [*Echo*] Up or down?

LESLIE: Down or up? [LESLIE *sits at dresser.*]

GIRL: [*Cutting in*] You're so damn sloppy; if you've got to smoke . . .

LESLIE: [*Cutting in*] I don't *have* to smoke, I *prefer* to smoke.

GIRL: [*Cutting in*] . . . got to smoke you could at least take a few elementary precautions not to burn the place down.

BOY: Up.

GIRL: Not to burn the place up.

LESLIE: [*Cutting in*] I am a very nervous person and I have to have something to do with my hands and I *prefer* to smoke, if you don't mind! If you don't *mind!*

GIRL: Well, you can buy your own cigarettes; don't expect

me to supply cigarettes for you, and don't think I don't
notice when you steal mine.

LESLIE: I wouldn't touch yours. . . .

GIRL: You can march down to the store and buy your own
—if you're not ashamed to be seen there.

(*The* BOY *has laughed chidingly at "march."*)

LESLIE: Why would I be . . . [*Breaks off, turns to mirror.*]
Hmm. [*Hands to sides of eyes, testily*] Oh, not good.
Not good at all. All those spidery little wrinkles showing
your *a-g-e*. Exposing yourself, aren't you? And a gray
hair or two—and your whole face just collapsing. Built
like a disaster. [*Turning mirror away*] Oh, do go away.
[*To the back of mirror*] You should be preserved somewhere. You are a very rare specimen that should be
saved for posterity. *Lowered* into the La Brea tar pits in
a time capsule as a little piece of the twentieth century
that didn't quite come off. Along with an Olivetti typewriter and a can of—cream of celery soup. [*Turning
mirror back again*] Whatever you're telling me I don't
want to hear it. I've heard it before from every bitchy
queen alive. The old fey mare ain't what she used to
be. But she's well preserved, you've got to give her that.
A *line or two,* but holding together. By a thread. [*Rising*]
But she can sing like a nightingale. Well, nearly. And
dance like Giselle. Giselle was a little willie—a willie is
a fairy who dances in the woods. [*Almost as though
telling a story to the* BOY *and* GIRL] And, well, they tried
to make Giselle's husband dance all night and she
danced all night in his place. [*Aside*] Didn't you, Giselle?
You did. You saved his life. [*To the walls*] Now, what
have I done for you? All my visitors—all the men who
have visited this stupid apartment for the last ten or so
years—what have I ever done for you? Well, let's face it,
what did you ever do for me? Look at it that way.
Precious little. [*Jumping onto the bed, tapping a finger
against a crossed out name*] Oh, you! Quentin! I scratched
your name off over a year ago; you gave me—what

particular social disease was it you gave me? You with
your neat little signature. Tight, like-a-spring-little-
signature. You can always tell a man by the way he
signs his name, and a tight signature is very, very
bad, Quentin.

BOY: How come?

LESLIE: [*Walking away. Only mildly scolding*] I have
studied graphology and believe me, it is very, very *bad*,
Quentin. You will undoubtedly give me some dreadful
social disease. And you, another meek little signature.
In pencil. But you were only an edge bashful, only shy.
For a meek little signature, Arnold Chrysler, you weren't
really bad. You were not Adam, but there was only one.
You were none of you like—anything like—Adam.
Well, Michael Delaney was wonderful indeed; marvelous
indeed, but he was not Adam. [*Cheek to Adam's name*]
You were everything. You are what I remember. Always
the dreams are you. [*Turning away, laughing*] Dreams?
Oh, my dear. Fantasies. Oh, you are definitely cracking.
[*Into mirror*] Mirror, you are—I am sorry to report—
cracking up. [*Frustrated*] I am losing my mind. I am. I
am losing my faggot mind. I'm going insane. [*The
Mozart returns, but never important—very distantly, and
only for a few bars.*] It's this stupid apartment and the
goddamned heat and *no one ever being at home!* [*To
telephone*] Why don't you answer? [*To himself*] You are
growing old and fat and insane and senile and old. [*Goes
to phone, dials. Ends the nervous note, says with the
phone:*] "The Lord is my"—yes, we know all that. [*Hangs
up. Dials.*] All of you are never, ever, ever at home.
[*Looking about the room as the phone rings on and on*]
You at least never had homes. You never lived in one
place more than a week. Bums and vagabonds, all of
you; even Adam, admit it. Tramp around the world,
hustling your box from Bermuda to Bangkok! From
Burma to Birmingham. How was Birmingham, Adam?
What? Oh, don't lie to me, *everyone* has hustled his box
in Birmingham. [*Notices the phone is in his hand, hangs
up.*] Never home. At least you can count on Dial-A-

Prayer being home. [*Tosses book on the desk.*] You, you
whores, tramp-the-street bitches. Dial-A-Prayer, and
weather and the correct time and Pan American Airways
travel information and TWA and American and Delta
and Ozark—and the public library. You can count on—
but an acquaintance? Don't count on it. There is no one
outside. [*Laughs.*] Well! [*To the* BOY *and* GIRL] A little
action, huh? [*They laugh, party-like.*] I hate beer, just a
Coke, please: Yes, I know they're both fattening, you
whore, I don't have to worry about that *yet!* Beauty isn't
everything! . . . But then what is? Come on.

GIRL: Come on.

(*A rock and roll record comes up.*)

BOY: Come on. Let's dance.
LESLIE: Let's dance. [GIRL *dances with* BOY, LESLIE *dances
with imaginary partner. The* BOY *talks both for himself
and* LESLIE's *partner. But* LESLIE *doesn't know the dance.*]
What is it? What on earth? Oh, God, I couldn't do that.
Zat new? Huh? Well, tell me the steps anyway.
BOY: Zeasy.
LESLIE: Walk through it once.
BOY: Just follow.
LESLIE: I'll try. Oh, God. [*Catching on, but not completely
getting it.*]
BOY: Zit.
LESLIE: Is it?

(*They continue to dance, very fast, very tiring, until the
end of the record and it goes off. General noise.*)

GIRL: Swell.
BOY: Thanks.

(*They walk away.*)

GIRL: Wheeh! It's so warm.
BOY: Yeah.

LESLIE: Is that all? Hell, it's over; put another quarter in. Ha! [*Comes out of it.*] Goddamn. Every time, all over sweat. You crazy loon. Stupid bitch. You should get dressed up and go down to the beach, it's so damn muggy and hot they must need a little something to liven up the beach about now. [*Makes a quick single enormous cabbage rose of the top sheet and puts it on his head as a fashionable hat—walks across the room as in a beauty contest, singing low:*] "There she is, Miss America. . . ." [*Takes rose from head, holds it to cover himself—a vision of total nudity, raises his eyes to the imaginary judge's bench. With sunny brightness.*] Good morning, Judge! [*Pause.*] Your Honor. [*Tosses it aside, goes to dresser.*] Oh, dear. [*Pause.*]

(BOY *and* GIRL *have been ignoring him.*)

BOY: [*To the actress quietly, privately*] Did you go somewhere?

LESLIE: [*Tossing the sheet back to the bed*] No.

GIRL: When?

BOY: Last night. Did you go out for a while?

GIRL: Oh, yes. I went for cigarettes.

BOY: I missed you. I rolled over for a second and stretched, you know—and you weren't there—and I thought where the hell—then I must have drifted off again. Got up and got dressed?

GIRL: I went out for a few minutes down to the drugstore.

BOY: I wondered.

GIRL: It was raining.

BOY: [*Faking a hurt voice*] Well, you might consider—I looked over expecting you to be there—and there was nothing but loneliness.

LESLIE: [*To himself—listening in spite of himself*] Loneliness. [*He is not looking toward them.*]

GIRL: You were asleep when I came back.

BOY: It's a terrible thing to wake up to loneliness. [LESLIE *looks sharply toward him at the word repeated.*]

GIRL: I came right back; it was wet as hell. You know?

LESLIE: You know nothing about loneliness. [*Long pause.*]
I should go out. [*Seeing name on the wall*] I should go
out and look for you. . . . [*Creeping up on the name*]
Mich-ael De-lan-ey— [*Grabbing the wall*] Gotcha!
[*Turning from the wall*] Good Lord—eight years ago—
you would be how old by now? Oh well, old hustlers
never die, they just start buying it back! [*Turning back
to the wall*] You were very good, I remember that. And
who else? [*Going over the names*] So-so; fair; clumsy,
but cute anyway; too intelligent; Larry; good, I remember; A-minus, and that's very good; undersized; very
nice; *over*sized, but I'm not complaining. [*Suddenly
angry*] Samuel Fitch! [*Runs to the desk for a pencil.*]
Samuel Fitch! [*Scratches the name off.*] No, I thought
you were gone! You bitch! You liar! You vicious faggot!
You *queer*! You were not a man, you were some worm.
Some smelly worm. [*Feeling better*] Of course, you
couldn't help it, you were *born* a worm. Once a worm
always a worm, I always say. [*Looking back at the erased
name*] Oh. Poor Samuel. You really couldn't help it,
could you? You were queer but you couldn't help it.
Domineering mother, probably. What was it—that was
sweet—you said. You said my body was smooth. [*The
Mozart is back, softly but getting louder.*] Hairless, that's
what you liked about it. You said I moved well, too,
didn't you? Well, *I do* move well. I move *exceptionally*
well. [*Sits on the side of the bed. Giselle music is added
to the Mozart, and in a moment the rock and roll also
begins.*] And I haven't a hair on my body. I'm as hairless
and smooth as a newborn babe. I shave, of course, my
underarms; no woman would go around with hair under
her arms. It's just not done. Lately. In America anyway.
[*Stretches his legs.*] And my legs—they're smooth. They
are. [*Feeling the backs of his legs*] I have—I [*Nervously*]
I have varicose veins in my legs. I can't wear hose. I
have hideous, dreadful legs. I have blue, purple, *black*
veins in my legs. They give me pain—they make me
limp, they ache, they're ugly. They used to be beautiful
and they are bony and ugly. Old veins. [*The BOY and

GIRL *begin to rub their legs and arms and to moan low.*]
Old legs, dancing legs; *but the veins!* They get tired.
And when they get [*Fast*] old they get tired and when
they get tired they get slow and when they get slow they
get stiff and when they get stiff they get brittle and when
they get brittle they break and the veins break and your
bones snap and your skin sags. . . . The veins in my
arms and legs—my veins are old and brittle and the
arteries break—your temples explode your veins break
like glass tubes—you can't walk you can't dance you
can't speak; you stiffen with age. Age takes you over
and buries you; it buries you under—under—*my veins,*
my arms, my body, my heart, my old callused hands; my
ugly hands; my face is collapsing. I'm losing my mind.
[*The* BOY *finally screams a long, low,* "Oh." *The* GIRL
screams nervously, "I'm going insane."] I'm going insane. I'm going insane!
BOY: My veins, my arteries.

(*The* BOY *and* GIRL *speak the next two lines simultaneously.*)

GIRL: I'm being buried.
BOY: I'm old; I'm growing old.
GIRL: [*Singing*] "Memories, memories."

(*The music has now reached its loudest point.*)

LESLIE: [*Speaking over* GIRL's *singing*] I'm losing my *mind.*
I'm losing my mind. Oh, God, I'm losing my mind! [*He
falls panting onto the bed. The only music left is the
Mozart, very far away. After a moment he gets up. He
notices his pants leg is pulled up; he slowly pulls it
down.*] I . . .
GIRL: [*Chattering madly*] If you must smoke you could at
least buy your own.
BOY: How did it go, memories and paper and addresses on
the walls and . . . ?
GIRL: And don't tell me . . .

LESLIE: [*Sits on side of the bed. To himself*] I should.

GIRL: And don't tell me you don't snatch mine; I've seen you. I sometimes count them, you know. Did you ever think about that?

LESLIE: I—I should go out. [*Rises, walks to desk, sits.*] That way insanity, Leslie. That way the funny farm, Lady Bright. The men in white, Mary. And watch it, because you know you look like a ghost in white. You have never, ever worn white well. [*Rising*] You should never be seen in any color other than pink. Candy pink. Candy pink and white candy stripes. Silk.

GIRL: Well, of course.

LESLIE: [*Walking toward the window*] Someone is playing their radio; I wonder what station plays Mozart all day long. [*The* BOY *has moved to beside the bed. He is buckling his belt.*] I know you don't understand it, but I do. Your pants are on the chair.

BOY: Yeah, I found them. You're good, I'll say that.

LESLIE: [*Pleased*] Sometimes I just like to stand and listen to the music from someone's radio. I've done that a lot this summer. I live alone. [*He continues to look out the window, away from the* BOY.]

BOY: I said you're good.

LESLIE: Well, of course. You see the names. Did you notice the names on the wall?

BOY: [*Seeing them*] Yeah. I mean I see them now. You do it?

LESLIE: Of course not! They're autographs. No one has refused me. And I'll want yours, too, of course.

BOY: My what?

LESLIE: Your name, your autograph.

BOY: On the wall?

LESLIE: Yes. Whenever you want to write it. There's an ink pen on the table if you haven't one.

BOY: [*Finding it and going to the wall*] Yeah. Okay you got it.

LESLIE: Don't tell me where. Move away now. [*He turns.*] Now. [*Surveying the walls*] There. Oh, so large, you egoist; it surely wasn't difficult to find it. Michael Delaney. You're Irish?

BOY: Yeah.

LESLIE: Irish. [*Distantly disappointed*] Well, it isn't romantic, is it? It's not Russian or Sicilian or one of those, but I've got nothing against the Irish. Anymore. You have raised my opinion of them, I'll admit, considerably. [*The* BOY *walks away, sits down.*] I thought you only drank a good deal, but I find you have a capacity for other things as well. And it's just as well to add a favorite nationality; I was guessing you as Jewish; you don't mind me saying that—the dark hair, you know—but with a name like Michael Delaney you couldn't be anything else. [*The music has faded slowly out.* LESLIE *looks out the window again.*] They've turned the radio down so I can't hear it now. I tell you [*A quick glance at the name*], Michael, it's no fun. It's no fun living here in this stupid apartment by myself listening to my few records and the neighbor's radio; I should like someone, I think sometimes [*Being delicate*], living here sometimes. Or maybe somehow not living here but coming here to see me often. Then I'd wash the walls— wash off everyone else. Wash them off and kiss them good-bye—good riddance. I've even thought I wouldn't mind, you know, just letting someone live here, scot- free; I could prepare the meals—and do things. I— want to *do* things for someone who could live here. And he could sleep here, every night. It's really lovely—or would be—with the music. I'd like something like that, it [*Turning*] gets so lonely here by . . . [*But of course, he's gone.* LESLIE *glances at the* BOY *sitting. To the* GIRL] This rumb room. [*To the walls*] Dumb! Mute! All you goddamned cobwebby corners, you stare down at me while I die of boredom; while I go insane because every- one I call is gone off somewhere. Once more. [*Goes to phone, dials, listens to the ringing.*] Once. Twice. Thrice. Quadrice. Screw. [*Limply he puts his finger on the cradle, clicking off. Raises it and dials from memory another number.*]

GIRL: Good afternoon, American Airlines. May we help you?

LESLIE: Yes. [*Pause.*] Fly me away from here. [*Clicks her off, leaving his finger on the phone. Long pause. Reflecting, bitchily*] Oh, well, fly yourself, fairy; you've got the wings. All God's chil'un got wings, Leslie. That's your disastrous body: wings and ass.

BOY: You've got a nice body. You know, a young body. How old are you, about nineteen? [LESLIE *is surprised, almost stunned by the line. The* BOY *repeats the cue.*] How old are you, about nineteen? [*The* BOY *has entered the room.*]

LESLIE: [*Sadly; remembering*] Twenty. [*The scene now is played with young, fresh buoyancy.*] And you're what? The same age about, aren't you?

BOY: Twenty-one. Get drunk legally, any state.

LESLIE: I've never—I'm almost embarrassed—I've never met anyone as—well, I'm never at a loss for words, believe me. I don't know what you have—anyone so good-looking as you are. [BOY *laughs.*] What do you do? Are you a weight lifter?

BOY: Who—me? I don't do nothing. Bum around.

LESLIE: Bum around.

BOY: Been in every state.

LESLIE: Just bumming around?

BOY: One state pays for the next, you know?

LESLIE: You hustle, I guess. I mean—do you only hustle? I . . .

BOY: [*Cutting in*] That's right. Oh, well, for kicks too; sometimes. Why not? When the mood hits me.

LESLIE: I wish to God it would hit you about now.

BOY: Yeah. Rough night, kid. Sorry.

LESLIE: Oh.

BOY: [*Looking around*] Come on, they'll be other nights. I said I like you; you're a nice kid. We'll make it. I'll promise you.

LESLIE: You will?

BOY: I'll promise you that.

LESLIE: Good. Then I'll wait.

BOY: How long you been in this pad?

LESLIE: About a month. Everything's new. I painted the walls myself.

BOY: You ever seen one of these?

LESLIE: What? A grease pencil? Sure, I used to work in the china department of this stupid store; we marked dishes with them.

BOY: Mind if I do something?

LESLIE: What am I supposed to say? [*Earnestly*] No. I don't mind if you do something. Anything.

BOY: Something to remember me by. [*Goes to wall.*]

LESLIE: What? *What?* Are you writing—your name? Hey, on my fresh wall? [*The* BOY *turns smilingly to him.*] What the hell, it looks good there.

BOY: Yeah. I'll see you around.

LESLIE: Where are you going? [*No answer.* LESLIE *is in the present now. The* BOY *walks to his chair and sits.*] Where are you going? Not you. Don't leave now. Don't. Adam. You're not leaving. Come back here, don't go away; you were the one I wanted. The only one I wanted, Adam! Don't go away! [*Wildly*] Don't go, Adam; don't go, Adam.

GIRL: Unrequited love is such a bore.

BOY: Sad.

GIRL: Left him flat, didn't he?

BOY: The only one he wanted.

LESLIE: Oh, God, that way, honey, is madness for sure. Think about Adam and you've had it, honey. Into the white coat with the wrap-around sleeves.

(*The following dialogue between the* BOY *and* GIRL *takes place simultaneously with* LESLIE's *next speech.*)

GIRL: It's sad, really.

BOY: It is. It really is. The only one he wanted really was Adam.

GIRL: And he never had him.

BOY: Never saw him after that.

GIRL: Of course he would have gone mad either way, don't you think?

BOY: Oh, yes.

GIRL: Drove himself to it, I mean. He couldn't have possibly lived a sane life like that.

BOY: Some pansies live a sane life and some don't. Like anyone else, I suppose.

GIRL: Well, not exactly.

BOY: I mean some go nuts and some don't. Some just go insane.

GIRL: Mad.

BOY: Nuts.

GIRL: Lose their balance, you know.

LESLIE: [*Over the above. Moves to the record player and goes through the records, finds one.*] What I should have is some music. I'm so sick of music for companionship. But it's better than [*Looks at the telephone*] you queens! Never-at-home sick queens! [*Puts a record on. It is Judy Garland, singing a fast, peppy number. The volume is kept very low.*] Now, that's better. That's a little better. I can dance to that one. [*He dances, as with a partner, but he dances a slow, sexy number as the music continues fast.*] There. I like the way you . . . Oh, you think I follow well. I'm glad you think I follow—I have a good sense of rhythm, I've always been told that I move well. I get lonely, but I've been told I move well. I sometimes just stare at the corners of my room, would you believe that, *and pray* . . . [*He stops dancing and stands still.*] *And pray for* . . . [*Stops, panting.*] I want—*I want* . . . [*But he can't say it.*]

GIRL: [*With comic remove*] He wants to die, I believe.

BOY: I think that's what he's trying to say.

GIRL: Well, it's easy to understand; I mean you couldn't expect him to live like that.

BOY: He's effeminate.

GIRL: No one can want to live if they're like that.

BOY: It's all right on girls.

LESLIE: Why do you let me live if you know it?

GIRL: [*To* BOY] What could we do?

LESLIE: Why?

BOY: No one should live who's like that.

LESLIE: Giselle. Giselle, you saved him. You danced all night and you danced till dawn and you saved him. You did, you saved him; you danced for him. They let you save him.

GIRL: He used to be an intelligent fellow.

BOY: He was. He was a bright kid.

GIRL: Quick-thinking.

LESLIE: Why do you let me live if you know it? Can't you see I'm going insane alone in my room, in my hot lonely room? Can't you see I'm losing my mind? I don't want to be the way I am.

GIRL: He doesn't like the way he is.

BOY: He'd like to be different.

GIRL: He looks different enough to me.

BOY: Extraordinary, I'd say.

LESLIE: You could have killed me as a child, you could have.

GIRL: Christ! How can you play those goddamned records? Do you have to blare that *music? Do you? You dance around in your room all day*. Do something worthwhile, why don't you?

LESLIE: You could have.

GIRL: Do something worthwhile.

LESLIE: [*As before to Michael Delaney*] I'd like to do something. [*Suddenly*] No. We won't have this music. [*He's wild now, excited.*] We won't have this music. [*Strip music comes in over the Garland.*] We'll have a party. We'll have a show. I'll give you a show!

BOY: He's going to give you a show. I think.

GIRL: Turn that off!

(LESLIE *goes to music. He turns it by accident to full volume, gets nervous, scratches the needle all the way across the record, at full volume. It clicks off. The other music goes off too.*)

LESLIE: [*Turning to them*] What would you like?

BOY: [*To* GIRL] What would you like?

GIRL: [*To* LESLIE] What would you like?

LESLIE: [*Happily*] Oh, me! God. I—would—like . . . We won't have a show, we'll have a royal dance; a cotillion; a nice beautiful dance.

GIRL: A ball! Wonderful!

BOY: Lady Bright requests your presence . . .

LESLIE: A beautiful party. [*Grabs the sheet and winds it around himself.*]

BOY: May I have the pleasure?
GIRL: I hardly know what to say.

(*Mozart music comes up.*)

LESLIE: And I shall be the queen! I dance with the most
grace. I will be selected queen by popular demand. I
dance like a flower on the water. [*Mozart up. They
dance around in a whirl.*] I dance like a flower. I shall
dance with Adam and you shall dance with whom you
please. No, I have no more room on my program, I
am dreadfully sorry, young man. . . . [*Still dancing*] I
am dancing tonight with only one man, you know what
that means.
GIRL: She's so lovely.
BOY: She's so beautiful.
GIRL: Did you catch her name?
LESLIE: My name is Giselle! I am Giselle! [*Running to
mirror*] I'm the fairest at the ball. I am the loveliest. *I
am young. I am young and lovely. Yes, I am young!*
[*He bends over the dressing table and returns to the
mirror. He takes up lipstick and smears it across his lips,
half his face.*] I am young tonight. I will never be old.
I have all my faculties tonight. [*The people have continued to dance.* LESLIE *returns and they whirl about.
Other music joins the Mozart—Giselle, the rock and
roll, the strip number.*] I am beautiful. I am happy!
[LESLIE *falls down. They continue to dance about him.
The music stops. Then comes on. Stops. Returns. A
pulsating effect.*] Excuse me, I must have . . . [*Music
continues loudly.*] My arms are so tired. My legs. I have
bad legs; I don't walk too well. The veins in my legs
are getting old, I guess. . . . [*This is light, chattery talk.*]
I grow tired easily. *I grow brittle and I break. I'm losing
my mind, you know. Everyone knows when they lose
their mind. But I'm so lonely!* [*The music stops.* LESLIE
looks up. The BOY *and* GIRL *exit to opposite sides. As if
to a man standing over him*] I'm sorry. I just slipped
and . . . [*Turning to the other side. There is a "man"
there, too.*] Oh, thank you. [*Allowing the man to help*

him up, still with the sheet as a gown; softly to the man, intimately] I'm sorry—I hate to trouble you, but I—I believe I've torn my gown. I seem to have ripped . . . Oh, no, it can be repaired. Yes, I'm sure it can. But would you take me home now, please? [*There is a pause.*] Just take me home, please; take me home, please. Take me home now. Take me home. *Please take me home.* [*The music now comes on and builds in a few seconds to top volume.* LESLIE *screams above it. He drops the sheet; it falls down around him.*] TAKE ME HOME, SOME-ONE! TAKE ME HOME! [*The music stops.* LESLIE *has run to the wall, to a far-off area, leaning against the wall. The Mozart is the only music remaining. Softly, whispering against the wall—to himself.*] Take me home. Take me home. Take me home. Take me home. Take me home. Take me home. Take me home. Take me home. Take me home. . . .

(*The lights fade out slowly.*)

CURTAIN

ENTERTAINING
MR. SLOANE
A Play in Three Acts

by
Joe Orton

———————— ◆ ◆ ————————

To Kenneth Halliwell

Entertaining Mr. Sloane was first presented in London at the New Arts Theatre on May 6, 1964, by Michael Codron Ltd and at Wyndham's Theatre on June 29, 1964, by Michael Codron and Albery, with the following cast:

KATH .... *Madge Ryan*
SLOANE .... *Dudley Sutton*
KEMP .... *Charles Lamb*
ED .... *Peter Vaughan*

Directed by Patrick Dromgoole
Designed by Timothy O'Brien
Costumes supervised by Tazeena Firth

Entertaining Mr. Sloane was revived as part of the "Joe Orton Festival" at the Royal Court Theatre, London, on April 17, 1975, subsequently transferring to the Duke of York's Theatre. The cast was as follows:

KATH .... *Beryl Reid*
SLOANE .... *Malcolm McDowell*
KEMP .... *James Ottaway*
ED .... *Ronald Fraser*

Directed by Roger Croucher
Designed by John Gunter
Costumes by Deirdre Clancy

ACT I

A room. Evening.

KATH *enters followed by* SLOANE.

KATH: This is my lounge.

SLOANE: Would I be able to use this room? Is it included?

KATH: Oh, yes. [*Pause.*] You mustn't imagine it's always like this. You ought to have rung up or something. And then I'd've been prepared.

SLOANE: The bedroom was perfect.

KATH: I never showed you the toilet.

SLOANE: I'm sure it will be satisfactory. [*Walks around the room examining the furniture. Stops by the window.*]

KATH: I should change them curtains. Those are our winter ones. The summer ones are more of a chintz. [*Laughs.*] The walls need redoing. The Dadda has trouble with his eyes. I can't ask him to do any work involving ladders. It stands to reason.

(*Pause.*)

SLOANE: I can't give you a decision right away.

KATH: I don't want to rush you. [*Pause.*] What do you think? I'd be happy to have you.

(*Silence.*)

SLOANE: Are you married?

KATH: [*Pause.*] I was. I had a boy . . . killed in very sad circumstances. It broke my heart at the time. I got over it, though. You do, don't you?

(*Pause.*)

201

SLOANE: A son?

KATH: Yes.

SLOANE: You don't look old enough.

(*Pause.*)

KATH: I don't let myself go like some of them you may have noticed. I'm just over . . . As a matter of fact I'm forty-one.

(*Pause.*)

SLOANE: [*Briskly.*] I'll take the room.

KATH: Will you?

SLOANE: I'll bring my things over tonight. It'll be a change from my previous.

KATH: Was it bad?

SLOANE: Bad?

KATH: As bad as that?

SLOANE: You've no idea.

KATH: I don't suppose I have. I've led a sheltered life.

SLOANE: Have you been a widow long?

KATH: Yes, a long time. My husband was a mere boy. [*With a half-laugh*] That sounds awful, doesn't it?

SLOANE: Not at all.

KATH: I married out of school. I surprised everyone by the suddenness of it. [*Pause.*] Does that sound as if I had to get married?

SLOANE: I'm broad-minded.

KATH: I should've known better. You won't breathe a word?

SLOANE: You can trust me.

KATH: My brother would be upset if he knew I told you. [*Pause.*] Nobody knows around here. The people in the nursing home imagined I *was* somebody. I didn't disillusion them.

SLOANE: You were never married, then?

KATH: No.

SLOANE: What about—I hope you don't think I'm prying?

KATH: I wouldn't for a minute. What about—?

SLOANE: . . . the father?

KATH: [*Pause.*] We always planned to marry. But there were difficulties. I was very young and he was even younger. I don't believe we would have been allowed.

SLOANE: What happened to the baby?

KATH: Adopted.

SLOANE: By whom?

KATH: That I could not say. My brother arranged it.

SLOANE: What about the kid's father?

KATH: He couldn't do anything.

SLOANE: Why not?

KATH: His family objected. They were very nice but he had a duty, you see. [*Pause.*] As I say, if it'd been left to him I'd be his widow today. [*Pause.*] I had a last letter. I'll show you some time. [*Silence.*] D'you like flock or foam rubber in your pillow?

SLOANE: Foam rubber.

KATH: You need a bit of luxury, don't you? I bought the Dadda one but he can't stand them.

SLOANE: I can.

KATH: You'll live with us, then, as one of the family?

SLOANE: I never had no family of my own.

KATH: Didn't you?

SLOANE: No. I was brought up in an orphanage.

KATH: You have the air of lost wealth.

SLOANE: That's remarkable. My parents, I believe, *were* extremely wealthy people.

KATH: Did Dr. Barnardo give you a bad time?

SLOANE: No. It was the lack of privacy I found most trying. [*Pause.*] And the lack of real love.

KATH: Did you never know your mamma?

SLOANE: Yes.

KATH: When did they die?

SLOANE: I was eight. [*Pause.*] They passed away together.

KATH: How shocking.

SLOANE: I've an idea that they had a suicide pact. Couldn't prove it of course.

KATH: Of course not. [*Pause.*] With a nice lad like you to take care of you'd think they'd've postponed it. [*Pause.*] Criminals, were they?

SLOANE: From what I remember they was respected. You

know, H.P. debts. Bridge. A little light gardening. The usual activities of a cultured community. [*Silence.*] I respect their memory.

KATH: Do you? How nice.

SLOANE: Every year I pay a visit to their grave. I take sandwiches. Make a day of it. [*Pause.*] The graveyard is situated in pleasant surroundings so it's no hardship. [*Pause.*] Tomb an' all.

KATH: Marble? [*Pause.*] Is there an inscription?

SLOANE: Perhaps you'd come with me this trip?

KATH: We'll see.

SLOANE: I go in the autumn because I clean the leaves off the monument. As a tribute.

KATH: Yes.

SLOANE: That's the main task I set myself.

KATH: Any relations?

SLOANE: None.

KATH: Poor boy. Alone in the world. Like me.

SLOANE: You're not alone.

KATH: I am. [*Pause.*] Almost alone. [*Pause.*] If I'd been allowed to keep my boy I'd not be. [*Pause.*] You're almost the same age as he would be. You've got the same refinement.

SLOANE: [*Slowly*] I need . . . understanding.

KATH: You do, don't you? Here, let me take your coat. [*Helps him off with his coat.*] You've got a delicate skin. [*Touches his neck. His cheek. He shudders a little. Pause.*]

KATH: [*Kisses his cheek.*] Just a motherly kiss. A real mother's kiss. [*Silence. Lifts his arms and folds them about her.*] You'll find me very sentimental. I upset easy. [*His arms are holding her.*] When I hear of . . . tragedies happening to perfect strangers. There are so many ruined lives. [*Puts her head on his shoulder.*] You must treat me gently when I'm in one of my moods.

(*Silence.*)

SLOANE: [*Clearing his throat.*] How much are you charging? I mean—I've got to know.

(*He drops his arms. She moves away.*)

KATH: We'll come to some arrangement. A cup of tea?
SLOANE: Yes, I don't mind.
KATH: I'll get you one.
SLOANE: Can I have a bath?
KATH: Now?
SLOANE: Later would do.
KATH: You must do as you think fit.

(*A door slams.* KEMP's *voice is heard off.*)

KEMP: You there?
KATH: [*Calls.*] I'm in here. Don't stand about. Sit down.
Go on. We don't charge. [SLOANE *sits on the settee.*]
That's a lovely shade of blue on your woolly. I'll fetch
you one down later that I knitted for my brother. [KEMP
enters. KATH, *loudly*] We have a visitor, Dadda.
KEMP: Eh?
KATH: A visitor.
KEMP: [*Stares, lifts his glasses, and stares again.*] Oh . . .
It's Eddie?
KATH: You are the limit. You show me up no end. It isn't
Ed. [*Pause.*] You behave like a sick child. I'm just about
tired of it. Afraid to have a guest or a friend in the
house. You put them off, Dadda. Let him shake your
hand. Go on.

(KEMP *shakes* SLOANE's *hand.*)

KEMP: What's he want, then?
KATH: Mr. Sloane is going to stay with us.
KEMP: Stay with us?
KATH: That's what I said.
KEMP: He can't. We've no room.
KATH: Make an effort, will you? What will the gentleman
think? He'll think you're a rude old man. [*Exchanges
looks with* SLOANE.] I'm going to have you apologize for

your boorish attitude. Do you feel embarrassed, Mr. Sloane?

SLOANE: It's all right.

KATH: No, it isn't. [*To* KEMP] Pull yourself together! [*Silence*.] Can I trust you to behave yourself while I get something to eat? [KEMP *does not answer*.] Entertain Mr. Sloane now. Give him the benefit of your experience. [*Pause*.] You want to learn manners. That's what you want. [*Picks up a basket of provisions from the floor*.] I'm a good mind to give you no tea. [*To* SLOANE] I'd not care to wonder what you must think of us. [*Takes a packet of crumpets from the basket. Hands it to* KEMP.] Here, toast these. Give yourself something to do. [*Exits*.]

(KEMP *goes to fire. Begins to toast crumpets*.)

SLOANE: Haven't we met before?

KEMP: Not to my knowledge.

SLOANE: Your face is familiar. Have I seen your photo in the paper? In connection with some event?

KEMP: No.

SLOANE: Do you pop into the pub at the end of the road?

KEMP: I don't drink.

SLOANE: Are you a churchgoer?

KEMP: Not at the moment. I used to be. In the old days I'd knock up the vicar at all hours. But then I lost touch.

SLOANE: I've seen you somewhere. I very rarely forget a face.

KEMP: Y've got me confused with another person.

SLOANE: Perhaps.

KEMP: Forget it, son. I'm not seen about much.

SLOANE: [*Pause*.] You don't resent my being in the house, do you?

KEMP: Not at all.

SLOANE: I thought you did. Just now.

KEMP: No.

SLOANE: This seems a nice place. Friendly atmosphere. [*Pause*.] How many children have you?

KEMP: Two.

SLOANE: Is your daughter married?

KEMP: She was. Had a terrible time. Kiddy died.

SLOANE: You have a son, don't you?

KEMP: Yes, but we're not on speaking terms.

SLOANE: How long is it?

KEMP: Twenty years.

SLOANE: 'Strewth!

KEMP: You perhaps find that hard to believe?

SLOANE: I do actually. Not speaking for twenty years? That's coming it a bit strong.

KEMP: I may have exchanged a few words.

SLOANE: I can believe that.

KEMP: He was a good boy. Played some amazing games as a youth. Won every goal at football one season. Sports mad, he was. [*Pause.*] Then one day, shortly after his seventeenth birthday, I had cause to return home unexpected and found him committing some kind of felony in the bedroom.

SLOANE: Is that straight?

KEMP: I could never forgive him.

SLOANE: A puritan, are you?

KEMP: Yes.

SLOANE: That kind of thing happens often, I believe. For myself, I usually lock the door.

KEMP: I'd removed the lock.

SLOANE: Anticipating some such tendencies on his part?

KEMP: I'd done it as a precautionary measure.

SLOANE: There are fascinating possibilities in this situation. I'd get it down on paper if I were you. [*Goes to the window.*]

KEMP: Admiring the view?

SLOANE: A perfect skyline you've got here. Lord Snowdon would give you something for a shot of that. Stunning it is. Stunning. Was this house a speculation?

KEMP: Not exactly.

SLOANE: Who built it, then? Was he a mad financier? The bloke who conceived the idea of building a house in the midst of a rubbish dump?

KEMP: It was intended to be the first of a row.

SLOANE: Go on. What happened?

KEMP: They gave up.

SLOANE: Lost interest?

KEMP: There were financial restrictions.

SLOANE: What a way to carry on!

KEMP: We've tried putting in complaints, but it's no good. Look at it out there. An eyesore. You may admire it. I don't. A woman came all the way from Woolwich yesterday. A special trip she made in order to dump a bedstead. I told her, what do you want to saddle us with your filthy mess for? Came over in a shooting brake. She was an old woman. Had her daughter with her. Fouling the countryside with their litter.

SLOANE: What you want is someone with pull on the council.

KEMP: If my boss were here I'd go to him.

SLOANE: Wealthy, was he?

KEMP: He had holdings in some trust. He didn't go into details with me.

SLOANE: How old was he?

KEMP: Forty.

SLOANE: Early middle age?

KEMP: Yes.

SLOANE: Dead, is he?

KEMP: Yes.

SLOANE: Did he die for his country?

KEMP: No. He was murdered. On the unsolved crimes list, he is.

SLOANE: A murderer not brought to justice. That's a sobering thought. [*Pause.*] Why can't they find the murderer? Didn't they advertise?

KEMP: Yes. They took a piece in the local paper.

SLOANE: How long ago was all this?

KEMP: Two years.

SLOANE: Do they have any clue to the murderer's identity?

KEMP: He was a young man with very smooth skin.

SLOANE: [*Pause.*] Was your boss a small man?

KEMP: Yes. Wavy hair. Wore a tweed tie.

SLOANE: What was his profession?

KEMP: He was a photographer. Specialized in views of the river.

SLOANE: You were employed in his service?

KEMP: Yes. As a general handyman. [*Pause.*] We gave the murderer a lift on the night of the crime.

SLOANE: [*Pause.*] You saw him, then?

KEMP: Yes.

SLOANE: Why didn't you go to the police?

KEMP: I can't get involved in that type of case. I might get my name in the papers.

SLOANE: I see your point of view. [*Pause.*] They won't find the killer now.

KEMP: I should very much doubt it.

SLOANE: No, the scent's gone cold. [*He watches* KEMP *in silence.*] Have you ever toasted a crumpet before?

KEMP: Yes.

SLOANE: I thought it was your first time from the way you're messing that about.

(KEMP *does not reply.*)

KEMP: [*Pause.*] Come here.

SLOANE: Why?

KEMP: I want to look at you.

SLOANE: What for?

KEMP: I think we have met before.

SLOANE: No, Pop. I'm convinced we haven't. I must have been getting you mixed up with a man called Fergusson. He had the same kind of way with him. Trustworthy.

KEMP: You think that?

SLOANE: Yes. [*Laughs.*]

KEMP: [*Pause.*] Fetch me a plate, will you?

SLOANE: Where from?

KEMP: The dresser. Back there.

(SLOANE *goes to the dresser. Fetches a plate. Comes to* KEMP, *bends down to give him the plate.* KEMP *seizes* SLOANE's *arm, pulls him toward him.*)

SLOANE: What's this!

KEMP: We have met before! I knew we had.

SLOANE: I've never met you.

KEMP: On my life. I remember.

SLOANE: Your eyes aren't good.

KEMP: I could still identify you.

SLOANE: [*Pause.*] Identify me?

KEMP: If it was necessary.

SLOANE: How could it be necessary?

KEMP: It might be.

SLOANE: Do lay off, Pop. You couldn't identify a herring on a plate!

KEMP: Don't speak to me like that, sonny. You'll find yourself in trouble.

SLOANE: Go on, you superannuated old prat!

KEMP: I'll have somebody to you. See if I don't.

(SLOANE *turns away.*)

SLOANE: Why don't you shut your mouth and give your arse a chance? [KEMP *lunges at* SLOANE *with the toasting fork.* SLOANE *gives a squeal of pain.*] Oh, you bleeding maniac! My leg. My leg.

KEMP: You provoked me!

SLOANE: [*Sinks into an armchair.*] I'll be in a wheelchair for life. [*Examines his leg.*] Oh, you cow. I'm covered in blood! Call somebody!

KEMP: [*Goes to the door, shouting.*] Kathy! Kathy!

KATH: [*Runs on, drying her hands on her apron, sees* SLOANE, *screams.*] What've you done?

KEMP: It wasn't intentional. [*Comes forward.*]

KATH: [*Shoos him away.*] Is there pain?

SLOANE: I can't move.

KATH: Are you hurt bad?

SLOANE: He's got an artery. I must be losing pints. Oh, Christ!

KATH: Come on. You'll be better on the settee. [*He allows her to guide him over. She settles him.*] What happened? Did he attack you? He's never shown signs before.

KEMP: I thought he was farther off. I can't judge distances.

KATH: Let Mr. Sloane speak for himself.

SLOANE: He ought to be in Colney Hatch. He's a slate off. Throwing things about.

KATH: Throw them, did he?

SLOANE: I don't know what he did.

KATH: I'm ashamed of you, Dadda. Really ashamed. I think you behave very badly. Lie down, Mr. Sloane. [*To* KEMP] Go and get the Dettol and some water. Make yourself useful. [KEMP *shuffles off.*] I never realized he was antagonistic to you, Mr. Sloane. Perhaps he's jealous. We were getting on so well. [*Pause*] Is it hurting you?

SLOANE: Can you get a bandage?

KATH: I will. [*Goes to the sideboard and rummages in a drawer. Rummages again. Repeat. Second drawer. Takes out and places on top of the sideboard a Boots folder containing snapshots and negatives, a reel of cotton, a piece of unfinished knitting, a tattered knitting pattern, a broken china figure, a magazine, a doorknob, and several pieces of silk.*]

SLOANE: [*Calling impatiently*] There's blood running on your settee. You'll have a stain, I can see it coming.

KATH: [*Runs back with a piece of silk. Lifts his leg. Spreads the silk under the bloody patch.*] This'll do. It's a piece of material my brother brought back. It's good stuff. I was intending to make a blouse but there's not enough.

SLOANE: What's he doing with that Dettol? Is he gone to Swansea for it?

KATH: [*Shouting*] What are you doing, Dadda? He gets that thick. [*Goes to sideboard.* KEMP *enters with a bottle of Dettol.* KATH *takes it from him.*] You done enough damage for one day. Make yourself scarce. [*He shuffles off.*] And don't be eating anything out there. [*Pushes past him. Returns with a saucepan full of water. After hunting in sideboard finds a torn towel. Comes to* SLOANE. *Kneels.*] What a lovely pair of shoes you got. [*Unlacing his shoes, she takes them off and places them under the settee.*]

SLOANE: I think I'm going to spew. [KATH *hastily holds the saucepan under him.*] No. I'll be all right.

KATH: I wonder, Mr. Sloane, if you'd take your trousers off? I hope you don't think there's anything behind the request. [*Looks at him. He unloosens his belt.*] I expect you guessed as much before I asked. If you'll lift up I'll pull them off. [KATH *tugs the trousers free.* SLOANE *tucks*

211

the tail of his shirt between his legs.] That's right. [*Pause.*]
Where is it, then?

SLOANE: Here. [*Pointing and lifting his leg.*]

KATH: He attacked you from behind? If you ask me it's
only a deep scratch. [*Pause.*] I don't think we'll require
outside assistance. [*Pause.*] Don't be embarrassed, Mr.
Sloane. I'd the upbringing a nun would envy and that's
the truth. Until I was fifteen I was more familiar with
Africa than my own body. That's why I'm so pliable.
[*Applies Dettol.*]

SLOANE: Ouch!

KATH: Just the thing for the germs. [*Pause.*] You've a skin
on you like a princess. Better than on those tarts you see
dancing about on the telly. I like a lad with a smooth
body. [*Stops dabbing his leg. Takes up the bandage.
Rises. Fetches a pair of scissors. Cuts bandage. Ties it
around* SLOANE's *leg.*] Isn't it strange that the hairs on
your legs should be dark?

SLOANE: Eh?

KATH: Attractive, though.

SLOANE: Dark?

KATH: Yes. You being a blond.

SLOANE: Oh, yes.

KATH: Nature's a funny thing.

(*Ring on the doorbell.*)

SLOANE: Who's that?

KATH: Keep your voice down. [*Pause.*] It's probably her
from the shops. I'll not answer it. She's only got one
subject for talk.

SLOANE: She'll hear.

KATH: Not if you keep your voice down.

(*Prolonged ringing.*)

SLOANE: What about Pop?

KATH: He won't answer. I don't want her in here. She

tells everybody her business. And if she found me in this
predicament she'd think all kinds of things. [*Pause.*] Her
daughter's involved in a court case at the moment. Tells
every detail. The details are endless. I suffer as she
recounts. Oh, Mr. Sloane, if only I'd been born without
ears. [*Silence. Finishes tying the bandage and squats on
her haunches looking up at him. Pause.*] Is that bandage
too tight?

SLOANE: No.

KATH: I wouldn't want to restrict your circulation.

SLOANE: It's okay.

(*She picks up his trousers.*)

KATH: I'll sponge these, and there's a nick in the material.
I'll fix it. [*Puts Dettol, bandage, etc., into the sideboard.*]
This drawer is my medicine cabinet, dear. If you wants
an occasional aspirin help yourself. [*She comes back. He
lies full length; she smiles. Silence. Confidentially*] I've
been doing my washing today and I haven't a stitch on
. . . except my shoes . . . I'm in the rude under this dress.
I tell you because you're bound to have noticed . . .
[*Silence.* SLOANE *attempts to reach his trouser pocket.*]
Don't move, dear. Not yet. Give the blood time to steady
itself. [SLOANE *takes the nylon stocking from between
cushions of settee.*] I wondered where I'd left it.

SLOANE: Is it yours?

KATH: Yes. You'll notice the length? I've got long legs.
Long, elegant legs. [*Kicks out her leg.*] I could give one
or two of them a surprise. [*Pause.*] My look is quite
different when I'm in private. [*Leans over him.*] You can't
see through this dress, can you? I been worried for fear
of embarrassing you. [SLOANE *lifts his hand and touches
the point where he judges her nipple to be.* KATH *leaps
back.*] Mr. Sloane—don't betray your trust.

SLOANE: I just thought—

KATH: I know what you thought. You wanted to see if my
titties were all my own. You're all the same. [*Smirks.*]
I must be careful of you. Have me naked on the floor if

213

I give you a chance. If my brother was to know . . .
[*Pause.*] . . . he's such a possessive man. [*Silence. Stands
up.*] Would you like to go to bed?

SLOANE: It's early.

KATH: You need rest. You've had a shock. [*Pause.*] I'll
bring your supper to your room.

SLOANE: What about my case?

KATH: The Dadda will fetch it. [*Pause.*] Can you get up
the stairs on your own?

SLOANE: Mmmm.

KATH: [*Motions him back. Stands in front of him.*] Just a
minute. [*Calls.*] Dadda! [*Pause.*] Dadda!

(KEMP *appears in the doorway.*)

KEMP: What?

KATH: Turn your face away. Mr. Sloane is passing. He
has no trousers on. [*Quietly to Sloane*] You know the
room?

SLOANE: Yes.

(*Silence.* SLOANE *exits.*)

KATH: [*Calling after him*] Have a bath if you want to, dear.
Treat the conveniences as if they were your own. [*Turns
to* KEMP.] I want an explanation.

KEMP: Yes. Kathy . . .

KATH: Don't Kathy me.

KEMP: But he upset me.

KATH: Upset you? A grown man?

KEMP: I've seen him before.

KATH: You've seen the milkman before. That's no cause
to throw the shears at him.

KEMP: I didn't throw them.

KATH: Oh? I heard different. [*Picks up her handbag and
takes out money.*] Go and fetch his case. It'll be about
fivepence on the bus. [*Presses the money into his hand.*]
The address is 39 St. Hilary's Crescent.

KEMP: Where's that?

KATH: [*Losing her temper*] By the Co-op! Behave yourself.

KEMP: A teetotal club on the corner is there?

KATH: That's the one. Only it is closed. [*Pause.*] Can you find it?

KEMP: I expect so.

(*There is a noise of tapping.*)

KATH: [*Goes to the window. Over her shoulder.*] It's Eddie.

KEMP: What's that?

KATH: [*Speaking to someone outside*] Why don't you come round the right way?

ED: [*Outside the window*] I rung the bell but you was out.

KATH: Are you coming in?

ED: I'll be round. [*Closes the window.*]

KATH: It's Eddie.

KEMP: I'm not going to talk to him!

KATH: I don't expect he wants you to.

KEMP: He knows I'm in always on Friday. [*Pause.*] I'm signing nothing, you can tell him that.

KATH: Tell him what?

KEMP: That I'm not signing nothing.

ED: [*Entering*] Is he still on? What's the matter with you? [KEMP *does not reply.*] Always on about something.

KEMP: I'm not speaking to him.

ED: [*Patiently*] Go on, get out of it afore I kicks you out. Make me bad, you do. With your silly, childish ways.

(KEMP *does not reply.*)

KATH: Do what I told you, Dadda. Try not to lose yourself. Follow the railings. Then ask somebody.

(KEMP *exits.* KATH *dips towel in saucepan, begins to sponge bloody patch on settee.*)

ED: [*Watches her. Takes a drag of his cigarette.*] What's this I heard about you?

KATH: What?

ED: Listening, are you?

KATH: Yes, Eddie, I'm listening.

ED: You've got a kid staying here.

KATH: No . . .

ED: Don't lie to me.

KATH: He's a guest. He's not a lodger.

ED: Who told you to take in lodgers?

(*Pause.*)

KATH: I needed a bit extra.

ED: I'll give you the money.

KATH: I'm taking Dadda away next year.

(*Pause.*)

ED: I don't want men hanging around.

KATH: He's a nice young man.

ED: You know what these fellows are—young men with no fixed abode.

KATH: No.

ED: You know what they say about landladies?

KATH: No, Eddie.

ED: They say they'd sleep with a broom handle in trousers, that's what they say.

KATH: [*Uneasy*] I'm not like that.

ED: You're good natured, though. They mistake it.

KATH: This young man is quite respectable.

ED: You've got to realize my position. I can't have my sister keeping a common kip. Some of my associates are men of distinction. They think nothing of tipping a fiver. That sort of person. If they realized how my family carry on I'd be banned from the best places. [*Pause.*] And another thing . . . you don't want them talking about you. An' I can't guarantee my influence will keep them quiet. Nosy neighbors and scandal. Oh, my word, the looks you'll get. [*Pause.*] How old is he?

KATH: He's young.

ED: These fellows sleep with their landladies automatic. Has he made suggestions? Suggested you bring him supper in bed?

KATH: No.

ED: That's what they do. Then they take advantage.

KATH: Mr. Sloane is superior to that.

ED: Where did you find him?

KATH: In the library.

ED: Picked him up, did you?

KATH: He was having trouble. With his rent. [*Pause.*] His landlady was unscrupulous.

ED: How long have you been going with him?

KATH: He's a good boy. [ED *sees trousers, picks them up*.] It was an accident.

ED: Had the trousers off him already, I see. [*Balls his fist and punches her upper arm gently.*] Don't let me down, darlin'. [*Pause.*] Where is he?

KATH: Upstairs.

ED: You fetch him.

KATH: He hurt his leg.

ED: I want to see him.

KATH: He's resting. [*Pause.*] Ed, you won't tell him to go?

ED: [*Brushing her aside*] Go and fetch him.

KATH: I'm not misbehaving. Ed, if you send him away I shall cry.

ED: [*Raising his voice*] Let's have less of it. I'll decide. [*She exits.* ED *calls after her.*] Tell him to put his trousers on. [*Picks up the trousers and flings them after her.*] Cantering around the house with a bare bum. Good job I came when I did. [*Pause.*] Can't leave you alone for five minutes.

KATH: [*Off.*] Mr. Sloane! Would you step down here for a minute? My brother would like to meet you. [*Reenters.*] He's trustworthy. Visits his parents once a month. Asked me to go with him. You couldn't object to a visit to a graveyard? The sight of the tombs would deter any looseness. [*Sniffs. Shrugs. Picks through the junk on the sideboard, finds a sweet, and puts it in her mouth.*] He hasn't any mamma of his own. I'm to be his mamma. He's an orphan. Eddie, he wouldn't do wrong. Please don't send him away.

ED: It'd crease me if you misbehaved again. I got responsibilities.

KÁTH: Let him stay.

ED: Kid like that. Know what they'll say, don't you?

(*Pause.*)

KÁTH: He's cultured, Ed. He's informed. [ED *turns and lights another cigarette from the butt of the one he is smoking. Opens the windows. Throws the butt out.* SLOANE *enters.*] This is my brother, Mr. Sloane. He expressed a desire to meet you.

ED: [*Turns, faces* SLOANE.] I . . . my sister was telling me about you. [*Pause.*] My sister was telling me about you being an orphan, Mr. Sloane.

SLOANE: [*Smiling*] Oh, yes?

ED: Must be a rotten life for a kid. You look well on it, though.

SLOANE: Yes.

ED: I could never get used to sleeping in cubicles. Was it a mixed home?

SLOANE: Just boys.

ED: Ideal. How many to a room?

SLOANE: Eight.

ED: Really? Same age, were they? Or older?

SLOANE: The ages varied by a year or two.

ED: Oh well, you had compensations, then. Keep you out of mischief, eh? [*Laughs.*] Well, your childhood wasn't unhappy?

SLOANE: No.

ED: Sounds as though it was a happy atmosphere. [*Pause.*] Got anything to do, Kath?

KATH: No.

ED: No beds to make?

KATH: I made them this morning.

ED: Maybe you forgot to change the pillow slips?

KATH: [*Going*] Eddie, don't let me be upset, will you? [*Exits.*]

ED: I must apologize for her behavior. She's not in the best of health.

SLOANE: She seems all right.

ED: You can't always go on appearances. She's . . . well,
I wouldn't say unbalanced. No, that'd be going too far.
She suffers from migraine. That's why it'd be best if you
declined her offer of a room.

SLOANE: I see.

ED: When are you going?

SLOANE: But I like it here.

ED: I dare say you do. The fact is my sister's taking on too
many responsibilities. She's a charming woman as a rule.
Charming. I've no hesitation in saying that. Lost her
husband. And her little kid. Tell you, did she?

SLOANE: She mentioned it.

ED: [Wary] What did she say?

SLOANE: Said she married young.

ED: She married a mate of mine—a valiant man—we were
together in Africa.

SLOANE: In the army?

ED: You're interested in the army, eh? Soldiers, garrison
towns, etc. Does that interest you?

SLOANE: Yes.

ED: Good, excellent. How old are you?

SLOANE: Twenty.

ED: Married?

SLOANE: No.

ED: [Laughs.] Wise man, eh? Wise man. [Pause.] Girl
friends?

SLOANE: No.

ED: No. You're a librarian?

SLOANE: No.

ED: I thought she said—

SLOANE: I help out at Len's . . . the tobacconist. Give him
a hand. I'm not employed there.

ED: I was told you were.

SLOANE: I help out. On Saturdays.

ED: I see. I've been mistaken. [Silence.] Well, as I just
said . . . I don't think it'd suit you. What with one thing
and another. [Pause.] To show there's no hard feelings
I'll make it worth your while. Call it a gift.

SLOANE: That's decent of you.

ED: Not at all. [*Pause.*] I'd like to give you a little present. Anything you care to name. Within reason.

SLOANE: What's within reason?

ED: [*Laughs.*] Well . . . no . . . Jags. [*Laughs.*] . . . No sports cars. I'm not going as far as that.

SLOANE: [*Relaxing*] I was going to suggest an Aston Martin.

ED: [*Walks from the window looking for an ashtray. He does not find one.*] I wish I could give you one, boy. I wish I could. [*Stubs out his cigarette into a glass sea-shell on the sideboard.*] Are you a sports fan? Eh? Fond of sport? You look as though you might be. Look the . . . outdoor type, I'd say.

SLOANE: I am.

ED: I'd say you were. That's what struck me when you walked in. That's what puzzled me. She gave me the impression you were . . . well, don't be offended. . . . I had the notion you were a shop assistant.

SLOANE: Never worked in a shop in my life.

ED: No. [*Pause.*] I see you're not that type. You're more of a . . . as you might say . . . the fresh-air type.

SLOANE: I help out on Saturdays for a mate of mine. Len. You might know him. Lifeguard at the baths one time. Nice chap.

ED: You're fond of swimming?

SLOANE: I like a plunge now and then.

ED: Body-building?

SLOANE: We had a nice little gym at the orphanage. Put me in all the teams they did. Relays . . . [ED *looks interested.*] soccer . . . [ED *nods.*] pole vault . . . long distance . . . [ED *opens his mouth.*] 100 yards, discus, putting the shot. [ED *rub his hands together.*] Yes. Yes. I'm an all-rounder. A great all-rounder. In anything you care to mention. Even in life . . . [ED *lifts up a warning finger.*] Yes, I like a good workout now and then.

ED: I used to do a lot of that at one time. With my mate . . . we used to do all what you've just said. [*Pause.*] We were young. Innocent too. [*Shrugs. Pats his pocket. Takes out a packet of cigarettes. Smokes.*] All over now. [*Pause.*] Developing your muscles, eh? And character. [*Pause.*] . . . Well, well, well. [*Breathless*] A little body-

builder, are you? I bet you are. . . . [*Slowly*] . . . Do you
. . . [*Shy*] exercise regular?

SLOANE: As clockwork.

ED: Good, good. Stripped?

SLOANE: Fully.

ED: Complete. [*Striding to the window*] How invigorating.

SLOANE: And I box. I'm a bit of a boxer.

ED: Ever done any wrestling?

SLOANE: On occasions.

ED: So, so.

SLOANE: I've got a full chest. Narrow hips. My biceps are—

ED: Do you wear leather . . . next to the skin? Leather
jeans, say? Without . . . aah . . .

SLOANE: Pants?

ED: [*Laughs.*] Get away! [*Pause.*] The question is are you
clean-living? You may as well know I set great store by
morals. Too much of this casual bunking up nowadays.
Too many lads being ruined by birds. I don't want you
messing about with my sister.

SLOANE: I wouldn't.

ED: Have you made overtures to her?

SLOANE: No.

ED: Would you?

SLOANE: No.

ED: Not if circumstances were ripe?

SLOANE: Never.

ED: Does she disgust you?

SLOANE: Should she?

ED: It would be better if she did.

SLOANE: I've no interest in her.

(*Pause.*)

ED: I've a certain amount of influence. Friends with
money. I've two cars. Judge for yourself. I generally
spend my holidays in places where the bints have got
rings through their noses. [*Pause.*] Women are like
banks, boy, breaking and entering is a serious business.
Give me your word you're not vaginalatrous?

SLOANE: I'm not.

221

ED: [*Pause.*] I'll believe you. Can you drive?

SLOANE: Yes.

ED: I might let you be my chauffeur.

SLOANE: Would you?

ED: [*Laughs.*] We'll see. . . . I could get you a uniform. Boots, pants, a guaranteed 100 per cent no-imitation jacket . . . an . . . er . . . a white brushed-nylon T-shirt . . . with a little leather cap. [*Laughs.*] Like that? [SLOANE *nods. Silence.*] Kip here a bit. Till we get settled. Come and see me. We'll discuss salary arrangements and any other business. Here's my card. [*Gives* SLOANE *a card.*] Have you seen my old dad?

SLOANE: I spoke to him.

ED: Wonderful for his age. [*Pause.*] Call her in, will you?

(SLOANE *exits.*)

SLOANE: [*Off*] I think you're wanted. [*Reenters.*]

ED: You'll find me a nice employer. [*Pause.*] When you come to see me we must have a drink. A talk.

SLOANE: What about?

ED: Life. Sport. Love. Anything you care to name. Don't forget.

SLOANE: I'm looking forward to it.

ED: Do you drink?

SLOANE: When I'm not in training.

ED: You aren't in training at the moment, are you?

SLOANE: No.

ED: I wouldn't want you to break your training. Drinking I don't mind. Drugs I abhor. You'll get to know all my habits.

(KATH *enters.*)

KATH: What you want?

ED: A word with you afore I go.

KATH: Are you staying, Mr. Sloane?

ED: 'Course he's staying.

KATH: All right, is it?

ED: He's going to work for me.

KATH: [*Pause.*] He isn't going away, is he?

ED: Offered him a job, I have. I want a word with my sister, Sloane. Would you excuse us?

(SLOANE *nods, smiles, and turns to go.*)

KATH: [*As he exits*] Have a meal, Mr. Sloane. You'll find a quarter of boiled ham. Help yourself. You better have what's left 'cause I see he's been wolfing it. An' you heard me ask him to wait, di'n't you? I told him.

(*Exit* SLOANE. *Silence.*)

ED: You picked a nice lad there. Very nice. Clean. No doubt upright. A sports enthusiast. All the proper requisites. Don't take any money from him. I'll pay.

KATH: Can I buy him a shirt?

ED: What do you want to do that for?

KATH: His own mamma can't.

ED: He can buy his own clothes. Making yourself look ridiculous.

(*Pause.*)

KATH: When it's Christmas can I buy him a little gift?

ED: No.

KATH: Send him a card?

ED: Why?

KATH: I'd like to. I'd show you beforehand. [*Pause.*] Can I go to his mamma's grave?

ED: If you want. [*Pause.*] He'll laugh at you.

KATH: He wouldn't, Eddie.

(*Silence.*)

ED: I must go. I'll have a light meal. Take a couple of Nembutal and then bed. I shall be out of town tomorrow.

KATH: Where?

ED: In Aylesbury. I shall dress in a quiet suit. Drive up in the motor. The commissionaire will spring forward.

There in that miracle of glass and concrete my colleagues and me will have a quiet drink before the business of the day.

KATH: Are your friends nice?

ED: Mature men.

KATH: No ladies?

(*Pause.*)

ED: What are you talking about? I live in a world of top decisions. We've no time for ladies.

KATH: Ladies are nice at a gathering.

ED: We don't want a lot of half-witted tarts.

KATH: They add color and gaiety.

ED: Frightening everyone with their clothes.

(*Pause.*)

KATH: I hope you have a nice time. Perhaps one day you'll invite me to your hotel.

ED: I might.

KATH: Show me round.

ED: Yes.

KATH: Is it exquisitely furnished? High up?

ED: Very high. I see the river often. [*A door slams.*] Persuade the old man to speak to me.

KEMP: [*Off*] Is he gone?

KATH: Speak to him, Dadda. He's something to ask you.

(*Silence.*)

ED: [*Petulant*] Isn't it incredible? I'm his only son. He won't see me. [*Goes to the door. Speaks through.*] I want a word with you. [*Pause.*] Is he without human feelings? [*Pause. Brokenly.*] He won't speak to me. Has he no heart?

KATH: Come again.

ED: I'll get my lawyer to send a letter. If it's done legal he'll prove amenable. Give us a kiss. [*Kisses her. Pats her bottom.*] Be a good girl now. [*Exit.*]

KATH: Cheerio. [*Pause.*] I said cheerio. [*Door slams.* KATH *goes to door.*] Why don't you speak to him? [KEMP *enters. He does not reply.*] He invited me to his suite. The luxury takes your breath away. Money is no object. A waitress comes with the tea. [*Pause.*] I'm going to see him there one day. Speak to him, Dadda.

KEMP: No.

KATH: Please.

KEMP: Never.

KATH: Let me phone saying you changed your mind.

KEMP: No.

KATH: Let me phone.

KEMP: No.

KATH: [*Tearfully*] Oh, Dadda, you are unfair. If you don't speak to him he won't invite me to his suite. It's a condition. I won't be able to go. You found that address?

KEMP: I got lost, though.

KATH: Why didn't you ask? [*Pause.*] You had a tongue in your head. Oh, Dadda, you make me so angry with your silly ways. [*Pause.*] What was the house like?

KEMP: I didn't notice.

KATH: He said it was a hovel. A boy like him shouldn't be expected to live with the rougher elements. Do you know, Dadda, he has skin the like of which I never felt before. And he confesses to being an orphan. His story is so sad. I wept when I heard it. You know how soft-hearted I am.

(*Silence.*)

KEMP: I haven't been feeling well lately.

KATH: Have you seen the optician?

KEMP: My eyes are getting much worse.

KATH: Without a word of a lie you are like a little child.

KEMP: I'm all alone.

KATH: You have me.

KEMP: He may take you away.

KATH: Where to?

KEMP: Edinburgh.

KATH: Too cold.

KEMP: Or Bournemouth. You always said you'd go somewhere with palms.

KATH: I'd always consult you first.

KEMP: You'd put me in a home. [*Pause.*] Would you be
tempted?

(*Silence.*)

KATH: You ought to consult an oculist. See your oculist at
once. [*Pause.*] Go to bed. I'll bring you a drinkie. In the
morning you'll feel different.

KEMP: You don't love me.

KATH: I've never stopped loving you.

KEMP: I'm going to die, Kath. . . . I'm dying.

KATH: [*Angrily*] You've been at that ham, haven't you?
Half a jar of pickles you've put away. Don't moan to
me if you're up half the night with the tummy ache. I've
got no sympathy for you.

KEMP: Good night, then.

KATH: [*Watches him out of the door. Looks through into
the kitchen.*] All right, Mr. Sloane? Help yourself . . .
all right? [*Comes back into the room. Takes lamp from
sideboard and puts it onto table beside settee. Goes to
record player, puts on record. Pulls curtains across
alcove and disappears behind them. The stage is empty.
The record plays for a few seconds and then the needle
jumps a groove, slides across record. Automatic change
switches record off.* KATH *pokes her head from behind
curtain, looks at record player, disappears again. Re-
appears wearing a transparent negligee. Picks up aerosol
spray, sprays room. Calls through door.*] Have you
finished, Mr. Sloane, dear?

SLOANE: [*Off*] Ugh?

KATH: You have? I'm so glad. I don't want to disturb you
at your food. [*Sees knitting on sideboard, picks it up.*]
Come into the lounge if you wish. I'm just at a quiet
bit of knitting before I go to bed. [SLOANE *enters wiping
his mouth.*] A lovely piece of ham, wasn't it?

SLOANE: Lovely.

KATH: I'll give you a splendid breakfast in the morning. [*Realizes that there is only one needle in the knitting. Searches in the junk and finds the other. Takes it to the settee.* SLOANE *sits on one end. Pause.*] Isn't this room gorgeous?

SLOANE: Yes.

KATH: That vase over there come from Bombay. Do you have any interest in that part of the world?

SLOANE: I like Dieppe.

KATH: Ah . . . it's all the same. I don't suppose they know the difference themselves. Are you comfortable? Let me plump your cushion. [*Plumps a cushion behind his head. Laughs lightly.*] I really by rights should ask you to change places. This light is showing me up. [*Pause.*] I blame it on the manufacturers. They make garments so thin nowadays you'd think they intended to provoke a rape. [*Pause.*] Sure you're comfy? [*Leans over him.*]

(SLOANE *pulls her hand toward him. She laughs, half in panic.*)

SLOANE: You're a teaser, ent you?

KATH: [*Breaks away.*] I hope I'm not. I was trying to find the letter from my little boy's father. I treasure it. But I seem to have mislaid it. I found a lot of photos, though.

SLOANE: Yes.

KATH: Are you interested in looking through them? [*Brings the snapshots over.*]

SLOANE: Are they him?

KATH: My lover.

SLOANE: Bit blurred.

KATH: It brings back memories. He reminds me of you. [*Pause.*] He too was handsome and in the prime of manhood. Can you wonder I fell. [*Pause.*] I wish he were here now to love and protect me. [*Leans her arm on his shoulder. Shows him another snap.*] This is me. I was younger then.

SLOANE: Smart.

KATH: Yes, my hair was nice.

SLOANE: Yes.

KATH: An' this . . . I don't know whether I ought to let you see it. [SLOANE *attempts to seize it.*] Now then!

SLOANE: [*Takes it from her.*] A seat in a wood?

KATH: That seat is erected to the memory of Mrs. Gwen Lewis. She was a lady who took a lot of trouble with invalids. [*Pause.*] It was near that seat that my baby was thought of.

SLOANE: On that seat?

KATH: [*Shyly*] Not on it exactly. Nearby . . .

SLOANE: In the bushes? . . .

KATH: [*Giggles.*] Yes. [*Pause.*] He was rough with me.

SLOANE: Uncomfortable, eh?

KATH: I couldn't describe my feelings. [*Pause.*] I don't think the fastening on this thing I'm wearing will last much longer. [*The snapshots slip from her hand.*] There! you've knocked the photos on the floor. [*Pause: he attempts to move; she is almost on top of him.*] Mr. Sloane . . . [*Rolls onto him.*] You should wear more clothes, Mr. Sloane. I believe you're as naked as me. And there's no excuse for it. [*Silence.*] I'll be your mamma. I need to be loved. Gently. Oh! I shall be so ashamed in the morning. [*Switches off the light.*] What a big heavy baby you are. Such a big heavy baby.

CURTAIN

ACT II

Some months later. Morning.

SLOANE *is lying on the settee wearing boots, leather trousers, and a white T-shirt. A newspaper covers his face.* KATH *enters. Looks at the settee.*

SLOANE: Where you been?

KATH: Shopping, dear. Did you want me?

SLOANE: I couldn't find you.

KATH: [*Goes to the window. Takes off her headscarf.*] What's Eddie doing?

SLOANE: A bit of servicing.

KATH: But that's your job.

(SLOANE *removes the newspaper.*)

KATH: He shouldn't do your work.

SLOANE: I was on the beer. My guts is playing up.

KATH: Poor boy. [*Pause.*] Go and help him. For mamma's sake.

SLOANE: I may go in a bit.

KATH: He's a good employer. Studies your interests. You want to think of his position. He's proud of it. Now you're working for him his position is your position. [*Pause.*] Go and give him a hand.

SLOANE: No.

KATH: Are you too tired?

SLOANE: Yes.

KATH: We must make allowances for you. You're young. [*Pause.*] You're not taking advantage, are you?

SLOANE: No.

KATH: I know you aren't. When you've had a drinkie go and help him.

SLOANE: If you want.

(*Pause.*)

KATH: Did mamma hear you were on the razzle?

SLOANE: Yes.

KATH: Did you go up West? You were late coming home. [*Pause.*] Very late.

SLOANE: Three of my mates and me had a night out.

KATH: Are they nice boys?

SLOANE: We have interests in common.

KATH: They aren't roughs, are they? Mamma doesn't like you associating with them.

SLOANE: Not on your life. They're gentle. Refined youths. Thorpe, Beck, and Doolan. We toured the nighteries in the motor.

KATH: Was Ed with you?

SLOANE: No.

KATH: Did you ask him? He would have come.

SLOANE: He was tired. A hard day yesterday.

KATH: Ask him next time.

(*Pause.*)

SLOANE: We ended up at a fabulous place. Soft music, pink shades, lovely atmosphere.

KATH: I hope you behaved yourself.

SLOANE: One of the hostesses gave me her number. Told me to ring her.

KATH: Take no notice of her. She might not be nice.

SLOANE: Not nice?

KATH: She might be a party girl.

(*Pause.*)

SLOANE: What exactly do you mean?

KATH: Mamma worries for you.

SLOANE: You're attempting to run my life.

KATH: Is baby cross?

SLOANE: You're developing distinctly possessive tendencies.

KATH: You can get into trouble saying that.

SLOANE: A possessive woman.

KATH: A mamma can't be possessive.

SLOANE: Can't she?

KATH: You know she can't. You're being naughty.

SLOANE: Never heard of a possessive mum?

KATH: Stop it. It's rude. Did she teach you to say that?

SLOANE: What?

KATH: What you just said. [SLOANE *makes no reply*.] You're spoiling yourself in my eyes, Mr. Sloane. You won't ring this girl, will you?

SLOANE: I haven't decided.

KATH: Decide now. To please me. I don't know what you see in these girls. You have your friends for company.

SLOANE: They're boys.

KATH: What's wrong with them? You can talk freely. Not like with a lady.

SLOANE: I don't want to talk.

(*Pause.*)

KATH: She might be after your money.

SLOANE: I haven't got any.

KATH: But Eddie has. She might be after his.

SLOANE: Look, you're speaking of a very good-class bird.

KATH: I have to protect you, baby, because you're easily led.

SLOANE: I like being led. [*Pause.*] I need to be let out occasionally. Off the lead.

(*Pause.*)

KATH: She'll make you ill.

SLOANE: Shut it. [*Pause.*] Make me ill!

KATH: Girls do.

SLOANE: How dare you. Making filthy insinuations. I won't have it. You disgust me, you do. Standing there without your teeth. Why don't you get smartened up? Get a new rig-out.

(*Pause.*)

KATH: Do I disgust you?

SLOANE: Yes.

KATH: Honest?

SLOANE: And truly. You horrify me. [*Pause.*] You think I'm kidding. I'll give up my room if you don't watch out.

KATH: Oh, no!

SLOANE: Clear out.

KATH: Don't think of such drastic action. I'd never forgive myself if I drove you away. [*Pause.*] I won't anymore. [*He attempts to rise.* KATH *takes his hand.*] Don't go, dear. Stay with me while I collect myself. I've been upset and I need comfort. [*Silence.*] Are you still disgusted?

SLOANE: A bit.

KATH: [*Takes his hand, presses it to her lips.*] Sorry, baby. Better?

SLOANE: Mmmm.

(*Silence.*)

KATH: How good you are to me. [KEMP *enters. He carries a stick. Taps his way to the sideboard.*] My teeth, since you mentioned the subject, Mr. Sloane, are in the kitchen in Stergene. Usually I allow a good soak overnight. But what with one thing and another I forgot. Otherwise I would never be in such a state. [*Pause.*] I hate people who are careless with their dentures.

(KEMP *opens a drawer.*)

KEMP: Seen my tablets?

KATH: If you're bad go to bed.

KEMP: I need one o' my pills. [*He picks his way through the junk.*]

SLOANE: [*Goes over to him.*] What you want?

KEMP: Let me alone.

SLOANE: Tell me what you want.

KEMP: I don't want no help. [*Pause.*] I'm managing.

232

SLOANE: Let me know what you want and I'll look for it.
KEMP: I can manage.

(SLOANE *goes back to the settee. Silence.*)

KATH: What a lot of foreigners there are about lately. I
see one today. Playing the accordion. They live in a
world of their own, these people.
KEMP: Colored?
KATH: No.
KEMP: I expect he was. They do come over here. Raping
people. It's a problem. Just come out o' jail, had he?
KATH: I really didn't stop long enough to ask. I just com-
mented on the tune he was playing.
KEMP: Oh, they're all for that.
KATH: [*Leans over* SLOANE.] Mamma has something special
to say to you.
KEMP: All for that.
SLOANE: [*Touches her hair.*] What?
KATH: [*To* KEMP, *louder*] I don't think he was dark enough
to be colored, Dadda. Honestly I don't.
KEMP: They should send them back.
SLOANE: What's your news?
KATH: Can't you guess.
SLOANE: No.
KATH: I know you can't.
KEMP: You should've put in a complaint.
KATH: Oh, no, Dadda.
KEMP: Playing his bloody music in the street.
KATH: What language! You should be a splendid example
to us. Instead of which you carry on like a common
workman. Don't swear like that in my presence again.

(*Silence.* SLOANE *attempts to grab her shopping bag. She
rises,* SLOANE *touches her up. She grunts. Smacks his
hand.*)

KEMP: What's up?
KATH: Nothing. Aren't the tulips glorious this year by the

municipal offices. What a brave showing. They must spend a fortune.

SLOANE: What have you bought me?

KATH: Mamma is going to have a . . . [*Makes a rocking motion with her arms.*]

SLOANE: What? [*Pause.*] What?

KATH: A little—[*Looks over to* KEMP. *Makes the motion of rocking a baby in her arms. Purses her lips. Blows a kiss.* SLOANE *sits up. Points to himself.* KATH *nods her head. Presses her mouth to his ear: whispers.*] A baby brother.

KEMP: What are you having?

KATH: A . . . bath, Dadda. You know that woman from the shops? [*Pause.*] You wouldn't believe what a ridiculous spectacle she's making of herself.

KEMP: Oh.

KATH: [*To* SLOANE] 'Course it's ever so dangerous at my age. But Doctor thinks it'll be all right.

SLOANE: Sure.

KATH: I was worried in case you'd be cross.

SLOANE: We mustn't let anyone know.

KATH: It's our secret. [*Pause.*] I'm excited.

KEMP: Are you having it after tea, Kath?

KATH: Why?

KEMP: I thought of having one as well. Are you there?

KATH: Yes.

KEMP: Have you seen them pills?

KATH: Have I seen his pills. They're where you left them, I expect. [*Goes to the sideboard. Finds bottle. Gives it to* KEMP.] How many you had today?

KEMP: Two.

KATH: They're not meant to be eaten like sweets, you know. [*He exits.*] I been to the Register Office.

SLOANE: What for?

KATH: To inquire about the license.

SLOANE: Who?

KATH: You.

SLOANE: Who to?

KATH: Me. Don't you want to? You wouldn't abandon me? Leave me to face the music.

SLOANE: What music?

KATH: When Eddie hears.

SLOANE: He mustn't hear.

KATH: Baby, how can we stop him?

SLOANE: He'd kill me. I'd be out of a job.

KATH: I suppose we couldn't rely on him employing you any longer.

SLOANE: Don't say anything. I'll see a man I know.

KATH: What? But I'm looking forward to having a new little brother.

SLOANE: Out of the question.

KATH: Please . . .

SLOANE: No. In any case I couldn't marry you. I'm not the type. And all things being equal I may not be living here much longer.

KATH: Aren't you comfy in your bed?

SLOANE: Yes.

KATH: [*Folds her arms around him. Kisses his head.*] We could marry in secret. Couldn't you give me something, baby? So's I feel in my mind we were married?

SLOANE: What like?

KATH: A ring. Or a bracelet? You got a nice locket. I noticed it. Make me a present of that.

SLOANE: I can't do that.

KATH: As a token of your esteem. So's I feel I belong to you.

SLOANE: It belonged to my mum.

KATH: I'm your mamma now.

SLOANE: No.

KATH: Go on.

SLOANE: But it was left to me.

KATH: You mustn't cling to old memories. I shall begin to think you don't love mamma.

SLOANE: I do.

KATH: Then give me that present. [*Unhooks the chain.*] Ta.

SLOANE: I hate parting with it.

KATH: I'll wear it for ever.

(ED *enters. Stands smoking a cigarette. Turns. Exits. Reenters with a cardboard box.*)

ED: This yours?

KATH: [*Goes over. Looks in the box.*] It's my gnome.

ED: They just delivered it.

KATH: The bad weather damaged him. His little hat come off. I sent him to the Gnomes' Hospital to be repaired.

ED: Damaged, was he?

KATH: Yes.

ED: Well, well. [*Pause.*] It's monkey weather out there.

SLOANE: I wasn't cold.

ED: You're young. Healthy. Don't feel the cold, do you?

SLOANE: No.

ED: Not at all?

SLOANE: Sometimes.

ED: Not often. [*Pause.*] I expect it's all that orange juice.

KATH: Mr. Sloane was coming out, Eddie. I assure you.

ED: I know that. I can trust him.

KATH: You've a lovely color. Let me feel your hand. Why, it's freezing. You feel his hand, Mr. Sloane.

ED: He doesn't want to feel my hand. [*Pause.*] When you're ready, boy, we'll go.

SLOANE: Check the oil?

ED: Mmn.

SLOANE: Petrol?

ED: Mmn. [*Pause.*] Down, en it?

SLOANE: Down?

ED: From yesterday. We filled her up yesterday.

SLOANE: Did we? Was it yesterday?

ED: Mmn. [*Pause.*] We used a lot since then.

SLOANE: You ought to get yourself a new car. It eats petrol.

(*Pause.*)

ED: Maybe you're right. You didn't use it last night, did you?

SLOANE: Me?

ED: I thought you might have.

SLOANE: No.

ED: Funny.

(*Silence.*)

KATH: I see a woolly in Boyce's, Mr. Sloane. I'm giving it
  you as a birthday present.

ED: What do you want to do that for?

KATH: Mr. Sloane won't mind.

ED: Chucking money about.

KATH: Mr. Sloane doesn't mind me. He's one of the family.

ED: Hark at it. Shove up, boy.

SLOANE: [*Moves.*] Sit by me.

ED: [*Sits next to him.*] You didn't use my motor last night,
  then?

SLOANE: No.

ED: That's all I wanted. As long as you're telling the truth,
  boy. [*He takes* SLOANE's *hand.*] You've an honest hand.
  Square. What a grip you got.

SLOANE: I'm improving.

ED: Yes, I can tell that. You've grown bolder since we met.
  Bigger and bolder. Don't get too bold, will you? Eh?
  [*Laughs.*] I'm going to buy you something for your
  birthday as well.

SLOANE: Can I rely on it?

ED: Aah.

SLOANE: Will it be expensive?

ED: Very. I might consider lashing out a bit and buying
  you a . . . um, er, aahhh . . .

SLOANE: Thank you. Thank you.

ED: Don't thank me. Thank yourself. You deserve it.

SLOANE: I think I do.

ED: I think you do. Go and put that box in the kitchen.

KATH: It's no trouble, Eddie.

ED: Let the boy show you politeness.

KATH: But he does. Often. He's often polite to me. [SLOANE
  picks up the box and exits.] I never complain.

(*Pause.*)

ED: Where was he last night?

KATH: He watched the telly. A program where people
  guessed each other's names.

ED: What else?

KATH: Nothing else.

ED: He used the car last night.

KATH: No.

(*Pause.*)

ED: If he's not careful he can have his cards.

KATH: He's only young.

ED: Joy-riding in my motor.

KATH: He's a good boy.

ED: Act your age. [*Pause.*] Encouraging him. I've watched you. What you want to keep him in here for all morning?

KATH: I didn't want him here. I told him to go and help you.

ED: You did? And he wouldn't?

KATH: No. Yes.

ED: What do you mean?

KATH: I thought it was his rest period, Eddie. You do give him a rest sometimes. I know, 'cause you're a good employer. [*Sits beside him.*]

ED: What do I pay him for?

KATH: To keep him occupied, I suppose.

ED: [*Makes no reply. At last, irritated.*] You're a pest, you are.

KATH: I'm sorry.

ED: [*Glances at her.*] Keeping him in when he ought to be at work. How do you expect him to work well with you messing about?

KATH: He was just coming.

ED: Taking him from his duty. Wasting my money.

KATH: I won't anymore.

ED: It's too late. I'll pay him off. Not satisfactory.

KATH: No.

ED: Not the type of person that I had expected.

KATH: He likes his work.

ED: He can go elsewhere.

KATH: He's a great help to me. I shall cry if he goes away. [*Pause.*] I shall have to take a sedative.

238

ED: I'll find someone else for you.

KATH: No.

ED: An older man. With more maturity.

KATH: I want my baby.

ED: Your what?

KATH: I'm his mamma and he appreciates me. [*Pause.*] He told me.

ED: When? When?

KATH: I can't remember.

ED: He loves you?

KATH: No, I didn't say that. But he calls me Mamma. I love him 'cause I have no little boy of my own. And if you send him away I shall cry like the time you took my real baby.

ED: You were wicked then.

KATH: I know.

ED: Being rude. Ruining my little matie. Teaching him nasty things. That's why I sent it away. [*Pause.*] You're not doing rude things with this kiddy, are you, like you did with Tommy?

KATH: No.

ED: Sure?

KATH: I love him like a mamma.

ED: I can't trust you.

KATH: I'm a trustworthy lady.

ED: Allowing him to kip here was a mistake.

(*Silence.*)

KATH: I never wanted to do rude things. Tommy made me.

ED: Liar!

KATH: Insisted. Pestered me, he did. All summer.

ED: You're a liar.

KATH: Am I?

ED: He didn't want anything to do with you. He told me that.

KATH: You're making it up.

ED: I'm not.

KATH: He loved me.

ED: He didn't.

KATH: He wanted to marry me.

ED: Marry you? You're a ridiculous figure and no mistake.

KATH: He'd have married me only his folks were against it.

ED: I always imagined you were an intelligent woman. I find you're not.

KATH: He said they was.

ED: Did he? When?

KATH: When the stork was coming.

ED: [*Laughs.*] Well, well. Fancy you remembering. You must have a long memory.

KATH: I have.

ED: Let me disillusion you.

KATH: Don't hurt me, Eddie.

ED: You need hurting, you do. Mr. and Mrs. Albion Bolter were quite ready to have you marry Tommy.

KATH: No they wasn't.

ED: Allow me to know.

KATH: [*Pause.*] He wouldn't have lied, Ed. You're telling stories.

ED: I'm not.

KATH: But he said it was 'cause I was poor. [*Pause.*] I couldn't fit into the social background demanded of him. His duty came between us.

ED: You could have been educated. Gone to beauty salons. Learned to speak well.

KATH: No.

ED: They wanted you to marry him. Tommy and me had our first set-to about it. You should have heard the language he used to me.

KATH: I was loved. How can you say that?

ED: Forget it.

KATH: He sent me the letter I treasure.

ED: I burned it.

(*Pause.*)

KATH: It was his last words to me.

ED: And that kiddy out there. I'm not having him go the same way.

KATH: [*Goes to the window.*] Did you burn my letter?

ED: Yes. [*Pause.*] And that old photo as well. I thought you was taking an unhealthy interest in the past.

KATH: The photo as well?

ED: You forget it.

KATH: I promised to show it to someone. I wondered why I couldn't find it.

ED: You wicked girl.

KATH: I'm not wicked. I think you're wicked. [*Sniffs without dignity.*]

ED: [*Lights a cigarette. Looks at her.*] While I'm at it I'll get the old man to look at those papers. [*Pause.*] Get my case in, will you? [*She does not reply. He stands up. Exits. Returns with briefcase.*] I made a mark where he's to sign. On the dotted line. [*Laughs.*] I'll be glad when it's over. To use an expression foreign to my nature —I'll be bloody glad. [*Stares at* KATH *as she continues to cry. Turns away. Pause.*] Quit bawling, will you? [KATH *blows her nose on the edge of her apron.*] You should be like me. You'd have something to cry over then, if you got responsibilities like me. [*Silence.*] Haven't you got a hankie? You don't want the boy to see you like that? [*Silence.* SLOANE *enters.*] Put it away, did you?

SLOANE: Yes.

ED: That's a good boy.

(*Pause.*)

KATH: Mr. Sloane.

SLOANE: What?

KATH: Can *I* call you boy?

SLOANE: I don't think you'd better.

KATH: Why not?

ED: I'm his employer, see. He knows that you're only his landlady.

(SLOANE *smiles.*)

KATH: I don't mean in front of strangers. [*Pause.*] I'd be sparing with the use of the name.

ED: No! [*Sharply*] Haven't you got anything to do? Standing there all day. [KATH *exits*.] Getting fat as a pig, she is.

SLOANE: Is she?

ED: Not noticed?

SLOANE: No.

ED: I have.

SLOANE: How old is she?

ED: Forty-one. [*Shrugs*.] Forty-two. She ought to slim.
I'd advise that.

SLOANE: She's . . .

ED: She's like a sow. Though she is my sister.

SLOANE: She's not bad.

ED: No?

SLOANE: I don't think so.

(ED *goes to the window. Stands. Lost. Pause.*)

ED: Where was you last night?

SLOANE: I told you—

ED: I know what you told me. A pack of lies. D'you think
I'm an idiot or something?

SLOANE: No.

ED: I want the truth.

SLOANE: I went for a spin. I had a headache.

ED: Where did you go?

SLOANE: Along the A40.

ED: Who went with you?

SLOANE: Nobody.

ED: Are you being entirely honest?

(*Pause.*)

SLOANE: Three mates come with me.

ED: They had headaches too?

SLOANE: I never asked.

ED: Cheeky. [*Pause.*] Who are they? Would I want them
in my motor?

SLOANE: You'd recognize Harry Thorpe. Small, clear-
complexioned, infectious good humor.

ED: I might.

SLOANE: Harry Beck I brought up one night. A Wednesday it was. But Doolan no. You wouldn't know him.

ED: Riding around in my motor all night, eh?

SLOANE: I'd challenge that.

ED: What type of youth are they?

SLOANE: Impeccable taste. Buy their clothes up West.

ED: Any of them wear lipstick?

SLOANE: Certainly not.

ED: You'd notice, would you? [*Throws over a lipstick.*] What's this doing in the back of the motor?

(*Silence.*)

SLOANE: [*Laughs.*] Oh . . . you jogged my memory . . . yes . . . Doolan's married . . . an' we took his wife along.

ED: Can't you do better than that?

SLOANE: Straight up.

ED: [*Emotionally*] Oh, boy. . . . Taking birds out in my motor.

SLOANE: Would you accept an unconditional apology?

ED: Telling me lies.

SLOANE: It won't happen again.

ED: What are your feelings toward me?

SLOANE: I respect you.

ED: Is that the truth?

SLOANE: Honest.

ED: Then why tell me lies?

SLOANE: That's only your impression.

(*Pause.*)

ED: Was this an isolated incident?

SLOANE: This is the first time.

ED: Really.

SLOANE: Yes. Can you believe me?

(*Pause.*)

ED: I believe you. I believe you're regretting the incident already. But don't repeat it. [*Silence.*] Or next time I won't be so lenient. [*Pause.*] I think the time has come for us to make a change.

SLOANE: In what way?

ED: I need you on tap.

SLOANE: Mmmn . . .

(*Pause.*)

ED: At all hours. In case I have to make a journey to a distant place at an unexpected and inconvenient hour of the night. In a manner of speaking it's urgent.

SLOANE: Of course.

ED: I got work to do. [*Pause.*] I think it would be best if you leave here today.

SLOANE: It might be.

ED: Give it a trial. [*Pause.*] You see my way of looking at it?

SLOANE: Sure.

ED: And you shouldn't be left with her. She's no good. No good at all. A crafty tart she is. I could tell you things about—the way these women carry on. [*Pause.*] Especially her. [*Opens window. Throws cigarette out.*] These women do you no good. I can tell you that. [*Feels in his coat pocket. Takes out a packet of mints. Puts one in his mouth. Pause.*] One of sixteen come up to me the other day—which is a thing I never expected, come up to me and said she'd been given my address. I don't know whether it was a joke or something. You see that sort of thing . . .

SLOANE: Well . . . ?

ED: You could check it.

SLOANE: I'd be pleased.

ED: Certainly. I got feelings.

SLOANE: You're sensitive. You can't be bothered.

ED: You got it wrong when you says that. I seen birds all shapes and sizes and I'm most certainly not . . . um . . . ah . . . sensitive.

SLOANE: No?

ED: I just don't give a monkey's fart.

SLOANE: It's a legitimate position.

ED: But I can deal with them same as you.

SLOANE: I'm glad to hear it.

ED: What's your opinion of the way these women carry on?

(*Pause.*)

SLOANE: I feel . . . how would you say?

ED: Don't you think they're crude?

SLOANE: Occasionally. In a way.

ED: You never know where you are with half of them.

SLOANE: All the same it's necessary.

ED: Ah well, you're talking of a different subject entirely. It's necessary. Occasionally. But it's got to be kept within bounds.

SLOANE: I'm with you there. All the way.

ED: [*Laughs.*] I've seen funny things happen and no mistake. The way these birds treat decent fellows. I hope you never get serious with one. What a life. Backache, headache, or her mum told her never to when there's an *R* in the month. [*Pause. Stares from window.*] How do you feel, then?

SLOANE: On the main points we agree.

ED: Pack your bags.

SLOANE: Now?

ED: Immediate.

SLOANE: Will I get a rise in pay?

ED: A rise?

SLOANE: My new situation calls for it.

ED: You already had two.

SLOANE: They were tokens. I'd like you to upgrade my salary. How about a little car?

ED: That's a bit [*Laughs.*] of an unusual request, en it?

SLOANE: You could manage it.

ED: It all costs money. I tell you what—I'll promise you one for Christmas.

SLOANE: This year?

ED: Or next year.

SLOANE: It's a date.

ED: You and me. That's the life, boy. Without doubt I'm glad I met you.

SLOANE: Are you?

ED: I see you had possibilities from the start. You had an air. [*Pause.*] A way with you.

SLOANE: Something about me.

ED: That's it. The perfect phrase. Personality.

SLOANE: Really?

ED: That's why I don't want you living here. Wicked waste. I'm going to tell you something. Prepare to raise your eyebrows.

SLOANE: Yes.

ED: She had a kiddy once.

SLOANE: Go on.

ED: That's right. On the wrong side of the blanket.

SLOANE: Your sister?

ED: I had a matie. What times we had. Fished. Swam. Rolled home pissed at two in the morning. We were innocent, I tell you. Until she came on the scene. [*Pause.*] Teaching him things he shouldn't 'a done. It was over . . . gone . . . finished. [*Clears his throat.*] She got him to put her in the family way, that's what I always maintain. Nothing was the same after. Not ever. A typical story.

SLOANE: Sad, though.

ED: Yes, it is. I should say. Of course, in a way of looking at it, it laid the foundation of my success. I put him to one side, which was difficult because he was alluring. I managed it, though. Got a grip on myself. And finally become a success. [*Pause.*] That's no mean achievement, is it?

SLOANE: No.

ED: I'm proud.

SLOANE: Why shouldn't you be?

ED: I'm the possessor of two bank accounts. Respected in my own right. And all because I turned my back on him. Does that impress you?

SLOANE: It impresses me.

ED: I have no hesitation in saying that it was worth it. None.

(*The door opens slowly,* KEMP *stands waiting, staring in, listening.*)

SLOANE: What is it, Pop?

(KEMP *enters the room, listens, backs to the door. Stops.*)

KEMP: Is Ed there with you? [*Pause.*] Ed?

ED: [*With emotion*] Dad . . . [*He goes to* KEMP, *puts an arm around his shoulder.*] What's come over you? [KEMP *clutches* ED'*s coat, almost falls to his knees.* ED *supports him.*] Don't kneel to me. I forgive you. I'm the one to kneel.

KEMP: No, no.

ED: Pat me on the head. Pronounce a blessing. Forgive and forget, eh? I'm sorry and so are you.

KEMP: I want a word with you. [*He squints in* SLOANE'*s direction.*] Something to tell you.

ED: Words. Dad. A string of words. We're together again.

(*Pause.*)

KEMP: Tell him to go.

ED: Dad, what manners you got. How rude you've become.

KEMP: I got business to discuss.

SLOANE: He can speak in front of me, can't he, Ed?

ED: I've no secrets from the boy.

KEMP: It's personal.

SLOANE: I'd like to stay, Ed . . . in case . . .

KEMP: I'm not talking in front of him.

SLOANE: Pop . . . [*Laughs.*] . . . Ed will tell me afterwards. See if he doesn't.

(*Pause.*)

247

KEMP: I want to talk in private.

(ED *nods at the door,* SLOANE *shrugs.*)

SLOANE: Give in to him, eh, Ed? [*Laughs.*] You know,
Pop . . . well . . . [*Pause.*] Okay, have it your own way.
[*Exits.*]

KEMP: Is he gone?

ED: What's the matter with you?

KEMP: That kid—who is he?

ED: He's lived here six months. Where have you been?

KEMP: What's his background?

ED: He's had a hard life, Dad. Struggles. I have his word
for it. An orphan deserves our sympathy.

KEMP: You like him?

ED: One of the best.

(*Silence.*)

KEMP: He comes to my room at night.

ED: He's being friendly.

KEMP: I can't get to sleep. He talks all the time.

ED: Give an example of his conversation. What does he
talk about?

KEMP: Goes on and on. [*Pause.*] An' he makes things up
about me. [*He rolls up his sleeve, shows a bruise.*] Give
me a thumping, he did.

ED: When? [*Pause.*] Can't you remember?

KEMP: Before the weekend.

ED: Did you complain?

KEMP: I can't sleep for worry. He comes in and stands by
my bed in the dark. In his pyjamas.

(*Pause.*)

ED: I'll have a word with him.

KEMP: [*Lifts his trouser leg, pulls down his sock, shows an
Elastoplast.*] He kicked me yesterday.

SLOANE: [*Appears in the doorway.*] There's a man outside
wants a word with you, Pop. [*Pause.*] Urgent, he says.

KEMP: Tell him to wait.

SLOANE: How long?

KEMP: Tell him to wait, will you?

SLOANE: It's urgent.

KEMP: What's his name?

SLOANE: Grove. Or Greeves, I don't know.

KEMP: I don't know nobody called that.

SLOANE: He's on about the . . . [*Pause.*] . . . whether he can dump something. You'd better see him.

KEMP: [*Swings around, tries to bring* SLOANE *into focus.*] Oh . . .

ED: [*Nods, winks.*] In a minute, boy. [SLOANE *closes door, exits. Silence.*] Dad . . .

KEMP: He's in bed with her most nights. People talk. The woman from the shop spotted it first. Four months gone, she reckons.

(*Pause.*)

ED: That's interesting.

KEMP: She's like the side of a house lately. It's not what she eats. [*Silence.*] Shall I tell you something else?

ED: Don't.

(*Pause.*)

KEMP: He's got it in for me.

ED: . . . don't—tell me anything—

KEMP: It's because I'm a witness. To his crime.

ED: What crime?

SLOANE: [*Enters carrying a suitcase. Puts it on the table. Opens it.*] Man en half creating, Pop. You ought to see to him. Jones or Greeves or whatever his name is. He's out the back.

ED: Go and see to him, Dad. [SLOANE *exits.*] See this man, Dad. Go on.

KEMP: There's no man there.

ED: How do you know? You haven't been and looked, have you?

KEMP: It's a blind. [*Pause.*] Let me tell you about the boy.

ED: I don't want to hear. [*Pause.*] I'm surprised to find you spreading stories about the kiddy. Shocked. [SLOANE *returns with a pile of clothes.*] That's slander. You'll find yourself in queer street. [SLOANE *begins to pack the case.*] Apologize. [KEMP *shakes his head.*] The old man's got something to say to you, boy.

SLOANE: [*Smiling*] Oh, yes?

ED: [*To* KEMP] Haven't you? [*Pause.*] Do you talk to him much? Is he talkative at night?

SLOANE: We have the odd confab sometimes. As I dawdle over my cocoa.

ED: You go and talk to that man, Dad. See if you can't get some sense into him. Dumping their old shit back of the house. [*They watch* KEMP *exit. Silence.*] He's just been putting in a complaint.

SLOANE: About me?

ED: I can't take it serious. He more or less said you . . . well, in so many words he said . . .

SLOANE: Really?

ED: Did you ever kick him?

SLOANE: Sometimes. He understands.

ED: An' he said . . . Is she pregnant?

(*Pause.*)

SLOANE: Who?

ED: Deny it, boy. Convince me it isn't true.

SLOANE: Why?

ED: So's I—[*Pause.*] Lie to me.

SLOANE: Why should I?

ED: It's true, then? Have you been messing with her?

SLOANE: She threw herself at me.

(*Silence.*)

ED: What a little whoreson you are, you little whoreson. You are a little whoreson and no mistake. I'm put out, my boy. Choked. [*Pause.*] What attracted you? Did she

250

give trading stamps? You're like all these layabouts.
Kiddies with no fixed abode.

SLOANE: I put up a fight.

ED: She had your cherry?

SLOANE: No.

ED: Not the first time?

SLOANE: No.

ED: Or the second?

SLOANE: No.

ED: Dare I go on?

SLOANE: It's my upbringing. Lack of training. No proper
parental control.

ED: I'm sorry for you.

SLOANE: I'm glad of that. I wouldn't want to upset you.

ED: That does you credit.

SLOANE: You've no idea what I've been through. [*Pause.*]
I prayed for guidance.

ED: I'd imagine the prayer for your situation would be
hard to come by. [*Pause.*] Did you ever think of locking
your bedroom door?

SLOANE: She'd think I'd gone mad.

ED: Why didn't you come to me?

SLOANE: It's not the kind of thing I could—

ED: I'd've been your confessor.

SLOANE: You don't understand. It gathered momentum.

ED: You make her sound like a washing machine. When
did you stop?

SLOANE: I haven't stopped.

ED: Not stopped yet?

SLOANE: Here, lay off.

ED: What a ruffian.

SLOANE: I got my feelings.

ED: You were stronger than her. Why didn't you put up
a struggle?

SLOANE: I was worn out. I was overwrought. Nervous.
On edge.

(*Pause.*)

ED: You're a constant source of amazement, boy, a never ending tale of infamy. I'd hardly credit it. A kid of your age. Joy-riding in an expensive car, a woman pregnant. My word, you're unforgivable. [*Pause.*] I don't know whether I'm qualified to pronounce judgment.

(*Pause.*)

SLOANE: I'm easily led. I been dogged by bad luck.

ED: You've got to learn to live a decent life sometime, boy. I blame the way you are on emotional shock. So perhaps [*Pause.*] we ought to give you another chance.

SLOANE: That's what I says.

ED: Are you confused?

SLOANE: I shouldn't be surprised.

ED: Never went to church? Correct me if I'm wrong.

SLOANE: You got it, Ed. Know me better than I know myself.

ED: Your youth pleads for leniency and, by God, I'm going to give it. You're pure as the Lamb. Purer.

SLOANE: Am I forgiven?

ED: Will you reform?

SLOANE: I swear it . . . Ed, look at me. Speak a few words of forgiveness. [*Pause.*] Pity me.

ED: I do.

SLOANE: Oh, Ed, you're a pal.

ED: Am I?

SLOANE: One of my mates.

ED: Is that a fact? How refreshing to hear you say it.

SLOANE: You've a generous nature.

ED: You could say that. I don't condemn out of hand like some. But do me a favor—avoid the birds in future. That's what's been your trouble.

SLOANE: It has.

ED: She's to blame.

SLOANE: I've no hesitation in saying that.

ED: Why conform to the standards of the cowshed? [*Pause.*] It's a thing you grow out of. With me behind you, boy, you'll grow out of it.

SLOANE: Thanks.

ED: Your hand on it. [SLOANE *holds out his hand.* ED *takes it, holds it for a long time, searches* SLOANE'*s face.*] I think you're a good boy. [*Silence.*] I knew there must be some reasonable explanation for your otherwise inexplicable conduct. I'll have a word with the old man.

SLOANE: Gets on my nerves, he does.

ED: Has he been tormenting you?

SLOANE: I seriously consider leaving as a result of the way he carries on.

ED: Insults?

SLOANE: Shocking. Took a dislike to me, he did, the first time he saw me.

ED: Take no notice.

SLOANE: I can't make him out.

ED: Stubborn.

SLOANE: That's why I lose my temper.

ED: I sympathize.

(*Pause.*)

SLOANE: He deserves a good belting.

ED: You may have something there.

SLOANE: I thought you might be against me for that.

ED: No.

SLOANE: I thought you might have an exaggerated respect for the elderly.

ED: Not me.

SLOANE: I've nothing against him. [*Pause.*] But he's lived so long, he's more like an old bird than a bloke. How is it such a father has such a son? A mystery. [*Pause.*] Certainly is. [ED *pats his pockets.*] Out of fags again, are you?

ED: Yes.

SLOANE: Give them up. Never be fully fit, Ed. [ED *smiles, shakes his head.*] Are you going to the shop?

ED: Yes.

SLOANE: Good. [*Silence.*] How long will you be?

ED: Five minutes. Maybe ten.

SLOANE: Mmmm. [*Pause.*] Well, while you're gone I'm going to have a word with Pop.

ED: Good idea.

SLOANE: See if we can't find an area of agreement. I'll hold out the hand of friendship an' all that. I'm willing to forget the past. If he is. [*Silence.*] I'd better have a word with him. Call him.

ED: Me?

SLOANE: No good me asking him anything, is there?

ED: I don't know whether we're speaking.

SLOANE: Gone funny again, has he?

ED: [*Goes to the window, opens it, looks out. Calls.*] Dad! [*Pause.*] I want a word with you.

KEMP: [*Off*] What's that?

(*Pause.*)

ED: Me—me—I want to see you. [*He closes the window.*] He gets worse. [*Silence.*] Appeal to his better nature. Say you're upset. Wag your finger perhaps. I don't want you to be er, well . . . at each other's throats, boy. Let's try . . . and . . . well, be friends. [*Pause.*] I've the fullest confidence in your ability. [*Pause.*] Yes . . . well, I'm going out now. [*Pause.*] . . . it's a funny business, en it? . . . I mean . . . well, it's a ticklish problem. [*Pause.*] Yes . . . it is. [*Exit.*]

(SLOANE *sits, waits. Pause.* KEMP *enters.* SLOANE *rises, steps behind* KEMP, *bangs door.* KEMP *swings around, backs.*)

KEMP: Ed? [*Pause.*] Where's Ed?

SLOANE: [*Takes hold of* KEMP's *stick, pulls it away from him.* KEMP *struggles.* SLOANE *wrenches stick from his hand. Leads* KEMP *to a chair.*] Sit down, Pop. [KEMP *turns to go.* SLOANE *pushes him into the chair.*] Ed's not here. Gone for a walk. What you been saying about me?

KEMP: Nothing, sonnie.

SLOANE: What have you told him? What were you going to tell him?

KEMP: I—[*Pause.*] Business.

SLOANE: What kind of business? [KEMP *does not reply.*] Told him she's up the stick, did you? [*No reply.*] Why did you tell him?

KEMP: He's her brother. He ought to know.

SLOANE: Fair enough.

KEMP: Got to know sometime.

SLOANE: Right. [*Silence.*] What else did you tell him? [KEMP *attempts to rise,* SLOANE *pushes him back.*] Did you say anything else? [KEMP *attempts to rise.*] Eh?

KEMP: No.

SLOANE: Were you going to?

KEMP: Yes.

SLOANE: Why?

KEMP: You're a criminal.

SLOANE: Who says I am?

KEMP: I know you are. You killed my old boss. I know it was you.

SLOANE: Your vision is faulty. You couldn't identify nobody now. So long after. You said so yourself.

KEMP: I got to go. [*Pause.*] I'm expecting delivery of a damson tree.

SLOANE: Sit still! [*Silence.*] How were you going to identify me?

KEMP: I don't have to. They got fingerprints.

SLOANE: Really?

KEMP: All over the shop.

SLOANE: It was an accident, Pop. I'm innocent. You don't know the circumstances. . . .

KEMP: Oh . . . I know. . . .

SLOANE: But you don't.

KEMP: You murdered him.

SLOANE: Accidental death.

(*Pause.*)

KEMP: No, sonnie . . . no.

SLOANE: You're prejudging my case.

KEMP: You're bad.

SLOANE: I'm an orphan.

KEMP: Get away from me. Let me alone.

SLOANE: [*Puts the stick into* KEMP's *hand.*] I trust you, Pop. Listen. Keep quiet. [*Silence.*] It's like this, see. One day I leave the home. Stroll along. Sky blue. Fresh air. They'd found me a likable permanent situation. Canteen facilities. Fortnight's paid holiday. Overtime? Time and a half after midnight. A staff dance each year. What more could one wish to devote one's life to? I certainly loved that place. The air round Twickenham was like wine. Then one day I take a trip to the old man's grave. Hic Jacets in profusion. Ashes to Ashes. Alas the fleeting. The sun was declining. A few press-ups on a tomb belonging to a family name of Cavaneagh, and I left the graveyard. I thumbs a lift from a geyser who promises me a bed. Gives me a bath. And a meal. Very friendly. All you could wish he was, a photographer. He shows me one or two experimental studies. An experience for the retina and no mistake. He wanted to photo me. For certain interesting features I had that he wanted the exclusive right of preserving. You know how it is. I didn't like to refuse. No harm in it, I suppose. But then I got to thinking . . . I knew a kid once called MacBride that happened to. Oh, yes . . . so when I gets to think of this I decide I got to do something about it. And I gets up in the middle of the night looking for the film, see. He has a lot of expensive equipment about in his studio, see. Well, it appears that he gets the wrong idea. Runs in. Gives a shout. And the long and the short of it is I loses my head, which is a thing I never ought to a done with the worry of them photos an' all. And I hits him. I hits him. [*Pause.*] He must have had a weak heart. Something like that, I should imagine. Definitely should have seen his doctor before that. I wasn't to know, was I? I'm not to blame.

(*Silence.*)

KEMP: He was healthy. Sound as a bell.

SLOANE: How do you know?

KEMP: He won cups for it. Looked after himself.

SLOANE: A weak heart.

KEMP: Weak heart, my arse. You murdered him.

SLOANE: He fell.

KEMP: He was hit from behind.

SLOANE: I had no motive.

KEMP: The equipment.

SLOANE: I never touched it.

KEMP: You meant to.

SLOANE: Not me, Pop. [*Laughs.*] Oh, no.

KEMP: Liar . . . lying little bugger. I knew what you was from the start.

(*Pause.*)

SLOANE: What are you going to do? Are you going to tell Ed? [KEMP *makes no reply.*] He won't believe you. [KEMP *makes no reply.*] He'll think you're raving.

KEMP: No . . . you're finished. [*Attempts to rise.* SLOANE *pushes him back.* KEMP *raises his stick,* SLOANE *takes it from him.*]

SLOANE: You can't be trusted, I see. I've lost faith in you. [*Throws the stick out of reach.*] Irresponsible. Can't give you offensive weapons.

KEMP: Ed will be back soon. [*Rises to go.*]

SLOANE: He will.

KEMP: I'm seeing him then.

SLOANE: Are you threatening me? Do you feel confident? Is that it? [*Stops. Clicks his tongue. Pause. Leans over and straightens* KEMP's *tie.*] Ed and me are going away. Let's have your word you'll forget it. [KEMP *does not reply.*] Pretend you never knew. Who was he? No relation. Hardly a friend. An employer. You won't bring him back by hanging me. [KEMP *does not reply.*] Where's your logic? Can I have a promise you'll keep your mouth shut?

KEMP: No.

(SLOANE *twists* KEMP's *ear.*)

KEMP: Ugh! aaah . . .

SLOANE: You make me desperate. I've nothing to lose, you see. One more chance, Pop. Are you going to give me away?

KEMP: I'll see the police.

SLOANE: You don't know what's good for you. [*He knocks* KEMP *behind the settee. Kicks him.*] You bring this on yourself. [*He kicks him again.*] All this could've been avoided. [KEMP *half-rises, collapses again. Pause.* SLOANE *kicks him gently with the toe of his boot.*] Eh, then. Wake up. [*Pause.*] Wakey, wakey. [*Silence. He goes to the door and calls.*] Ed! [*Pause.*] Ed!

(KATH *comes to the door. He pushes her back.*)

KATH: [*Off*] What's happened?

SLOANE: Where's Ed? Not you! I want Ed!

CURTAIN

ACT III

Door slams off.

ED: [*Entering*] What is it? [*Sees* KEMP *lying on the floor.
Kneels.* SLOANE *enters, stands in the doorway.* KATH *tries
to push past. Struggle.* SLOANE *gives up. She enters.*]

SLOANE: Some kind of attack.

ED: What did you do?

KATH: If only there were some spirits in the house. Unfortunately I don't drink myself. [*She loosens* KEMP's
collar.] Somebody fetch his tablets.

(*Nobody moves.*)

ED: He's reviving.

KATH: Speak to me, Dadda. [*Pause.*] He's been off his food
for some time. [*Pause.*] He's cut his lip.

ED: [*Lifts* KEMP.] Can you walk?

KEMP: [*Muttering*] Go away . . .

ED: I'll carry you upstairs. [KATH *opens the door, stands in
the passage.*] He'll be better in a bit. Is his bed made?

KATH: Yes. Let him lie still and he'll get his feelings back.
[ED *exits with* KEMP. *Slowly*] Mr. Sloane, did you strike
the Dadda?

SLOANE: Yes.

KATH: You admit it? Did he provoke you?

SLOANE: In a way.

KATH: What a thing to do. Hit an old man. It's not like
you. You're usually so gentle.

SLOANE: He upset me.

KATH: He can be aggravating, I know, but you shouldn't
resort to violence, dear. [*Pause.*] Did he insult you?
[*Pause.*] Was it a bad word? [*Pause.*] I don't expect you
can tell me what it was. I'd blush.

SLOANE: I hit him several times.

259

KATH: You're exaggerating. You're not that type of young man. [*Pause.*] But don't do it again. Mamma wouldn't like it. [ED *enters.*] Is he all right?

ED: Yes.

KATH: I'll go up to him.

ED: He's asleep.

KATH: Sleeping off the excitement, is he? [*Exit.*]

ED: [*Taking* SLOANE *aside.*] How hard did you hit him?

SLOANE: Not hard.

ED: You don't know your own strength, boy. Using him like a punch bag.

SLOANE: I've told you—

ED: He's dead.

SLOANE: Dead? His heart.

ED: Whatever it was, it's murder, boy. You'll have some explaining to do. [*Lights a cigarette.* KATH *enters with a carpet sweeper, begins to sweep.*]

KATH: I'd take up a toffee, but he only gets them stuck round his teeth.

ED: You're not usually at a loss, surely? You can conjure up an idea or two.

KATH: Let Mr. Sloane regain his composure, Ed. Let him collect his thoughts. Forget the incident. [*She goes upstage, begins to hum "The Indian Love Call."*]

(SLOANE *looks at* ED. ED *smiles, shakes his head.*)

ED: That isn't possible, I'm afraid.

KATH: He meant no harm.

ED: What are you doing?

KATH: My housework. I mustn't neglect my chores.

ED: Can't you find a better time than this?

KATH: It's my usual time. Guess what's for dinner, Mr. Sloane.

SLOANE: I'm not hungry.

ED: He doesn't want any.

KATH: Guess what Mamma's prepared?

ED: Let him alone! All you think of is food. He'll be out of condition before long. As gross as you are.

260

KATH: Is he upset?

ED: Tell her.

SLOANE: I'm really upset.

ED: Turned your stomach, has it?

KATH: Will you feel better by this afternoon?

SLOANE: I don't know.

ED: He's worried.

KATH: The Dadda won't say anything, dear, if that's what's on your mind. He'll keep quiet. [*Pause.*] That new stove cooks excellent, Eddie.

ED: Does it?

KATH: Yes. I cooked a lovely egg yesterday. Mr. Sloane had it. I think they ought to have put the grill different, though. I burned my hand.

ED: You want to look what you're doing.

KATH: It's awkwardly placed.

ED: Cooking with your eyes shut.

KATH: [*Pause.*] You haven't guessed yet what's for dinner. Three guesses. Go on.

SLOANE: I don't know!

KATH: Chips.

SLOANE: Really?

KATH: And peas. And two eggs.

SLOANE: I don't give a sod what's for dinner!

ED: Don't use those tones to my relations, Sloane. Behave yourself for a change. [*Lights a cigarette.*]

SLOANE: Can I see you outside?

ED: What do you want to see me outside for?

SLOANE: To explain.

ED: There's nothing to explain.

SLOANE: How I came to be involved in this situation.

(KATH *puts the Ewbank away.*)

ED: I don't think that would be advisable. Some things will have to be sorted out. A check on your excesses is needed.

SLOANE: Are you sure he's—

ED: As forty dodos. I tried the usual methods of ascertaining; no heartbeats, no misting on my cigarette case. The finest legal brains in the country can't save you now.

(KATH *reenters.*)

SLOANE: I feel sick.

KATH: It's the weather.

SLOANE: No.

KATH: Take a pill or something. I had some recommended me the other day. [*Opens a drawer, searches. She finds the tablets, shakes out two into her hand. Offers them to* SLOANE.] Take them with a glass of water. Swallow them quick. They'll relieve the symptoms.

SLOANE: I don't want them! [*He knocks them from her hand.*] I don't want pills! [*Exits.*]

KATH: He's bad, isn't he?

ED: A very bad boy.

KATH: [*Picks up one tablet, searches for the others, gives up.*] Somebody will tread on them. That's the reason for these stains. Things get into the pile. The Dadda dropped a pickled walnut and trod it into the rug yesterday. If only we had a dog we wouldn't have so much bother.

ED: You're not having a dog.

KATH: Eddie, is Mr. Sloane ill?

ED: He may be.

KATH: He looks pale. I wonder if he isn't sickening for something.

ED: He might have to go away. Something has happened which makes his presence required elsewhere.

KATH: Where?

ED: I'm not sure. Not for certain.

KATH: Is he in trouble?

ED: Dead trouble.

KATH: It was an accident, surely?

ED: You know, then?

KATH: The Dadda told me about it. Mr. Sloane was unfortunate. He was joking, I expect.

ED: He never jokes.

KATH: No, he's remarkably devoid of a sense of fun. Dadda was full of it.

ED: I don't understand you.

KATH: Oh, I said he had no proof. I didn't waste my energy listening to him. Sometimes I think he makes up these things to frighten me. He ought to curb his imagination. [*Exits.*]

ED: I should have asked for references. I can see that now. The usual credentials would have avoided this. An attractive kid, so disarming, to—to tell me lies and—

KATH: [*Enters carrying a china figure.*] This shepherdess is a lovely piece of chinawork. She comes up like new when I give her a wash.

ED: Now?

KATH: The crack spoils it, though. I should have it mended professionally. [*Exit. Reenters carrying large vase.*] Dadda gets up to some horrible pranks lately. Throwing things into my best vase now. The habits of the elderly are beyond the pale. [*She exits.* ED *sits on the settee.*]

ED: I must sort out my affairs and quick.

SLOANE: [*Enters, glances at* ED. ED *does not look up.*] Accept my apology, Ed. Sorry I was rude, but my nerves won't stand much more, I can tell you. [*He opens the suitcase. Begins to pack.*] She's got two of my shirts in the wash. Good ones. [*Opens sideboard, takes out cardigan.*] Can't risk asking her for them. [*Looks under sideboard, finds canvas shoes.*] She's been using this razor again. [*Holding up razor.*] I can tell. That's not hygienic, is it?

ED: What are you doing?

SLOANE: Packing.

ED: Why?

SLOANE: I'm going away.

ED: Where?

SLOANE: With you.

ED: No, boy. Not with me.

SLOANE: It was settled.

ED: I can't allow you to take up abode in Dulverton Mansions now.

SLOANE: Why not?

ED: What a fantastic person you are. You've committed a murder!

SLOANE: An accident.

ED: Murder.

SLOANE: Those pills were undermining his constitution. Ruining his health. He couldn't have lasted much longer.

ED: Attacking a defenseless old man!

SLOANE: He had his stick.

ED: He wasn't strong enough to use it.

SLOANE: I blame that on the pills. Who prescribed them?

ED: His doctor.

SLOANE: Reputable, is he?

ED: He's on the register. What more do you want?

SLOANE: You'll find medical evidence agrees with my theory.

ED: The pills had nothing to do with it. You've no excuse. None.

SLOANE: What kind of life is it at his age?

ED: You've abused my trust.

SLOANE: I did him a service in a manner of speaking.

ED: You'll have to face the authorities.

SLOANE: Look, I'm facing no one.

ED: You've no choice.

SLOANE: I'll decide what choice I have.

ED: Get on the blower and call the law. We're finished.

SLOANE: You wouldn't put me away, would you?

ED: Without a qualm.

SLOANE: You're my friend.

ED: No friend of thugs.

SLOANE: He died of heart failure. You can't ruin my life. I'm impressionable. Think what the nick would do to me. I'd pick up criminal connections.

ED: You already got criminal connections.

SLOANE: Not as many as I would have.

ED: That's a point in your favor.

SLOANE: Give me a chance.

ED: You've had several.

SLOANE: One more.

ED: I've given you chances. Expected you to behave like a civilized human being.

SLOANE: Say he fell downstairs.

ED: What kind of a person does that make me?

SLOANE: A loyal friend.

ED: You'll get me six months. More than that. Depends on the judge.

SLOANE: What a legal system. Say he fell.

ED: Aiding and abetting.

SLOANE: Fake the evidence.

ED: You're completely without morals, boy. I hadn't realized how depraved you were. You murder my father. Now you ask me to help you evade Justice. Is that where my liberal principles have brought me?

SLOANE: You've got no principles.

ED: No principles? Oh, you really have upset me now. Why am I interested in your welfare? Why did I give you a job? Why do thinking men everywhere show young boys the straight and narrow? Flash check books when delinquency is mentioned? Support the Scout movement? Principles, boy, bleeding principles. And don't you dare say otherwise or you'll land in serious trouble.

SLOANE: Are you going to help me?

ED: No.

SLOANE: We must find a basis for agreement.

ED: There can be no agreement. I'm a citizen of this country. My duty is clear. You must accept responsibility for your actions.

SLOANE: [Sits beside ED. Lays a hand on his knee.] I accept responsibility.

ED: Do you?

SLOANE: Fully.

ED: Good. Remove that hand, will you?

SLOANE: Certainly.

ED: What you just said about no principles—that's really upset me. Straight. Really upset me.

SLOANE: Sorry, Eddie, sorry.

ED: One thing I wanted to give you—my principles. Oh, I'm disillusioned. I feel I'm doing no good at all.

SLOANE: I'm very bad. Only you can help me on the road to a useful life. [Pause.] A couple of years ago I met a man similar to yourself. Same outlook on life. A dead ringer for you as far as physique went. He was an expert on the adolescent male body. He'd completed an exhaustive study of his subject before I met him. During the course of one magical night he talked to me of his principles—offered me a job if I would accept them. Like a fool I turned him down. What an opportunity I lost, Ed. If you were to make the same demands, I'd answer loudly in the affirmative.

(*Pause.*)

ED: You mean that?

SLOANE: In future you'd have nothing to complain of.

ED: You really mean what you say?

SLOANE: Let me live with you. I'd wear my jeans out in your service. Cook for you.

ED: I eat out.

SLOANE: Bring you your tea in bed.

ED: Only women drink tea in bed.

SLOANE: You bring me my tea in bed, then. Any arrangement you fancy.

(KATH *screams loudly offstage. Pause. Screams again nearer. She enters.*)

KATH: Ed!

ED: Come here.

KATH: Ed, I must—[ED *takes her arm, she pulls back.*] It's Dadda—he's dead. Come quick.

ED: Sit down. [*To* SLOANE] Bring the car round. We'll fetch the doctor.

KATH: Eddie, he's dead.

ED: I know. We know. Didn't want to upset you.

(SLOANE *exits.*)

KATH: I can't believe he's dead. He was in perfect health.

ED: He was ill.

KATH: Was he?

ED: You told me he was.

KATH: I didn't believe it. I only took his word for it.

ED: Didn't he say he was ill?

KATH: Often. I took no notice. You know how he is. I thought he was having me on.

ED: He was telling the truth.

KATH: [*Begins to sniff.*] Poor Dadda. How he must have suffered. I'm truly ashamed of myself. [*She wipes her eyes on her apron.*] It's all the health scheme's fault. Will I have to send his pension book in?

ED: Yes.

KATH: I thought I would.

ED: Now listen—

KATH: Eddie.

ED: —carefully to what I say. [*He passes a hand across his mouth.*] When the doctor comes what are you going to tell him?

KATH: Me?

ED: He'll want to know.

KATH: I'll say Dadda had an attack. He passed away sudden.

ED: What about the cuts on his face?

KATH: He was rude to Mr. Sloane, Eddie. Provoked him.

ED: They won't wear that.

KATH: Won't they? [*Pause.*] I shall never get in my black. I've put on weight since we buried Mamma.

ED: They'll get the boy for murder.

KATH: They'd never do that, would they?

ED: They'll hang him.

(*Pause.*)

KATH: Hang him?

ED: They might. I'm not sure. I get confused by the changes in the law.

KATH: Is it bad?

ED: Awful. You wouldn't see him again. You understand?

KATH: The Dadda was rude. He said a rude word about me.

ED: That's no excuse in the eyes of the law. You must say he fell downstairs.

KATH: I couldn't.

ED: I would never suggest deceiving the authorities under normal circumstances. But we have ourselves to think of. I'm in a funny position. I pay his wages. That's a tricky situation.

KATH: Is it?

ED: I'm compromised. My hands are tied. If the situation was different I might say something. Depend on it.

KATH: Wouldn't they make an exception? If we gave him a good character?

ED: He hasn't got a good character.

KATH: We could say he had.

ED: That would be perjury.

KATH: He has nice manners when he wants. I've seen them.

ED: I feel bad doing this. You see the position? He went too far. But he did it out of respect for you. That's some consideration.

KATH: He did it out of love for me?

ED: You should be grateful. No doubt of that. [*Pause.*] Do you polish that lino?

KATH: Eh?

ED: On the stairs?

KATH: No, never. I have to think of the Dadda.

ED: Go and polish them.

KATH: Doctor will be cross.

ED: Let him be.

KATH: He'll think I'm silly. He'll think I caused Dadda's fall.

ED: It doesn't matter as long as he thinks it was an accident.

KATH: [*Bites her lip, considers.*] Shall I put Dadda's new shoes on him?

ED: Now you're using your initiative. Slippery, are they?

KATH: He only wore them once.

ED: Good girl.

(SLOANE *enters.*)

SLOANE: Ready? Come on, then.

(ED *nods to* KATH, *waiting. She looks from one to the other. Notices the case.*)

KATH: Why is he taking his case?
ED: He's coming with me. He can't stay here.
KATH: Why not?
ED: They'll suspect.

(*Pause.*)

KATH: When is he coming back?
ED: Day after next.
KATH: He doesn't need that big case. [*She exits.*]
ED: Get in the car, boy.
SLOANE: How about my shirts?
ED: I'll see about buying a couple.
KATH: [*Off*] Why is he taking his clothes?
ED: What are you on about?

(KATH *returns.*)

KATH: I've just checked. They aren't in the laundry basket.
ED: Snooping around. Don't you trust me?
KATH: You're taking him away.
SLOANE: We thought I ought to live in.
KATH: Do you want to leave?
SLOANE: I'll be back when this has blown over.
KATH: Why are you leaving your mamma? There's no need for him to go away, Eddie. Doctor knows he lives here.
ED: He'll instigate proceedings.
KATH: Doctors don't do that. He wants to stay.
ED: Ask him. [*To* SLOANE] Do you want to stay?
SLOANE: No.
ED: The question is answered.
KATH: Ed—
ED: Send a wire—
KATH: I've something to tell you. [*She lifts her apron. Shyly.*] I've a bun in the oven.
ED: You've a whole bloody baker's shop in the oven from the look of that.
KATH: Mr. Sloane was nice to me. Aren't you shocked?
ED: No, it's what I expect of you.
KATH: Aren't you angry with Mr. Sloane?

269

Joe Orton

ED: I'm angry with you.

KATH: Are you?

ED: Mr. Sloane's already explained.

KATH: What did he explain?

ED: How you carried on.

KATH: I didn't carry on! What a wicked thing to say.

ED: Seducing him.

KATH: Did he say that?

ED: Told me the grisly details.

(Silence.)

KATH: Mr. Sloane, dear, take back your locket.

ED: What locket?

KATH: He gave me a locket. [*She takes off the locket.* SLOANE *attempts to take it.*] I don't believe he'd take it if you weren't here, Ed. [*She puts the locket back. To* SLOANE] How could you behave so bad. Accusing me of seducing you.

SLOANE: But you did!

KATH: That's neither here nor there. Using expressions like that. Making yourself cheap. [SLOANE *turns to the suitcase.*] I see the truth of the matter. He's been at you. Isn't that like him?

ED: He wants to come with me.

KATH: Let him decide for himself.

ED: He's got problems. Needs a man's hand on his shoulder.

KATH: I'm afraid you're unduly influencing him.

ED: You've been found out.

KATH: Found out?

ED: Exposed.

KATH: Rubbish!

ED: Making a spectacle of yourself. Corrupting a kid young enough to be your son.

KATH: He loves me.

ED: Prove it.

KATH: A woman knows when she's loved.

ED: I blame myself for letting him stay. Knowing your character.

270

KATH: My character will stand analysis.

ED: You're older than him.

KATH: I'm a benign influence. A source of good.

ED: You spoil him.

KATH: Who tucks him up at night? And he likes my cooking. He won't deny that.

ED: No.

KATH: See, I'm right.

ED: I can't argue with you.

KATH: You can't.

ED: You don't make sense.

KATH: I do.

ED: You have no logical train of thought.

KATH: What is that?

ED: No power of argument.

KATH: I keep his trousers pressed nice. He's been smarter since I knew him.

ED: He's lost with you.

KATH: I gave him everything.

ED: No backbone. Spineless.

KATH: He's lovely with me. Charming little baby he is.

ED: No, he's soft. You softened him up.

KATH: I gave him three meals a day. Porridge for breakfast. Meat and two veg for dinner. A fry for tea. And cheese for supper. What more could he want?

ED: Freedom.

KATH: He's free with me.

ED: You're immoral.

KATH: It's natural.

ED: He's clean-living by nature; that's every man's right.

KATH: What are you going to give him?

ED: The world.

KATH: [*Comes around the case, looks in.*] The state of this case. Mr. Sloane, dear, you can't even pack. See how he needs me in the smallest things? Can't manage without a woman.

ED: Let him try.

KATH: Women are necessary.

ED: Granted.

KATH: Where's your argument?

271

ED: In limited doses.

KATH: You're silly, Eddie, silly. . . .

ED: Let him choose. Let's have it in black and white, boy.

SLOANE: I'm going with Ed.

(ED *nods, smacks* SLOANE's *shoulder, laughs.*)

KATH: Is it the color of the curtains in your room?

SLOANE: No.

KATH: Is it because I'm pregnant?

SLOANE: No. Better opportunities. A new life.

KATH: You vowed you loved me.

SLOANE: Never for a second.

KATH: I was kind to you.

SLOANE: Yes.

KATH: Are you grateful?

SLOANE: I paid.

KATH: I paid too. Baby on the way. Reputation ruined.

SLOANE: You had no reputation.

KATH: Is that what he's taught you?

ED: I taught him nothing. He was innocent until you got your maulers onto him.

KATH: He'd packed the experience of a lifetime into a few short years.

ED: Pure in heart, he was. He wouldn't know where to put it.

KATH: I attracted him instantly.

ED: You couldn't attract a blind man.

KATH: He wanted to marry me.

ED: What a bride!

KATH: We were to ask your consent.

ED: Look in the glass, lady. Let's enjoy a laugh. [*He takes her to the mirror.*] What do you see?

KATH: Me.

ED: What are you?

KATH: My hair is nice. Natural. I'm mature, but still able to command a certain appeal.

ED: You look like death! [*She shakes him off. He drags her back to the mirror.*] Flabby mouth. Wrinkled neck. Puffy hands.

KATH: It's baby coming.

ED: Sagging tits. You cradle snatcher.

KATH: He said I was a Venus. I held him in my arms.

ED: What a martyrdom!

KATH: He wanted for nothing. I loved him sincerely.

ED: Your appetite appalled him.

KATH: I loved him.

ED: Insatiable.

KATH: [*To* SLOANE] Baby, my little boy . . .

ED: He aches at every organ.

KATH: . . . Mamma forgives you.

ED: What have you to offer? You're fat and the crow's-feet under your eyes would make you an object of terror. Pack it in, I tell you. Sawdust up to the navel? You've nothing to lure any man.

KATH: Is that the truth, Mr. Sloane?

SLOANE: More or less.

KATH: Why didn't you tell me?

ED: How could he tell you? You showed him the gate of hell every night. He abandoned hope when he entered there.

KATH: [*Snaps the suitcase shut.*] Mr. Sloane, I believed you were a good boy. I find you've deceived me.

SLOANE: You deceived yourself.

KATH: Perhaps. [*She holds out her hand.*] Kiss my hand, dear, in the manner of the theater. [*He kisses her hand.*] I shall cry. [*She feels for a handkerchief.*]

ED: On with the waterworks.

KATH: I'm losing you forever.

SLOANE: I'll pop round.

KATH: I'll not be able to bear it.

SLOANE: You'll have the baby.

KATH: I shall die of it, I'm sure.

ED: What a cruel performance you're giving. Like an old tart grinding to her climax.

(SLOANE *kisses* KATH'*s cheek*.)

KATH: Baby . . . [*She holds him close. Looks at* ED *over* SLOANE'*s shoulder*.] Before you go, Mr. Sloane, we must straighten things out. The Dadda's death was a blow to me.

SLOANE: [*Releases her.*] Ed can vouch for me. You can support his story.

KATH: What story?

SLOANE: The old man fell downstairs.

KATH: I shall never under any circumstances allow anyone to perjure me. It was murder.

(*Pause.* SLOANE *releases her. Pause.*)

SLOANE: He was ill.

KATH: Ah, you know as well as I he was perfectly healthy this morning.

SLOANE: Ed will give me an alibi.

KATH: He wasn't there, dear. Respect the truth always. It's the least you can do under the circumstances.

SLOANE: He'll say he was a witness.

KATH: It's not in accordance with my ideas of morality.

SLOANE: Look—Mamma . . . see—

KATH: When Doctor comes he'll want to know things. Are you asking me to deceive our G.P.? He's an extremely able man. He'll notice discrepancies. And then where will we be? He'd make his report and Mamma would be behind bars. I'm sure that isn't your idea. Is it?

SLOANE: Ed is supporting me.

KATH: He must decide for himself. I won't practice a falsehood.

SLOANE: You're not going back on your word?

KATH: You know how I go to pieces under cross-examination.

SLOANE: Make an effort.

KATH: Who for?

SLOANE: Me.

KATH: You won't be here.

SLOANE: I'll come and see you.

KATH: No. Call me names if you wish, but I won't tell stories. I'm a firm believer in truth.

ED: Look . . . Kathy—say you were out when the accident occurred.

KATH: No.

ED: Down the shops.

KATH: But I wasn't.

ED: You didn't see him fall.

KATH: I would have heard him.

ED: Say you were out of range.

KATH: No.

ED: Forget the whole business.

KATH: No.

ED: Go to the police, then. What will you achieve? Nothing. This boy was carried away by the exuberance of youth. He's under age.

KATH: [*Hands the suitcase to* ED.] You struck the Dadda down in cold blood, Mr. Sloane. In the course of conversations before his death he told me one or two things of interest.

SLOANE: Concerning whom?

KATH: We talked only of you. I could hardly give credence to the report of your crimes. I didn't believe the old man. I'm paid for it now.

ED: The last word, eh? Using your whore's prerogative?

KATH: Stay with me.

SLOANE: No.

KATH: Hold me tight again.

SLOANE: No.

KATH: There's no need to go away, dear. Don't make me unhappy.

SLOANE: I'm going with Ed.

KATH: I was never subtle, Mr. Sloane. . . . If you go with Eddie, I'll tell the police.

SLOANE: If I stay here he'll do the same.

ED: It's what is called a dilemma, boy. You are on the horns of it.

(*Silence.*)

KATH: You see how things are, Mr. Sloane?

(SLOANE *smacks her face; she screams.*)

275

Joe Orton

ED: What are you doing?

SLOANE: Leave her to me.

KATH: Don't attempt to threaten me.

ED: There's no suggestion of threats.

KATH: What's he doing, then?

ED: Let her alone, boy.

SLOANE: Keep out of this! [ED *lays a hand on* SLOANE's *shoulder, tries to pull him away from* KATH. SLOANE *turns, shoves* ED *from him.*] Did you hear what I said? Keep out of it!

ED: Don't be violent. No violence at any cost. [SLOANE *gets* KATH *into a corner; struggles with her.*] What's this exhibition for? This is gratuitous violence. Give over, both of you!

SLOANE: [*Shakes* KATH.] Support me, you mare! Support me!

KATH: Make him stop! I shall be sick. He's upsetting my insides.

ED: [*Runs around.*] What did you want to provoke him for?

(SLOANE *shakes* KATH *harder. She screams.*)

KATH: My teeth! [*She claps a hand over her mouth.*] My teeth. [SLOANE *flings her from him. She crawls around the floor, searching.*] He's broke my teeth! Where are they?

ED: Expensive equipment gone west now, see? I'm annoyed with you, boy. Seriously annoyed. Giving us the benefit of your pauperism. Is this what we listen to the Week's Good Cause for? A lot of vicars and actresses making appeals for cash gifts to raise hooligans who can't control themselves? I'd've given my check to the anti-Jewish League if I'd known.

KATH: [*Reaching under the settee.*] I'll still forgive and forget.

ED: Coming in here as a lodger. Raised in a charity home. The lack of common courtesy in some people is appalling.

SLOANE: She's won! The bitch has won!

(*He grips* ED's *arm.* ED *shrugs him away.*)

ED: We'll discuss the matter.

SLOANE: We need action, not discussion. Persuade her. Cut her throat, but persuade her!

ED: Don't use that tone of voice to me, boy. I won't be dictated to. [*Pause.*] Perhaps we can share you.

SLOANE: Deal with her.

ED: We'll think of something.

SLOANE: She must be primed. Get her evidence correct.

ED: Don't worry. I'm in perfect control of the situation.

SLOANE: You're in control of nothing! Where are your influential friends? Ring them, we need protection.

KATH: It's his nerves. He doesn't know what he's doing.

ED: Put your teeth in, will you? Sitting there with them in your hand.

KATH: He's broke them.

ED: They're only chipped. Go on, turn your back.

KATH: [*Puts her teeth in.*] What are we going to do, Eddie?

ED: Stand up. We can't conduct a serious discussion from that position.

KATH: Help me up, Mr. Sloane. Thank you, baby. See, Ed, he hasn't lost respect for me.

ED: An arrangement to suit all tastes. That is what's needed.

KATH: I don't want to lose my baby.

ED: You won't lose him.

KATH: But—

ED: [*Holds up a hand.*] What are your main requirements? I take it there's no question of making an honest woman of you? You don't demand the supreme sacrifice?

SLOANE: I'm not marrying her!

ED: Calm down, will you?

SLOANE: Remember our agreement.

ED: I'm keeping it in mind, boy.

SLOANE: Don't saddle me with her for life.

KATH: He's close to tears. Isn't he sweet?

ED: Yes, he's definitely attractive in adversity. Really, boy, what with one thing and another . . . I warned you

against women, didn't I? They land you in impossible
predicaments of this nature.

SLOANE: You can solve it, Ed.

ED: You believe that, do you? I hope so. Marriage is a
non-starter, then?

KATH: He's led me on.

ED: Are you repentant now? Truly ashamed of yourself?

SLOANE: I am.

ED: You aren't going to press your claims, are you? Even
if he thee worshiped with his body, his mind would be
elsewhere. And a wife cannot testify against her husband.

KATH: Can't she?

ED: No, a minor point.

KATH: I don't mind about marriage as long as he doesn't
leave me.

ED: Fine. [*Pause.*] I think, boy, you'd better go and wait in
the car. Keep the engine running. I won't be long. I
want a private talk with my sister.

SLOANE: Is it going to be okay?

ED: Well . . . perhaps.

SLOANE: I'll be grateful.

ED: Will you?

SLOANE: Eternally.

ED: Not eternally, boy. Just a few years. [*He pats* SLOANE
on the shoulder. SLOANE *exits.*] What will the story be?

KATH: Like you said—he fell downstairs.

ED: That will explain the cuts and bruises. You'd better
say you were out. Stick to that. You know nothing. I'll
manage the doctor.

KATH: Yes, Ed.

ED: Can I trust you?

KATH: Yes.

ED: Then let's have no more threats. You'll support him?

KATH: As long as he stays here.

ED: You've had him six months; I'll have him the next
six. I'm not robbing you of him permanently.

KATH: Aren't you?

ED: No question of it. [*Pause.*] As long as you're prepared
to accept the idea of partnership.

278

KATH: For how long?

ED: As long as the agreement lasts.

KATH: How long is that?

ED: By the half-year.

KATH: That's too long, dear. I get so lonely.

ED: I've got no objections if he visits you from time to time. Briefly. We could put it ˙in the contract. Fair enough?

KATH: Yes.

ED: I'd bring him over myself in the car. Now, you'll be more or less out of action for the next three months. So shall we say till next August? Agreed?

KATH: Perfect, Eddie. It's very clever of you to have thought of such a lovely idea!

ED: Put it down to my experience at the conference table.

(*Car sounds off.*)

KATH: Can he be present at the birth of his child?

ED: You're not turning him into a midwife.

KATH: It deepens the relationship if the father is there.

ED: It's all any reasonable child can expect if the dad is present at the conception. Let's hear no more of it. Give me that locket.

KATH: It was his present to me.

ED: You'll get it back in March. [*She hands him the locket. He puts it on.*] And behave yourself in future. I'm not having you pregnant every year. I'll have a word with him about it. [*He kisses her cheek, pats her bottom.*] Be a good girl.

KATH: Yes, Ed.

ED: Well, it's been a pleasant morning. See you later. [*He exits. The front door slams.* KATH *goes to the sideboard and rummages in drawer; takes out a sweet, unwraps it, and puts it into her mouth. Sits on settee.*]

CURTAIN

279

A LATE SNOW
A Play in Two Acts

by
Jane Chambers

A Late Snow was produced at Clark Center for the Performing Arts, New York City, in 1974. Produced by Playwrights Horizons; directed by Nyla Lyon; costumes by Sally Blankfield; lighting design by Patrika Brown. In the original cast:

QUINCEY .... *Carolyn Cope (replaced by Lin Shaye)*
PAT .... *Susan Sullivan*
ELLIE .... *Susanne Wasson*
MARGO .... *Anita Keal*
PEGGY .... *Marilyn Hamlin*

CHARACTERS

In order of appearance:

QUINCEY: Mid-twenties, pleasant, open, honest, a young writer.

PAT: Mid-thirties, tall, attractive, witty. A charming alcoholic.

ELLIE: Mid-thirties, attractive, cool. A college professor.

MARGO: Forties, a well-known writer, attractive, self-contained, super-charming.

PEGGY: Mid-thirties, a chic suburban housewife trying to do everything "right."

ACT I

It is late afternoon in early spring. As the curtain rises, we see the interior of a cabin by a lake.

Downstairs, a living room and a kitchen, somehow separated from one another. The living room has a fireplace, although we need not see the fire. It also has a big window overlooking the lake, which can be the "fourth wall."

The second floor, which can be indicated by risers, has two small bedrooms and a door leading to a bath. There should be steps of some kind from one level to the other, indicating a stairway.

Downstairs, there are two doors: a front door, off the living room; a back door, off the kitchen.

Furnishings are comfortable and worn. Books and artifacts are tossed comfortably around. There is a bar area in the living room and a set of wind chimes in the master bedroom window.

QUINCEY *opens the door to the living room from the outside with a key.*

QUINCEY: I hope you can get that truck back out of here.
PAT'S VOICE: Oh, sure. It's got four-wheel drive. Just prop the door open.

(QUINCEY *does so.*)

PAT'S VOICE: I've got the tailgate down. We can roll it in. Come on.

(QUINCEY *goes back out. We hear the sound of something heavy being moved.*)

QUINCEY'S VOICE: It weighs a ton.

PAT'S VOICE: You wouldn't listen. I tried to sell you something nice and light—an end table, a dry sink. . . .

QUINCEY'S VOICE: This is the piece she wants. She talks about it all the time.

(*They appear, pushing an antique Dutch cupboard.*)

PAT'S VOICE: Lift it over the sill.

QUINCEY: [*Looking at the heavy object*] Lift it over the sill.

PAT: Come on.

(*With a mighty effort,* QUINCEY *does so.*)

QUINCEY: *Mother of God.*

PAT: Good. Now we just roll it into place.

QUINCEY: It goes over there.

PAT: I know where it goes.

QUINCEY: Watch the rug.

PAT: Push!

QUINCEY: Don't scratch it!

PAT: Just push, will you?

QUINCEY: Don't scrape the floor!

PAT: You're really uptight, aren't you? [*She pushes the piece into place, scraping the floor.*]

QUINCEY: You scraped the floor! [*She looks closely.*] Shit.

PAT: Spit on it. [QUINCEY *looks at her, puzzled.*] Spit on it and rub it with your finger.

QUINCEY: [*Does so.*] It's a gouge.

PAT: It's a scratch. She'll never notice. You can't hurt these floors. [QUINCEY *continues to spit and rub.*] What does she do, beat you?

QUINCEY: I'm not even supposed to be out here. I mean, she's never said, "Here are the keys, go out to the cabin."

PAT: Aren't you here every weekend?

QUINCEY: With Ellie. After all, it's her house.

PAT: It's her house. [*She looks around.*] It looks the same. I miss it. [*Quickly*] I never did like that piece. It's junk.

QUINCEY: Why did you take it?

PAT: Because Ellie wanted it. I figured some sucker would buy it.

QUINCEY: Ellie says you took half the stuff in the place.

PAT: Well, half of it was mine. She took the lamp. I wanted that. [*She indicates a Tiffany shade.*] That's worth something—a couple of hundred.

QUINCEY: Don't touch that!

PAT: Just looking.

QUINCEY: [*About scratch*] I hope she won't notice.

PAT: She will.

QUINCEY: You said she wouldn't!

PAT: [*Smiles.*] I lied. [*She examines shade closely.*] If I put this in the shop tomorrow morning, it'd be sold by noon. Three hundred, easy.

QUINCEY: Come on, don't touch that!

PAT: Red glass is rare. Do you know why?

QUINCEY: Leave it alone!

PAT: They use gold to make red glass. Gold.

QUINCEY: Please. I never should have brought you out here.

PAT: You wanted delivery. You drove a hard bargain.

QUINCEY: Bullshit. I paid you twice what that piece is worth.

PAT: That's true. Actually, you paid much more than twice. Ellie and I found that piece of junk in an abandoned barn, four years ago.

QUINCEY: [*Defensively*] She loves it. She's always saying, "I wish I had my old cupboard." She kept her papers in it, I think.

PAT: Her private treasure chest. I used to love to go through it when she was out of the house. She kept little notebooks. . . .

QUINCEY: She still does. She has an old library table in the apartment. She keeps her notebooks in the drawer.

PAT: "Pat drunk seventeen days this month. Rash on my right hand getting worse. Psychological? Order a cord of wood by the thirtieth." A veritable font of information, huh?

QUINCEY: I don't know. I never look.

PAT: You should. Ellie rarely tells you what she's really thinking. "Pat's stories too pat. Something's going on."

QUINCEY: I shouldn't have brought you out here.

PAT: I still have keys.

QUINCEY: She changed the lock.

PAT: She take a Peace Bond out on me, too?

QUINCEY: Ellie says you'd steal the gold from your grand-mother's teeth.

PAT: [*Grins.*] There's a lot of stuff here I'd like to have.

QUINCEY: It belongs to Ellie.

PAT: It belongs to both of us.

QUINCEY: Not any more.

PAT: Where'd you get those keys?

QUINCEY: I took them out of her bureau drawer.

PAT: Before you establish your territorial prerogative, you'd better get your own keys. [*She goes to bar.*] Want a drink?

QUINCEY: We can't stay.

PAT: Why'd you come to my shop?

QUINCEY: To buy that cupboard.

PAT: Really?

QUINCEY: It's our anniversary. Our first anniversary. I want to give her something special.

PAT: When is it?—your anniversary? What's the date?

QUINCEY: The eighteenth.

PAT: Amazing. Sure you won't join me? [*She continues to case the house as she drinks.*]

QUINCEY: We've got to go.

PAT: No hurry. I've closed shop for the day.

QUINCEY: We shouldn't stay out here.

PAT: The eighteenth of April. Ours was June twenty-fourth. It wasn't really, but I convinced Ellie it was—it was close enough. All my anniversaries are June twenty-fourth. It's the only way I can remember: 6–24—the first three digits of my social security number. [*She picks up an object.*]

QUINCEY: Come on. Don't.

PAT: Why'd you come to my shop?

QUINCEY: [*Taking object from her*] It was the only way to get the cupboard.

PAT: There are a couple of cupboards just like that every weekend at the flea market.

QUINCEY: That cupboard is special.

PAT: It looks like all the others. She wouldn't know the difference. . . . You've walked by before. I've seen you.

QUINCEY: You lived with her for five years. You were an important part of her life.

PAT: [*Satisfied*] I never should have let her buy me out.

QUINCEY: You made her buy you out!

PAT: She wouldn't let me live here and I needed the money. We laid these floors ourselves—and framed the windows—

QUINCEY: We've got to go now.

PAT: Ellie's mother sent us those drapes.

QUINCEY: It'll be dark soon.

PAT: So what? You said she won't be back until Sunday.

QUINCEY: The conference isn't over until Saturday night. She's flying back on Sunday.

PAT: When we bought this place there was no insulation, no paneling, you could see the ground through the floorboards.

QUINCEY: Please, Pat, let's go.

PAT: She's really got you tied up, hasn't she? Little Miss Step and Fetch It. Ellie loves to give orders. I never took them. [*She goes back to bar.*] Are you a teetotaler, too?

QUINCEY: No. Are you going to be able to drive?

PAT: My reputation precedes me.

QUINCEY: Ellie says you have a problem.

PAT: [*Pours them each a drink.*] Ellie says I'm a drunk. She's at a conference?

QUINCEY: In Philadelphia. University department heads.

PAT: She go alone?

QUINCEY: With the other university department heads.

PAT: I never knew a conference to end on a Saturday night. [*She hands* QUINCEY *a drink.*] Cheers. [*At window*] When did the ice go this year?

QUINCEY: Sometime last week, I think.

PAT: We used to bet on the day.

QUINCEY: We weren't out here.

PAT: Ever see it go?

QUINCEY: No.

PAT: It starts melting around the edges. For a few days, it's slush for maybe fifteen, twenty feet around the shoreline. Then the circle of ice that's left in the middle of the lake gets gray, then black—then WHOOSH. It goes under in ten seconds. The black lake turns navy, then sky blue. And it's spring. [*She surveys the cabin.*] You a student of Ellie's?

QUINCEY: I was—last year when I was in grad school. I'm a writer.

PAT: Published?

QUINCEY: No.

PAT: How do you earn a living?

QUINCEY: I edit a throwaway.

PAT: What?

QUINCEY: A rag. One of those four-page weekly papers with neighborhood news and a lot of ads that you find in your mailbox.

PAT: I didn't know Ellie was into seducing her students.

QUINCEY: She's not. She didn't seduce me. I pursued her. It wasn't easy. She wasn't over you.

PAT: Oh?

QUINCEY: I lived with your ghost for months.

PAT: She never answered my letters. She hung up when I called her.

QUINCEY: Five years is a long time.

PAT: Yes, it is.

QUINCEY: It takes a while to get over it. She's over it now.

PAT: Chilly in here. Let's start a fire.

QUINCEY: Let's go.

PAT: There's wood in the crib by the fireplace. You know how to start a fire?

QUINCEY: Of course.

PAT: Well, do it. I'm going to take a look upstairs.

QUINCEY: No.

PAT: [*Charming*] She'll never know.

QUINCEY: No.

PAT: For old times' sake.

QUINCEY: No.

PAT: [*Handing her the starter wood*] Placate me. Lonely,

nearing middle age, with a slight tendency to imbibe, a
pitiful figure . . . [QUINCEY *laughs in spite of herself.*]
Good girl.

QUINCEY: Don't take anything!

PAT: [*Going upstairs*] You can frisk me when I come down.

(QUINCEY *begins to make a fire. We hear a car motor,
see lights flash across the kitchen.* QUINCEY *looks up
quizzically as the key turns in the back door.*

ELLIE *enters.*)

QUINCEY: Oh, shit.

ELLIE: Quincey!

QUINCEY: You're back early!

(QUINCEY *embraces* ELLIE, *who responds perfunctorily,
then pulls nervously away.* ELLIE *is dismayed by*
QUINCEY's *unexpected presence but tries valiantly not
to show it.*)

QUINCEY: I wanted to surprise you!

ELLIE: You did.

(QUINCEY *pulls* ELLIE *to the cupboard.*)

QUINCEY: With this. [*She hugs* ELLIE.] Happy First
Anniversary!

ELLIE: Quincey, where did you get this?

(*At the back door,* MARGO *appears, suitcase in hand.
She stands there, unnoticed.*)

QUINCEY: [*About the cupboard*] Surprise!

ELLIE: Where did you get it?

QUINCEY: It's what you wanted!

ELLIE: It's just like the old one.

QUINCEY: It *is* the old one.

MARGO: May I come in?

(ELLIE *looks from* MARGO *to* QUINCEY, *back to* MARGO. *She is flustered.*)

QUINCEY: Hello.

MARGO: Hello.

ELLIE: [*Recovering*] This is Quincey Evans, a former student of mine. Quincey, Margo.

QUINCEY: Margo. *The* Margo?

MARGO: The only one I know.

QUINCEY: *A Memory of Autumn, The Last Question, Miller's Breach, Afternoon in* . . .

MARGO: Amazing.

QUINCEY: I took a course in you. Ellie teaches a course in you.

ELLIE: It's true.

MARGO: I never thought of myself as a multiple-choice answer.

QUINCEY: You're always an essay. I thought you were retired [*Catches herself.*]—a recluse. I thought you never came out in public.

MARGO: Only after dark.

QUINCEY: I mean, you never give interviews or . . . [*Shrugs.*] I'm getting in deeper, aren't I? Sorry. Welcome. [*To* ELLIE] Where did you find her?

ELLIE: Margo was the guest lecturer at the conference. We flew back together.

MARGO: She's trying to coerce me into teaching.

ELLIE: A lecture series. Wouldn't that be a coup?

QUINCEY: Terrific. You're a kind of cult among the undergrads.

MARGO: It terrifies me.

QUINCEY: I have everything you've ever written.

ELLIE: I asked Margo to spend the day here tomorrow—so I can do my sales pitch.

QUINCEY: It's like seeing a legend come to life.

ELLIE: I promised her a quiet day by the lake.

QUINCEY: I hope we'll have time to talk. I have a thousand questions.

ELLIE: I have yet to sell her on the joys of university life.

QUINCEY: I'm a writer, too, you know. Fledgling but good, I think.

MARGO: Ellie, I'm tired . . . and a little uncomfortable. Can I change?

ELLIE: Of course. Upstairs. Excuse us, Quincey.

(ELLIE *picks up* MARGO's *bag, starts up the stairs. She encounters* PAT *on her way down.* ELLIE *is startled and angry at* PAT's *presence.*)

PAT: Hi.

ELLIE: What are you doing here?

PAT: I came with the cupboard.

QUINCEY: She insisted: free delivery.

PAT: [*To* ELLIE] Thank you?

ELLIE: Thank you. Excuse us, please.

(*She leads* MARGO, *bewildered, upstairs.* MARGO *stops at the master bedroom.*)

MARGO: What a cozy room. And a beautiful view of the lake.

ELLIE: Yes. [*Pause.*] Put your things anywhere.

MARGO: But this is your room, isn't it?

ELLIE: It's the nicest room. The guest room is kind of sparse. I'll sleep there.

MARGO: No.

ELLIE: Please. I insist.

MARGO: No. It's your room.

ELLIE: The guest room overlooks the compost heap. Please?

MARGO: All right.

ELLIE: It's the least I can do. [*Pause.*] I'm sorry. I didn't expect anyone to be here.

MARGO: [*Smiles.*] It's a regular party, isn't it?

ELLIE: They'll be leaving soon.

MARGO: It's all right.

ELLIE: It's not all right. I promised you a quiet weekend.

MARGO: They're your friends. I'm sure they're interesting people. [*She starts to undress.*] Aren't they?

ELLIE: [*Ignoring that*] I know how you feel about meeting strangers.

MARGO: That's my problem. I'm a big girl now. I can take care of myself.

ELLIE: I'm sorry about Quincey. She's young and exuberant. She didn't mean to embarrass you.

MARGO: Embarrass me? I was flattered. Would you hand me that shirt, please?

(*Downstairs.*)

PAT: [*To* QUINCEY] Well, well. Aren't you glad we stuck around?

QUINCEY: Cool it. That's business.

PAT: I'll say.

QUINCEY: Don't you know who she is?

PAT: I heard your eulogy.

QUINCEY: She's like a myth. I've never seen a picture of her. I've read everything she's ever written, but I never knew what she looked like before.

PAT: You won't forget.

QUINCEY: Ellie has many business associates. That's what this is. I know Ellie.

PAT: I guess I don't. I thought she was true-blue-lou.

QUINCEY: She is.

(*Upstairs,* ELLIE *is uncomfortable watching* MARGO.)

ELLIE: They won't stay long.

MARGO: Will you stop worrying?

ELLIE: Sorry. I'll go downstairs and take care of it. [*Pause.*] Are you all right?

MARGO: I'm fine. Just fine.

(ELLIE *descends the stairs as* PAT *is pouring another drink.*)

ELLIE: Quincey? Thank you. [*She hugs* QUINCEY *warmly*.] I'm sorry I was abrupt—I was just stunned to find you here.

QUINCEY: It's all right.

ELLIE: It was an opportunity that I couldn't pass up, honey. Every university in the country has tried to get Margo on faculty. No one's ever succeeded. We seemed to hit it off at the conference. . . .

QUINCEY: It's important to you, isn't it?

ELLIE: Honey, she doesn't know. . . . I mean, I haven't said anything. So, play it cool?

QUINCEY: I hate doing that.

ELLIE: Please?

PAT: [*Entering their area*] So, how are you, Ellie?

ELLIE: Fine, Pat. And you?

PAT: Fine.

ELLIE: Good.

PAT: You look well.

ELLIE: So do you.

PAT: The house looks good.

ELLIE: It's a nice house.

PAT: It always was, I miss it.

ELLIE: Don't give me that. You made me buy you out.

PAT: I needed the money.

ELLIE: I didn't have it, if you remember.

PAT: You got it, though. You could always get money if you had to.

ELLIE: Sure. At eight percent interest.

PAT: The pleasures of a good credit rating.

ELLIE: It's been good seeing you, Pat. I appreciate your bringing the cupboard out. You don't mind giving Quincey a ride back to town, do you?

PAT: [*Pause.*] I see.

ELLIE: I have work to do.

QUINCEY: I'd like to stay, Ellie. I'd like to talk to her.

ELLIE: If I get her to sign a contract, you'll have lots of chance to talk to her. [*Pause.*] It wouldn't look good, honey. I'm sorry, Quincey.

(PAT *grins.* MARGO *comes down the stairs, sloppy, comfortable.*)

MARGO: This is the real person. That other lady is a sham.

PAT: Hi.

ELLIE: Oh. Margo, this is Pat Leonard.

PAT: I've read your work.

MARGO: And?

PAT: You're good.

QUINCEY: Great.

MARGO: You really are a fan, aren't you?

QUINCEY: An admirer. Fan sounds—childish.

PAT: You must be used to adulation.

MARGO: Not at all. I don't see many people. That's one of the things that distresses me about Ellie's idea.

QUINCEY: Lecturing?

MARGO: It terrifies me. All those people!

QUINCEY: Adoring you.

MARGO: Why? For what?

QUINCEY: For being one of the best writers in the world.

MARGO: She's tenacious.

PAT: Ellie can testify to that.

ELLIE: I don't know what you're talking about.

PAT: Quincey told me about your first meeting.

MARGO: Oh? [*Pause.*] Well?

QUINCEY: It's not a very interesting story. I want to talk to you. If I could have picked any writer in the world to interview, it would have been you: and here you are.

MARGO: I'm overwhelmed. I'm also hungry. I never could eat that airline food. How about some supper?

ELLIE: Pat and Quincey have to get back to town.

MARGO: We bought plenty of food—Ellie and I stopped in this marvelous little country store. . . .

PAT: O'Brien's.

MARGO: You know it?

PAT: Well.

MARGO: And I'm cooking.

ELLIE: No.

MARGO: Yes. Does that tempt you?

QUINCEY: Ellie . . . ?

PAT: We'd love to stay.

MARGO: Good!

QUINCEY: We'll leave right after supper.

MARGO: You [*To* ELLIE] go upstairs and change. Get comfortable. You two [*To* PAT *and* QUINCEY] bring in the groceries. [ELLIE, *reluctantly, starts for stairs.*] Go on! [PAT *grins and goes for the groceries.* QUINCEY *tries to elicit some response from* ELLIE, *but* ELLIE *goes upstairs. To* QUINCEY] I neglected to mention that I haven't cooked since Thanksgiving three years ago when my sister was having her fifth baby.

QUINCEY: How do you eat?

MARGO: I live in a hotel. There's a restaurant downstairs.

QUINCEY: That must be expensive.

MARGO: Money buys time. And time is something a writer never has enough of. You'll find that out.

QUINCEY: You live alone?

MARGO: Yes.

QUINCEY: I don't think I'll ever want to live alone.

MARGO: You never have?

QUINCEY: No. My family, then college, then—roommates.

MARGO: You should try it alone. Everyone should. Builds an independent person.

QUINCEY: I always want to have a lover.

MARGO: Just don't get married and have babies. It drains your creative juices.

QUINCEY: That isn't exactly what I had in mind.

MARGO: You have a boyfriend?

QUINCEY: Well, I have had a boyfriend. A lot of them, as a matter of fact.

MARGO: I should think so. You're a nice-looking girl.

(PAT *enters with groceries.*)

PAT: You're not doing your share, Quincey, friend.

QUINCEY: Oh. Sorry. I'll get the rest.

PAT: That's it.

MARGO: Don't stand there like Samson. Those must be heavy. Put them down. [PAT *does.*] I hope there's no one here with a weight problem. [*She takes spaghetti out of the bag.*]

QUINCEY: Ellie.

MARGO: Ellie? She's on her own, then. We're having spaghetti. Fan—admirer—want to help?

QUINCEY: Sure.

PAT: You never got that fire going, did you?

(*Without waiting for an answer,* PAT *heads to the fireplace.*

ELLIE *comes down the stairs.*)

ELLIE: [*To kitchen*] Everything under control?

MARGO: Fine. The fan—

QUINCEY: Admirer.

MARGO: —is helping.

ELLIE: What can I do?

MARGO: Nothing. Out of the kitchen! Too many cooks . . .

ELLIE: You're sure? If you need me . . .

(*As* ELLIE *enters living room:*)

PAT: I need you. Give me some newspapers off that pile.

ELLIE: [*Doing so*] You always had a talent for that.

PAT: You haven't had a fire since.

ELLIE: Don't flatter yourself. I've managed.

PAT: You still think I'm a scoundrel, don't you?

ELLIE: Aren't you?

PAT: I never thought so.

ELLIE: Pat, I don't want to get into that.

PAT: I didn't mean to be.

ELLIE: It's over, let's forget it. Okay?

PAT: It's not over. The ice sank last week.

ELLIE: I didn't see it.

PAT: It's going to be spring.

ELLIE: It looks like snow to me.

PAT: All dead things come to life.

ELLIE: No. It looks like snow.

PAT: I'm sorry. You never gave me a chance to say I'm sorry. You wouldn't see me, talk to me. You never gave us a chance.

ELLIE: [*Pause.*] Did you give Cassie a chance?

PAT: I never loved her.

ELLIE: You made love to her—drunk. You wrapped her in a car around a walnut tree and you walked away.

PAT: It was an accident.

ELLIE: She was my friend.

PAT: You hated her.

ELLIE: I hated her for having an affair with you, for making a fool out of me, for lying to me. For loving you.

PAT: It didn't mean anything, Ellie. It never meant anything.

ELLIE: Cassie's dead, Pat. That means something.

PAT: It was an accident.

ELLIE: Everything's an accident. It's an accident you drink too much. It's an accident you fall into bed with the nearest available woman. It's an accident that they all fall in love with you, even when you don't want them. Cassie is dead and you say, it was an accident.

PAT: Don't you think I feel anything?

ELLIE: I don't know.

PAT: I didn't want to kill anybody. I never wanted to hurt anybody. I'm sorry Cassie's dead. I'm sorry, sorry, sorry, I've said it a million times, asleep and awake. I know there's no price on a human life but I've paid, Ellie, I've paid. The court wiped out my trust fund; my father, the compassionate bastard, wiped me out of his will. I lost my home, I nearly lost my business. And I lost you.

ELLIE: I was just someone to come home to between binges, between affairs. Not much of a loss, Pat.

PAT: I loved you.

ELLIE: [*Pause.*] I loved you.

PAT: What happened to us?

ELLIE: Maybe five years is too long.

PAT: I wanted to be with you for a lifetime. I had a
dream: two crochety old ladies rocking on that front
porch, waiting for the ice to go. [*Pause.*] She's not enough
for you, Ellie. You need more than that.

ELLIE: She's bright and honest—and she loves me.

PAT: She's there when you come home. Faithful and comfortable. Only a year and you're bored to death.

ELLIE: That's not true.

PAT: Then why the house guest?

ELLIE: The house guest is here on business. I don't know
anything about her—personal preferences.

PAT: But you've got a feeling, haven't you?

(QUINCEY *enters the living room.*)

QUINCEY: Ellie, do we have a garlic press?

PAT: [*Smartly*] Bottom drawer on the left, under the sink.

QUINCEY: Ellie?

ELLIE: That's right.

(QUINCEY *exits.*)

PAT: Little Miss Step and Fetch It. But cute. I'll admit that.
Cute.

ELLIE: You're jealous.

PAT: Not of her.

ELLIE: She's good for me.

PAT: She worships you. Good for your ego.

ELLIE: You won't give up, will you?

PAT: She's no challenge. That's what makes the knees
tremble and the wind chimes ring: the challenge. Without it, boredom.

ELLIE: If challenge means sitting up night after night
wondering in whose bed you'll find your drunken lover,
I've had enough challenge for a lifetime, thanks.

(*From the kitchen,* MARGO's *voice.*)

MARGO: All right, you two. I need some help!

PAT: [*To* ELLIE] Obviously, you haven't. [*To* MARGO] Coming!

(*They go into the kitchen.*)

MARGO: [*To* ELLIE] I understand you make magnificent sauce.
PAT: She does.
MARGO: [*To* PAT] And what are you good at?
PAT: [*Grinning*] My specialty is—mixing drinks.
ELLIE: [*Warning*] Pat . . .
MARGO: Mine is drinking them. [*To* ELLIE, *about the kitchen*] It's all yours. Let me know when you're ready for the spaghetti to go in.

(PAT *and* MARGO *go into the living room,* ELLIE *looking worriedly after them.*)

QUINCEY: [*To* ELLIE] Hi. I love you. I missed you.

(ELLIE *smiles nervously, proceeds to make sauce.* QUINCEY *presses garlic, cuts bread, etc.*

In the living room:)

MARGO: Straight up. A shot glass is fine.
PAT: I can tell you're my kind of woman.

(*In the kitchen:*)

QUINCEY: I'm jealous.
ELLIE: Don't be silly. I don't even know the woman.
QUINCEY: Not her. Pat.
ELLIE: I was crazy for five years. I won't go back.
QUINCEY: Sometimes I think you're still in love with her.
ELLIE: [*Ignoring that*] She's getting drunk, Quincey. You've got to get her out of here right after supper. Can you drive that truck of hers?
QUINCEY: I suppose so.

ELLIE: She's uncontrollable when she's drunk. She talks too much.

QUINCEY: That could be embarrassing.

ELLIE: And she'll try to seduce anyone—if she thinks it'll hurt me.

QUINCEY: Don't worry. I wouldn't fall for that.

(*In the living room:*)

MARGO: [*At window*] It looks like snow.

PAT: No way. It's too late in the season.

MARGO: It's a snow sky. [*She accepts drink.*] Thank you. So, exactly who are you?

PAT: [*Looking at sky*] A friend.

MARGO: Oh?

PAT: An ex-friend.

MARGO: You don't know which?

PAT: Like the weather up here, it could change any minute.

MARGO: You're from this area?

PAT: I lived here for five years. In this house.

MARGO: Oh. Ellie bought it from you?

PAT: Partly.

MARGO: What do you do?

PAT: I restore old things. Antiques.

MARGO: How about old writers?

PAT: I could open a department. [*Pause.*] You're not old.

MARGO: No? I had my success so early. I peaked at twenty-five—and there are too many years left after that. Girl Genius goes dry.

PAT: You're still writing.

MARGO: Trying. Strange. I had so much to say when I was twenty-five.

PAT: Does a writer write from imagination or experience?

MARGO: Experience first. That triggers the imagination.

PAT: And you're short on experience?

MARGO: [*Pause.*] Interesting.

PAT: Are you?

MARGO: Yes. Ten years ago I closed the door. I'd had as much experience as I could bear. Enough to last, I thought. [PAT *pours another drink, looks questioningly at* MARGO.] Not yet. But meeting Ellie this week . . .

PAT: Yes?

MARGO: So full of life, of ideas. I never thought of teaching.

PAT: Ellie loves it.

MARGO: It frightens me.

PAT: It's a challenge.

MARGO: Ellie makes me feel that I can do it. She makes me feel alive again—brave. I almost want to live.

PAT: I see.

MARGO: [*Quickly, to kitchen*] How are you doing in there?

(*From kitchen:*)

ELLIE: Under way. [*To* QUINCEY] Go in the living room, honey. Relax.

QUINCEY: I'd rather stay with you.

ELLIE: I'd rather you kept an eye on Pat.

QUINCEY: [*Reluctantly*] Oh. [*She gives* ELLIE *a kiss as she goes into the living room.* ELLIE *gives her a warning look.*] Sorry. Just doing what comes naturally. [*She goes into the living room.*]

MARGO: Whatever it is, it smells good.

QUINCEY: It'll be good. Ellie's a super cook.

PAT: [*To* QUINCEY] You think everybody's just wonderful, don't you?

QUINCEY: [*To* PAT] Not necessarily.

MARGO: [*Quickly*] I'm sure Ellie cooks as well as she does everything else.

PAT: We're obviously all aware of Ellie's talents.

QUINCEY: [*Confused, quickly*] Tell me about the conference.

MARGO: The conference?

QUINCEY: In Philadelphia.

MARGO: Oh. Well, I gave a timid little lecture and Ellie led the applause.

QUINCEY: Where did you stay?

MARGO: The Concord.

QUINCEY: So did Ellie.

MARGO: Yes. Everyone at the conference stayed at the Concord. It's a lovely old hotel.

QUINCEY: I've never been there. I've never been to a conference.

PAT: You haven't missed a thing.

QUINCEY: What happens? What do you do?

MARGO: You meet, have assemblies, lectures. . . .

QUINCEY: Day and night?

MARGO: Days mostly. There was a terrible dinner the first night—a command performance. Shoeleather butterfly steaks, frozen vegetables and speakers. Deadly. Everyone glued themselves to the bar afterward, I'm told. The turnout at the early session the next morning must have been very small.

QUINCEY: Ellie doesn't drink.

MARGO: We didn't stay. We spent the evening talking.

QUINCEY: In your room?

MARGO: In hers. [*To* PAT] Would you freshen this?

QUINCEY: Me, too.

PAT: [*To* QUINCEY] Oh. Sorry. [*She starts to mix drink.*] We need ice. I'll get it. [*She goes to kitchen.*]

ELLIE: [*To* PAT] Will you take it easy?

PAT: Nag, nag. I'm just being the genial host.

ELLIE: —ess.

PAT: [*Prissy*] Hostess.

ELLIE: The trouble with you is you don't like women.

PAT: Are you kidding?

ELLIE: You don't. Not really. You don't like yourself and you don't like other women.

PAT: Stop philosophizing and keep cooking. [*She slaps* ELLIE *on the ass and exits to living room with ice.*]

MARGO: I know that I'd enjoy working with Ellie.

PAT: [*Entering*] Ice, coming up.

(*In the kitchen,* ELLIE *tosses her apron on the sink and heads to the living room.*)

MARGO: But I'm nervous about making a commitment—to teaching.

ELLIE: [*Entering*] The sauce is simmering. You can put on the water for the spaghetti.

MARGO: [*Charmingly to* QUINCEY] Would you?

ELLIE: [*Before* QUINCEY *can answer*] Thanks, honey.

(QUINCEY, *irritated, goes to kitchen.*)

PAT: We were having a fascinating conversation: how you and Margo discovered one another across a crowded room in Philadelphia.

MARGO: That's not quite what I said.

PAT: And changed the course of one another's lives.

ELLIE: Pat!

MARGO: Of my life. I said that meeting you was meaningful to me. [*An awkward pause.*] And it might well change the course of my life. [*Laughs.*] It's a course that could use some changing, believe me.

PAT: [*To* ELLIE] Your boundless enthusiasm and zest for challenge has sparked new life, presented new horizons.

ELLIE: I've always admired Margo's work.

PAT: The sun rises brightly over the bay: a new day, a new world. . . .

ELLIE: I was in awe when I met her.

MARGO: Were you really?

PAT: Presto! A marriage—of talents.

ELLIE: [*To* MARGO] Oh, yes.

MARGO: I liked you instantly—and trusted you. That's rare for me.

ELLIE: You don't seem like a skeptic.

MARGO: Not a skeptic. A wounded woman.

PAT: Tell me about it.

ELLIE: Will you shut up?

MARGO: I felt you really liked me.

ELLIE: I did. I do.

MARGO: I like you, too.

(*They smile at each other.*)

PAT: Put some music to that and we'll dance to it. [*In frustration*] Where's the poker? I want to stoke the fire.

ELLIE: [*Crossing to the window*] I don't know. In the crib. Look for it.

MARGO: Pat used to live here, she was telling me.

ELLIE: She was?

PAT: We used to live here together.

MARGO: I thought perhaps something like that. [ELLIE *looks at her quickly.*] You're snippy with each other. You must know each other very well.

PAT: Perceptive.

MARGO: It goes with being a writer. Occupational handicap—or advantage. Depends on your point of view.

PAT: She lives with Quincey now.

(ELLIE *looks sharply at* PAT.)

MARGO: Oh?

ELLIE: [*Quickly*] We share an apartment near the university. Rents are very high.

MARGO: And you. Do you have a roommate, Pat?

PAT: Sometimes. And sometimes not.

MARGO: I guess I'm the only loner here. I have had roommates though. [ELLIE *and* PAT *look with interest.*] I remember my college roommate. [*She laughs.*]

PAT: I never had a college roommate. Ellie did.

MARGO: Mine had peroxide hair. Frizzy. She lost her virginity in the entrance hall, after hours, her freshman year. Bled all over the bathroom. Put me in a state of terror: I was sure that going to bed with a man was tantamount to a seige of battle.

PAT: Wasn't it?

(MARGO *just smiles.*)

ELLIE: My college roommate was beautiful. The most beautiful girl on campus. The jocks used to line up in the lounge, waiting for her. She gave them all a hard time.

PAT: Perfect Peggy. [*To* MARGO] You'll excuse my attitude but I've heard this story a thousand times.

MARGO: You're about to hear it again. I'm interested.

ELLIE: No. [*Pause.*] She was just perfect, that's all.

MARGO: [*Easily*] And you loved her.

ELLIE: [*Taken aback*] Yes.

MARGO: It's nice to remember friends we've loved. What happened to her?

PAT: Perfect Peggy panicked. She got married.

MARGO: That's nice. Do you hear from her?

ELLIE: Christmas cards, now and then.

MARGO: You should look her up. It's fun to see how people change.

ELLIE: I'd rather remember her.

PAT: You can control your memories. You don't have to remember that she had a large wart on the back of her ear. . . .

ELLIE: She didn't have any warts!

PAT: Or she picked her nose.

ELLIE: Pat!

PAT: Or she drank a little too much. [*She pours herself another drink.*]

ELLIE: Stop it.

PAT: Or she fooled around. . . . [*She offers* MARGO *a drink.* MARGO *refuses.*] You can shine memories up real nice. But live people—they're a little harder to control.

ELLIE: [*Quickly*] I wrote to her recently, as a matter of fact. I told her about the cabin and invited her to bring her family up some weekend.

PAT: No kidding?

ELLIE: I don't know why I did that. I was—

PAT: Bored. [ELLIE *looks sharply at* PAT.] I'd like to meet Perfect Peggy.

ELLIE: I hope that can be avoided. [QUINCEY *enters, pours another drink.*] How's it going, Quincey? [QUINCEY *doesn't respond.*] Take it easy. You're not a drinker. [QUINCEY *slugs it.*] Are you all right?

QUINCEY: I think I'm not going to feel so good.

ELLIE: Go upstairs and lie down.

QUINCEY: Not on your life.

MARGO: We were talking about college roommates. Did you have a college roommate, Quincey?

PAT: Yeah. The professor.

QUINCEY: I only lived in the dorm six months. It wasn't my style. I couldn't feel free there. It's an up-tight school. [*To* ELLIE] Sorry, it's true.

MARGO: What do you mean, "up-tight"?

PAT: It means closed up tight, constipated.

ELLIE: Pat!

MARGO: I know what the word means. I haven't been dead —just cloistered.

QUINCEY: For instance: [*A pause. She doesn't know whether to go ahead or not.*] One person, a sophomore, tried to form a Gay Lib group. . . .

MARGO: Gay Lib? [*To* PAT] I know what it means.

PAT: I figured you did.

MARGO: [*To* QUINCEY] And?

QUINCEY: They kicked her out of the dorm.

MARGO: Who did?

QUINCEY: The administration. The rest of the kids, we rallied and picketed and the trustees had a hearing. They let her stay in school—if she lived off campus. She couldn't live in the dorm.

ELLIE: Quincey . . .

QUINCEY: It's true, isn't it?

ELLIE: It was four years ago. The administration has changed. There are some radical groups on campus now.

QUINCEY: The faculty's still in the closet.

MARGO: Ellie tells me there's a professed Communist on the staff. That's a far cry from my college days.

QUINCEY: There may be a two-headed donkey, too, but there sure as hell aren't any homosexuals!

ELLIE: It's a conservative school. This is a conservative state.

QUINCEY: Somebody has to make change happen. Somebody who believes in the goodness of themselves, of what they are.

PAT: So do it.

QUINCEY: [*Frantically*] I can't! Everything I do reflects on Ellie. I want to be honest and free and proud . . .

ELLIE: Quincey, that's enough. [QUINCEY *turns and runs upstairs to the bedroom.*] She's not used to drinking.

MARGO: She seems to be really upset.

ELLIE: I'll go. [*Follows* QUINCEY *upstairs.*]

MARGO: [*To* PAT] Well. I'm not sure I know what all that was about.

PAT: I expect you do.

MARGO: Young people are all crusaders these days.

PAT: Come on, Margo. Don't give me that "Lawsy, Miss Scarlett, I don't know nothing about birthing babies" act.

MARGO: I don't know what you're talking about. [*Rises.*] I'd better check on the spaghetti. I hope Quincey will feel like eating. I made enough for six people. [*She passes the window.*] See? I told you it looked like snow.

PAT: [*Looking out window*] Well, I'll be damned.

(MARGO *goes to kitchen, leaving* PAT *in living room.* PAT *pours another drink. Upstairs:*)

ELLIE: Quincey . . .

QUINCEY: Why'd you put her in our room?

ELLIE: It's the nicest room. She's a special guest.

QUINCEY: You really want to impress her, don't you?

ELLIE: I did.

QUINCEY: I'm sorry. I couldn't help it. I didn't say anything about you.

ELLIE: If she doesn't know now, she's retarded.

QUINCEY: What difference does it make? She may be, herself. If she's not, so what? I love you. I want the world to know it.

ELLIE: I could lose my job.

QUINCEY: Oh, Ellie.

ELLIE: It makes people uncomfortable. They don't understand.

QUINCEY: It's time we made them understand.

ELLIE: Quincey, I know you're right.

QUINCEY: Then, why won't you do something about it? Aren't you proud? Don't you like yourself?

ELLIE: I like being a woman.

QUINCEY: A woman who loves other women.

ELLIE: Quincey, listen to me! When I was your age, "lesbian" was a dictionary word used only to frighten teen-age girls and parents. Mothers fainted, fathers became violent, landlords evicted you, and nobody would hire you. A lesbian was like a vampire: she looked in the mirror and there was no reflection.

QUINCEY: You're scared.

ELLIE: Of course I'm scared. I don't want to be different. I don't want people pointing fingers at me, misguided altruists feeling sorry for me.

QUINCEY: You're a VIP on campus. You could be a figurehead.

ELLIE: I don't have the courage to be a figurehead, Quincey. I'm sorry. [*She starts to leave.*]

QUINCEY: Ellie? I hope I didn't screw things up for you. I don't want to hurt you. I love you. I love you, love you, love you. [ELLIE *holds her.*] It's just that I'm so fucking tired of living in a closet!

ELLIE: [*Pause.*] Are you going to be all right?

QUINCEY: As long as I'm here.

ELLIE: Think you can come downstairs?

QUINCEY: Give me a minute. [ELLIE *releases her, starts to leave.*] I'm sorry.

ELLIE: So am I.

QUINCEY: Someday.

ELLIE: I hope so. [*She comes down the stairs, into the kitchen. To* MARGO] She's all right. Just a little too much to drink. She'll be down for supper.

MARGO: Good.

ELLIE: Can I help?

MARGO: In a minute.

(ELLIE *goes into living room.*)

ELLIE: It's snowing.

PAT: Hard and fast. So I was wrong. I'm not often wrong.

ELLIE: You'd better go right after supper, Pat. I don't want you marooned here all night.

PAT: Don't worry. I've got four-wheel drive. Is the kid all right?

ELLIE: She's not a kid.

PAT: Sorry. Is the young woman all right?

ELLIE: She'll be fine. She doesn't have your tolerance for alcohol.

PAT: She doesn't have my experience.

ELLIE: Thank God.

PAT: You're not in love with her.

ELLIE: I love her.

PAT: It's not the same thing.

ELLIE: It's a lot more reliable.

PAT: What are you going to do, bounce her off your knee when you hear the wind chimes again? Dump her?

ELLIE: No. I'm not going to hurt her.

PAT: You won't be able to help yourself. [*Pause.*] I'd rather you stay with Quincey.

ELLIE: What?

PAT: I'll still have a chance then.

ELLIE: Stop it.

PAT: That one [*Indicating kitchen*] is real competition. I don't want to see that happen.

ELLIE: You don't have anything to do with it.

PAT: Don't I?

(*From the kitchen:*)

MARGO: Okay, set the table!

(ELLIE *begins to do so,* PAT *pours another drink in the living room.* QUINCEY *comes down the stairs,* PAT *sees her, motions her in.*)

PAT: How're you feeling?

QUINCEY: Better.

PAT: This stuff is poison. You got to work up a tolerance, takes years.

QUINCEY: You ought to know.

PAT: What are you going to do?

QUINCEY: About what?

PAT: Your celebrity rival in there.

QUINCEY: She's no rival.

PAT: I wouldn't jump to that conclusion.

QUINCEY: Ellie says you're a troublemaker.

PAT: Do you believe everything Ellie says?

QUINCEY: Most of it. She's as honest as she can be. She wouldn't hurt me.

PAT: She wouldn't mean to. [*Pause.*] I know a game that will nip that in the bud.

QUINCEY: No games. I don't play games.

PAT: It's your funeral.

QUINCEY: [*Pause.*] What is the game?

PAT: I'll come on to you, see. She'll get jealous . . .

QUINCEY: No.

PAT: It'll work.

QUINCEY: No.

PAT: Couldn't hurt.

QUINCEY: No. I won't play games with Ellie.

(ELLIE *enters.*)

PAT: We're getting to know each other.

ELLIE: How about earning your supper?

QUINCEY: I'll get the flatwear.

PAT: Want another drink first, Quincey?

ELLIE: She's had enough.

PAT: Oh, listen to Mommy.

QUINCEY: I don't want another drink.

ELLIE: [*At window*] It's really coming down.

(PAT *is at bar.*)

PAT: A late snow. Something like a last chance, wouldn't you say?

(MARGO *enters.*)

MARGO: What was that?

PAT: A late snow. Something like a last chance.

MARGO: [*Pause.*] I suppose so.

(*Car lights outside, a horn.*)

310

ELLIE: What's that?

QUINCEY: [*At back door*] A car outside.

MARGO: A stranded motorist, probably. The roads must be slippery.

(*A voice calls,* "Ellie!")

ELLIE: [*At door*] Who is it?

VOICE: [*Offstage*] Ellie, I've been driving for hours. I thought I'd never find you. I know I should have called but I just couldn't. I hope you don't mind.

ELLIE: Peggy? [PEGGY's *at the door.*] Peggy!

(PEGGY *pours into* ELLIE's *arms.*)

PEGGY: I'm so glad to see you. I thought I was going to slide into a ditch, it's like driving on glass and my snow tires are old, they hardly have any tread. . . .

ELLIE: You look just the same.

PEGGY: You're lying. I look older.

ELLIE: A year or two.

PEGGY: [*Handing* ELLIE *her suitcase*] Here. Is it just terrible of me to come barging in?

ELLIE: No. Of course not.

PEGGY: I didn't have time to call. I walked out on Jim again. The second time this year. I just got in the car, I didn't know where I was going, then I remembered your letter was in my pocketbook, so I followed the directions and here I am. The directions were very good, I usually get lost a dozen times.

ELLIE: Come in.

PEGGY: Oh, you've got company. How stupid of me. I should have called, shouldn't I?

ELLIE: This is Pat, Quincey, Margo, Peggy.

PAT: Perfect Peggy. What do you know.

PEGGY: What?

PAT: Ellie used to talk about you—a lot. I called you Perfect Peggy. [*Pause.*] Forget it.

MARGO: Nice to meet you.

QUINCEY: Hi.

MARGO: Fortunately, we have plenty of food. Join us.

ELLIE: There's a guest bedroom, off to the right, upstairs. Can you manage that?

PEGGY: I managed to get it down the stairs, I guess I can get it up.

ELLIE: Make yourself comfortable, I'll be right up. [PEGGY *goes up the stairs. To* QUINCEY, PAT, MARGO] Can you handle everything down here?

PAT: I don't know. It's getting damned complicated.

MARGO: Go ahead. Five minutes till supper.

ELLIE: I'm sorry about all this, Margo.

MARGO: One has to learn to roll with the punches. I'm rather enjoying it; it's quite educational.

ELLIE: I'll figure something out.

MARGO: I'm sure you will.

(MARGO *smiles as* ELLIE *mounts the stairs.*

PAT *is at the window with* QUINCEY.)

PAT: The trouble with a late snow is—it's unexpected and messy as hell.

CURTAIN

ACT II

MARGO *is lying down in the living room, reading. Outside, the noise of grinding gears and an occasional "Push!" "Rock it!" from* PAT *and* QUINCEY.

ELLIE *and* PEGGY *are in the kitchen, finishing dishes.*

It is dark outside.

PEGGY: . . . The first three or four years were good, Ellie. I had the kids, we bought the house, we had dreams. Jimmy was the bright young man in college, you remember.

ELLIE: I remember. "Most likely to succeed." Most popular girl weds boy "most likely."

PEGGY: Well, the world is full of colleges and every year thousands of bright young men, all of them "most likely," descend on the corporate world, swarming towards offices labeled "Executive Vice-President" like salmon dashing for the mating grounds. Head of Northeastern Sales is as far as Jimmy got.

ELLIE: That sounds impressive.

PEGGY: Not to Jimmy. It's a middle-management job. Nobody gets promoted from there. Jimmy says it's the slot reserved for failures. Eight years ago, he quit. He needs success, Ellie, he hungers for it the way kids cry for love. He opened his own business. We borrowed from his folks and my folks and we took the kids' tuition money we'd saved—he opened a luxury hardware business.

ELLIE: Luxury hardware?

PEGGY: You know, fancy shelves, early American doorknobs, drawer pulls, drop latches, indirect lighting systems, self-stick bulletin boards, velvet contact paper.

ELLIE: Luxury hardware.

PEGGY: Jimmy has always been farsighted. The time was ripe. So many people living in apartments now, doing their own decorating.

ELLIE: Luxury hardware.

PEGGY: Listen, it was a good idea. Unfortunately, the manager of Woolworth's dime store across the street was also farsighted and sold the same merchandise for 8 percent less. Jimmy went back to Hamilton Die, Head of Northeastern Sales. He thinks of himself as a failure.

ELLIE: And you?

PEGGY: [*Not responding*] I've been working at a thrift shop downtown, four days a week. Lois is a senior this year. She wants to go to Bard but it's out of the question. They only give half scholarships. If she works this summer, between her salary and mine, we'll just be able to get her through a year at State.

ELLIE: You wanted a house on Mulhaven Drive with a maid and a garden out back. In the driveway . . .

PEGGY: [*Joining in the litany*] . . . the *circular* driveway . . .

ELLIE: . . . lined with towering elms . . .

PEGGY: . . . and paved with . . .

ELLIE: Gold.

PEGGY: No. Slate.

ELLIE: You'd sit in the late afternoon, your exquisite straw hat casting perfect shadows on your perfect features . . .

PEGGY: . . . sipping tall, cool drinks . . .

ELLIE: . . . served on a silver tray, while planning that evening's formal dinner for the town dignitaries . . .

PEGGY: . . . and considering how someone in my position could help the less fortunate.

ELLIE: The fairy princess.

PEGGY: [*Laughing*] No. "Most popular girl weds boy most likely." I never got my circular drive: we have a carport —and a cleaning woman once a week.

ELLIE: Dreams rarely come true.

PEGGY: Yours did. You wanted to teach in a university.

ELLIE: You thought it was a dull, old-maid thing to do.

PEGGY: And to live in a funky apartment with mobiles and wall hangings.

ELLIE: I do.

PEGGY: And to have a funny shack somewhere to get away from it all.

ELLIE: This is it.

PEGGY: Your dreams came true.

ELLIE: Not wholly. I wanted someone to share it with, someone to be a part of it, from the beginning to the end. I always wanted that.

PEGGY: Well, you can't have everything. You got the most important part.

ELLIE: Did I?

PEGGY: And you did it yourself. You didn't depend on someone else. I could never have done that.

ELLIE: Of course you could.

PEGGY: No. I could never have done that. [*She laughs.*] The curse of a fairy princess.

ELLIE: You wanted to be a buyer. Remember how we used to go over the want ads on Sunday mornings. You were going to be a buyer for the fanciest store in town and I was going to teach. We'd live in a town house with high ceilings and hanging plants—

PEGGY: And mobiles and wall hangings? No, not me. That was you. I never wanted that.

ELLIE: Sometimes you did.

PEGGY: Never.

ELLIE: But the circular drive with the towering elms won out.

PEGGY: Actually, it's a development.

ELLIE: With a carport.

PEGGY: Yes. But it's my life. Mine and Jimmy's.

ELLIE: Why did you leave?

PEGGY: Eddie's at military school. Jim's father pays the tuition. "Make a man out of him." Frankly, I think it's making a jerk out of him. He's so damned disciplined, he doesn't know how to be a kid. Twelve years old and he gives orders like a five-star general. He won't stop at Head of Northeastern Sales.

ELLIE: Why did you leave, Peggy?

PEGGY: When a man thinks he's failed in business, he has to succeed somewhere. His job takes him on the road a lot so he has plenty of opportunity. I've never said a word about it, it's been going on for years. Oh, I haven't been lonely. I have a friend, Wanda. She works with me at the thrift shop. We go out to dinner and to the movies together. I've found letters from his girl friends and phone numbers in his wallet. He hasn't been home for a birthday or anniversary in years but I never accused him. I never accused him. How dare he accuse me!

ELLIE: Of having an affair?

PEGGY: How dare he?

ELLIE: Have you?

PEGGY: Why should he care if I did?

ELLIE: Did you?

PEGGY: He says, if you've thought about it, it's the same as doing it. I haven't done it!

ELLIE: You obviously want to.

PEGGY: Wanda thinks I should leave him.

ELLIE: What do you think?

PEGGY: I think he's a son of a bitch. I've put most of my life into this marriage. The kids will be out of school in a few years. I don't know. I don't know what I want. I guess that's why I came here. You're the only person I know who'll understand. You and Wanda.

ELLIE: [*Meaningfully*] Wanda?

PEGGY: You sound like Jim! Wanda is my friend, like you were my friend. I love her, like I loved you.

ELLIE: We loved each other—a step beyond friendship.

PEGGY: We were friends. Best friends. I never felt so close to anyone, until Wanda.

ELLIE: What you're feeling isn't friendship, Peggy. What we felt together wasn't friendship.

PEGGY: Of course it was! We loved each other.

ELLIE: We were in love with each other.

PEGGY: I'm not like that.

ELLIE: We made love.

PEGGY: That's not true!

ELLIE: Not often, we were both too scared. But we did make love. After the Saint Patrick's Party, New Year's Eve in New Hampshire, your birthday our senior year—I remember every time. I remember it because it was new and pure and perfect. It was always exciting, to the very end it was exciting. It was perfect.

PEGGY: You were going with Danny Rogers and I was going with Morton Tate—until the end of our senior year when I met Jim. We were good friends, Ellie. That's all. [*Pause.*] Danny Rogers is an assemblyman now. They say he's going to run for Congress. You missed a good bet. He married a mouse.

(*The door opens and* QUINCEY *and* PAT *enter, coats drenched from the snow.*)

QUINCEY: No luck.

PAT: We pushed and rocked and spun. It's already four inches and icing up. Nobody's going anywhere tonight.

PEGGY: Too bad Jim's not here. He could get it out.

ELLIE: You may not believe that this drunken woman is an ace mechanic, but she is. If Pat can't move that car, nobody can.

PEGGY: I've always felt that men were just naturally better suited for some things.

QUINCEY: I don't believe I heard that.

PAT: [*Flirting with* PEGGY] She doesn't have a wart behind her ear. Has she been picking her nose?

PEGGY: What?

ELLIE: Never mind. Take off that wet coat, Quincey.

PAT: [*To* QUINCEY] Mind Mama. [*To* PEGGY] Want a drink?

PEGGY: Why not?

PAT: Follow me.

(*They go into living room.*)

MARGO: And?

PAT: Can't budge it. Want a drink?

MARGO: No, thanks. I've got coffee.

PAT: Party pooper. Now, what do you want, Perfect Peggy?

PEGGY: An after-dinner drink would be fine.

PAT: Ugh.

PEGGY: Creme de cocoa.

PAT: Really?

PEGGY: I like it.

PAT: I'll see if there's some in the kitchen. [*Goes to kitchen.*]

PEGGY: Excuse me, I hope you won't think I'm rude but . . . [MARGO *looks up.*] are you one of them?

MARGO: I beg your pardon?

PEGGY: You know. One of them.

MARGO: One of what?

PEGGY: Do you like men?

MARGO: Some men.

PEGGY: Do you sleep with them?

MARGO: Men?

PEGGY: Yes.

MARGO: I've probably slept with more men than you've ever met.

PEGGY: Oh, good. It looks like we're all going to have to stay over. You and I can share a room.

PAT: [*Entering with bottle*] That's the first proposition of the night.

PEGGY: [*About bottle, quickly*] That looks fine. That's a very good brand.

PAT: Nothing but the best, baby. Nothing but the best.

(*In the kitchen:*)

QUINCEY: Are you all right?

ELLIE: I'm worried.

QUINCEY: About Pat?

ELLIE: Who's going to be the victim. It's Pat's pattern. Step One: Seduce somebody. Step Two: Hurt somebody else by doing it. It's called "See how much everybody loves me? Anybody who loves me deserves to be punished."

QUINCEY: She wanted me to play a game with her.

ELLIE: A game?

QUINCEY: To pretend I was attracted to her, to Pat. It was supposed to make you pay attention to me.

ELLIE: [*Smiling*] I know that game. It's designed not to make me pay attention to you—but to her.

QUINCEY: I don't understand.

ELLIE: You're too honest. I hope you never understand.

QUINCEY: Something's happening and I'm frightened.

(*In the living room:*)

PEGGY: Are you really an auto mechanic?

PAT: Nope. I'm an antique dealer. A multifaceted human being.

PEGGY: I love antiques. Do you do appraisals?

PAT: Sure. Where do you live?

PEGGY: Oh, I'm too far. About seventy miles.

PAT: I travel.

PEGGY: Maybe you could recommend someone in my area.

PAT: You left your husband, huh?

PEGGY: I need some time to think things over.

PAT: You're bored.

PEGGY: I don't think so.

PAT: You're bored with him, with your marriage.

PEGGY: Maybe I am.

PAT: It happens to everybody. How long have you been bored?

PEGGY: [*Laughs.*] About ten years.

PAT: When the kids started school.

PEGGY: How do you know?

PAT: I've heard it before. I've known a few disgruntled wives.

PEGGY: I'm not just a disgruntled wife. There's a lot more to it.

PAT: There always is.

MARGO: [*Irritated, rises.*] Excuse me. [*She goes upstairs, into the bathroom.*]

PAT: Tell me about you and Ellie.

PEGGY: We were good friends.

PAT: She says you were the most beautiful girl in the school.

PEGGY: My daughter looks just like me. She's beautiful. [*Smiles.*] Things change.

PAT: You're probably more beautiful now.

PEGGY: You are drunk.

PAT: I think women get better with age. Like good wine . . .

PEGGY: Ellie got prettier. She was gawky in college. I never went through that gawky stage. I guess I'm going through it now.

PAT: She really loved you.

PEGGY: We were good friends.

PAT: Romeo and Juliet, Damon and Pythias, Jonathan and David, Gertrude and Alice . . .

PEGGY: We were good friends.

PAT: Nobody could ever live up to you.

PEGGY: No. We were friends. Not that I'm passing judgment on your life-style, but we were just friends.

PAT: That's all?

PEGGY: That's all.

PAT: Another creme de cocoa?

(*In the kitchen:*)

QUINCEY: Let's go to bed. Let's just go upstairs and go to bed and let them all do whatever it is that they're going to do.

ELLIE: I can't. When Pat is drunk, she not only plays her games—she's also likely to set the house on fire, turn on the gas without lighting it, leave the grate off the fireplace, fall through the storm door.

QUINCEY: I don't understand why you stayed with her for five years.

ELLIE: It wasn't always like this. Sometimes she'd go for months without drinking. When we were first together, she hardly drank at all. We were so happy and so much in love—and when the drinking started again, I knew what it could be like, what we could have together—and I kept hoping it would come back. I suppose I thought it was my fault.

QUINCEY: It wasn't.

ELLIE: No. It's just the way life is. The wind chimes stop.

QUINCEY: Wind chimes?

ELLIE: The excitement goes, the thrill, the lust, whatever you want to call it.

QUINCEY: But that's just the beginning. That's when a relationship starts: when you stop lusting and start loving.

ELLIE: Is it?

QUINCEY: You have to work at it.

ELLIE: How would you know? You've never had a relationship. You've gone from college affair to college affair.

QUINCEY: We're a relationship.

ELLIE: You've stopped lusting?

QUINCEY: [*Grins.*] Not entirely. When I first saw you at campus orientation, my knees shook. You were at a picnic table, hostessing. I sat down on the grass about twenty yards away and stared. I stared for two hours. For four years, I stared. You were my fantasy. When I finally got into a class of yours, my first grad year, your face was drawn and pained. Your hands shook. I wanted to run to the front of the room and hold you in my arms.

ELLIE: I remember that day. It was the day after the accident.

QUINCEY: I watched you fall apart that year, piece by piece —and piece by piece, put yourself back together: stronger. I loved you for five years before I made love to you. And even then, your thoughts were somewhere else. I know that. I don't care. You're mine now.

ELLIE: Quincey. Go on to bed, honey.

QUINCEY: Where?

ELLIE: In my room. I'll have to move Margo.

QUINCEY: You can't do that.

ELLIE: Would you rather sleep with Perfect Peggy?

QUINCEY: I'd rather sleep with you. In our room.

ELLIE: I'll be up as soon as I get Pat settled.

QUINCEY: Not too long.

ELLIE: At the rate she's drinking, she won't be able to stand up much longer.

(QUINCEY *goes upstairs,* ELLIE *goes into living room.*)

PEGGY: Come on in, Ellie. Have a drink. Pat and I were discussing old times.

PAT: [*To* ELLIE] Your old times. [*To* PEGGY] Ellie doesn't drink.

PEGGY: I remember when she did. On the front porch of the frat house, you drank half a pint of Bourbon and did God-knows-what with Sammy Kincaid while poor Danny was out beating the bushes for you.

ELLIE: That's why I don't drink.

PAT: Peggy says your college days together were right out of *A Date with Judy*—Jane Powell and Shirley Temple, giggling girl friends.

PEGGY: Well, Ellie did have a crush on me. I remember that. You were very jealous of Jim.

ELLIE: Of course I was!

PEGGY: And you used to give me the answers in Economics III. I only took that course because all the brightest boys did.

ELLIE: The most-likely-to-succeeds? [*Pause.*] Morty wanted to sleep with you and you told him you couldn't because you were in love with me.

PEGGY: He was a creep. I wanted to shock him.

ELLIE: He spread it all over the campus.

PEGGY: It was a kick. Well, it wasn't true. Anyone who knew me, knew that.

ELLIE: I didn't.

PEGGY: The jocks used to line up in the lounge to see me.

ELLIE: Yes. And Saint Patrick's night our sophomore year, you got into my bed.

PEGGY: I was drunk. I thought you were Jim.

ELLIE: You hadn't even met Jim then.

PEGGY: Well, I thought you were Morty.

PAT: Morty was a creep.

ELLIE: New Year's Eve. Remember New Year's Eve? You were engaged to Jim. At midnight, everybody kissed. You didn't kiss Jim. You kissed me. In front of the whole fucking fraternity house. Jim walked out. You didn't see him again until spring semester.

PEGGY: I didn't meet him until spring semester.

PAT: Will the real Perfect Peggy please stand up?

PEGGY: It didn't happen! Not like that.

ELLIE: It did. And it's happening again. With Wanda.

PEGGY: I'm not a lesbian! [*She runs upstairs to the guest bedroom, stage left.*]

PAT: It wasn't real.

ELLIE: It was!

PAT: Even if it happened, it wasn't real. Unadmitted, without commitment.

ELLIE: It was so perfect.

PAT: You never faced the bills together, you never faced joblessness together, you never built a house together, a life together. You never faced death together. It wasn't real. We were real.

ELLIE: We didn't work.

PAT: Why? I don't know why. I love you.

ELLIE: You don't love you.

PAT: All right. I never wanted to be a woman. It's a crappy thing to be. You can't do anything! I saw my father raking in the money, playing big business, flying to Europe, to the Caribbean, buying booze and women in every part of the globe while my mother ran the diaper brigade for eight kids. She never got farther than the corner A&P. Her conversation was limited to baby talk and what she heard on the radio. My father met Al Capone—met him! While my mother was scrubbing underwear on a washboard. Here's your choice, kiddies. Which one would you rather be?

ELLIE: Your father was a crook. What's good about that?

PAT: Is a crook. A successful one. The main man in Boston. My mother's dead of a heart attack.

ELLIE: I didn't know.

PAT: Last year.

ELLIE: I didn't know.

PAT: It doesn't matter. She's been dead for forty years. We finally buried her. But he goes on. And so do I. And I don't know why anymore. . . . Give us a chance, Ellie.

ELLIE: It's too late.

PAT: Can't you remember how it was? We built a home together: we made love on that beach at midnight and sailed that broken-down boat under the stars until dawn. We were safe from the world.

ELLIE: For a while.

PAT: Then you started teaching. You were gone so much, seeing new people. That's why I went out with other women, Ellie. To make you know how much you loved me.

ELLIE: The wind chimes stopped. And we didn't know how to make it work. Too much has happened. We can't go back.

PAT: Let me come home, Ellie.

ELLIE: I'm sorry. This isn't your home anymore.

(PAT *lunges for the front door and exits as* MARGO *comes down the stairs.*)

MARGO: [*To* PAT] Hey! It's cold out there. [*To* ELLIE] Shouldn't you go after her?

ELLIE: She's safer outside than in. She's very drunk, Margo. She'll wander around in the snow until she gets cold and wet enough to come in. As long as she can't move the car, she's safe.

MARGO: You know her very well.

ELLIE: I thought I did.

MARGO: Are you still in love with her? [ELLIE *turns, shocked.*] I'm not blind.

ELLIE: I'm sorry. I didn't intend to bring you into all of this.

MARGO: Are you?

ELLIE: I love her. I remember being in love with her. [*Pause.*] No.

MARGO: Quincey?

ELLIE: She loves me.

MARGO: That wasn't the question.

ELLIE: Quincey says that once the thrill goes, when the knees stop trembling and the wind chimes stop tinkling, it's a job. You've got to work at it.

MARGO: She's right.

ELLIE: Pat and I didn't know how to do that.

MARGO: But Quincey does.

ELLIE: Probably. But I think you have to hear the chimes first.

MARGO: And you haven't?

ELLIE: Not with Quincey. I love her, I appreciate her, I'm thankful for her. But no chimes. Ever.

MARGO: I was married to a man once, much like Pat. Worse, I guess. He was not only a drunk but a violent drunk. And I loved him. I loved him long after I left him. And I loved again. A woman. She died ten years ago.

ELLIE: [*Surprised*] I'm sorry.

MARGO: I haven't written a publishable book since that time. I haven't let another human being touch me since that time. Oh, I've slept with a few. I picked up a salesman in the bar downstairs from my hotel room. He was from Detroit. I never saw him again. Another time, a bellhop. And a woman reporter from a newspaper up-state. She was in town for the afternoon to interview me. But they didn't touch me: not emotionally, not really physically. I made love to them. . . . It's hard to make anything last, Ellie. A job, a talent, a marriage.

ELLIE: A lot of people do it.

MARGO: A lot of people hold on to dead things. But to make something last—and live . . . It's harder with a woman. There are no rules. And the stakes are so very high. [*They look at each other for a moment.*] We worked at it. We worked very hard at it. We brought new things into our relationship, we challenged one another with ideas, with goals. We weren't always successful. We had bad years, years when I was sure it was over, when I thought it should be over. But we survived them, some-how. It was good again, it was working. [*Pause.*] I think I hated her for dying, for leaving me. And I was very frightened. I still am.

ELLIE: But you've learned to be alone.

MARGO: I don't do it very well. I need to share, to be a part of something. I, too, miss the wind chimes.

ELLIE: But they don't last. It doesn't last. You start to

build—and it's over. You start again—and it's over. Why bother?

MARGO: Because you need it. I need it. And we keep hoping, all of us: men and women, women and women, men and men, that we can make it work. What do you want, Ellie?

ELLIE: Someone to grow with. Someone to build with.

MARGO: You can do that with Quincey. What do you want, Ellie?

ELLIE: I want it all. I want the chimes, I want to tremble. I want that kind of crazy desire that surmounts reason. I want someone to live for, to die with. Someone to climb mountains for, slay dragons for, someone to snuggle with by a fire when the world is cold. Someone to show the first marigold of spring. I want a lover consumed by the greatest passion, a partner possessed of the greatest loyalty, a friend committed to the greatest love. I want it all.

With Pat, there was passion. With Quincey, there is loyalty. I don't want to settle. I want it all.

I thought I'd had it all with Peggy. Passion, loyalty, friendship. I thought it had been perfect. But it was so long ago and I was so young. I knew less then. Maybe I needed less, too.

MARGO: Does she remember it as perfect?

ELLIE: She doesn't remember it at all.

[QUINCEY *appears at the head of the stairs.*]

QUINCEY: Are you coming up?

ELLIE: In a minute.

[QUINCEY *comes down the stairs.*]

QUINCEY: Where's Pat?

MARGO: She's outside. Waiting for spring.

QUINCEY: Is she all right?

ELLIE: I want to wait and see. Go back to bed, honey. I'll be up in a minute.

QUINCEY: Okay. Hurry. [*She goes back up the stairs.*]

MARGO: What are you going to do, Ellie?

ELLIE: I don't want to hurt anybody.

MARGO: Why did you ask me here?

ELLIE: [*Pause.*] Because I liked you.

MARGO: Liked me?

ELLIE: Because I felt something. The night we talked in my hotel room, I felt something.

MARGO: What?

ELLIE: I don't know. Something. A beginning.

MARGO: And what are you going to do about it?

ELLIE: [*Pause.*] Wait.

MARGO: Why?

ELLIE: Because I'm scared. Because I'm tonguetied when I talk to you, and my knees feel weak. When I stand near you there's electricity between us like a living thing. Because something great is growing here and I'm afraid for it to start. I don't want it to end. And I don't know what you want.

MARGO: [*After a long moment*] I want you. [*Holds out her arms.*] Don't settle, Ellie. Let's reach for all of it.

(ELLIE *goes into* MARGO's *arms as* PAT *comes quietly in the back door, wet and drunken. She sees what is happening and sneaks quietly up the stairs to* PEGGY's *room.* PEGGY *is staring out the window at the lake.*)

PAT: Hi, there.

PEGGY: It's the abominable snowman.

PAT: The boat has a hole in it.

(*From the bedroom:*)

QUINCEY: Ellie?

(*In the living room:*)

327

ELLIE: [*To* MARGO] I've got to go.
MARGO: Not yet.

(*Upstairs:*)

PAT: [*Crossing the hallway to* QUINCEY'S *room*] Hi.
QUINCEY: Hi.
PAT: [*Explaining*] The boat has a hole in it.
QUINCEY: What?
PAT: Ellie wants you downstairs.

(QUINCEY *gets up as* PAT *goes back to* PEGGY'S *room.*)

PEGGY: Don't sit on the bed. You're all wet.
PAT: You want me to take them off?
PEGGY: No!

(*Downstairs:*)

MARGO: You've got to make a decision, Ellie.

(*Upstairs:*)

PAT: I will if you will.
PEGGY: Stop it! [*She starts to cry.*]
PAT: Hey, I'm sorry.

(*Downstairs:*)

MARGO: I have something at stake here, too, you know. I have everything at stake.

(*Upstairs:*)

PAT: Come on, cut the waterworks.
PEGGY: Hold me. Please hold me. I'm so afraid.
PAT: [*Doing it*] Perfect Peggy.

(QUINCEY *comes down the stairs, unsuspectingly turns the corner.*)

QUINCEY: Ellie? [*She sees* ELLIE *and* MARGO. *Turns, runs up the stairs.*]

ELLIE: Quincey!

QUINCEY: No! [*She runs into the room, slams and locks the door.* ELLIE *follows.*]

ELLIE: Quincey! Quincey?

QUINCEY: No!

MARGO: [*At the foot of the stairs*] Leave her alone, Ellie. Let her go.

(ELLIE *slowly comes down the steps, follows* MARGO *to the sofa, where they lie down together as the lights dim slowly, then cross-fade to dawn.*

PAT'S *in the hallway, greeting the morning.*)

PAT: Rise and shine! [QUINCEY *in her room and* PEGGY *in hers hear and rise and hurriedly begin to dress.*] The birds are chirping, the sun is shining and the late snow is melting into spring.

MARGO: [*Sitting up*] Why aren't you hung over?

ELLIE: [*Sleepily*] She never is.

MARGO: It's criminal.

PAT: Rise and shine, Ellie, put on the coffee! We itinerates have to get packing.

MARGO: Make it yourself, you chauvinist pig.

ELLIE: Believe me, you wouldn't want to drink it.

(PAT'S *in the kitchen, getting the pot out.*)

PAT: The pot, coffee, measuring cup: all ready! [ELLIE *rises, goes to the kitchen.* PAT *countercrosses to the living room. To* MARGO] Sleep well?

MARGO: Fine, thank you. What about you? Did you sleep in the snow?

PAT: I came in. [*Pause.*] Upstairs with Perfect Peggy.

MARGO: You're very sure of yourself, aren't you?

PAT: Not at all. I know what I want.

MARGO: Not Peggy.

PAT: Not Peggy. . . . I'm a gambler. Are you?

MARGO: No.

PAT: I can tell. Your odds are bad. She's a three-time loser. And I know the track. Are you betting win, place, or show?

MARGO: Across the board.

PAT: Want some advice?

MARGO: No.

PAT: Come back to town with me. I'll take you to dinner, we'll get to know each other. I'm a very interesting person.

MARGO: [*Smiles.*] No.

PAT: I'd make a great character for a book. You can study me.

MARGO: [*Smiles.*] No.

PAT: I can't take you out of the running, huh?

MARGO: [*Smiles.*] No.

(ELLIE *has put on the coffee and goes upstairs. She knocks on* QUINCEY's *door.*)

ELLIE: Quincey?

PAT: I'm going out to start the car. But I'm not going far. Ever.

(*Upstairs:*)

ELLIE: Quincey.

(QUINCEY *unlocks the door, admits* ELLIE.

Downstairs:)

PAT: Consider yourself warned.

(*Upstairs:*)

ELLIE: Quincey.

QUINCEY: That's why you brought her here.

ELLIE: No.

QUINCEY: It wasn't enough in Philadelphia.

ELLIE: That's not how it happened.

QUINCEY: And Chicago and Des Moines and how many other cities, how many other conferences, how many other business trips? I've been sitting home like an idiot, believing you.

ELLIE: It never happened before.

QUINCEY: What was I? A convenient place to rest?

ELLIE: I wanted it to work with us, Quincey.

QUINCEY: You never worked at it. My whole life is constructed around you. I can't write what I want to, it reflects on you. I can't be who I am, you'll lose your job. "May I ask someone home for supper? May I have the key to the cabin? May I use the car? May I, may I, may I?" Ellie decides everything. What Ellie wants, what Ellie needs, how Ellie wants to live. I don't even exist!

ELLIE: I'm sorry.

QUINCEY: Sorry isn't good enough! You made a commitment to me!

ELLIE: I didn't want to. Do you remember that? I didn't want to.

QUINCEY: I thought you'd learn to love me.

ELLIE: I wanted to. I really wanted to.

QUINCEY: We're good together!

ELLIE: No. It isn't enough, Quincey. It's bad for me—it's bad for you. You have so much love to give.

QUINCEY: I love you.

ELLIE: I love you. But not the right way.

QUINCEY: Is this just an affair? A week? A month? I'll wait.

ELLIE: No.

QUINCEY: I'm good for you.

ELLIE: But I'm not good for you. You're young, you can be free, you can be open, you can build the kind of life you want. You can fight for what you believe in. You can make a difference, Quincey. There's a world of women out there, young women, who'll stand with you.

QUINCEY: I want you.

ELLIE: I can't.

QUINCEY: Are you in love with her?

ELLIE: I don't know yet. I think so.

QUINCEY: Then you're not in love with me. You've never been in love with me. [*Pause.*] I guess I've always known that. I thought I could make it happen.

ELLIE: I never lied to you.

QUINCEY: Not in words. By holding me, living with me, making love to me. You lied to me. [*She hits the wind chimes at the window.*] I heard them. You didn't.

ELLIE: I kept hoping I would.

QUINCEY: No. You just wanted a comfortable place to wait.

ELLIE: Quincey . . .

QUINCEY: You used me. That's the most degrading part of all.

ELLIE: I'm sorry.

QUINCEY: I have some sweaters and things in the drawers. I'd like to pack them. [*Pause.*] Can I use that duffel bag?

ELLIE: [*Nods. Going to her.*] Quincey . . .

QUINCEY: [*Pulling away*] For God's sake, leave me with some dignity.

(ELLIE *backs from the room, watching* QUINCEY *for a moment, then closes the door.*

PEGGY *comes out of the bathroom, dressed.*)

PEGGY: Good morning. [*She goes into her bedroom, gets her suitcase.*] Ready to go. Hope I can get my car out.

ELLIE: You're leaving?

PEGGY: I'm going home.

ELLIE: Oh.

PEGGY: I have a life there. It's not what I had in mind, but it's mine.

ELLIE: With Jim?

PEGGY: He won't change. Neither can I.

ELLIE: And Wanda?

PEGGY: Wanda is my friend. That's all. That's the way it's going to stay. I can't deal with it, Ellie. It takes courage: a kind I haven't got.

ELLIE: You came here for help. I'm afraid I didn't offer much.

PEGGY: I came looking for an answer. An answer that worked for me. I found it. I have a nice house, two lovely children, a good job. I'll settle for that. [*She proceeds down the stairs with her suitcase.*]

(PAT *enters from the yard.*)

PAT: Car's started. We'll have no problem getting out.
PEGGY: What about mine?
PAT: It's only a couple of feet from the road.
PEGGY: Would you do it for me?
PAT: My pleasure.
PEGGY: Now.
PAT: Don't you want a cup of coffee first?
PEGGY: I'll stop on the road. I want to go home. Before I change my mind. [*She extends her hand.*] Ellie, thanks. Don't go to any more New Year's Eve parties. It gets everybody in a lot of trouble.

(PEGGY *and* PAT *exit.*

QUINCEY *comes down the stairs, carrying the duffel bag. She and* ELLIE *look at one another for a minute.*)

QUINCEY: I want the apartment. I decorated it and I want it.
ELLIE: [*Meekly*] All right.
QUINCEY: Call me when you want to pick up your things. I won't be there. [*She pauses, looks at the Dutch cupboard, touches it.*] To remember me by. [*She looks at* MARGO.] I suppose I'll see you around campus. [*She crosses to the door.*] Work at it. [*She exits.*]
MARGO: [*After a moment*] There is no painless way.
ELLIE: Will we have this moment?
MARGO: There are no guarantees.
ELLIE: Perfect Peggy settled.
MARGO: Some people have to. [*Pause.*] And some people can't.

333

(ELLIE *pours a cup of coffee and hands it to* MARGO.)

ELLIE: The snow's almost gone.

(PAT *enters brightly, takes the coffee out of* MARGO's *hand, sips it.*)

PAT: Thanks. Well, Peggy's on her way. You always had good taste, Ellie. [*She pockets a piece of paper.*] Her phone number. She needs an occasional appraisal. [*She gulps the rest of* MARGO's *coffee, hands her the empty cup.*] Quincey's waiting in the car.

ELLIE: Thanks for delivering the hutch.

PAT: It's okay. I overcharged her. [*To* MARGO] Across the board?

MARGO: Across the board.

PAT: I'll be waiting at the finish line. [*She kisses* ELLIE *on the cheek.*] See you soon, Ellie.

ELLIE: No.

PAT: [*Shaking* MARGO's *hand*] Good luck.

MARGO: We're running on a long track, Pat.

PAT: I've got a lot of patience.

(PAT *exits.*

ELLIE *watches them go.*

MARGO *pours two cups of coffee.*)

MARGO: Black?

ELLIE: Fine.

MARGO: [*Gives the coffee to* ELLIE.] Where will you live?

ELLIE: I'll find an apartment.

MARGO: I'll need to live near campus. How would that look, our living together?

ELLIE: Do you care?

MARGO: No.

ELLIE: Neither do I. I'm tired of living a half-life.

MARGO: So am I.

ELLIE: I can't march. But I won't hide. [*She starts up the stairs,* MARGO *follows.*] What's your favorite color?
MARGO: Blue.
ELLIE: Favorite flower?
MARGO: Marigold.
ELLIE: Favorite season?
MARGO: Summer.
ELLIE: Favorite food?
MARGO: Pineapple.

(*In the bedroom:*)

ELLIE: Pineapple?
MARGO: [*Smiling*] Pomegranate?

(ELLIE *looks out the window.* MARGO *sits on the bed.*)

ELLIE: The snow is gone. The sun is out. [*She opens the window.*] Favorite person? [*The wind chimes tinkle in the breeze. They both laugh.* MARGO *holds out her arms.*] Let's try to keep it that way.

CURTAIN

THE KILLING OF SISTER GEORGE
A Comedy in Three Acts

by
Frank Marcus

The Killing of Sister George was first presented by the Bristol Old Vic at the Theatre Royal, Bristol, by arrangement with Michael Codron. It was subsequently presented at the Duke of York's Theatre, London, on June 17, 1965, by Michael Codron in association with Bernard Delfont with the following cast:

(In order of appearance)

ALICE "CHILDIE" MC NAUGHT .... *Eileen Atkins*
JUNE BUCKRIDGE (SISTER GEORGE) .... *Beryl Reid*
MRS. MERCY CROFT .... *Lally Bowers*
MADAME XENIA .... *Margaret Courtenay*

It was first presented in the United States on October 5, 1966, at the Belasco Theatre, New York, by Helen Bonfils and Morton Gottlieb, by arrangement with Michael Codron in association with Bernard Delfont, with the original cast, except for Madame Xenia, played by Polly Rowles.

British Production designed by Catherine Browne
American Production supervised by William Ritman
Directed by Val May

ACT I

*The living room of a West End flat in London. A bay
window at the back overlooks roofs. The furniture, an in-
congruous mixture of antique, nineteen-thirtyish and modern, looks expensive but ill-assorted. There is a large radio,
bearing trophies and framed certificates; elsewhere there
are embroidered cushions in profusion, various bric-a-brac;
and Victorian dolls are on the chairs and in the corner of
a chintz-covered settee. Downstage right an arch leads to
the hall and entrance; upstage left a door leads to the bedroom; a passage off up left leads to the bathroom, and
another door downstage leads to the kitchen. The curtain
rises on an empty stage. It is a Tuesday afternoon in late
September. Presently the front door bangs, and* JUNE BUCK-
RIDGE *enters. She is a rotund, middle-aged woman, wearing
a belted white mackintosh. She is very agitated.*

ALICE: [*Calling from the kitchen*] George? . . . George,
is that you? [JUNE *opens a cigar box, finds it empty, and
throws it down.* ALICE *throws up the hatch between the
kitchen and the living room.* ALICE *is a girl-woman in
her thirties, looking deceptively young. She conveys an
impression of pallor: her hair, eyes, and complexion are
all very light. She is wearing a sweater and jeans, with
a plastic apron and orange rubber gloves, having been
in the middle of the washing up. She is very surprised.*]
George, what on earth . . . ? [JUNE *throws a doll to the
floor.*] George, what are you doing at home at this time
of the afternoon?

(JUNE *lights a cheroot from a box on the mantelpiece.*)

JUNE: [*After a pause*] They are going to murder me.
ALICE: What—
JUNE: I've suspected it for some time.
ALICE: What?
JUNE: Will you kindly close that hatch?

339

ALICE: [*Closing the hatch and entering the sitting room from the kitchen*] What are you talking about?

JUNE: [*Brutally*] Shut up. You know nothing. [ALICE, *silenced, watches* JUNE *puffing nervously on her cigar.*] That Australian bitch, that Sheila, let it out. . . .

ALICE: The one who used to be a lady cricketer?

JUNE: [*With disgust*] Yes—the lolloping great trollop!

ALICE: So, what did she say?

JUNE: [*Very excited now*] It was in the tea break, when she gave me a cup of tea. "I trust you're in good health," she said, with a sly wink.

ALICE: There's nothing wrong with that.

JUNE: I knew what she meant. I got the message.

ALICE: It might have been quite innocuous—

JUNE: Innocuous! They are trying to kill me, and you call that innocuous! [*Pacing up and down*] Somebody's leaked it to her—another Australian. They're everywhere: the place is rampant with them; they multiply like rabbits.

ALICE: You're imagining things.

JUNE: No, not rabbits, opossums! ! Dreary little pests.

ALICE: Well, anyway, what did you *do?*

JUNE: I left.

ALICE: [*Alarmed*] You walked out of rehearsal?

JUNE: [*Subdued*] I wasn't going to let some illiterate bitch wink at me. . . .

ALICE: [*Biting her lip*] They won't like it. . . .

JUNE: I've given six years' devoted service to that program.

ALICE: You said yourself: they don't like contract artists to have tantrums—

JUNE: [*Getting excited again*] They have no right to do this to me. I'm a senior member of the cast. If they wanted to—[*She swallows.*] write me out, they should have called me to the office in the proper manner—

ALICE: Nobody wants to write you out. It's unthinkable. Applehurst couldn't survive without you. . . .

JUNE: Don't you be too sure. Applehurst is more than a village, you know—it's a community, a way of life. It doesn't depend on individuals. There's many a stone in that churchyard. . . .

340

ALICE: You talk as if it was real—

JUNE: [*Raising her voice again*] It's real to millions! It stands for the traditional values of English life—tenacity —common sense—our rural heritage—

ALICE: Oh, belt up.

JUNE: You're getting above yourself, Missy.

ALICE: But you *are* the serial! It would be nothing without you—

JUNE: Stranger things have happened. Only the other day Ronnie said, "There'll have to be some changes, you know."

ALICE: He probably meant the story line—

JUNE: No—no—it's the ax again! We're losing listeners, and they've got to have a scapegoat. It's over a year since old Mrs. Prescott was kicked by a horse. . . .

ALICE: Yes, and remember the rumpus there was over that! And she was only a minor character—

JUNE: She had her following.

ALICE: She hardly had a line to say from one week to the next.

JUNE: What about the time I nursed her back to health, when she had concussion?

ALICE: That was exceptional.

JUNE: No, no, no. She had nice little bits—here and there. Remember that time she found the stray dog, and the village adopted it—[*A dark thought occurs to her.*]— until it was run over by a tractor. [*She shudders.*]

ALICE: There is no comparison. Mrs. Prescott—

JUNE: [*Shouting*] Mrs. Prescott had a following.

ALICE: [*Shrugging her shoulders*] All right: Mrs. Prescott had a following.

JUNE: The subject is now closed.

(*Pause.*)

ALICE: But she was expendable.

JUNE: [*Exploding*] Are you trying to aggravate me? Are you deliberately trying to annoy me?

ALICE: You're the most popular character in it—

341

JUNE: Don't screech at me. It's an ugly, grating sound.

ALICE: Well, look at your ratings.

JUNE: They are down! Four percent last week—I'm slipping! Now do you understand?

(*Pause.*)

ALICE: You still get the most fan mail, don't you?

JUNE: Only just. . . . Ginger, the pubkeeper, is close on my heels. Ever since he had that win on the Premium Bonds, and lent the money to Farmer Bromley, so as they wouldn't turn his place into a factory farm—

ALICE: What about young Rosie?

JUNE: [*Conspiratorially*] Aha. [ALICE *looks puzzled.*] She's preggers.

ALICE: No! You mean the actress—

JUNE: No, the character, blockhead! We reckon that'll bring some listeners.

ALICE: [*Intrigued*] Who was responsible?

JUNE: We haven't been told yet. I think it was Lennie, her steady. If so, it'll be absolutely splendid. They can get married—everybody loves a wedding. But Arthur thinks it was Roy.

ALICE: Who's Roy?

JUNE: That soldier—from the army camp at Oakmead. He took her to that dance, remember?

ALICE: [*Concerned*] What's she going to do . . . about the baby?

JUNE: She's going to confide in me about it—in the next installment. Comes to me in tears; wants to get rid of it . . . [*Sighing*] Don't know what the younger generation's coming to. . . .

ALICE: What do you tell her?

JUNE: What *don't* I tell her! She gets a dressing-down from me that she won't forget in a hurry! [*In her country accent*] Where is he? Mr. Clever Lad? Show me where he is, so's I can tear some strips off him, the fine young fellow. Just don't you aggravate yourself, my dear—leave it to me! My dear, who was it? Just tell me who it was!

ALICE: And does she tell you?

JUNE: No. [*Pause.*] But I'll wheedle it out of her, never fear. Give me three installments and I'll do it.

ALICE: [*Tensely*] They shouldn't talk about . . . things like that.

JUNE: [*Happier now*] It's nice, though, the way they come to me . . . with their troubles. . . . Oh, they know they'll get straight talking from me—no lard ever passed my lips. No, sir, fine words butter no parsnips.

ALICE: What the hell are you on about?

JUNE: They *need* me. Get that into your thick head: Applehurst needs a district nurse. Who'd deliver the babies, who'd look after the old folk, I'd like to know?!

ALICE: Exactly! Nobody's suggesting—

JUNE: What do you mean, nobody's suggesting? Why did that woman ask about my health, then? Why did she wink at me, eh?

ALICE: Perhaps she fancies you.

JUNE: This is no time for jesting.

ALICE: How am I to know why she winked at you. Perhaps she has a nervous twitch?

JUNE: She's Australian, dunce! They're extroverts, not neurotic townsfolk like us. They come from the bloody bush!

ALICE: [*Becoming exasperated*] Well, I don't know why she winked at you!

JUNE: Oh, shut up! Stupid bitch. [*She goes to the radio and reads out one of the framed certificates.*] "And in recognition of your devoted work and care for the old and sick, we name the Geriatric Ward the Sister George Ward." [ALICE *applauds slowly and ironically.*] Take care, Childie, you're trailing your coat. . . .

ALICE: [*Giggling*] You're the bull. . . .

JUNE: [*Dangerously*] We're very cocky all of a sudden!

ALICE: [*Mock-innocently*] Who, me?

JUNE: Yes, you. Anyway, what the hell are you doing at home on a Tuesday afternoon? Why aren't you at work?

ALICE: Mr. Katz gave us the day off. It's a Jewish holiday.

JUNE: [*Suspiciously*] Oh, really. What holiday?

ALICE: I don't know. The Feast of the Contamination, or something.

JUNE: You seem to have more holidays than workdays just lately.

ALICE: Not my fault.

JUNE: [*Still suspicious*] He hasn't "had a go" at you again, your Mr. Katz, has he?

ALICE: [*Primly*] Certainly not.

JUNE: I bet he has.

ALICE: He hasn't. I'd tell you.

JUNE: I wonder. [*Self-pityingly*] Nobody tells me anything.

ALICE: That's because you always make a stupid fuss about things.

JUNE: All right, I won't make a fuss. Go on, tell me.

ALICE: There's nothing to tell.

JUNE: [*Venomously*] You expect me to believe that! After what happened last time?

ALICE: Nothing happened!

JUNE: Oh, no? A four-inch tear and three buttons off your blouse—you call that nothing?

ALICE: I told you. I got it caught in the Xerox.

JUNE: Don't lie to me, Childie.

ALICE: I'm not lying.

JUNE: Why do you avoid my eyes, then?

ALICE: Because . . . because— Oh! You're impossible, George. [*She runs off into the bathroom.*]

JUNE: Don't throw tantrums with me, young lady. [*Roaring*] Come out! Come out this instant!

ALICE: [*From the bathroom*] I shan't.

JUNE: [*Picking up one of the Victorian dolls*] Can you hear me, Childie? I've got Emmeline here, your favorite doll. [*Softly, but clearly*] And if you don't come out of the bathroom AT ONCE . . . I'll pull Emmeline's head off. . . .

ALICE: [*Tear-stained, rushes into the room, tears the doll out of* JUNE's *hands, and hugs it.*] Monster. . . .

JUNE: There, that's better. [*Pause.*] And now: apologize.

ALICE: What for?

JUNE: For causing me unnecessary aggravation.

ALICE: I'm sorry.

JUNE: You don't sound it.

ALICE: Look, I know that you're worried and everything, but that's no reason—

JUNE: Don't answer back. Don't be cheeky.

ALICE: Look, George—

JUNE: Has Mr. Katz "had a go" at you?

ALICE: [*Screaming*] No ! ! !

JUNE: Don't screech at me! Apologize this instant, or there'll be severe chastisement.

ALICE: I'm sorry.

JUNE: That's better. Now—down on your knees.

ALICE: Must I?

JUNE: Yes. [ALICE, *still hugging the doll, goes on her knees.*] Come on—show your contrition.

ALICE: How?

JUNE: [*Pointing to the ashtray*] Eat the butt of my cigar.

ALICE: I couldn't: it would make me sick.

JUNE: [*Standing over* ALICE] Are you arguing with me?

ALICE: Okay. Hand it over.

JUNE: Good girl. Now eat it.

ALICE: Can I take the ash off?

JUNE: You may take the ash off, but you must eat the paper.

(*With an expression of extreme distaste,* ALICE *eats the cigar butt.*)

ALICE: It tastes vile.

JUNE: Good. That'll teach you to be rude.

(*The telephone rings.*)

ALICE: [*Rushing to answer it, relieved to be let off her punishment*] Hello, yes, this is Miss June Buckridge's flat. One moment, please.

JUNE: [*Apprehensive*] Who is it?

ALICE: I don't know.

JUNE: Why didn't you ask, fathead? [*She takes the receiver.*] Hello, this is Miss June Buckridge. . . . Who wants her? Yes, of course. . . . Yes, I'll hold on. . . . [*Putting her hand over the mouthpiece*] God Almighty, Childie, it's the BBC.

ALICE: [*Trembling*] Oh, Lord, I hope it's nothing serious. . . .

JUNE: [*On the telephone*] Hello? Hello, Mrs. Mercy, dear. . . . No, of *course* not. . . . Quite. . . . Quite. Oh, I'm *feeling* all right. . . . Yes, I . . . Well, as a matter of fact, there *is* something. . . . Perhaps we'd better have a man-to-man—You have something to say to *me*? No, I'm not doing anything at the moment. . . . Well, I'd rather not come back to BH today. . . . Yes, yes, that a *splendid* idea! Love to see you! That's right: Devonshire Street . . . top floor. You press the bell, and one of those "I speak your weight" machines answers— [*A rather forced laugh.*] Yes, you know the kind of thing— [*Intoning a deep voice*] "You are thirteen stone ten"—no, no, of course not—I wasn't implying . . . Yes, that'll be lovely . . . *any* time . . . 'Bye [*She hangs up, wipes her brow.*] She's coming round. [*Nervously lighting another cheroot*] She'll be here in a minute. God, I'm for it!

ALICE: Who was it?

JUNE: The Assistant Head . . . Mrs. Mercy Croft—

ALICE: The one who has that weekly spot on Woman's Hour?

JUNE: "Ask Mrs. Mercy"—that's her!

ALICE: But she sounds awfully nice on the radio—at least, her advice is sort of . . . sensible.

JUNE: She is nice. . . . [*Trying to convince herself*] Mrs. Mercy is a *nice woman*.

ALICE: Well, then.

JUNE: She's coming to me, you understand? At first, she asked me to see her in her office. . . .

ALICE: [*After a pause*] Did she seem friendly?

JUNE: [*Tensely*] Yep.

ALICE: It'll be a good thing to clear the air—

JUNE: You don't know what you're talking about! She

wants to see me on an urgent matter. We must brace ourselves for the worst—

ALICE: Will she expect some tea?

JUNE: Tea, yes of course. You must make her something special—at the double.

ALICE: There's that piece of Dundee cake that Mother sent—

JUNE: That'll be absolutely first class. And make her some of your Scotch scones! And when you're serving, look cheerful, keep your shoulders back, try to make a good impression. And if she speaks to you don't open your mouth about things you don't understand.

ALICE: I can quite easily go out.

JUNE: What, and leave me to pour tea and all that pansy stuff? Not likely. You'll stay here and do some work.

ALICE: Look, George. Try not to show how worried you are. You always get sort of . . . aggressive when you're nervous.

JUNE: Go on. Back to the kitchen where you belong!

ALICE: I wish you'd do relaxing exercises, or something. [*Exits.*]

JUNE: [*Shouting after her*] I'll do relaxing exercises on your behind, if you're not careful! Now then. [*She goes to arrange the display on the radio.*] "Personality of the Year"—I'll put that in a prominent position. . . . The English Village Preservation Society . . . the Association of British Nursing Sisters . . . the Variety Club of Great Britain . . . "Miss Humanity" nominated by the *Daily Mirror*. . . . There's something missing. . . . [*Calling*] Alice!

ALICE: [*From the kitchen*] I'm busy!

JUNE: [*Imperiously*] Come here! I want you.

ALICE: [*Reentering*] What is it now? You're always interrupting . . .

JUNE: There's one missing. [*She points to the trophies.*]

ALICE: I haven't touched anything—

JUNE: There's one missing, isn't there? Go on—*have a look!* I want to hear you tell me, in your own words, which one is missing.

ALICE: [*Without looking*] I don't know.

JUNE: [*Softly, with deadly emphasis*] Where's the Honorary "Stag"?

ALICE: [*Uncertainly*] What—

JUNE: [*As before*] What have you done with it? [*No reply from* ALICE.] I give you ten seconds to confess. [*She waits, breathing heavily.*]

ALICE: Let me get on with the tea. She'll be here in a minute. . . .

JUNE: You've destroyed it. haven't you? [*Pause.*] Where is the Honorary "Stag"?

ALICE: I threw it away.

JUNE: You . . . *what?*

ALICE: [*Slightly hysterically*] I hated it! A cut-off stag's head. Impaled on a pike! You had no right to keep such abominations in the house—you know I like animals!

JUNE: When did you throw it away?

ALICE: Last night. [*She has started to cry, silently.*]

JUNE: It meant a lot to me—being elected an Honorary "Stag" . . .

ALICE: [*Very contrite now*] I'll get it back; I'll get another.

JUNE: [*Tragically*] Too late.

ALICE: I'll telephone to the Town Hall—the Borough Litter Disposal Unit—

JUNE: [*Still tragically*] You mean the dustmen, don't you . . . why can't you bloody well say so? . . . [*The buzzer rings.*] It's her: the bitch, the cow, the plague spot, the bossed carbuncle—[JUNE *answers the buzzer.*] Hello, Mrs. Mercy, dear. Expecting you. Yes, top floor. [*She switches off.*] Don't stand about gawping! Blow your nose. Pull your sweater straight: you look disgusting. Now, remember: be polite and keep mum. I'll speak to you later. [*Pause.*] Where the hell has she got to?

ALICE: Maybe she got stuck in the lift.

JUNE: [*Aghast*] The lift door! I think I forgot to close the door.

ALICE: [*Rushing to the door*] I'll do it!

JUNE: [*In a hoarse whisper*] Don't—it's too late! She'll either walk, or . . .

(*The doorbell rings.*)

ALICE: [*Suddenly scared*] Let's not open the door!

(JUNE *throws* ALICE *a glance expressing contempt, and strides out to open the door.*)

JUNE: [*Offstage*] Oh, hello, Mrs. Mercy! I'm so sorry— I'd only just remembered that the lift was out of order. . . .

MRS. MERCY: [*Entering, cheerfully*] Not at all—I never use the lift. [*Seeing* ALICE] Oh?

(MRS. MERCY *is a well-groomed lady of indeterminate age, gracious of manner, and freezingly polite. She is wearing a gray two-piece suit, matching hat and accessories, and a discreet double string of pearls around her neck. She carries a briefcase.*)

JUNE: May I introduce—Miss Alice McNaught, Mrs. Croft.

MRS. MERCY: [*Extending her hand*] How do you do? [*Turning to* JUNE] Yes, I always say: we get far too little exercise these days. If we walked the stairs, instead of using lifts, those extra inches would disappear.

ALICE: [*Trying to be helpful*] I sometimes walk—

MRS. MERCY: You don't need to lose any weight, my dear—

JUNE: Alice is just preparing the tea—

MRS. MERCY: Oh, that is nice. I do hope I haven't put you to any trouble—inviting myself out of the blue.

JUNE: Rubbish.

ALICE: Not at all. [*Goes to the kitchen.*]

MRS. MERCY: May I look around? I *adore* looking at other people's flats—they do reflect their occupiers' personalities in an uncannily accurate way. [*Looking around*] To be perfectly honest, I imagined your home to be . . . different.

JUNE: Really?

MRS. MERCY: This charming Victoriana . . . the dolls . . .
Somehow—

JUNE: [*Slightly embarrassed*] They're Miss McNaught's.

MRS. MERCY: Oh, of course, that would explain it. They
just weren't *you*. I didn't know—

JUNE: [*Rather sheepishly*] Yes, I have a flatmate. . . .

MRS. MERCY: [*Sympathetically*] How nice. It's so important
to have . . . companionship—especially when one's an
artist. . . .

JUNE: These are mine—I collect brasses.

MRS. MERCY: How useful. . . . May I look out from your
window? I love overlooking things. I've always adored
heights; in my young days, my husband and I often used
to go mountaineering—in the Austrian Alps for prefer-
ence. [*She has gone to the window.*] Oh! [*A sudden yell
of delight.*] There's BH! You can see Broadcasting House
from your window—isn't that . . . *super!* To have that
reassuring presence brooding over you, seeing that you
don't get into mischief!

ALICE: [*Lifting the hatch and looking into the room*]
Ready in a minute.

MRS. MERCY: Oh—good!

JUNE: Would you kindly close the hatch. [ALICE *shuts the
hatch.*] There are times when I have an almost irresistible
urge to decapitate her.

MRS. MERCY: Oh, poor Miss McNaught. I do like your
settee cover—a homely pattern. I love floral design—I
know it's old-fashioned, but . . .

JUNE: Childie—Miss McNaught—made them.

MRS. MERCY: Really. How clever of her—they're beautifully fitted. You're fortunate to have such a handy companion.

JUNE: [*With a bitter look at the trophies*] Yes, she's good
with the needle, I'll say that for her.

MRS. MERCY: [*Lightly*] That was Sister George speaking.

JUNE: [*Self-conscious*ly] One can't helping slipping—

MRS. MERCY: But you are Sister George far more than
Miss June Buckridge to all of us at BH.

JUNE: Jolly nice of you to say so. [*Motions her to sit.*]

MRS. MERCY: Thank you. You have made the part completely your own—it was obvious—even at the first auditions. I remember it quite clearly, although it must be, oh—

JUNE: Almost six years ago. I was scared stiff, too.

MRS. MERCY: How charming! One can't imagine you scared stiff!

JUNE: I don't mind physical danger, I even like it. I manned an anti-aircraft during the war.

MRS. MERCY: Lovely!

JUNE: None of that sissy troop entertainment for yours truly!

MRS. MERCY: It wasn't that bad. As a matter of fact, I did a bit of organizing for ENSA myself. . . .

JUNE: I'm sorry. No offense meant.

MRS. MERCY: None taken. Now, Miss Buckridge—or may I call you Sister George, like everybody else?

JUNE: Certainly.

MRS. MERCY: As you know, I hold a monthly surgery in my office, when I welcome people to come to me with their problems. I've always made it a rule to be approachable. In some cases, involving matters of special importance, I prefer to visit the subjects in their own homes, so that we can talk more easily without any duress. That's why I'm here today.

JUNE: [*In her country accent*] Ah well, farmer's footsteps are the best manure!

MRS. MERCY: Quite. There's rather a serious matter I wish to discuss with you.

ALICE: [*Entering with tea*] Sorry I took so long.

MRS. MERCY: Ah, *lovely!* [*To* JUNE] We'll continue our little chat after tea.

ALICE: If you'd rather—

JUNE: You can speak quite freely, Mrs. Mercy. Miss McNaught and I have no secrets from each other.

MRS. MERCY: Well, let's all have tea first. . . . [*As* ALICE *lays the table*] I say, what delicious-looking scones!

ALICE: They're Scotch scones.

351

Frank Marcus

JUNE: They're Childie's specialty. Copied from her grandmother's recipe.

MRS. MERCY: They look delish! May I try one?

ALICE: Help yourself. Here's the jam.

MRS. MERCY: They're what we used to call girdle scones—

JUNE: Or drop scones—

ALICE: It's important not to get the girdle too hot, or the outside of the scones will brown before the inside is cooked.

MRS. MERCY: They're a lovely even color. . . .

ALICE: [*Very animated*] I always cool them in a towel—

MRS. MERCY: Do you?

ALICE: Yes, and I wait till the bubbles rise to the surface before I turn them over—

MRS. MERCY: They're very successful.

ALICE: I use half a teaspoon of bicarbonate of soda—

MRS. MERCY: Now you're giving away trade secrets.

ALICE: And one level teaspoon of cream of tartar—

JUNE: [*Rising*] Shut up!

(*There is a moment's silence.*)

ALICE: Eight ounces of flour—

JUNE: [*Exploding*] Shut up!

ALICE: [*Softly*] And one egg.

JUNE: Shut up! ! [*Hurls a cake in ALICE's direction.*]

MRS. MERCY: [*Continuing to eat, unperturbed*] Now then, girls—temper!

ALICE: She hates me to talk about food. [*Confidentially to MRS. MERCY*] She's a wee bit overwrought—

JUNE: Overwrought, my arse!

ALICE: [*Chiding*] Now, that wasn't nice—that was not a nice thing to say.

MRS. MERCY: [*Smiling indulgently*] I expect she picked it up in the army.

ALICE: She swears like a trooper—

MRS. MERCY: But she has a heart of gold.

ALICE: One day, she got into such a temper, I wrote a poem about it.

JUNE: [*Bitterly*] Yes, she fancies herself as a poetess. Goes to the City Lit. every Wednesday night, to learn about meter and things—

MRS. MERCY: What a nice hobby.

JUNE: As a poetess, she makes a good cook.

MRS. MERCY: It's still a question of mixing the right ingredients to make a tasty whole.

ALICE: That night she came back in a raging temper—

JUNE: Thank you very much, we don't want to hear anything about that—

ALICE: I wrote this poem. It began:
"Fierce as the wind
Blows the rampaging termagant . . ."

MRS. MERCY: Very expressive [*To* JUNE] And how did you like being compared to the wind?

(JUNE *blows a raspberry.*)

ALICE: [*To* MRS. MERCY] Slice of cake, Mrs. Mercy?

MRS. MERCY: Just a teeny one. Mustn't be greedy.

JUNE: Her mother made it.

MRS. MERCY: You can always tell if it's home-baked; it tastes quite different.

JUNE: You'd be surprised if you knew what Mother Mc-Naught put into it.

MRS. MERCY: I'm not even going to ask.

JUNE: I'm delighted to hear it! [*Laughs.*]

MRS. MERCY: [*Enjoying herself*] Oh dear, this is just like a dormitory feast—all this girlish banter. [*To* JUNE] I bet you were a terror at school!

JUNE: I was captain of the hockey team and a keen disciplinarian—God help the girl I caught making me an apple-pie bed! [*She chuckles.*]

MRS. MERCY: Ah, there's Sister George again! It's wonderful how over the years the character *evolved.* . . .

ALICE: Who first thought of putting her on a motorbike?

JUNE: That was because of sound effects. As long as I was on the old bike, listeners never knew whether I was static or mobile.

353

MRS. MERCY: A unique sound—Sister George on her motor-bike, whizzing through the countryside, singing snatches of hymns—

JUNE: One day I got into trouble because I sang a hymn which sounded like "On the Good Ship Venus."

MRS. MERCY: A traditional air—?

JUNE: I've found it safer to stick to hymns. Once I tried a pop song, and d'you know, hundreds of letters came in, protesting.

MRS. MERCY: We learn from experience. . . . but we don't want Applehurst falling behind the times.

JUNE: No—no—of course not.

MRS. MERCY: But we must constantly examine criticism, and if it's constructive, we must act on it. Ruthlessly.

JUNE: What sort of criticism?

MRS. MERCY: Oh, nothing in particular . . . at least . . .

JUNE: But what?

MRS. MERCY: Well, that brings me—I'm afraid—to the un-pleasant part of my business. . . .

ALICE: Oh dear—

MRS. MERCY: [*Rising*] But first, would you show me to the little girls' room?

JUNE: Alice, show Mrs. Mercy to the . . .

ALICE: This way, Mrs. Mercy.

JUNE: —little—girls'—

(MRS. MERCY *exits, accompanied by* ALICE. JUNE *catches sight of her briefcase, looks round furtively, and opens it as* ALICE *returns.*)

ALICE: [*Aghast*] What are you doing?

JUNE: [*Rummaging in the case*] Keep a lookout!

ALICE: You can't. You mustn't!

JUNE: [*Taking a folder*] My personal file.

ALICE: [*In a hysterical whisper*] Put it back!

JUNE: [*Perusing some papers*] Quiet! [*She takes an envelope from the file. Reads.*] "Sister George. Confidential."

ALICE: She's coming!

JUNE: [*Quickly replaces the folder in the briefcase, realizes too late that she has still got the envelope in her hand:*

354

puts it behind the nearest cushion.] . . . So Emmeline said, "I don't want any girdle scones . . . thank you very much."

MRS. MERCY: [*Reentering*] I got on the scales, to see if I've put on any weight.

JUNE: I don't suppose . . .

MRS. MERCY: [*Takes her briefcase, while* JUNE *and* ALICE *stand rigid with suspense.*] Now then . . .

ALICE: I'll make myself scarce. . . . [*Goes into kitchen.*]

MRS. MERCY: Please sit down. [JUNE *sits.*] You won't hold it against me if I speak plainly?

JUNE: Please do.

MRS. MERCY: It's my unpleasant duty to haul you over the coals, and administer a severe reprimand.

JUNE: Oh?

MRS. MERCY: Believe me, Sister George, I'd much rather let bygones be bygones—

JUNE: [*In a country accent*] Let sleeping dogs lie—

MRS. MERCY: Precisely. . . . But I must remind you of the little chat we had just about a year ago, after that unfortunate incident in the club . . . involving a lady colleague of mine.

JUNE: Let's not rake over old embers.

MRS. MERCY: I don't intend to. But in the light of recent events, it's difficult to forget an incident as vivid as the pouring of a glass of beer over the Assistant Head of Talks. I had hoped one black mark would have been enough for you, but this morning [*Takes a sheet of paper from the folder.*] I received this memo from the Director of Religious Broadcasting. [*She hands the paper to* JUNE.] I should like to have your comments.

JUNE: [*Excitedly reads the paper, flushes, and jumps up violently.*] It's a lie! It's an utter, bloody lie!

MRS. MERCY: [*Firmly*] Please calm yourself, Miss Buckridge. Kindly hand me back the paper. [JUNE *hands over the paper.*] I take it you're not denying that you were drinking in the Coach and Horses on the night of the nineteenth?

JUNE: How the hell should I remember? [*Calling*] Alice! Come here!

ALICE: [*Enters, wide-eyed and worried*] You want me?

JUNE: Where was I on the night of the nineteenth?

MRS. MERCY: I'm sorry to involve you in this, Miss Mc-Naught—

ALICE: [*Quietly*] That was a Wednesday: I was at the City Lit.

JUNE: You bloody well would be. [*To* MRS. MERCY] All right; it seems I was at the Coach and Horses on the night in question, having a drink with some of the boys. That's no crime.

MRS. MERCY: Miss Buckridge . . . according to this letter from the mother superior of the Convent of the Sacred Heart of Jesus, you boarded a taxi stopping at the traffic lights at Langham Place—

JUNE: I thought it was empty.

MRS. MERCY: [*Reading*] A taxi bearing as passengers two novitiate nuns from Ireland who had just arrived at Kings Cross Station—

JUNE: How was I to know?

MRS. MERCY: You boarded this taxi in a state of advanced inebriation and [*Consulting the paper*] proceeded to assault the two nuns, subjecting them to actual physical violence!

ALICE: [*To* JUNE] You didn't really!

JUNE: No, no, no. Of course not. I'd had a few pints. . . . I saw this cab, took it to be empty, got in—and there were these two black things screaming blue murder!

MRS. MERCY: Why didn't you get out again?

JUNE: Well, I'd had a very nasty shock myself! What with their screaming and flapping about—I thought they were bats, you know, vampire bats! It was they who attacked me. I remember getting all entangled in their skirts and petticoats and things . . . the taxi driver had to pull me free. . . .

MRS. MERCY: A deplorable anecdote. According to the mother superior, one of the nuns required medical treatment for shock, and is still under sedation. She thought it was the devil.

ALICE: George, how could you!

JUNE: Don't you start on me! [*Clapping her hands*] Back to the kitchen! Washing up! Presto!

ALICE: [*Firmly*] No, I'm staying. This concerns me, too.

JUNE: It was all a ghastly mistake.

MRS. MERCY: No doubt, but it'll take some explaining.

JUNE: Fancy informing the Director of Religious Broadcasting. What a nasty thing to do for a holy woman!

MRS. MERCY: The mother superior is responsible for the nuns in her charge—

JUNE: Then she should jolly well teach them how to behave in public! I got the fright of my life, in there! Those nuns were like *mice*—albino mice—with white faces and little red eyes. And they were vicious, too. They scratched and they bit! Look—you can still see the tooth marks— [*She points to her arm.*]—do you see that? I've a good mind to make a counter-complaint to the mother superior: they deserve to be scourged in their cells.

MRS. MERCY: [*Wearily*] I can hardly put through a report to the Controller, informing him of your allegation that you were bitten by two nuns!

JUNE: No, well you could say—

MRS. MERCY: Let's be practical, Sister George—we're concerned with retaining the trust and respect of the public. Now, people understand perfectly well that artists frequently work under great emotional stress. We do all we can to gloss over the minor disciplinary offenses. But we simply cannot tolerate this sort of behavior. It's things like this which make people resent paying more for their wireless licenses! Thousands of pounds spent on public relations, and you jeopardize it all with your reckless and foolish actions. Really, Sister George, we have reason to be very, very angry with you.

JUNE: [*Beaten*] What do you want me to do?

MRS. MERCY: You must write a letter immediately to the mother superior. You must sincerely apologize for your behavior and I suggest you offer a small donation for some charity connected with the convent. Then you must send a copy of your letter to the Director of Religious

Broadcasting, with a covering note from you, couched in suitable terms.

JUNE: You mean humbling myself.

ALICE: Don't worry, Mrs. Mercy. I'll see she does it and I'll make quite sure she doesn't get into any mischief in the future.

MRS. MERCY: There speaks a true friend. [*To* JUNE] You're very lucky to have someone like Miss McNaught to rely on. Treasure her.

JUNE: [*Bitterly*] I'll treasure her, all right!

ALICE: I'll see to it that the letters are written and sent off right away!

MRS. MERCY: [*Rising*] Good. That's what I like to hear. [*To* JUNE] I'll leave you in Miss McNaught's expert charge.

JUNE: What about Applehurst?

MRS. MERCY: [*Noncommittally*] That's another, rather more complex problem. . . .

JUNE: But . . . has anything been decided about the future?

MRS. MERCY: I'm afraid I can't say anything about that at the moment.

JUNE: It comes as a bit of a shock to me, you know, all this.

MRS. MERCY: It comes as a bit of a shock to me too, I assure you—especially as I understand that you often open church bazaars—

ALICE: I'll look after her—I'll keep her away from convents.

MRS. MERCY: You keep her on a tight rein, and all will be well.

ALICE: Of course I will. Between us we'll keep her in order.

MRS. MERCY: She won't have a chance, will she?

JUNE: Look here—I'm sorry—you know—if I've been a bad boy.

MRS. MERCY: [*Turning to* JUNE *and shaking hands*] Well, good-bye, dear Sister George. Keep your chin up. Things are never as bad as they seem—

JUNE: [*Listlessly, in her country accent*] Every cloud has a silver lining. . . .

MRS. MERCY: That's the spirit! And [*Whispering confiden-tially*] no more walkouts at rehearsals, eh? If you have any complaints do come and see me about them.

JUNE: [*In her country accent*] Well, it's the creaking gate that gets oiled. . . .

MRS. MERCY: [*Reflecting for a moment*] A somewhat un-fortunate simile. . . . [*To* ALICE] So nice to have met you—

ALICE: Nice to have met *you*, Mrs. Mercy. What's the sub-ject of your talk tomorrow? Is it a secret, or are you allowed to tell?

MRS. MERCY: [*Smiling graciously*] It's family planning this week—and foundation garments next!

(*She sails out, followed by* ALICE. JUNE *nervously lights a cheroot. There are sounds of conversation from out-side, then the front door closes.* ALICE *returns and gives* JUNE *a meaningful look.*)

ALICE: Well!

JUNE: [*Alarmed*] Did she say anything? Did she drop any hints behind my back?

ALICE: No. Just general comments—you know—about nuns in taxis.

JUNE: What do you mean?

ALICE: Nuns. You know, n-u-n-s. Brides of Christ.

JUNE: Oh, I see, that's what's biting you.

ALICE: [*In an outburst*] How could you! How could you make such an exhibition of yourself!

JUNE: For heaven's sake, Childie, grow up. Don't be so bloody . . . *squeamish.*

ALICE: [*Primly*] I think you owe me some sort of explana-tion.

JUNE: [*Chuckling*] All those petticoats . . .

ALICE: It's the sort of thing you used to do when I first knew you. In that club in Notting Hill Gate: I remember how you used to go clomping about, without a bra, hitting girls over the head.

JUNE: Kindly keep those foul-mouthed recollections to yourself. In my young days . . .

ALICE: Your young days were spent in a cul-de-sac in Al-
dershot, with the Band of Hope on one side and the foot
clinic on the other. You told me so yourself.

JUNE: How dare you. This is a respectable house—and
don't you forget who's paying the rent!

ALICE: Not much longer, perhaps.

JUNE: They wouldn't dare get rid of me because of this
. . . of this trivial incident. . . .

ALICE: [*Imitating* JUNE'*s country accent*] We none of us
know what the future holds for us.

JUNE: [*After a pause, puffing on her cigar*] I'm worried. I
really am worried, Childie. Please, do me a favor. . . .

ALICE: What?

JUNE: Go and ask Madame Xenia to come up. She's an
expert on the future.

ALICE: She's probably got a client—

JUNE: Maybe she's between appointments. Go on.

ALICE: I can't just barge in—

JUNE: Why not? You've done it before. Remember when
I was bitten by that Lakeland terrier and you thought I
had the rabies! She always knows what's going to happen.
Go on.

ALICE: Oh.

JUNE: This is an emergency. Extreme measures must be
taken at once! Go and get her at once!

ALICE: I can't. She hates my guts.

JUNE: Madame Xenia? Why?

ALICE: She thinks I'm after her lodger. [JUNE *rises menacingly.*] It's complete fantasy.

JUNE: [*Ominously, in the voice of Sister George*] There's
no smoke without fire!

ALICE: Just like the last one you scared off.

JUNE: I could see which way the wind was blowing. I
nipped it in the bud.

ALICE: I only helped him with his homework. He was a
mere boy.

JUNE: [*Decisively*] There's nothing mere about boys. . . .
Now go and fetch her at once and watch your step.

ALICE: [*Going*] You've always got to have someone doing
your dirty work.

JUNE: Thanks, you're a pal. [*Alice goes.* JUNE *reads the inscription on a frame on the table.*] ". . . and for your devoted work and care for the old and sick." [*Gets out the envelope from behind the cushion. Looks at it, puts it back.*]

ALICE: [*Offstage*] I'm sorry to drag you away . . .

MADAME XENIA: That's all right. I know. I know. George! [*Enter* MADAME XENIA, *a hawk-faced, elderly lady of foreign origin, hennaed and hung with beads.* ALICE *follows.*] George? Darling? What is the matter?

ALICE: Madame was in the middle of a consultation with a client—

JUNE: Oh, I *am* sorry.

XENIA: Never mind. You are my friend. Always you come first. Now, darling, what's the trouble?

JUNE: Madame Xenia, I'm worried out of my wits. . . . It's the BBC. They're driving me mad—

XENIA: They will suffer for it. I will put curses on them. [*Professionally*] Sit down; make yourself at home.

JUNE: Thanks.

XENIA: I forget; I always say it to people to make them relax. Right—[*To* JUNE] Would you draw the curtains, please?

JUNE: [*Goes to draw the curtains.*] Certainly.

XENIA: [*To* ALICE] And you: will you please sit facing the east?

ALICE: Which way's the east?

XENIA: [*Pointing*] There. Towards Great Portland Street.

ALICE: [*Sitting*] Yes, of course.

XENIA: [*Facing* JUNE] I require a personal possession from you [JUNE *looks startled*] to hold in my hand. To connect with your vibrations. Anything—a piece of jewelry—

JUNE: I don't wear jewelry. Will a hankie do?

XENIA: [*Taking* JUNE's *handkerchief*] Beautiful. Now, to work. . . . First, a warning. Next week will be tough for Sagittarians. Mars is in conjunction with Venus. And I don't have to tell you what that means. [*She sits down and shuffles a pack of cards.*] Cut the cards.

JUNE: [*Cutting the cards*] All right?

XENIA: Again. [JUNE *cuts again*.] And once more, just for luck—

ALICE: —as the bishop said to the actress.

JUNE: [*Sternly*] We can dispense with observations from the east.

XENIA: [*Scrutinizing the cards*] A short journey to see a friend; a pleasant surprise; unexpected money; the Queen of Spades—a woman in black you do not like?

ALICE: The mother superior?

JUNE: Shut up!

XENIA: Whoever it is—keep out of her way—she's no good to you.

JUNE: [*Stuttering*] What—what is she going to do?

XENIA: [*Consulting the cards*] She's asking you to a big do.

JUNE: [*Incredulous*] The mother superior?

(ALICE *giggles*.)

XENIA: I see lots of people, lots of drink, dancing. . . .

ALICE: [*Brightly*] I know! It's not the convent—it's the drag ball at Richmond!

XENIA: [*She continues laying the cards*.] Maybe a slight emotional upset—nothing serious. You hear of a broken romantic association. . . . You catch a cold. A very bad cold!

JUNE: [*Alarmed*] When?

XENIA: [*Thoughtfully*] Maybe it's because I'm holding your handkerchief. . . . Forget the cold. What else—? [*She looks at the cards again*.]

JUNE: My career . . .

XENIA: I can see a red-headed man.

JUNE: Ginger the pubkeeper! What's he doing?

XENIA: I'm afraid it's not very clear. . . . Ah! I see a letter —a very important letter. . . .

ALICE: [*Suddenly remembering*] The envelope!

JUNE: [*Jumping up, panic-stricken*] The envelope!

ALICE AND JUNE: [*Gasping*] The envelope. . . .

XENIA: [*Helpfully*] It could be a postcard.

ALICE: [*Snatches the hidden letter from behind the cushion. To* JUNE] Here it is! Do you want to open it?

JUNE: [*Anguished*] No.

ALICE: Let's send it back to her, tell her she must have dropped it out of her bag.

JUNE: No, no. It's fallen into our hands; we'd better read it.

XENIA: May I see the envelope?

JUNE: Yes, of course. Do you—do you get any . . . vibrations?

XENIA: [*Carefully*] Mmm . . . It's difficult to say. It could mean one of two things. . . .

JUNE: [*Squaring her shoulders*] Give it to me! I'm going to open it. [*She takes the envelope from* MADAME XENIA, *and tears it open.*] What must be, must be. . . . [*She glances at the contents, and collapses onto the settee.*] Oh, my God!

ALICE: [*Rushing to comfort her*] George! What's the matter? George! [JUNE *remains impassive;* MADAME XENIA *has taken the letter and looks at it.*] What does it say?

XENIA: "Memo from Audience Research. Latest Popularity Ratings: Sister George 64.5 percent. Ginger Hopkins 68."

JUNE: That's the weapon they've been waiting for. Now they'll kill me.

CURTAIN

ACT II

Scene 1

A week later. It is 4 A.M. By the dim light of a table lamp
JUNE *can be discerned, sitting at the table. She is wearing*
a dressing gown; in front of her is a tumbler and a bottle
of gin. She is roused from her torpor by the ringing of an
alarm clock in the bedroom.

JUNE: [*Startled*] What . . . ? It must be morning. . . . I
must have dropped off. . . . [*Calling*] Childie! Rise and
shine—that's if you persist in this ridiculous enterprise!
Childie? I'm in the living room.

ALICE: [*Dressed only in brassiere and pants, carrying a*
bundle of clothing in her arms, comes running in. She
throws her clothes on the settee, and attacks JUNE.]
Pinch, punch, first of the month!

JUNE: [*Jumping up*] Are you out of your mind?

ALICE: [*Squashed*] It's the first of the month . . . October. . . .

JUNE: You could have given me a heart attack.

ALICE: Sorry.

JUNE: Gawd Almighty. . . . What's the time?

ALICE: Ten to four.

JUNE: When are you supposed to get there?

ALICE: There's no rush; the gang gets there at about five.
Have you made out your list?

JUNE: No.

ALICE: [*Annoyed*] Well, why didn't you? Are you sure
you don't want me to try for *Swan Lake*?

JUNE: Positive. I can't stand those bloody little cygnets
prancing about—in their tutus—

ALICE: All right, all right. Nobody's forcing you.

JUNE: [*Rising, stretching out her arms*] My sympathy's
entirely with Von Rothbart—

ALICE: I'll just try for *Giselle*, then.

JUNE: Yeah, you try. And *Petrushka;* don't forget *Petrushka.*

ALICE: You told me last night you didn't want to see *Petrushka!*

JUNE: Did I? Well, I changed my mind. . . .

ALICE: [*Exasperated, getting hold of the program*] Oh, you are a nuisance! I'd put a tick against *Petrushka* and then I crossed it out, and now I've got to put a tick again . . . and now I can't find it—

JUNE: You're annoying me, you know. . . . Stop getting so . . . so het-up about your bloody ballet.

ALICE: It's all very well for you to talk—you'll be sitting at home. There's a big queue, and if you don't know what to ask for—

JUNE: You've got hours to decide what to ask for! You're only queuing for your queue tickets now.

ALICE: I know. But we've all got our lists. Anyway, there's no certainty that we get what we ask for: you only get so many for Fonteyn and Nureyev—

JUNE: In that case: why make a list?

ALICE: [*On the brink of hysteria*] You've got to ask for it first, even if you don't get it!

JUNE: You'll get something you're *not* asking for in a minute.

ALICE: Anyway, it wouldn't have hurt you to have come with me. You're up.

JUNE: I wouldn't be seen dead with that mob. What a collection!

ALICE: There's nothing wrong with them. They're very nice, the regulars, I've known some of them for fifteen years. Do you know: there's a woman there who follows Anya Linden everywhere. . . .

JUNE: *Everywhere?*

ALICE: Oh, shut up.

JUNE: Anyway, I did come with you one day—remember? Never again. All that gossip and name-dropping—

ALICE: The only reason you didn't like it was because you were embarrassed by the lorry driver.

JUNE: What lorry driver?

ALICE: The one that called at you, "That's a nice pair of head lamps."

JUNE: I had totally forgotten. Besides, he was paying me a compliment—unlike the gentleman in Soho, who suggested that you should wear a pair of sunglasses for a brassiere!

ALICE: Don't be disgusting.

JUNE: [*Jeering*] You're my flatmate in more senses than one.

ALICE: [*Incensed*] George, don't drink any more.

JUNE: [*Dangerously*] Mind your own business.

ALICE: Night after night I find you sitting up—with the bottle of gin and that old press-cuttings book. And then you wonder why you're tired.

JUNE: I can't sleep.

ALICE: You don't try. You must try to relax, to unwind—

JUNE: [*Imitating her caustically*] Relax! Unwind! It's easy for you to talk—

ALICE: You've been impossible ever since that day Mrs. Mercy came to tea—

JUNE: Well, I'm more impossible since I ran into her again yesterday.

ALICE: Where?

JUNE: At BH.

ALICE: Was she friendly?

JUNE: She smiled at me—with the same expression as my old cat Tiddles had when she used to look in a goldfish bowl. Until one Sunday my parents and I came home from church, and there on the table lay the goldfish—all five of them—neatly laid out, like sardines. . . .

ALICE: Did she . . . say anything to you?

JUNE: I'll show you what she did. Get up. Go on, stand up a minute. [ALICE *stands up*.] You're me. I was just coming out from the studio, on my way to the canteen, when I turned a corner rather sharply, and ran slap into her. Go on—bump into me.

ALICE: No, I don't want to do that.

JUNE: Don't be sloppy. . . . Go on—bump into me! [ALICE *brushes against* JUNE.] Oh, God help us! No, properly, stupid. Hard. Try again.

ALICE: I've got to go in a minute.

JUNE: You'll bloody well stay till I've done with you. Now then—you're coming down the corridor. [*She claps her hands.*] Start!

ALICE: [*Takes a run, bumps into* JUNE, *and floors her.*] Sorry!

JUNE: [*Rises.*] "Oh, it's you." [*She surveys her with* MRS. MERCY'S *half-smile.*] "Chin up, Sister George." [*She pats her arm, and walks past her.*] Chin up, indeed, the lousy old cow. You noticed the way she patted my arm—as if to say: "Sorry, it can't be helped."

ALICE: You're imagining things again.

JUNE: She's been avoiding me, I tell you, and I know why. . . .

ALICE: She was probably in a hurry to get somewhere. A committee meeting or something.

JUNE: They've had that. And I found out what happened.

ALICE: [*Alarmed*] What?

JUNE: I've been written out of next Tuesday's episode.

ALICE: What?

JUNE: Are you deaf? I said—

ALICE: I heard. So what—it's happened before. Every time you go on holiday—

JUNE: But I'm not going on holiday, am I? [ALICE *is silent.*] Sister George is confined to her bed . . . with a bad cold. . . .

ALICE: That in itself—

JUNE: [*Cutting her short*] That in itself could mean it's a dress rehearsal for my extinction.

ALICE: Nothing of the sort.

JUNE: They want to see what it sounds like without me . . . if I am expendable. . . .

ALICE: What about the following episodes?

JUNE: [*Grimly*] We shall know soon. The new scripts are due in the post this morning. I can see what's going to happen. That cold's going to get worse—I can feel it in my bones. It'll turn into bronchitis, then pneumonia, and before I know where I am I shall be out like a light.

ALICE: [*Only half-convinced*] You are making a moun-

tain out of a molehill. You've missed episodes before . . .
it's nothing to lose sleep over—

JUNE: That's what you think. . . . Anyway, I'm not the
only one.

ALICE: What do you mean?

JUNE: Did you know that you talk in your sleep?

ALICE: I don't.

JUNE: You do. I heard you distinctly. Last night and again
tonight. You woke me up.

ALICE: [*Nervously*] What did I say?

JUNE: You were tossing about, and mumbling something.
And then out it came, loud and clear.

ALICE: [*Unconvinced*] What?

JUNE: [*In a plaintive, high-pitched voice*] "Take me!"

ALICE: You're lying!

JUNE: [*As before*] "Take me, Isadore!"

ALICE: That's a filthy lie, and you know it!

JUNE: The "Isadore" wasn't any too distinct: it might have
been another name.

ALICE: I don't believe a word of this.

JUNE: [*More in sorrow than in anger*] You're having an
affair with someone, aren't you?

ALICE: I wish I were.

JUNE: [*Crushed*] That was very . . . unkind.

ALICE: Well, you asked for it. Always nagging me. Even
if I did shout "Take me" in my sleep—and I am not
aware of it—

JUNE: You couldn't be: you were asleep at the time.

ALICE: All right: even if I did, it might have meant "Take
me for a walk" or [*Brightly*] "Take me to the ballet!"

JUNE: A likely story!

ALICE: You always put the nastiest interpretation on what
people say.

JUNE: In nine cases out of ten it's true. [*Sipping her gin*]
Are you making yourself some breakfast?

ALICE: Just a cup of coffee. I usually have a hot pie later
on with the gang. In one of the workmen's cafés. It's
ever such fun, really! You get the ballet crowd and the
night shift from Covent Garden market all mixing
together.

JUNE: Sounds scintillating.

ALICE: It's ever so lively. Why don't you get dressed and come? They'd be thrilled to see you, and everyone would ask for your autograph!

JUNE: [*High-pitched*] "Take me!"

ALICE: Oh, George!

JUNE: No, you run along and enjoy yourself. . . . I'm all right where I am . . . waiting for the scripts to arrive.

ALICE: I don't know what's the matter with you just lately! You've become really . . . morbid. You used to be such fun.

JUNE: What are you talking about? We're going to the fancy dress ball tonight, aren't we? I bet it'll be you who'll be tired and wan tonight—after getting up at this unearthly hour!

ALICE: I'm glad you said that. I must take my iron pills. That'll help to keep me awake! [*She takes a bottle from the sideboard, shakes a pill out, and swallows it.*]

JUNE: Let me see them.

ALICE: What for?

JUNE: [*Emphatically*] Let me see them!

ALICE: [*Handing her the bottle*] All right. . . .

JUNE: [*Examining it*] Why doesn't it say what they are? [ALICE *looks nonplussed.*] There's no name on the label!

ALICE: I don't know.

JUNE: [*Scrutinizing it*] All it says [*She has difficulty in deciphering the writing in the dark.*] is "One to be taken every day, as prescribed." [*She sniffs the bottle.*] I don't believe these are iron pills at all. . . . They're those birth pills—

ALICE: Oh, really? Dr. Kunjaghari gave them to me. Why don't you go and ask him?

JUNE: [*Viciously*] Because I don't trust Dr. Kunjaghari, that's why. He's a quack. He's like those Indians who come to the door in a turban, flogging brass bangles for rheumatism!

ALICE: Perhaps you'd like to have them chemically analyzed.

JUNE: It would shake you if I did, wouldn't it?

ALICE: You can do what you like—you'd only make yourself ridiculous. Like that time you rang at the office, pretending to be Mrs. Katz.

JUNE: It served its purpose—it gave him a fright!

ALICE: It very nearly got me the sack. He knew it was you.

JUNE: He couldn't prove it.

ALICE: He's a solicitor—he could prove anything! [*Rummaging among her clothes*] Can't find my socks.

JUNE: I say— [*Regarding her benignly*] Seeing you in black pants reminds me of the army. We all had to wear regulation black woollen pants. We used to refer to them as blackouts. One day, a chap came to talk to us on the subject "What not to do with our blackouts down." He couldn't understand why we kept giggling. . . .

ALICE: [*Putting on her socks*] Found them!

JUNE: Your legs are unusually white—luminous white. Loo-minous. . . . I don't think I've ever seen such white legs.

ALICE: They don't get much sun on them.

JUNE: There's something uniquely touching about white legs . . . especially when they are loo-minous white. . . . You're very pale altogether. You're anemic—you ought to take iron pills. [ALICE *throws her a meaningful glance.*] I mean proper pills . . . not that muck. [*She pours herself another gin.*]

ALICE: Haven't you had enough?

JUNE: [*Quickly*] No. [*Chuckling, raising her glass*] To absent friends. Your health, albino mice!

ALICE: You *are* naughty.

JUNE: Say that again.

ALICE: What?

JUNE: What you just said.

ALICE: You *are* naughty.

JUNE: That's it. The same inflection. Takes me back years. . . .

ALICE: You mean—

JUNE: When we first met—in Mrs. Goodbody's tastefully furnished bed-sitters. . . . I used to watch you come and go—for weeks I watched you—and never said a word to you.

ALICE: You were different then—you hadn't become famous.

JUNE: Every morning I used to watch you go to work. Punctually at ten past nine every morning. You were always in a rush.

ALICE: I had to get on the underground at twenty past—

JUNE: Often you were in such a hurry you would fall over the doorstep; or, if it had been raining, you'd come slithering out, shouting "Oops"—

ALICE: I had no idea you were watching me.

JUNE: One night, I went into the bathroom just after you'd had a bath. The mirrors were all steamed up, and the bath mat was moist and glistening where you'd stood on it. There was a smell of talcum powder and of bath crystals—it was like an enchanted wood. . . . I stood quite still on that mat—in your footsteps—and I saw that you'd left your comb behind. It was a small pink plastic comb, and it had your hairs in it. I took that comb back to my room and kept it as a souvenir. . . . And all this time I'd never spoken a word to you. . . .

ALICE: You soon made up for it.

JUNE: That night your boyfriend saw you home. . . . I knew I'd have to strike quickly.

ALICE: That was Roger. He wanted to marry me.

JUNE: [Bitterly] That's what they all said— and you fell for it, silly goose.

ALICE: Some of them meant it; Roger meant it.

JUNE: What are you talking about? Roger was already married!

ALICE: [Adamantly] He still meant it. I liked Roger; he had a ginger mustache. . . .

JUNE: What a lot of rubbish. His mustache was ginger because he used to singe it with his cigarettes—you told me so yourself. You told me that being kissed by him tasted all sort of burnt and beery.

ALICE: I might have had babies. . . .

(Long pause.)

JUNE: [*Quietly*] You haven't been lonely, exactly.

ALICE: [*Changing the subject*] There's a performance of *Petrushka* on the nineteenth. I might try for that.

JUNE: [*Suddenly*] Shh! Shh! Was that the post?

ALICE: At this time in the morning? It won't be here for hours yet. You really ought to go to bed. . . .

(*There is a pause.*)

JUNE: [*Seriously*] They're driving me round the bend.

ALICE: You're driving yourself round the bend! Why don't you go to bed?

JUNE: Because I can't sleep.

ALICE: Shall I get you some hot milk?

JUNE: Urghh!

ALICE: You'll catch a cold, you know, sitting up like this.

JUNE: I've already got a cold.

ALICE: Well, keep your throat covered up, then. Put your dressing gown on properly. It's time we got you a new one—this collar is all frayed . . . come on, tuck it in. . . . I'll put some new braid on it tomorrow . . . there, better?

JUNE: Thanks.

ALICE: Shall I put the bottle away?

JUNE: No, I just want to hold it for a moment.

ALICE: I ought to be going—it's half past four. Will you be all right?

JUNE: Childie, they won't do it, will they? They *can't*, after all I've done for them.

ALICE: Of course they can't, George. You must stop brooding about it, you'll make yourself ill. Why don't you go to bed and sleep it off? You can set the alarm to wake you for rehearsal.

JUNE: There's no rehearsal tomorrow.

ALICE: All right, then. Good. You can get a nice long rest. Now, George, I've got to go.

JUNE: No, wait a minute—

ALICE: Oh, George, they'll be waiting for me, I'll be at the back of the queue.

JUNE: You can't go like *that*, you know.

ALICE: Like what?

JUNE: [*Pointing to the knapsack*] You're not going on a hike, you know. Mind you: donkeys are best for loading.

ALICE: There's only a change of clothes in it, to take to the office. And a few provisions. Please, may I go now?

JUNE: Did you speak?

ALICE: Yes, I said, "May I go now?"

JUNE: [*Considering the request*] Not before you have made your obeisance to me in the proper manner.

ALICE: [*Alarmed*] What do you mean?

JUNE: [*Breathing heavily and alcoholically for a few moments*] Kiss the hem of my garment. [*With an imperious gesture*] On your knees. Go on! Down, boy, down! [*She snaps her fingers.*]

ALICE: [*Picks up her knapsack, looks at her watch, and shrugs her shoulders.*] Oh, all right. [*She goes on her knees.*]

JUNE: Now repeat after me: I hereby solemnly swear—

ALICE: [*Mechanically*] I hereby solemnly swear—

JUNE: That I will not allow—

ALICE: That I will not allow—

JUNE: Anybody whosoever, including Mr. Katz, gratification of his fleshly instincts with me today or at any other time.

ALICE: [*Quickly*] All right, all right, I swear.

JUNE: Mind you remember, or may the curse of Satan fall on your head.

ALICE: [*Quickly reiterating*] That's one *Giselle*, one *Petrushka*, and no *Lac*—

JUNE: [*With enormous effort*] *Rien de Lac de Cygnes. C'est juste.* [*Holds on to* ALICE'S *scarf*] *Mon petit chou.*

ALICE: George, let go. Let go!

JUNE: What's this?

ALICE: What?

JUNE: [*Looking at the label on scarf*] This isn't yours, is it? Where did you get it?

ALICE: George, give it back.

JUNE: Who is J. V. S. Partridge?

ALICE: A young liberal. Satisfied?

JUNE: Far, far from satisfied. How long have you been entangled with this—youth?

ALICE: He's not a youth. He's forty-six.

JUNE: Bit long in the tooth for a young liberal? [*Fiercely*] Who is he?

ALICE: The chap downstairs, daftie. Madame Xenia's lodger.

JUNE: Ah—I thought there was some monkey business going on.

ALICE: There is not. I've only seen him twice.

JUNE: How did you get his scarf, then?

ALICE: I pinched it off the hallstand.

JUNE: D'you expect me to believe that?

ALICE: Look, George. I've never even spoken to him. It's nothing.

JUNE: That's what you said when you went off with that estate agent for a weekend in Birmingham.

ALICE: That was five years ago—

JUNE: It happened once—it can happen again—

ALICE: [*Almost screaming*] Nothing happened!

JUNE: What?

ALICE: *Nothing!*

JUNE: Well, nothing's going to happen with this one. I forbid you to speak to him again.

ALICE: You're raving mad. He's a neighbor, there's no harm in being friendly.

JUNE: [*Shouting*] I forbid you to speak to him, do you hear?

ALICE: [*Shouting back*] I'll flipping well speak to him if I want to—why shouldn't I?

JUNE: [*Venomously*] You fancy him, don't you?

ALICE: He seems perfectly agreeable— [*Sees* JUNE's *face contorted with suspicion.*] Yes, I do fancy him—he's a dish. [JUNE *threatens her.*] You keep away from me— you've no right to—

JUNE: I've got every right.

ALICE: I'm not married to you, you know. [*Long pause.*] I'm sorry, George, but you asked for it.

JUNE: You'd better run along, you'll be late.

ALICE: Look after yourself! Don't forget the party tonight!
[*Exits.*]

JUNE: [*Alone, wanders about the room. Surveys the scene
for a few moments, swaying slightly. Then, pulling a
chair center stage*] Ah, there's my beautiful bike. Mornin',
old friend! Just get you started in a minute. [*She sits
astride it, and makes a purring noise to indicate the
start of the engine.*] Prrrrrrrrrrrrrrrr—prr—prrr— [*She
waves.*] 'Bye, Jean, 'Bye, Rosie, tell your dad to look
after his gammy leg! Prrrr—prrrr— [*She starts singing.*]
"O God, our help in ages past"—prr—prr—"Our hope
for years to come"—Prrr—prrr—Morning, Ginger,
morning, Vicar, you're up early today—prrr—prrr—first
call old Mrs. Hinch—prrrr—prrrr—"Be thou our guard
while troubles last"—prrr—prrr—"And our eternal"—
prrr—"home."

Scene 2

Later the same day.
*The stage is empty when the curtain rises. Laughter and
shrieks can be heard from offstage.*

JUNE: [*Imperiously, offstage*] Pull yourself together. Try
again, and this time do it properly!

ALICE: [*Offstage*] I can't promise I'll get it right.

(*The well-known signature tune of Laurel and Hardy is
heard, laboriously played on the flute.* ALICE *and* JUNE
enter, in the costume of Laurel and Hardy.)

JUNE: [*Imitating* HARDY] And what, may I ask, are you
supposed to be doing?

ALICE: Nothing, Olly, just playing . . . a tune. . . .

JUNE: May I suggest that you stop playing a tune . . . and
get on with the next bit. A-one, a-two.

JUNE and ALICE: [*Doing a soft-shoes dance, side by side*]
"By the light—dum da dum da dum—of the silvery

moon—dum da dum—I used to—rum dum da dum da dum da dum—with my honey and—La da da. By the light—" [ALICE *bumps into* JUNE.]

JUNE: What was the meaning of that? [*Hits* ALICE *with her bowler hat.*]

ALICE: Nothing, Olly—I was only—practicing—

JUNE: [*Turning away in dismay, fluttering her tie*] Oh, fiddlesticks. . . .

ALICE: Did you say "fiddlesticks"? [*She rams the flute into* JUNE.]

JUNE: [*Forgetting her impersonation*] Ouch, that hurt! That was not funny!

ALICE: [*Giggling*] Sorry, Olly.

JUNE: [*Giving* ALICE *a great swipe*] Sorry, Stan.

ALICE: [*As herself*] That hurt!

JUNE: [*In the best Hardy manner, dusting her hands*] Let that be a lesson to you! [*She turns away, beaming.*]

ALICE: [*Again rams the flute against* JUNE. JUNE *seizes it viciously.* Be careful, it's Miss Broadbent's—

JUNE: [*Only half acting*] A very useful instrument. [*She hits* ALICE *over the head with it—fortunately she has her bowler on.*]

ALICE: [*Squaring up to* JUNE, *making sounds of frustrated rage*] You, oh . . .

JUNE: [*Under her breath*] That's not Laurel, daftie, that's the Three Stooges!

ALICE: Sorry, Olly. [*Brightly*] Olly—

JUNE: Yep?

ALICE: Give me your hat.

JUNE: What for, Stan?

ALICE: I just want to look at something.

JUNE: [*Thrusting her hat at* ALICE] Okay. [ALICE *spits on it, and puts it on* JUNE's *head again.* JUNE, *as herself*] What was that supposed to be?

ALICE: [*As herself*] Don't know. Just an idea. Horseplay, you know. . . . We're celebrating because you're back in the series, aren't we?

JUNE: [*With an evil glint in her eye*] Just because the scriptwriters have cured my cold . . . there's no need to go raving, bloody mad you know.

ALICE: I thought it was funny.

JUNE: You thought it was funny?

ALICE: Yes, I thought it was funny.

JUNE: You thought it was funny. Stan.

ALICE: Yes, Olly?

JUNE: Give me your hat.

ALICE: What for?

JUNE: I just want to look at something. Look up there, Stan.

ALICE: There's nothing up there, Olly.

JUNE: Try this, then, Stan.

(ALICE *hands over her bowler:* JUNE *with a righteous nod of the head goes to the table and squirts soda into* ALICE's *hat.* ALICE *stands, unconcernedly twiddling her thumbs.* JUNE *returns, and places the hat, brimful with soda water, on* ALICE.)

ALICE: You fool—now you've spoilt my costume! [*She attacks* JUNE, *pummeling her with her fists.*]

JUNE: [*Keeping her at arm's length*] Steady, now. Steady.

ALICE: What was the point of that?

JUNE: Just an idea. Horseplay you know.

ALICE: You are rotten. I'm all wet, Now I'll have to change.

JUNE: Nonsense, woman. A drop of good clear water never did anybody any harm.

ALICE: All right. [*She takes some flowers out of a vase, and approaches* JUNE, *menacingly holding the vase.*]

JUNE: Don't come near me! I warn you: keep away.

ALICE: I want to show you something, Olly.

JUNE: Childie, stop it. Be your age. [*She backs away.*]

ALICE: Take your punishment like a man!

JUNE: [*Shouting*] All right. [*She stands stock-still, squaring her shoulders.*] Go on—what are you waiting for? [*They laugh, and struggle with the vase.*]

ALICE: [*Losing her nerve.*] Never mind. [*She puts the vase on the table.*]

JUNE: Go on—I'm not afraid of a drop of water! Ugh, you're like a marshmallow.

(The doorbell rings.)

ALICE: It's Madame Xenia, to fetch us. She's ordered a cab. She's early.

JUNE: Well, don't stand and gape. Open the door! [*She propels* ALICE *to the door with a kick.*]

ALICE: [*Offstage*] Oh! Oh, I'm sorry. . . . We were expecting—[*She ushers in* MRS. MERCY CROFT.]

MRS. MERCY: I'm sorry to intrude. I do hope it's not inconvenient. . . .

JUNE: [*Taken aback*] Not at all. I'm sorry we're . . .

MRS. MERCY: Playing charades?

ALICE: As a matter of fact, we were just getting ready to go out—to a fancy dress ball.

JUNE: Ball—fancy—

MRS. MERCY: Oh, I'll come back another time when it's more convenient. Perhaps Miss Buckridge could come to see me tomorrow morning, before rehearsal?

JUNE: We're not in a rush. We can talk now. Would you have a drink?

MRS. MERCY: No thank you.

ALICE: [*Cordially*] Do sit down, Mrs. Mercy.

MRS. MERCY: Thank you, dear.

JUNE: If you had telephoned a little earlier—

MRS. MERCY: *I know.* It's most remiss of me, turning up unexpectedly like this. Actually, I've come straight from a meeting—felt I had to see you personally.

ALICE: [*Anxiously*] The nuns?

MRS. MERCY: Oh, didn't the office tell you? We had a most charming communication from the mother superior. All is forgiven. But there's still the matter of the charity.

JUNE: What charity?

ALICE: The donation you promised to give to the convent.

JUNE: Oh, that!

MRS. MERCY: It's only obliquely mentioned in the letter—

JUNE: [*With a wry smile*] I didn't expect her to forget about it. [*To* ALICE] Remind me to send her a check tomorrow. It'll keep her Irish novices in hair shirts!

MRS. MERCY: Very nice of you, Miss Buckridge. I'm relieved to see the matter settled.

JUNE: [*Going to the cigarette box*] May I offer you a small cigar?

MRS. MERCY: Oh, no . . . no, thank you. I gave up smoking years ago.

JUNE: You don't mind if I smoke?

MRS. MERCY: Well . . .

ALICE: [*Chiding*] You smoke far too much!

JUNE: [*With a mock bow*] Thank you for your touching concern.

MRS. MERCY: Well now, I'm afraid I have some bad news for you, Miss Buckridge.

JUNE: Bad news . . . ?

MRS. MERCY: You're the first to be told. It's only just been decided; or rather, it's only just received the official stamp of approval. . . .

ALICE: [*Terrified*] You can't mean—

JUNE: Be quiet, Childie.

MRS. MERCY: Yes. I'm sorry, Miss Buckridge: it's the end of Sister George.

(*There is a stunned pause.*)

ALICE: [*Suddenly shouting*] But why? Why?

MRS. MERCY: Believe me, dear Miss Buckridge, the decision is no reflection on your ability as an actress. You created a character that has become a nationwide favorite.

ALICE: [*Still incredulous*] But why kill her?

MRS. MERCY: Why do some of our nearest and dearest have to die? Because that's life. In Applehurst we try to re-create the flavor of life, as it is lived in hundreds of English villages—

ALICE: But she's the most popular character in it!

MRS. MERCY: [*Slightly uncomfortable*] I know. The BBC took that into consideration. They felt—and I must say I concurred—that only some dramatic event, something that would get into the news headlines, could save Applehurst. We felt that in their grief, robbed of one of their greatest favorites, listeners would return again to Applehurst with a new loyalty, with a—

JUNE: [*Interrupting dully*] How?

MRS. MERCY: [*Quietly*] It's not for another fortnight. It's scheduled for the twelfth.

JUNE: But how?

MRS. MERCY: [*Smiling benignly*] It's just an ordinary morning at Applehurst. The chaffinch on Sister George's window wakes her up as usual and is rewarded with its daily saucerful of crumbs—

JUNE: [*Under her breath, automatically*] Hello, Dicky. . . .

MRS. MERCY: Up in the road, in the Old Mill Farm, young Jimmy Bromley, the scamp, wakes up with a cough and doesn't want to go to school. "We'd better get Sister George in," says his mother—and he's up in a jiffy! Meanwhile, punctual to the minute, Sister George finishes her breakfast and packs a basketful of preserves and cottage cheese for old Mrs. Hinch, in bed with bronchitis. On with her bonnet and cape, and off she goes, striding purposefully through the autumn leaves—sound effects here—to the bicycle shed. The bolts are pushed back, and the door creaks open, and there's her prized possession—the motorbike.

JUNE: Good morning, old friend.

MRS. MERCY: Whiz—pop—the engine starts—and away she goes! Pop-pop-pop-pop . . . "Hurry up, Jimmy, you'll be late for school . . ." she calls out. "Tell Mrs. Pemberton to give you plenty of homework to keep you out of mischief!" "I will," the boy calls back—adding, as she drives out of earshot—"I don't think!"

JUNE: Cheeky little beggar!

MRS. MERCY: A chorus of greetings follow her as she heads out into the open country—the wind billowing in her cape—and bursts, as usual, into a snatch of her favorite hymn: "O God, Our Help in Ages Past." Honk-honk answers her hooter in a merry descant as she turns into Oakmead Road, and then—BANG! [*She claps her hands.*] Collision with a ten-ton truck.

JUNE: Oh, my God. . . .

ALICE: Is it—is it . . .

MRS. MERCY: Instantaneous. Never regains consciousness.

ALICE: [*Has started to cry.*] You can't, you can't . . .

MRS. MERCY: It so happens that your death will coincide with Road Safety Week: a cause which we know has been close to you for many years.

JUNE: [*Recovering slightly*] I've never ridden carelessly. [*Rising*] I protest—

MRS. MERCY: [*Anxious to placate her*] I know, I know. We're taking great care to establish it's the lorry driver's fault.

JUNE: [*Unconvinced*] But even so—a ten-ton truck . . .

MRS. MERCY: I'm sorry, but there it is.

JUNE: [*With dignity*] I think I have a right to a say about my own mode of death!

MRS. MERCY: [*Kindly*] Now, do leave it to us, dear Miss Buckridge. Leave it to the BBC. We know best. We've had experience in these matters.

JUNE: If I could die in the course of duty—from some infection, perhaps—an epidemic. Yes, that's it—I could go to nurse a patient somewhere up in the hills, someone suffering from some unspeakable disease. . . .

MRS. MERCY: I'm sorry, Miss Buckridge, the scripts have been typed.

JUNE: But they could be altered. . . .

MRS. MERCY: I'm afraid they've been officially approved.

JUNE: Then I shall take this to a higher authority—

ALICE: Yes, don't let them treat you like this. You've still got your public behind you: they won't let them kill you off.

MRS. MERCY: [*Annoyed*] I'm surprised at your attitude, Miss McNaught: I thought you'd be more sensible. I've come here of my own volition, as a gesture of courtesy to a valued and trusted colleague.

ALICE: But it's not fair!

JUNE: Shut up, Childie.

ALICE: I won't shut up.

MRS. MERCY: I was going to say that I'm sure the BBC will want to find some outlet for Miss Buckridge's talents.

JUNE: I'm still not satisfied about the—the accident.

MRS. MERCY: I'm afraid that decision is final.

ALICE: [*To* JUNE] Do you think you ought to lie down? You look awful. [*To* MRS. MERCY] She hasn't been sleeping well lately.

MRS. MERCY: Oh, I'm sorry to hear that.

JUNE: [*Pause.*] Will I be buried in the churchyard?

MRS. MERCY: [*Cheerfully.*] It'll be done in style! Don't you worry your head about that. There's some talk of a special memorial broadcast, with contributions from all sorts of famous people—but I shouldn't really be talking about that, as it's still in the planning stage.

JUNE: Would I be in it? In the memorial broadcast, I mean?

MRS. MERCY: Naturally. There will be lots of recorded extracts of Sister George.

JUNE: No, I meant: would I be able to tell the people how the character developed?

MRS. MERCY: Oh no! That would spoil the illusion.

JUNE: But you said just now you wanted to use me again.

MRS. MERCY: Yes, but not as Sister George.

JUNE: [*On the brink of hysteria*] What's wrong with Sister George?

MRS. MERCY: Nothing, dear Miss Buckridge. She'd be dead, that's all.

(*Pause.*)

ALICE: [*To* JUNE] Come on, George, come and lie down. Come on—come on.

MRS. MERCY: In due course, I hope to discuss ideas for a new serial with you. We'll do something really exciting; I'm sure of it!

JUNE: Mrs. Mercy: I would like to thank you for coming personally to tell me of the . . . decision. I don't really feel up to discussing new ideas for serials at the moment.

MRS. MERCY: Of course you don't!

JUNE: Please don't go. Childie—Miss McNaught—will make you a cup of tea or something. I'll go and lie down for a bit, I think. I'll put that away, in the . . . cabinet. [*Taking gin bottle.*]

ALICE: Will you be all right, George?

JUNE: [*Stopping in the doorway*] What did you say?

ALICE: I said: Will you be all right?

JUNE: You called me "George" then, didn't you? You'll have to get out of that habit. [*She exits.*]

MRS. MERCY: [*Rising*] I really don't think I should stay any longer.

ALICE: Please stay, Mrs. Mercy. I'd like you to.

MRS. MERCY: Well, of course . . . if I can be of any assistance—

ALICE: [*With an awkward laugh*] Just to have somebody to talk to . . .

MRS. MERCY: I expect it hasn't been easy for you . . . recently.

ALICE: [*Quietly, with an anxious look to the door*] She's been impossible. Life's been absolute hell. You've no idea.

MRS. MERCY: I thought as much.

ALICE: Night after night I found her sitting up, drinking. Said she couldn't sleep with worry—

MRS. MERCY: Did she keep you awake?

ALICE: Some nights she made such a din—singing and, you know, reciting and things—that the neighbors complained!

MRS. MERCY: I had no idea it was as bad as that!

ALICE: It's been . . . diabolical!

MRS. MERCY: I do feel sorry for you.

ALICE: When she gets excited, or nervous, or anything, she has to take it out on somebody. Who do you think bears the brunt? Yours truly.

MRS. MERCY: I'm amazed you put up with it.

ALICE: I have no alternative.

MRS. MERCY: Oh come, there must be lots of openings for a girl with your qualifications!

ALICE: I've been with George for seven years.

MRS. MERCY: Seven years—as long as that!

ALICE: Yes, she was quite unknown when we first met.

MRS. MERCY: I expect she was easier to get on with in those days.

ALICE: She was always very jealous; wouldn't let anyone come near me.

MRS. MERCY: What a shame. Especially as it's so important for someone with literary ability to have contact with a lot of people.

ALICE: How did you know that I—

MRS. MERCY: You mentioned your interest in poetry last time we met. You attend classes, I believe?

ALICE: Yes, every Wednesday.

MRS. MERCY: I'd like to read your poems, if I may?

ALICE: Would you? Would you really? Shall I get them now?

MRS. MERCY: No, we'd better not disturb Miss Buckridge now! Give me a ring at the BBC and my secretary will fix an appointment.

ALICE: Oh, thank you. It's really nice of you . . . to take an interest.

MRS. MERCY: Have you ever thought of writing for the radio?

ALICE: It has occurred to me. You know: sometimes one hears such tripe, and one thinks— [*She puts her hand over her mouth.*]

MRS. MERCY: [*With mock reproval*] I know what you were going to say!

ALICE: Sorry.

MRS. MERCY: Never mind. We all feel the same way at times. Anyway, I'm not responsible for *all* the programs!

ALICE: I'm sure yours are by far the best.

MRS. MERCY: [*Very pleased*] Flattery—

ALICE: No, honestly. Years ago, before I knew you had anything to do with Applehurst, I listened to your talks on the wireless about people's problems and honestly, they were really . . . understanding.

MRS. MERCY: [*Touched*] I'm so glad. [*Indicating the door*] You've got a little problem on *your* hands and no mistake!

ALICE: A big problem!

MRS. MERCY: What are we going to do?

ALICE: Don't know.

MRS. MERCY: [*Quietly sympathetic*] Is she always so difficult?

ALICE: Difficult! She gets very violent—especially after she's had a few pints! You've no idea the things she gets up to!

MRS. MERCY: Really?

ALICE: Oh yes. . . . [*She looks around a little wildly.*] Mrs. Mercy, I'm scared. I'm scared of what will happen.

MRS. MERCY: Now, don't be silly. Nothing will happen. You've been living through a rather difficult few weeks, that's all. It was the uncertainty that made her nervous. Now that she knows the worst she'll be much more bearable, you'll see.

ALICE: You don't know George! I don't know how I'll survive the next fortnight. . . .

MRS. MERCY: I'll do what I can to help.

ALICE: I hope she won't get in a rage and murder me.

MRS. MERCY: [*Startled*] Are you serious?

ALICE: Dead serious. When she gets into a temper, she's capable of anything!

MRS. MERCY: Has she ever . . . attacked you?

ALICE: It happens all the time.

MRS. MERCY: But this is *outrageous!*

ALICE: She beats me, you know. She hits me with anything that comes into her hand.

MRS. MERCY: [*Horrified*] But why do you put up with it?

ALICE: [*After a pause*] I have nowhere else to go. . . .

MRS. MERCY: Surely there's somewhere. . . .

ALICE: I couldn't face living alone. Not anymore.

MRS. MERCY: [*Overcome*] My poor girl. This is terrible. . . . Look, if there's any more trouble, don't hesitate to give me a ring. Please regard me as your friend.

ALICE: Oh, you really are kind, Mrs. Mercy.

MRS. MERCY: And we must find somewhere for you to go.

ALICE: [*Gratefully*] Would you? Would you really?

MRS. MERCY: [*Squeezing* ALICE's *arm*] Leave it to me. [*Rising*] How pretty this room looks in the evening sunlight. . . . All these charming dolls—[*She picks up Emmeline.*]

ALICE: That's my favorite. Her name is Emmeline.

MRS. MERCY: [*Shaking the doll by the hand*] Hello, Emmeline.

(*Pause.*)

ALICE: Do you think I ought to go and see if George is all right?

MRS. MERCY: [*Speaking in a childish voice to the doll*] I should leave her where she is . . . the naughty woman. . . .

ALICE: I haven't offered you a cup of tea!

MRS. MERCY: We haven't time for a cup of tea. We have to go. [*To the doll*] Good-bye, little Emmeline.

ALICE: I wish you could stay.

MRS. MERCY: So do I. But I'm glad we had a chance to have a little chat. Now remember what I told you; if there's any trouble, get straight on the telephone to me! [ALICE *puts on the bowler hat.*] That's the spirit!

ALICE: [*In a Laurel voice*] Gee, I'm frightened. . . .

MRS. MERCY: [*Confidentially*] Don't let her bully you.

ALICE: [*As before*] She's a devil when roused. . . .

MRS. MERCY: Good-bye, dear. Must run. [*Waving from the door*] Have fun. [*Exits.*]

ALICE: [*Mechanically*] Must run . . . have fun . . . [*She looks toward the bedroom, undecided; picks up the flute and marches up to the bedroom, playing the Laurel and Hardy signature tune. No reply from* JUNE.] George? George, are you all right? [*Still no reply. She hammers on the bedroom door.*] George! George! ! [*Returning to the room pale with worry*] What am I going to do?

CURTAIN

ACT III

Heard in darkness before the curtain goes up is the sound of SISTER GEORGE's *motorbike, background of country noises, twittering of birds, mooing, neighing.*

SISTER GEORGE: [*Singing*] "O God, our help in ages past . . ."

    (*Fade out. Then the monotonous sound of the engine of a heavy lorry.*)

BILL: [*In a thick West Country accent*] You awake, Fred? [FRED *grunts something unintelligible.*] Won't do to fall asleep now. We're nearly there.

FRED: Not up to it anymore . . . this all-night driving.

BILL: There's the turning coming up now—don't miss it!

FRED: [*Sound of acceleration, and changing of gears.*] Let's get there fast—I'm hungry. . . .

BILL: [*Shouting*] Look out! [*Screeching of brakes, shouting, followed by an explosion. Near hysteria*] Fred! We hit her! Fred! We hit her!

    (*The sound of a car door slamming is heard.*)

FRED: It weren't my fault. I braked—

BILL: Is she—? My God, she looks bad.

FRED: A nurse, by the look of her. . . .

BILL: [*Calling*] Hey, there!

    (*Sound of heavy footsteps, coming nearer.*)

FARMER BROMLEY: [*Coming nearer*] What happened?

BILL: Bike came round the corner, fast!

FRED: I tried to brake. It weren't my fault!

FARMER BROMLEY: [*Panting*] I always did say it's a dangerous crossing. Is she badly—Holy saints! ! It's, it's Sister George!

FRED: It *were* . . .

(*The Applehurst theme swells up. The curtain rises.*)

(*Two weeks have passed. It is a sunny October morning. the room is littered with letters and telegrams, and there is an abundance of flowers.* MADAME XENIA, *discreetly dressed, is listening to Sister George's accident on a tape recorder. As the Applehurst theme swells up, she switches it off and wipes her eyes.*)

XENIA: [*Overcome*] Oi oi oi . . . poor George! [*The doorbell rings.*] All right, I come! [*She goes to the front door and opens it.*] . . . Yes, I will take them, but I don't know where I am going to put them. . . . [*Closes door and comes in with wreaths.*] Soon we shall not be able to move. [*Telephone.*] They are mad. I told them we were not accepting any more calls. [*She lifts the receiver.*] You are mad. I told you we are not accepting any more calls. A message from whom? The girls of your exchange? Yes, I will convey it. . . . Very nice of you. . . . Charming. Miss Buckridge will be very touched. Who am I? Never you mind—I am her temporary secretary. . . . No, I have nothing to do with Applehurst. . . . No, I am not the old gypsy woman who stole a pig! You are beginning to make me very upset. I will not speak anymore! And no more calls, if you please! [*She hangs up.*] Stupid nit.

(ALICE *enters, rubbing her eyes and yawning. She is wearing baby-doll pajamas.*)

ALICE: What time is it?

XENIA: [*With a black look*] Half past ten.

ALICE: Heavens—I'm going to be late for the funeral. [*Nearly trips over a wreath.*] Oh, not more flowers—I shall never find my things. . . .

XENIA: [*Pointedly*] I have been working for two hours.

ALICE: [*Hunting for clothes*] Where's George?

XENIA: Out.—Gone. I don't know where. I am very worried.

ALICE: Gone? When?

XENIA: Since early this morning. I came up with two wreaths and some lilies—she took one look, rushed into the lift, slammed the gate in my face, and went down like a captain on a sinking ship—but not saluting—swearing.

ALICE: I hope she is not going to do something awful?

XENIA: I think she could not stand to be in the flat another moment with all this. . . . [*She looks around at the flowers.*] She felt claustrophobia—I must get out! It has been terrible for her since the accident—nothing but the telephone—letters—reporters.

ALICE: She ought never to have listened to the accident—it was dreadful.

XENIA: Oi oi oi, I just listened to the tape again—that beautiful hymn—the screeching brakes, then [*Claps her hands.*] crash, bang, wallop!

ALICE: [*Covering her ears*] Don't!

XENIA: It was like a gasworks blowing up—horrible. [*Shudders.*] I cried again.

ALICE: Ought we to ring up the police or something?

XENIA: No. We must wait. And work. Everything must be right for her when she comes back. [*She bustles about. ALICE sinks into a chair.*]

ALICE: I feel so exhausted—I think it's the strain.

XENIA: Nonsense—it was the farewell party last night. You have no stamina. You are a—what you call it?—a milksop.

ALICE: I've probably caught a cold. George stuffed a peach melba down the back of my dress. Really, she's getting worse and worse. . . .

XENIA: Listen to this. [*Reading the inscription*] "Unforgotten, from the patients and staff of the Sister George Geriatrics Ward." Beautiful! I could cry!

ALICE: She'd like that.

XENIA: All wreaths against the wall. There. All beautifully organized.

ALICE: Honestly, Madame Xenia, you're a brick.

XENIA: Why do you say that?

ALICE: It's an expression; a friend, a help—

XENIA: I see. But I promised George I would take charge today, and I hold my promise.

ALICE: Could I look at some of the telegrams?

XENIA: If you're very careful and don't get them mixed up. One pile is personal, the other official. Over here it's doubtfuls.

ALICE: Let's see the doubtfuls.

XENIA: What I would like more than anything is a nice cup of tea. . . .

ALICE: [*Looking up from a telegram*] Oh, no!

XENIA: What?

ALICE: [*Bitterly*] Trust her to get in on the act. [*She crumples up the telegram.*]

XENIA: [*Chiding*] You must not do this.

ALICE: [*Very red in the face*] How dare she send telegrams after all these years!

XENIA: From what person . . . ?

ALICE: [*Reading*] "Heartfelt condolences. Love, Liz."

XENIA: Liz?

ALICE: A friend of George's. Before my time.

XENIA: Aha.

ALICE: An absolute cow. Kept writing sarcastic little notes at first; things like "Hope you are divinely happy" and "Hope this finds you as it leaves me—guess how?"

XENIA: [*Quietly*] What I would like more than anything is a nice cup of tea. . . .

ALICE: Anyway, she stole a fountain pen and a camera off George!

XENIA: Tut-tut.

ALICE: "Heartfelt condolences"—she's mocking her!

XENIA: [*Changing the subject*] Here is a nice one from my old friend the baroness. "Shall be thinking of you today. Best wishes for a triumphant funeral. Love, Augusta." She specially put off her hairdresser so that she can listen to it this morning. And she only met George once—at my Halloween party last year.

ALICE: Which one was the baroness?

XENIA: She came as Julius Caesar. At least, that's what we *thought* she was meant to be. . . .

ALICE: I hope George isn't going to be late. . . .

XENIA: I think it is a mistake for her to listen today. Psychologically it is a mistake.

ALICE: Oh, I don't know. She can't just play a character for six years, and miss her own exit.

XENIA: But it will upset her!

ALICE: All her old friends will be there—people she's worked with for years. There'll be tributes paid; there'll be a proper service! I mean to say: there's a right way and a wrong way of doing things. [*She sits on the settee.*]

XENIA: [*Shrugging her shoulders*] I do not understand you.

ALICE: Maybe in your country, people—

XENIA: [*Flaring up*] What do you mean: in my country? We had state funerals which could have taught you something: twenty-eight horses with black plumes, ha?

ALICE: [*Bitchily*] Well, you had lots of practice, didn't you? All those assassinations—

XENIA: Assassinations?

ALICE: Shooting people.

XENIA: Of course we shoot people we don't like! You send them to the House of Lords—what's the difference?

ALICE: Anyway, if you expect the BBC to lay on twenty-eight horses with black plumes, you're in for a disappointment!

XENIA: [*Furious*] Do you want me to go? Immediately I go downstairs—

ALICE: No, no—

XENIA: You can explain my absence to George when she comes back. *If* she comes back . . . [*She moves to the door,* ALICE *runs after her.*]

ALICE: No! Madame Xenia, please stay—I didn't mean to be rude. It's my nerves, I'm so worried about her—supposing she's really cracked up and thrown herself under a bus or something—what am I going to do?

XENIA: [*After a pause*] No, it is not a bus. [*Mysteriously*] I read the cards this morning . . . it is something to do with the head.

ALICE: The *head!* Oh, no . . . I can't bear it.

XENIA: [*Suddenly*] Shh! There's somebody at the door—

ALICE: George!

XENIA: Look cheerful—she must see happy faces.

ALICE: She'll kill me if she sees me walking about like this—[ALICE *rushes toward the bedroom, but trips over a large wreath on the way.*]

JUNE: [*Shouting off*] Open the windows and let the sunshine in!

XENIA: [*Apprehensively*] We are here, my darling. . . .

(ALICE *picks up the wreath and tries to hide behind it, as* JUNE *sails in, wearing an extravagant pink chiffon hat and carrying a large parcel.*)

JUNE: It's glorious out! [*To* XENIA] Darling—how sweet of you to hold the fort—I do hope you weren't pestered too much. . . . [ALICE's *wreath rustles.* JUNE *sees her.*] Oh, God, down in the forest something stirred.

XENIA: George, we were so worried—where have you been?

JUNE: Shopping. I picked up this marvelous bargain—a Christmas gift hamper packed full of goodies. [*Unpacking it*] Oh, two bottles of Veuve Clicquot '52.

XENIA: But—what for . . . ?

JUNE: I've decided to skip the funeral and have a celebration.

XENIA: Celebration?

JUNE: Yes, more a coming-out party, really.

XENIA: But who is coming out?

JUNE: I am!

XENIA: [*Looking at* JUNE's *hat*] I see you bought something else, as well. . . .

JUNE: Do you like it?

XENIA: It is *charming*! Where did you find it?

JUNE: That little shop on the corner. Saw it in the window and couldn't resist it.

XENIA: You were absolutely right! It does something for
you.

JUNE: Do you think so?

XENIA: It makes you look so young! Like eighteen years—
[ALICE *sniggers*.]

JUNE: [*Turning on* ALICE] What are you laughing at?
And why aren't you dressed yet? You look indecent.

ALICE: I overslept. Bit of a hangover.

JUNE: [*Incredulous*] A hangover? After two glasses of
shandy?

ALICE: I mixed it a bit.

JUNE: With what—ginger ale? [ALICE *does not reply*.] Do
you think it proper to entertain visitors in this—this
unseemly attire?

XENIA: [*Placating*] Oh, please, please.

JUNE: Did you make Madame Xenia a cup of tea?

XENIA: It really wasn't necessary. . . .

JUNE: What's the matter with you?

ALICE: Don't know.

JUNE: You should have been out and about for the last
three hours. Did you do your exercises?

ALICE: [*Defiantly*] No.

JUNE: [*To* MADAME XENIA] Oh, God, help us—she takes
a keep-fit course. You know: knee bends, running on
the spot, bicycling on her back. To judge by her condition it's been singularly ineffective! Go on—I want a
cup of tea *now*. And one for Madame Xenia. And get
dressed. And look sharpish about it. *Avanti!*

ALICE: [*Looking straight at* JUNE] I think your hat is a
mistake.

JUNE: [*Thundering*] What? [*No reply from* ALICE.] I can
see this day will end in tears.

ALICE: [*Shouting*] They won't be my tears! [*She runs off*.]

JUNE: The baggage. The little baggage.

XENIA: She is upset.

JUNE: She has no business to be upset: it's *my* funeral!

XENIA: She's taking it hard. Some people—

JUNE: She's no good in a crisis. I've seen it happen again
and again: people going to pieces in a crisis. During the
war—

XENIA: Ah, the war! I was an air-raid warden.

JUNE: I was in the army. Attached to the commandos. It was tough, but rewarding.

XENIA: It's lucky for her she wasn't old enough.

JUNE: Childie in the army? That'd be a bit of a giggle. . . . She'd have collapsed under the weight of her forage cap. [*She laughs.*]

XENIA: Would you like to go through the last tributes?

JUNE: If it's absolutely necessary.

XENIA: Look at this—from the patients and staff of the Sister George Geriatrics Ward. In that hospital your name will never die.

JUNE: [*Firmly*] *Her* name.

XENIA: Her name, your name. It's the same thing—

JUNE: Not any longer. George and I have parted company. And do you know, I'm glad to be free of the silly bitch. [*Pause.*] Honestly.

XENIA: George, what are you saying?

JUNE: I'm saying that my name is *June.* June Buckridge. I'm endeavoring to memorize it.

XENIA: You are incredible!

JUNE: Why?

ALICE: [*Entering with the tea tray*] I'm afraid one of the telegrams got crumpled up. You'd better read it.

JUNE: What telegram?

ALICE: Here. [*She serves the crumpled telegram on a bread plate.*] Will there be any reply, madam?

JUNE: [*Reads it.*] Liz . . . I don't believe it!

ALICE: [*Bitterly*] I thought you'd be pleased.

XENIA: [*Attempting to mediate*] It's always nice to hear from old friends.

ALICE: [*Starts to sing "Auld Lang Syne."*] Sugar, Madame Xenia?

XENIA: No, thank you. I take it neat.

JUNE: [*Reminiscing*] She was a real thoroughbred: stringy, nervy, temperamental. I remember I used to tease her because her hair grew down her neck, like a thin mane, between her shoulder blades— [ALICE *exits, banging the door behind her.*] I knew that would annoy her! [*She chuckles.*]

XENIA: She got out of bed with the left foot, this morning.

JUNE: Her behavior recently has left much to be desired. I may have to speak to her mother—

XENIA: She has her mother here?

JUNE: In Glasgow. Inoffensive old soul. Bakes cakes; minds her own business, but a terrific mumbler. Can't understand a word she says. [*She essays a few words of high-pitched, vaguely Scottish-sounding gibberish.*]

XENIA: Oh, you are a scream!

JUNE: Well, come on—let's open the champers. [*Looks at the flowers.*] Then we can clear out all the foliage. . . .

(*The doorbell rings.*)

XENIA: I go. Soon we shall need a greenhouse.

JUNE: It's awfully kind of you to help out today.

XENIA: My darling: for you I do anything. [*The doorbell rings.*] Perhaps this one is from Buckingham Palace?

JUNE: And about time too, they've been slacking! [*Opens the champagne.*]

XENIA: [*Off*] Did you want to see Miss Buckridge?

JUNE: Now then— [*The cork pops from the bottle.*]

MRS. MERCY: [*Enters. She is dressed in mourning, with a small veiled hat.*] I do hope I'm not disturbing you.

JUNE: [*Surprised*] Mrs. Mercy! No, of course not. . . .

MRS. MERCY: [*Handing over a bouquet*] Dear Sister George —for you—a little tribute—from all of us in admin. at BH.

JUNE: [*Nonplussed*] Oh. Thanks. Extremely decent of you. I—appreciate the thought. Would you be an angel, Madame, and put them in water? Oh, I'm terribly sorry: do you know each other? This is Madame Xenia—Mrs. Mercy Croft.

XENIA: [*Bearing down on* MRS. MERCY] What, *the* Mrs. Mercy?

JUNE: Of course, didn't you know—

XENIA: [*Softly to* MRS. MERCY] But I love you, my dear. [*Shouting*] I *adore* you!

MRS. MERCY: Have I had the pleasure?

XENIA: You don't know me from Adam, my darling, but for twenty years I have listened to you—every single week!

JUNE: How nice.

MRS. MERCY: Charming!

XENIA: [*Quite overcome*] I am—I cannot tell you—your advice is a hundred percent. A hundred and twenty percent! One senses—you have a heart, you have suffered—

MRS. MERCY: Well, we all have our ups and downs.

XENIA: But you have had more downs than ups—am I right?

MRS. MERCY: I shouldn't like—

XENIA: Of course I am! I knew it at once! Ask George here: am I ever wrong?

JUNE: Never. She is quite infallible. You see, Madame Xenia is a clairvoyant.

MRS. MERCY: Oh, really.

XENIA: A psychometrist.

JUNE: Oh, sorry.

XENIA: I write a syndicated column every week: star forecasts—hack work, but what-the-hell, one's got to live.

MRS. MERCY: I'm afraid I don't really believe in that kind of—

XENIA: [*Quickly*] Be careful what you do on the tenth. There's treachery around you. Don't sign any important documents before full moon—

MRS. MERCY: I'm obliged to you, but really—

XENIA: There's news from abroad—

MRS. MERCY: [*Turning to* JUNE] I thought you'd be all alone this morning. That's why I came—

JUNE: Very kind of you.

XENIA: You're inclined to suffer from digestive disorders. Don't worry, it's nothing serious—

JUNE: [*Apologetically*] Madame is helping me out today.

XENIA: A tall man doesn't like you. Avoid him.

MRS. MERCY: It would be somewhat difficult in my job to—

XENIA: An old association will be broken. Never mind: there are plenty of birds in the sky—

MRS. MERCY: [*Icily*] I think you mean fish in the sea.

XENIA: [*To herself*] Interesting. Must be born under Pisces. . . . [*Cheerfully*] Oh well, I'll get some water for the flowers. . . . [*She exits.*]

JUNE: She's been frightfully good: done all the organizing for me today.

MRS. MERCY: Isn't your friend—er—Miss—?

JUNE: Miss McNaught? She's not up yet! I'm afraid she's no good at times like these. No backbone. Ballast.

MRS. MERCY: [*Inspecting the wreaths*] What beautiful tributes! May I read some? I *adore* inscriptions.

JUNE: There's a whole lot more in the bathroom. As soon as Childie's dressed she can take the whole damn lot and dump them on the Cenotaph.

MRS. MERCY: But you can't do that! They're for *you*. [*Seriously*] Do you know the entire Applehurst Company turned up for the recording today in black? It was quite spontaneous.

JUNE: [*Annoyed*] They must be bonkers! I can just see old Mrs. Hinch. She must have looked like the Phantom of the Opera. . . . [*Sees* MRS. MERCY'*s black suit.*] Oh, I beg your pardon.

MRS. MERCY: We felt we couldn't let her go without some mark of respect. After all, she has been with us . . . how long?

JUNE: Six perishing years.

MRS. MERCY: Oh, come now—you know you enjoyed every minute of it.

JUNE: [*Getting exasperated*] Yes, but it's over—I just want to forget it—

MRS. MERCY: I don't think your public will let you. [*Indicating the wreaths*] You can see how much you meant to them.

JUNE: [*Trying to escape*] Actually, I was just on the point of changing. . . . [*Takes off hat.*]

MRS. MERCY: For the funeral?

JUNE: For the broadcast.

(MADAME XENIA *reenters, brandishing a large gilded vase in the shape of a galleon bearing* MRS. MERCY'*s flowers.*)

XENIA: All right?

JUNE: Wasn't there something a little more conservative?

XENIA: I can put them in a milk bottle, if you like. Or perhaps you'd prefer a bottle of gin? [*Piqued*] It is good to have one's hard work appreciated! Getting up early in the morning—

JUNE: Madame, darling—I'm eternally grateful. You've been a brick!

XENIA: Yes, so I've been told before.

MRS. MERCY: What a charming message. [*Reading*]
"Ever-present, spirit-like,
Harken! the familiar sound:
Sister George, astride her bike,
In the happy hunting ground."

(JUNE *mutters under her breath*.)

XENIA: [*About to go*] Well, happy hunting, Sister George!

JUNE: You're off then, are you, dear?

XENIA: I'm afraid my client is waiting. The moment you need me, just stamp on the floor.

JUNE: Don't worry about me—I'm feeling fine. If any more flowers come, you'd better shove them in the coalshed.

XENIA: Leave everything to me. *I am your friend!*

MRS. MERCY: [*Reading*] "Fare thee well. Go in peace, good woman."

XENIA: I can take a hint. [*She strides out, nose in the air.*]

JUNE: [*Blowing her a kiss*] Thank you, darling.

MRS. MERCY: You do have a lot of friends, don't you?

JUNE: I hope so. I like to think—

MRS. MERCY: Loneliness is the great scourge of our time.

JUNE: Too true.

MRS. MERCY: I had visions of you, sitting by your set, alone with your grief. . . .

JUNE: With Miss McNaught actually, but it comes to the same thing.

MRS. MERCY: Frankly, I'm amazed you're taking it like this.

JUNE: Like what?

MRS. MERCY: So calmly. Cheerfully.

JUNE: The uncertainty was the worst. Once that was over . . .

MRS. MERCY: You have a very strong character. [*After a pause*] Will you go on listening to the program now?

JUNE: I don't know. I hadn't really thought. Probably not. I mean—it might be rather—distressing—listening to all the old voices going on without me. . . .

MRS. MERCY: Isn't that a rather selfish attitude to take?

JUNE: Selfish?

MRS. MERCY: You died to save the series—surely you'll want to take an interest in its fortunes?

JUNE: Well . . .

MRS. MERCY: I think the next few episodes will be particularly fascinating. [*She warms to the subject.*] Your death means an enormous readjustment to the whole community. It will take them weeks, even months, to get over the shock. But eventually the gap must be filled, new leaders will arise—

JUNE: Leaders? What leaders? Who?

MRS. MERCY: [*Confidentially*] Well, it's not really for release yet, but between you and me—I believe Ginger—

JUNE: [*Horrified*] Ginger? [*Slipping into country accent*] He couldn't lead a cow down Buttercup Hill. He's weak! Weak as rotten apples dropping off a tree.

MRS. MERCY: Ginger will be our anti-hero.

JUNE: An anti-hero in Applehurst?

MRS. MERCY: Contemporary appeal. Applehurst is facing up to the fact that the old values have become outdated.

JUNE: I wonder how old Mrs. Hinch is going to take that?

MRS. MERCY: [*Quickly*] Not very well, I'm afraid. She passes away.

JUNE: [*Aghast*] What!

MRS. MERCY: It's due in the second week in December.

JUNE: How?

MRS. MERCY: It'll be a cold winter in Applehurst. She gets up in the middle of the night to let the cat in . . .

JUNE: And—?

MRS. MERCY: Bronchitis. Gone in two days.

JUNE: But you can't do this! After all the care I gave that woman—why, I've nursed her from gout to gastro-enteritis over the last six years.

MRS. MERCY: That's neither here nor there.

JUNE: I could have saved her—just as I saved old Mr. Burns last winter. He's three years older and look at him now, fit as a fiddle! At least, he was . . .

MRS. MERCY: I'm afraid he is due for a stroke next Friday.

JUNE: But why all this carnage, all this slaughter?

MRS. MERCY: We live in a violent world, Miss Buckridge, surrounded by death and destruction. It's the policy of the BBC to face up to reality.

JUNE: Who's going to look after the survivors?

MRS. MERCY: Nurse Lawrence.

JUNE: What!

MRS. MERCY: Yes, she arrives from the district hospital tomorrow to take over from you.

JUNE: But she's a probationer. She couldn't put a dressing on a salad! They won't stand for that, you know.

MRS. MERCY: On the contrary, Nurse Lawrence wins the trust and affection of the village, and becomes known, rather charmingly, I think, as Sister Larry.

JUNE: [*Rising*] You're going to make this ill-bred, uneducated slut—

MRS. MERCY: [*Shouting*] Contemporary appeal, Sister George! People like that *do* exist—and in positions of power and influence; flawed, credible characters like Ginger, Nurse Lawrence, Rosie—

JUNE: What about Rosie?

MRS. MERCY: She's pregnant.

JUNE: I know that. And as she's not married, that's about as flawed and credible as you can get!

MRS. MERCY: She's going to marry her boyfriend, Lennie.

JUNE: Oh good. I'm glad . . . I'm glad about that . . . glad—

MRS. MERCY: Mind you, it's not his baby.

JUNE: Eh?

MRS. MERCY: It's Roy's from the army camp at Oakmead. She tells Lennie, makes a full confession, and he forgives her, and they live happily ever after.

JUNE: Pardon me while I vomit.

ALICE: [*Enters. She is wearing a gaily colored dress.*] Oh, hello.

MRS. MERCY: [*Cordially*] Hello, dear. I was wondering where you were.

ALICE: I didn't go to work today.

MRS. MERCY: No, of course not.

ALICE: [*Sweetly, to* MRS. MERCY] Can I make you a cup of tea, Mrs. Mercy?

MRS. MERCY: I'd *adore* a cup of tea!

JUNE: [*Bitterly*] Mrs. Mercy came over to bring me the good news that I'm to be replaced by Nurse Lawrence.

ALICE: Nurse Lawrence—Nurse Lawrence? Do I know her?

JUNE: Don't be irritating. Of course you know her. That interfering busybody from Oakmead—

ALICE: [*With indifference*] Oh, her.

JUNE: Yes, her.

ALICE: [*To* JUNE] Anyway, it's not really your concern anymore what happens in Applehurst. You're out of it—

JUNE: [*Bellowing*] Don't you understand? Don't you understand anything? I built it up: I made it what it is! It's not *nice* to see one's life work ruined!

MRS. MERCY: I have one piece of cheering news for you, if you can bear to hear it.

JUNE: I can bear it. Pour out a glass of gin for me, Childie, while you're over at the sideboard. Sorry, Mrs. Mercy, you were saying . . .

MRS. MERCY: It concerns your future.

JUNE: My future, yes. You are quite right: we must talk of the future. Is there still time—?

MRS. MERCY: There's still nearly an hour to go.

JUNE: Did you want to stay for the . . . the . . .

MRS. MERCY: Broadcast?

JUNE: The funeral. Yes. . . .

MRS. MERCY: No, I'll have to get back to BH. We're having a little party, you know. Perhaps "party" isn't quite the right word.

ALICE: A wake?

MRS. MERCY: I suppose one could call it that. That's why

I want a quick word with you, Miss Buckridge. Mrs. Coote has promised to come. You know Mrs. Coote, don't you? She's in charge of Toddler Time.

JUNE: Yes, of course I know her, a charming woman.

MRS. MERCY: Well, dear, she's very anxious to have you.

JUNE: Really?

MRS. MERCY: What I'm telling you now is strictly off the cuff. Everything's still in the planning stage. I thought I'd nip over and tell you that there's a ray of sunshine on the horizon.

JUNE: I'm all ears.

(ALICE *exits to the kitchen.*)

MRS. MERCY: [*Very confidentially*] Well, dear, as you probably know, Toddler Time has been—what shall we say—a wee bit disappointing. Audience research figures —this is strictly *entre nous*, you understand—

JUNE: Yes, yes, of course.

MRS. MERCY: —show a slight but perceptible slide. Mrs. Coote, I may tell you, is worried out of her mind! She hasn't slept a wink for three weeks—

JUNE: Poor love!

MRS. MERCY: The scriptwriters are running around in circles—one of them's had a nervous breakdown: the one who wrote that series about Tiddlywink, the Cockerel, which, as you know, was taken off after only three installments. Anyway, to cut a long story short, there's been some agonizing reappraisal over Toddler Time. A completely new approach has been decided on—

JUNE: Don't tell me—marauding gollywogs, drunk teddy bears, and pregnant bunnies!

(ALICE *reenters with tea.*)

MRS. MERCY: [*Smiling enigmatically*] Not quite, dear. But we're preparing an absolutely super adventure serial, in which we've got loads of confidence, which will combine exciting narrative with a modern outlook. And you're being considered for the title role.

JUNE: What is it called?

MRS. MERCY: The World of Clarabelle Cow.

JUNE: [*Rising after a pause*] Am I to understand that this . . . this character is a cow?

MRS. MERCY: A very human one, I assure you: full of little foibles and prejudices—

JUNE: [*Slowly*] A . . . flawed . . . credible . . . cow?

MRS. MERCY: Credible in human terms, certainly. Otherwise the children wouldn't believe in her. Children are very discerning!

ALICE: Ought to be fun.

JUNE: I don't think I could have understood you correctly. I don't believe I really grasped the meaning of your words.

MRS. MERCY: I thought I made myself perfectly clear.

ALICE: Oh, don't be dense, George!

JUNE: [*To* ALICE] Be quiet! [*To* MRS. MERCY] Am I to take it that you have come here today—the day of the funeral of Sister George—to offer me the part of a cow?

MRS. MERCY: We've got to be practical, dear. None of us can afford to be out of work for too long.

JUNE: Childie, give me another gin! [*To* MRS. MERCY] You're not serious, are you? You're joking, aren't you?

MRS. MERCY: We don't joke about these things at the BBC, Miss Buckridge.

ALICE: [*To* JUNE] It's jolly nice of Mrs. Mercy to come over special to tell you.

MRS. MERCY: I thought it was a brilliant idea of Mrs. Coote's.

JUNE: [*Shouting and tearing her hair*] I can't stand it! I'm going mad!

XENIA: [*Enters with another wreath.*] One more for luck!

JUNE: [*Tonelessly*] From whom?

XENIA: [*Reading the inscription*] "I never thought I'd survive you." Signed: Mrs. Ethel Hinch.

MRS. MERCY: She doesn't know yet. . . .

JUNE: [*Distracted*] She's going to die, Madame Xenia— in two months' time! They're going to murder her, too. An old lady of eighty-five, who's never done anyone the slightest harm!

XENIA: How terrible! Are you sure?

JUNE: [*Wildly to* MRS. MERCY] Murderess! [*She lunges at* MRS. MERCY *and is held back by* ALICE *and* MADAME XENIA.]

MRS. MERCY: Really, Miss Buckridge! Restrain yourself!

JUNE: Is your blood lust sated? How many other victims are you going to claim?

MRS. MERCY: [*Shrilly*] Control yourself!

ALICE: George, you're drunk!

XENIA: My darling is upset. She's had a shock.

JUNE: [*Making a great effort to control herself*] With reference to Toddler Time, please thank Mrs. Coote for her kind interest—

MRS. MERCY: There's no need for you to decide today—

JUNE: —and tell her I cannot possibly accept the part in question.

MRS. MERCY: Very well, I'll tell her.

(*The buzzer sounds.*)

ALICE: Don't be silly, George. You can't afford to turn down—

JUNE: I'm not playing the part of a cow!

XENIA: A cow? What cow?

JUNE: [*Frantically*] I'M NOT PLAYING THE PART OF A COW! !

MRS. MERCY: I've taken your point, Miss Buckridge!

XENIA: . . . There are two nuns, to see Sister George.

JUNE: No! . . . NO!!

(*Groaning with dismay, she rushes off to the bathroom.*)

XENIA: [*To* MRS. MERCY] Nuns before noon is a good omen!

MRS. MERCY: I'll take your word for it.

ALICE: [*Following* JUNE] I'd better go and see what she's doing. [*Goes to the bathroom. Offstage*] . . . George: what are you doing?

XENIA: [*Into the speaker*] I'm sorry, Sister George is getting ready for her funeral.

404

ALICE: [*Long pause.*] George! . . . [*She reenters.*] She appears to be running a bath.

XENIA: Shall I go and speak to her?

MRS. MERCY: She won't do anything silly, will she?

XENIA: [*To* ALICE] See if she's all right! [ALICE *goes off again.*] I'm so worried.

MRS. MERCY: There was bound to be a reaction.

ALICE: [*Offstage*] George? . . . I can't hear what you're saying! Turn the bloody taps off!

(JUNE *mumbles offstage.*)

XENIA: Oi oi oi.

ALICE: [*Reentering*] Says she wants to be left alone.

XENIA: How did she sound?

ALICE: Like a walrus.

XENIA: [*Clapping her hands*] Thank God. Thank God she's herself again. [*Tidying up confusedly*] Oi, oi, what a morning!

(*She exits.* MRS. MERCY *and* ALICE *face each other for a few seconds. Then* MRS. MERCY *extends her arms, and* ALICE *flies to her, and bursts into tears.*)

MRS. MERCY: My poor child. . . . There, there. . . .

ALICE: I can't stand it anymore.

MRS. MERCY: I know, dear, I know. You've been under a terrible strain.

ALICE: You've no idea, Mrs. Mercy—

MRS. MERCY: I can imagine.

ALICE: She's been *terrible!*

MRS. MERCY: Hush, dear. She'll hear you.

ALICE: I was praying you'd come.

MRS. MERCY: I wasn't going to leave you alone with her today. [*She smiles.*] Besides, I had promised.

ALICE: Oh, I know, but I knew how busy you were.

MRS. MERCY: First things first.

ALICE: I knew I could rely on you. I felt it the first time I met you.

MRS. MERCY: And I felt that I was speaking to a proud and sensitive person, whose personality was being systematically crushed.

ALICE: Don't.

MRS. MERCY: And with a definite literary talent.

ALICE: Honestly? Do you really think so?

MRS. MERCY: I'm being quite objective.

ALICE: Gosh. Wouldn't it be marvelous?

MRS. MERCY: What, dear?

ALICE: If I could do some work for you—writing, I mean.

MRS. MERCY: We shall see what transpires. I'll certainly give you all the help I can.

ALICE: Oh, you are nice!

MRS. MERCY: And the other offer still stands.

ALICE: Yes, well . . . I think I've almost definitely decided. I'm sorry to be so vague. . . .

MRS. MERCY: Not at all.

ALICE: It's a bit of wrench, you know. I've been working for Mr. Katz for nearly four years. I'd have to give him a month's notice—

MRS. MERCY: There's no rush. I told you I'd keep the job open for a fortnight.

ALICE: And there's George.

MRS. MERCY: Yes.

ALICE: I mean: I don't know how she'd take it.

MRS. MERCY: You haven't told her, of course?

ALICE: God, no. She'd have murdered me!

MRS. MERCY: In view of what happened today, I think we were very wise—

ALICE: If she suspected I'd been to see you behind her back—

MRS. MERCY: But there was no reason why you shouldn't. You're perfectly entitled—

ALICE: Oh, I *know*. But she's so possessive. She never allows me anywhere near the BBC. I'm kept a guilty secret.

MRS. MERCY: She's shackled you to her. Anyway, you wouldn't be working for the BBC: you'd be working as my own private secretary, in my London flat.

ALICE: It sounds absolutely super. I'm sorry I'm being so
   slow about making up my mind.

MRS. MERCY: A thought has just occurred to me: if you're
   in any kind of trouble—you know, with George—you
   can always camp down at the flat. There's a divan—

ALICE: Oh, that'd be *wonderful!*

MRS. MERCY: It could serve as your temporary HQ. It's
   not luxurious, mind you.

ALICE: Never mind that. It would be an escape . . . if
   necessary. . . .

MRS. MERCY: That's what I thought. I only ever stay there
   if I've been kept late at a story conference, or something
   like that. I find it useful. . . . I suppose it's really a place
   to escape for me, too. . . .

ALICE: We'd be like prisoners on the run. . . .

MRS. MERCY: Do you really think you can escape?

ALICE: [*After a pause*] I don't know.

MRS. MERCY: It's very difficult for you.

ALICE: It's been so long, so many years. . . .

MRS. MERCY: It's hard to break the routine.

ALICE: It's little things one misses most.

MRS. MERCY: [*Smiling*] You could bring your dolls.

ALICE: [*Grabbing Emmeline*] I couldn't go anywhere without them. I even take them on holiday—and then I'm
   terrified they'll get lost or stolen. Sometimes George
   hides them—it's her idea of a joke. . . .

MRS. MERCY: A very cruel joke.

ALICE: [*Clutching* MRS. MERCY] Don't let her get at me,
   Mrs. Mercy! Stay here—don't go away!

MRS. MERCY: I can't stay here all day, dear.

ALICE: Don't leave me alone—I'm frightened of what she
   will do!

MRS. MERCY: Calm yourself, Alice. No one's going to hurt
   you. Here, put your head on my shoulder; close your
   eyes. . . . Relax—my goodness, you're trembling like a
   leaf. . . . [*She strokes* ALICE'*s hair.*]

ALICE: That's nice. . . .

MRS. MERCY: You're my little girl. You're going to be . . .
   my little girl. . . .

JUNE: [*Enters. She is wearing her bathrobe.*] What a touching sight. . . .

ALICE: [*Panic-stricken, breaking away from* MRS. MERCY] George!

JUNE: [*To* MRS. MERCY] I always did say she had nice hair. That's one thing I always said for her. . . .

ALICE: George, you don't understand!

JUNE: [*Grabbing the doll*] Your mummy says I don't understand. Did you see what your mummy was doing with that strange lady?

MRS. MERCY: She was overwrought, Miss Buckridge. I tried to comfort her.

JUNE: How absolutely sweet of you! And how well you have succeeded!

(ALICE *is trembling from head to toe.*)

MRS. MERCY: I hope you don't think—

JUNE: [*Sweetly*] Alice, Childie: come here a minute. I want to say something to you! . . . [ALICE *looks terrified.*] Come along, don't be frightened, I'm not going to hurt you.

ALICE: Why can't you tell me—in front of Mrs. Mercy?

JUNE: [*Feigning gaucheness*] Well, you know, boy's talk—

MRS. MERCY: Would you rather I left?

JUNE: Oh no, no. Whatever could have given you that idea? Come along, keep still. I only want to whisper it in your ear. [*She whispers something.*]

ALICE: [*Shouting*] No! [JUNE *whispers something else.*] No, I'm not going to do it!

JUNE: Yes or no, Childie? Yes or no?

ALICE: [*Frantically*] No, no, NO!

MRS. MERCY: [*White with indignation*] What are you asking her to do, Sister George?

JUNE: The appropriate treatment, that's all. The punishment that fits the crime. . . .

ALICE: [*Shrieking*] She wants me to drink her bath water!

MRS. MERCY: [*Astounded*] Her bath water?

ALICE: To humiliate me!

MRS. MERCY: [*Rising*] But this is preposterous! I've never heard of such an obscene suggestion!

JUNE: You're shut off from the world, Mrs. Mercy! "Ask Mrs. Mercy"—all your problems answered! "Dear Mrs. Mercy, what shall I do? My flatmate is nasty to me and wants me to drink her bath water. By the time you reply to me—glug, glug, glug—it may be too late—glug—and I might have drowned!"

MRS. MERCY: [*To* ALICE] I strongly advise you to leave this house at once!

JUNE: [*To* ALICE] Well, you have had the benefit of Mrs. Mercy's expert advice. Are you going to take it?

ALICE: I'm sorry, George, I can't stay with you any longer.

MRS. MERCY: Very sensible.

JUNE: Did you hear what your mummy said, Emmeline? Your mummy wants to leave us—

MRS. MERCY: I wish you wouldn't—

JUNE: [*Dangerously*] Mind what you're saying, Mrs. Mercy: this is between Alice and myself!

ALICE: [*Pleading*] Let me have Emmeline!

JUNE: Glug, glug, glug to you. [*She makes the doll point at* MRS. MERCY.]

MRS. MERCY: I don't know how you can be so cruel. The poor child—

JUNE: "The poor child!" As you're going to see quite a lot of "the poor child," I'd better put you in the picture about her—

ALICE: George, don't! George, please!

JUNE: "The poor child" likes to pretend she's a baby, but take a close look at her!

(ALICE *bursts into tears.*)

MRS. MERCY: Can't you see you're upsetting the child!

JUNE: [*Shouting*] The child? The child is a woman— she's thirty-four! [*A loud sob from* ALICE.] She's old enough to have a grandchild!

MRS. MERCY: Oh, really, now you're exaggerating—

JUNE: Am I? *Am I?*

ALICE: [*Whimpering*] Don't, George . . . don't . . .

JUNE: [*With disgust*] Look at you: whimpering and pleading! Have you no backbone, can't you stand up like a
man—

ALICE: [*Sobbing*] I can't . . . help it. . . .

JUNE: "I can't help it!" She'll never change—feckless,
self-indulgent—

ALICE: I'm going! I'm packing my bag! [*She runs to the
door, but* JUNE *bars the way.*]

JUNE: Come back here!

MRS. MERCY: Let her go! Let her go!

JUNE: [*To* MRS. MERCY] You've got yourself a prize packet
there, I can tell you!

ALICE: [*Screaming*] Let me go!

JUNE: She had an illegitimate child when she was eighteen.
She gave it away—to strangers! She has a daughter of
sixteen. . . . [ALICE *collapses on the floor in a heap.*] Do
what you like—you make me sick! [*She sits in an armchair.*]

MRS. MERCY: Stop crying, dear. Go and pack, quickly. You
needn't take everything now. Go along, hurry! I'll wait
for you here. . . . [ALICE *goes into the bedroom.*] I'm
sorry, Miss Buckridge, about all this. It'll be all for the
best, you'll see. . . . I do hope you're not bearing me any
grudge—[JUNE *shakes her head.*] Oh, good, good. Sometimes it's best to make a clean break—it's painful, but
that's the advice I always give in my program. Which
reminds me: it's almost time for the broadcast. Shall I
switch it on? [*She switches on the radio.*] Let it give you
strength, Miss Buckridge. Remember: Sister George was
not killed because she was hated, but because she was
loved! [ALICE *comes on, tear-stained, carrying a small
case.*] If you study anthropology you'll discover that in
primitive societies it was always the best-loved member
of the community who was selected as the sacrificial
victim. By killing him they hoped that the goodness and
strength of the victim would pass on to them. It was
both a purge and a rededication. What you will hear in

a few moments is the purge and rededication of Applehurst. Good-bye, Sister George.

(*From the radio comes the slow tolling of a bell.*)

ALICE: I think she's right in what she said: Mrs. Mercy, I mean. I love you, too, George, that's why I've got to leave you. You do understand, don't you. . . . I mean— [*She's starting to cry again.*] All right, Mrs. Mercy, I'm coming. Good-bye, George, and—you know—thanks for everything!

(ALICE *and* MRS. MERCY *exit.*)

ANNOUNCER'S VOICE: [*From the radio*] Applehurst: a chronicle of an English village. This is a sad day for Applehurst. The church bell is tolling for the funeral of Sister George, the well-beloved district nurse, whose forthright, practical, no-nonsense manner had endeared her to the community. But death comes to the best of us, and the picturesque village is today swathed in mourning. . . .

(*The church bell tolls again.*)

JUNE: [*A very plaintive sound*] Moo! . . . [*Louder*] Moo! Moo! [*A heart-rending sound.*]

CURTAIN

CORNBURY:
The Queen's Governor
A Comedy in Two Acts

by
William M. Hoffman and Anthony Holland

Cornbury: The Queen's Governor was first presented as a staged reading at the Public Theater in New York City, on April 12, 1976. It was produced by Joseph Papp and directed by Anthony Holland, with the following cast:

CORNBURY .... *Joseph Maher*
MARIE .... *Linda Lavin*
MARGARETA DE PEYSTER .... *Grayson Hall*
SPINOZA DACOSTA .... *Richard Bauer*
AFRICA .... *Risë Collins*
RIP VAN DAM .... *Christopher Guest*
PASTOR CORNELIUS VAN DAM .... *Macintyre Dixon*
MUNSEE .... *Ray Barry*
ANNA MARIA BAYARD .... *Sigourney Weaver*
ATTICUS .... *Ron McLarty*
MOLLY, QUEEN ANNE, SARAH ....*Sasha Von Scherler*
MARTHA, HESTER .... *Kate McGregor-Stewart*
NARRATOR, LOVELACE .... *Paul Dooley*

CHARACTERS

(In order of speaking. Roles with asterisks may be doubled and tripled, if necessary.)

NARRATOR*
SPINOZA DACOSTA*
EDWARD HYDE, Viscount Cornbury, Governor of New York and New Jersey
AFRICA
PASTOR CORNELIUS VAN DAM
RIP VAN DAM (the Pastor's son)
MARGARETA DE PEYSTER (née van Cortlandt)
MOLLY*
MARTHA*

414

MUNSEE*
ANNA MARIA BAYARD*
MARIE (Edward's wife)
ATTICUS*
QUEEN ANNE*
HESTER DE LANCEY*
SARAH VANDERSPIEGEL*
SIR RICHARD LOVELACE*
TOWNSPEOPLE,* CONGREGATION,* ACTORS,* SOLDIERS*

SETS: The curtain should be painted to depict the William Burgis panoramic view of New York in 1717. The sets are painted backdrops, two-dimensional in effect, representing the interiors required for each scene.

COSTUMES: Should be as accurately historical as possible. That is to say, the conflict of the baroque English court with Calvinist New York sobriety should be obvious.

MUSIC: Ranges from Korngold, Handel, Bach, to African chants. It is both live and prerecorded.

AUTHORS' NOTE: The style is jocular and always light. This play is meant to be done by a small company with great energy.

Cornbury, when recalled, was in prison for debt [in New York]. He had the name of a buffoon. When formerly he had been on the staff of Prince George he was always missing, and when at last politely exiled to New York he made his first appearance as governor, he was dressed as a woman. It seemed reasonable to ask why. "Because," the enquirer was told, "I represent Her Majesty the Queen."

—David Green, *Queen Anne*

ON THE PROSPECT OF PLANTING ARTS
AND LEARNING IN AMERICA

. . . In happy climes, the seat of innocence,
  Where nature guides and virtue rules;
Where men shall not impose for truth and sense
  The pedantry of courts and schools.

There shall be sung another golden age,
  The rise of empire and of arts,
The good and great inspiring epic rage:
  The wisest heads and noblest hearts.

Not such as Europe breeds in her decay;
  Such as she bred when fresh and young,
When heav'nly flame did animate her clay,
  By future poets shall be sung.

Westward the course of empire takes its way;
  The four first acts already past,
A fifth shall close the drama with the day:
  Time's noblest offspring is the last.
                                   —George Berkeley

Prologue

*As the audience is seated and before the lights dim, we hear
the lush Hollywood orchestrations of Erich Wolfgang Korngold's* Overture to The Sea Hawk—*1940. The lights dim
as the love theme begins; over this, in the darkness, the rich
synthetic baritone of the* NARRATOR *heightens the anticipation of the audience.*

NARRATOR: New York, seventeen hundred and eight. The royal colony, formerly New Amsterdam until its conquest by the English, teeters on the brink of open mutiny. It is the last year of Governor Cornbury's administration. Edward Hyde, Viscount Cornbury, first cousin to Queen Anne, a favorite of the late King William, and eldest son of the Earl of Clarendon, held in universal disdain by his subjects, was soon to be dismissed by history as a vain buffoon. An abomination to some, an angel to others, this is *his* story: Cornbury, the Queen's Governor.

(*Musical flourish as the curtain rises*)

ACT I

Scene 1

A chamber in the governor's mansion. LORD CORNBURY *and his secretary,* SPINOZA DACOSTA. EDWARD *is in his dressing gown preparing his toilette for the evening. During the course of the following dialogue,* EDWARD *dons a gown, wig, and furbelows, which transform him into an uncanny resemblance to the portrait of* QUEEN ANNE *painted in 1689 by Ludwig Kneller. A similar portrait of* LORD CORNBURY *may be found in the New-York Historical Society between the main floor lavatories. Ask the woman at the desk.* EDWARD *is forty-seven years old, heavy, masculine, and needs a shave.* SPINOZA *is a Jewish refugee from the latest Portuguese inquisition. He is simply dressed in period clothing. He wears a hat. Fifty years old, he is a man of deep learning and universal sympathy. He speaks English fluently, as well as Hebrew, Dutch, Portuguese, Spanish, French, Italian, and enough Turkish to get by.*

SPINOZA: But, my lord, we cannot afford further expenditures. The assembly demands an accounting of all moneys. We must not ignore—

EDWARD: Was it ill conceived to choose this blue manto, my dear Spinoza, when the willow green would have suited my eyes, or the scarlet given definition to my great determination? Kneller, Her Majesty's favorite painter, told me once, "A royal portrait is a royal portrait. Leave it to Sarah Churchill to be captured playing at cards, but royalty must stand like the gods. They must be metaphor." Well, we can't all be seen as Queen Anne in the role of Justice . . . [EDWARD *holds an imaginary sword and scales.*] admired by the three Graces while she's kicking Envy . . . [EDWARD *kicks Envy.*] with her gouty foot.

419

SPINOZA: Excuse me, your lordship, on the matters we
spoke of—

EDWARD: [*Arranging gown*] Still, I have other stuffs as fine
as this, and this is better than anything found in sad New
York. I wish I could be painted in all my favorite clothes.
My silver-tissue manto, lined with the palest sky-blue.
My crimson velvet under-petticoat with lace. My rich fox
muff. My cherry-colored silk nightgown, lined with lute-
string. I drink my chocolate in that and wipe my lips on
a fine Turkish handkercher embroidered in gold. You
must send for some amber powder and a paper of
patches.

SPINOZA: The treasury is empty, my lord.

EDWARD: *Sell Staten Island!* . . . Oh, what do these Dutch
women know, those somber gowns? Ladies, ladies, I have
seen enough black, enough mourning hangings, to last a
lifetime. Those Dutch have come and they even bring
their smell. Ah, me, memories.

SPINOZA: My lord, these same Dutch are—

(*We hear harpsichord music—Couperin—from another
room.*)

EDWARD: Those wretched towns we passed on the way to
The Hague. Even the winds of a new continent can't
blow away the stink of pickled fish. Well, these Dutch
broodmares have had a paragon, an example, for the last
seven years. A master-mistress, who would chide but who
could teach. And they have not learned, have rejected
the metaphor that I am. [*Striking a Baroque pose*] Civilization! The core is *male* . . . [*Breaking the pose into an
undulating deep curtsy*] the surface yielding.

SPINOZA: 'Tis true, my lord, we must yield. At this very
moment in Saint Mark's Church, your Dutch subjects
gather to voice their displeasure.

EDWARD: Of that, my good Jew, I am well aware and do
intend to inform myself further *in my own way*. Be at
ease. The light grows dark, and soon begins your Sabbath. You are excused.

420

SPINOZA: Good night, my lord . . . and take care. [*Exits bowing.*]

EDWARD: [*Puts on jewels and arranges his wig and details of his gown.*] In my seven bitter years as governor of this dismal town only Sarah Vanderspiegel seemed to soften, to turn, and Margareta van Cortlandt took to carrying a peacock fan till she became the wife of Abraham de Peyster. Milord de Peyster, from what Dutch swamp were you spawned? We have all been vomited on this continent. De Peyster was belched forth from a marsh, and I was hurled across an angry ocean by my cousin royal, Anne, the Queen.

As children we played together at Windsor, hide and seek in the garden at Saint James, and we told each other secrets in a little wilderness of yew and holly, away from the formal paths and fountains. [*Confidentially*] Once while we were whispering together we saw one of the footmen playing with his big thing, his breeches down. Lady Frances laughed when Anne told her; I, silly boy, followed him around the palace until . . . [*Mock embarrassment*] She was ever such a pasty-faced little girl. And later when her succession to the throne seemed more than possible, how solemn, dutiful, and, oh, so stubborn, she became. So Protestant princess—not like *ma cousine* her older sister, Mary, who blended the Stuart majesty of her royal father with the easy charm of her mother's family, *my* family, *our* family, the *Hyde* family. Who would have thought there would be so many queens among us? [*The music stops.*] Ah, me, Mary had William to guide her, lead her. She accepted his favorites, and even smiled when she stumbled on us romping together at the Old Palace. The Duke of Portland was furious because William wanted to bugger me and not him. Such a scene. And who should walk in but Mary, with some idea of founding a college.

(*Enter* AFRICA, *massaging her fingers like Wanda Landowska. She is a beautiful young black woman draped in her native garb. Although presently a slave, she is in no way obsequious or hostile.*)

EDWARD: Dearest Africa, you've practiced enough today. What seems to be the matter with the back of this gown? Is the clasp undone? Please do look at it.

AFRICA: The moths have eaten the stuff around the hook, your lordship.

EDWARD: Susanna Rhinelander must have brought them with her along with the pox.

AFRICA: It was a pretty belt. Well, all suffers alteration here. I was a princess of a proud people, and now I am your lordship's servant.

EDWARD: How many times have I told you that it is an honor to serve a person of quality? The noble serve the noble. In England the most powerful families vie to have one of their ladies attached to the queen. Surely you remember what I have told you: Sarah, the powerful Duchess of Marlborough, is the Queen's First Lady of the Chamber, and for that matter, *entre nous* . . . [EDWARD *makes an obscene gesture.*] And in France, where I spent a good part of my youth, it is deemed an honor to be with the King when he is taking a physic. How the French worship the enema. Quick, a looking glass.

AFRICA: [*Fetching a looking glass*] I had twenty slaves at home to do my bidding.

EDWARD: As an Englishman I abhor slavery, but the Dutch will have their filthy habits. I didn't bring you here; I found you here. Our late King William tried to have geography taught to young William—

AFRICA: Duke of Gloucester, Princess Anne's only surviving son—

EDWARD: A spindly thing with an enormous head. I remember the map his Majesty had drawn for the poor boy—the Niger rising from a great lake close to the Nile, running in a thick bold line straight to the Atlantic; places called Congoland, Nubia, and Abyssinia all beautifully printed. [*While* EDWARD *rambles on,* AFRICA *sings a tribal dirge.*] It did no good. Little Billy died. We all had to wear black again. And again. We were hardly ever out of mourning. Just when we started to wear something bright, Anne would have another miscarriage. I was ready to die myself when she had her eighteenth. Mercifully, she stopped trying for the Protestant cause after that. [*Puts down the mirror.*] Do stop that moaning; it puts me in ill humor.

Of what use is it to dress here? I haven't seen the *beau monde* for seven long years. Do they still wear their hair so, with curls placed here and there?

(AFRICA *starts singing a lively and rhythmic tune.*)

EDWARD: Ah, that's better. What does it signify?
AFRICA: "The lion has given us his nails, the snake his fangs, the *wambaku* his eyes—"
EDWARD: The *wambaku*?
AFRICA: Please not to interrupt, your lordship. I lose the thought . . . "The *tumba* his ears, and the tree spirit his wisdom. To trap our enemies, to kill our enemies, to eat their hearts."
EDWARD: I fancy that lively song.
AFRICA: In my land it is forbidden for a woman to sing it. But here . . . [*She shrugs.*]
EDWARD: I know. It's all topsy-turvy. Enemies, the prey, revenge—'tis the same all over the globe. My cloak, please. [AFRICA *fetches a ratty beaver cape.*] No, not the sheared beaver. Lordy, how I hate that fur. The black cape with the hood. I'll be late, late. Sing that tune again. "The lion has given us his nails." I go into the very mouth of the beast. Ah, and tell my good wife not to wait up for me.

(EDWARD *exits hurriedly wearing the hooded cape.* AFRICA *continues chanting for a beat, soon to be overlapped by the hymn of the next scene.*)

Scene 2

Church of Saint Mark's-on-the-Bouwerie. A meeting of Calvinists. The CONGREGATION, *soberly dressed in blacks and browns, standing, sings the following hymn, accompanied by organ. The style is Bach.*

CONGREGATION: A mighty fortress is our Lord:
Blood and guts anoint His sword.
The cannon's roar proclaims His Son.
Only by us will His will be done

The severed head still sings His name,
The broken arm salutes His fame.
Narrow the path, straight the gate,
The love of Him on earth is hate.

(*Enter* EDWARD, *hooded and unnoticed. He takes his place among the* CONGREGATION.)

A loaded pistol is our God;
On our necks His feet have trod.
A heavy weight is heavenly bliss,
Brushing our lips with a deadly kiss.
Hallelujah and amen.

PASTOR VAN DAM: [*From lectern. He looks like a hawk.*] We have gathered together that we may praise in proper Protestant prayer the goodness of the Lord and then sign a petition to Her English Majesty Queen Anne to remove the wicked Pharaoh Cornbury. [*Reading from petition*] "We the undersigned, all honest and loyal tax-paying subjects of the colony of New Amsterdam—"

RIP VAN DAM: [*An extremely handsome blond young man in his early twenties. Earnest.*] 'Tis called New York now, Father. That would offend the Queen.

PASTOR: York, York, York! Like geese in November. [*Ranting, he corrects the petition.*]

MARGARETA DE PEYSTER: [*A forceful widow of forty. She speaks with authority.*] Get to the meat of it, Cornelius.

PASTOR: "—do hereby request of Her Royal Highness that the Governor be removed from office, the reasons being the following:

"That Edward Hyde, Lord Cornbury, has demeaned his office by the disgusting and unnatural practice of dressing in women's attire at public functions, not to mention even more ungodly behavior in private, his explanation being that since he represents the person of a female sovereign he must dress like one."

VOICES: Shame! Shame!

PASTOR: [*Smugly smiling, he stops short the voices with a gesture.*] "That he openly tolerates Indians and Negroes, and encourages Jews to settle."

VOICE 1: Even his secretary is a Jew.

VOICE 2: Spinoza Dacosta.

VOICE 3: That bloodsucker!

PASTOR: "The governor has declared that the tint of one's skin and religious predilection are matters of chance, taste, and habit. And even worse, that the Bible-sanctioned practice of slavery is an evil that must be abolished."

VOICE 1: He would have us scrub our own floors!

VOICE 2: Who would till the fields?

PASTOR: "That he allows his wife to pray in the Popish manner and has permitted the erection of a brazen image of the Virgin of Rome within the confines of his official residence."

VOICE 3: To the stake with Lady Cornbury!

PASTOR: "That said wife is an inveterate thief, and is totally unable to control her vile habit of purloining the valuables of loyal subjects while on official visits."

(*This accusation provokes the greatest outrage.*)

WOMAN 1: She stole my brooch!

WOMAN 2: She stole my necklace!

WOMAN 3: She stole my chamberpot!

PASTOR: "And, finally, that Lord Cornbury is guilty of corruption in financial matters.

"Item: He has sold crown lands without Her Majesty's permission."

VOICE: He sold Staten Island three times to three different people.

PASTOR: "Item: He has publicly proclaimed the price of an audience with himself at two shillings sixpence for the first quarter hour—"

VOICE 1: The same price as the whores!

VOICE 2: And you have to pay the Jew another shilling!

PASTOR: "Item: He has borrowed vast sums and now refuses repayment on the grounds of sovereign immunity."

VOICE 1: Down with Cornbury!

VOICE 2: Out with the sodomite!

VOICE 3: Over with Hanover!

VOICE 4: New York is Dutch!

PASTOR: "Therefore we do petition Your Highness to provide the colonies with an honest yet fair, just yet merciful, *manly* new governor."

MARGARETA: Well said, Cornelius.

PASTOR: Thank you, Margareta.

RIP: This man is a menace to manhood. When he sees our petition he'll go at once.

PASTOR: We are agreed. But who will show it to him?

MARGARETA: Why not yourself, Cornelius?

PASTOR: He vowed to have me thrashed if I came into his sight.

VOICE: What new infamy is this?

PASTOR: He claims I stole some lands from the Indians—

VOICE 1: There wasn't an Indian left in the Bronx!

VOICE 2: That's no crime!

VOICE 3: He desecrates another tradition!

MARGARETA: Perhaps young Rip van Dam should present the petition. I think he would have no trouble gaining his lordship's audience—without charge, too.

RIP: But if we are alone he might—

MARGARETA: You are a Christian man. Defend yourself with your virtue—and wear a sword.

RIP: I shall do it. For the sake of our people!

PASTOR: For the sake of our Lord!

MARGARETA: For the sake of our money! Who will be the first to sign after me? [*She steps forward to sign the document.*]

PASTOR: Let us pray.

(*Hymn recommences.* EDWARD *exits furtively.*)

MARGARETA: [*Signing*] Margareta de Peyster.

DIRK GANSEVOORT: Dirk Gansevoort.

HENDRIK DE LANCEY: Hendrik de Lancey.

ANDRIAAN VANDERSPIEGEL: Andriaan Vanderspiegel.

(*The singing swells to full volume as the song of the following scene begins.*)

Scene 3

Fat Molly's, a Bouwerie dive. EDWARD, *still incognito, enters, as* MOLLY, *the slatternly owner, sings a duet with the bouncy barmaid,* MARTHA. *The ballad they sing refers to the notorious love affair between Queen Anne and the Duchess of Marlborough, Sarah Churchill.*

MARTHA: I'll always be true to you, my love,
      I'll always be true to you.

MOLLY: I favor this part, Martha, my sweet. Our good Queen, mighty though she is, has her portion of misery. Sarah Churchill is as wicked as you.

MARTHA: Wicked? You know you're first in my heart, Molly.

MOLLY: If not, dearie, it's back to the docks, where I found you. [*Slaps* MARTHA's *ass and sings, as Queen Anne:*]
      Though fashions change and treaties wane
      And couples pledge their troth in vain,
      I to you will constant be,

Faithful, kind, and husbandly.
I'll always be true to you, my love.
I'll always be true to you.

MARTHA: [*As Sarah Churchill*]
Honored thus, my gracious Queen,
You give me more than I could dream.
But grant you please your little mouse
A large and stately country house.
I'll always be true to you, my love,
I'll always be true to you.

MOLLY: Though Whigs and Tories assail my head,
And for my Prince these legs must spread,
'Tis you who's ever in my thoughts,
Though Spanish ships attack my ports.
I'll always be true to you, my love,
I'll always be true to you.

MARTHA: I take your pledge and give you mine,
My breasts, my twat, forever thine.
But for love's sake, my husband Anne,
Pray give the Churchills lots of land.
I'll always be true to you, my love,
I'll always be true to you.

EDWARD: [*Throwing back his hood. He recites an impro-vised verse.*]
So vowed the Queen to her fair maid,
And Mistress Churchill was well paid.
For thus she fought her husband's war,
Proved mother, wife, and damned fine whore.

(*All laugh.*)

MOLLY: That's a new one—and so naughty, Governor.
You deserve the best for that. [*She pours him a drink.
He surveys the empty bar.*] A bit early, milord?
EDWARD: Where is everyone, Moll?
MOLLY: It's those damned Hollanders. I thought this town
was English. Mind you, I hate no man so long as his coin
be true, but these herring-eaters should watch their
own itching privates and leave us to scratch our own.

428

It's getting so that as soon as you take your coffee and have your morning shit—begging your pardon—curfew begins. And if we should so much as light a candle past seven o'clock, some tallow-faced hymn-singer throws a rock through the windows. Mind you, milord, I'm a Christian woman, but 'tis sad to see the state to which the Bouwerie is fallen. Gone, all gone, the Captain's, the Nest, the Green Parrot, and One-Eyed Peg's—Lord knows I hated that low bitch but she knew her business well. New York was a jolly place: twelve roaring taverns on one road, each filled with lasses to do your biddin' and boyos to fill your pleasure. We had anything you could dream up, no matter how quaint your taste. [*She winks.*] If you know what I mean. [*She proposes a toast.*] Here's to the old days. [*Familiarly*] I never met a man who took his pleasures so keenly . . . [*She slaps* EDWARD *on the back.*] or was so choosy about what lay next to his skin. Here, Martha, feel this stuff. [MARTHA *does so.*] Beggin' your leave, Governor, when will this Calvinist physic be done with? The best have left for Philadelphia. So much revenue lost to your lordship. But your fat Moll is yet loyal. [*Digs in bosom and hands* EDWARD *a purse. He counts the coins in it.*] Let those hypocrites fart their righteousness down on us, here's one English bitch who won't give in.

(MARTHA *giggles.*)

EDWARD: [*Pocketing the money*] I'll see that you're not disturbed, good Moll. Be assured, it was not my notion to persecute my loyal friends. But the de Peysters and van Cortlandts, who were here before I came, must needs be reckoned with.

MOLLY: Like any pox that ruins a man's pleasure. But we'll not let them diminish ours. . . . [*She drinks from a bottle.*] Have you seen the latest step? 'Twas a Portuguese sailor taught it to our Martha—along with a few other tricks, I warrant. Come, girl, give his lordship a lesson.

(MOLLY *beats time and hums as* MARTHA *dances.* EDWARD *watches.*)

EDWARD: 'Tis a familiar step. It was introduced at court by Catherine of Braganza, and if my memory serves me, you turn thus . . . [*Now leading the dance*] . . . and thus. [*Curtsies.*]

MARTHA: The governor knows more than the sailor.

EDWARD: And wait! There's a *jeté* right here.

(EDWARD *gracefully dances his way into the next scene, the music for which has already begun.*)

Scene 4

A chamber in the governor's mansion. Offstage, AFRICA *is singing another native song.* EDWARD *throws off his cloak, revealing a scarlet court dress trimmed with jet. He reclines on a Queen Anne chaise longue.*

EDWARD: Africa, Africa! Cease that savage wailing! You know I can't stand primitive music.

(*Enter* AFRICA.)

AFRICA: That was the sacred Revenge and Fertility for Yams chant. Only a daughter of royal blood is permitted to lend her voice to it.

EDWARD: Africa, darling, we're in the New World now. Royal prerogative has no place in this mosquito-infested bog. We must alter our natures to suit the clime. How do I look?

AFRICA: Pearls, my lord.

EDWARD: Pearls? Pearls. Fetch them. [AFRICA *throws pearls to* EDWARD, *who divests himself of other jewelry by throwing it behind a screen. He puts on strands of pearls. Looking at himself in a mirror*] You're always right.

You're the only person with taste on this side of the ocean.

AFRICA: Why are you wearing such finery today?

EDWARD: I have a matter of importance to attend to. My unruly subjects are preparing an attack against my person; I am wearing suitable armor.

AFRICA: Prithee, let me watch this battle.

(*A loud knocking is heard.*)

EDWARD: That will be Master Rip van Dam. Bid him enter. And, of course, you may lend an ear behind the door if you wish some amusement, Princess.

(*Exit* AFRICA. EDWARD *tries out various feminine poses on the chaise. Reenter* AFRICA, *leading* RIP, *who is wearing a sword.*)

AFRICA: Master Rip van Dam, my lord.

(*Exit* AFRICA. RIP *stares speechless as* EDWARD *"adjusts" himself.*)

EDWARD: You don't like me in red. I knew it. It was definitely a day for blue.

RIP: My lord, I have here— [*Takes out petition.*]

EDWARD: Don't say it. You're aching to read me a billet-doux. Best keep it a secret. Whisper it, sing it softly as a lullaby, thrust it into the grate, but don't pronounce your words of love no matter how fiercely the arrows sear your heart.

RIP: [*Reading*] "We the undersigned—"

EDWARD: I know, the whole colony loves me. You've thought of no one but me since the day I set foot on shore. My eyes, my hair, my legs . . . Don't say it.

RIP: But, my lord, you disgust me.

EDWARD: I understand, foolish boy. You feel unworthy of me and thus mask your admiration. But we are alone now, Rip—may I call you Rip? You may call me—oh,

431

call me what you will. We are alone now. Bruise me with your words. Cornbury understands all. [*He seizes the petition and rips it up.*]

RIP: [*Outraged*] You, you—

EDWARD: Pervert. Say it, Rip!

RIP: You are a revolting—

EDWARD: Catamite. Say it, Calvinite!

RIP: May God damn you and strike you dead.

EDWARD: *Comprendre, c'est pardonner.* I can scarce accept your proposal for I am married.

RIP: Proposal? If I should touch you, I would—

EDWARD: Vomit. Vomit from love. Eros strikes each differently. Your ardor makes me blush. Which part of me pleases you most, Master Rip?

RIP: You are hideous from head to toe. A man is a man, a woman is a woman. You are a—

EDWARD: You find me *unique.* And that piques your interest. Here, see if you can *pique* mine. [EDWARD *suddenly rises and with manly gestures takes a sword from the wall. He assumes a fencing position.*] You worship Lord Cornbury. Admit it. [RIP *has drawn his sword.* EDWARD *strikes it. They duel.* EDWARD *duels superbly.* RIP's *efforts, in comparison, are clumsy.*] You adore Lord Cornbury. . . . [*They continue dueling.* EDWARD *is winning.*] You love Lord Cornbury. . . . [EDWARD *is at* RIP's *throat.*] You love Lord Cornbury, don't you, my boy? [*Deep and menacing*] Ah? Ah? Say it!!

RIP: [*From floor*] I love Lord Cornbury.

EDWARD: You may call me Edward. *Whom* do you love?

RIP: I love Edward.

EDWARD: [*Releasing him and suddenly coquettish*] Well, Edward loves you not and is shocked that you would be so forward. Africa! [AFRICA *appears immediately.*] Master van Dam wishes to depart. [*Tosses* RIP *his sword.*] Show him out, I pray you. [*Flings himself on the chaise longue and fans himself.*] We shall see you at the Queen Anne Birthday Ball. I promise you the second gavotte. Good night.

(*Blackout, covered by loud Korngold movie music.*)

432

Scene 5

The chamber of SPINOZA DACOSTA. SPINOZA *is at his small rough-hewn desk looking at an* INDIAN *seated on a stool. The Native American,* MUNSEE, *is of the Delaware tribe— a Lenape. He is tall, muscular, and imposing. He wears his long hair loose and oiled. He sports shell jewelry. He looks sexy in his animal-skin clothing. His chest is daubed with ocher.* SPINOZA *is holding up his hand, trying to learn the Lenape words for the numbers 1 through 7.*

MUNSEE: [*In Lenape*] N'gutti . . . nischa . . . nacha . . . newo . . . pal-enach . . . guttasch . . . nischasch.

SPINOZA: [*In Hebrew*] Echade . . . shtayim . . . shalosh . . . arba . . . chamesh . . . shesh . . . sheva.

(MUNSEE *gracefully describes the four seasons in sign language, giving each one their Lenape name.*)

MUNSEE: [*For spring*] Sickquan.

SPINOZA: Aviv.

MUNSEE: [*For summer*] Nippinge.

SPINOZA: Kayitz.

MUNSEE: [*For autumn*] Tacockque.

SPINOZA: Stav.

MUNSEE: [*For winter*] Wean.

SPINOZA: Choref. [*Indicating himself*] Man. Ish.

MUNSEE: [*Also indicating himself*] Leno.

SPINOZA: [*Describing the curves of a woman with hands*] Woman.

MUNSEE: Ochquen.

SPINOZA: [*Excited*] Adam and Eve! Abraham, Isaac, and Jacob! Cain and Abel! Israel! *Yerooshehlieeem!!* . . . I must control myself. I feel on the verge of a great discovery. God, Thou hast given Thy servant the joy of finding his brother—his lost brother—whom Thou in Thy wrath hast scattered across the earth to taste the bitter fruit of exile. Thy goodness doth prevail! Patience, I must have patience. [*Making broad, sweeping gestures*

433

in the air] The Lord is here. He surrounds us. Thou art my brother, lost Israel! [*Approaching* MUNSEE] You found refuge in this land until the moment the Lord should summon you to return. I am the instrument of His mercy and shall instruct you in the ways of our people! My brother, what do they call you? [*Indicating himself*] My name is . . . Spinoza Dacosta.

MUNSEE: [*In English*] Me . . . [*He howls like a wolf.*] Me Munsee.

SPINOZA: Wolf! I shall call you Zev, which means wolf in God's tongue. Zev! Zevi! [*He attempts to embrace his brother but is repelled by the body paint.*] Feh!

(*Enter* PASTOR VAN DAM *and* MARGARETA. *They are carrying a package which contains a beaver dressed for the pot. They are startled to find* DACOSTA *talking to* MUNSEE.)

MARGARETA: It's useless, Dacosta, to teach them anything. They are incapable of thought. [*She notices that* DACOSTA *is rubbing his hands.*] And that rancid fish oil they put on their bodies—ach!—how can you stand so close?

SPINOZA: [*Bows to them.*] Mistress de Peyster, Pastor van Dam, what a beautiful surprise.

MARGARETA: Cornelius, give Dacosta the package.

PASTOR: [*Does so.*] It is a beaver prepared for the pot. I'm sure your wife will put it to good use. You know the tail can be eaten as a Lenten dish—but then, that's not important to you.

SPINOZA: [*Gives beaver to* MUNSEE.] Take this to my good wife, Leah. You will find her in the kitchen. [*He quickly mimes a kitchen.* MUNSEE *leaves.*] I thank you, Mistress de Peyster. We are fortunate in having a less than severe winter. I remember last year the snow—

MARGARETA: Shall we dispense, Dacosta, with talk that is tiresome to all of us?

PASTOR: Better a cold winter than the fires of hell.

MARGARETA: [*In Dutch, to* PASTOR] *Hou je mond, domme dwaas!* (Be quiet, you stupid fool!) [*To* SPINOZA] If we had time enough there would be many things that would give delight to speak of, but let us get to the point.

SPINOZA: By all means, madam. A humble public servant is not often favored by a visit from the gentry.

MARGARETA: As you are aware, much of the land in East and West Jersey has been seized by the English crown—

SPINOZA: Madam, the landowners *voluntarily* surrendered their governmental powers to the crown in 1702. They retained some of their land rights.

PASTOR: They say that Queen Anne has Jewish blood.

MARGARETA: *Donder op, klootzak!* (Quiet, you asshole!) But such confusion resulted. Those dirty Swedes think they own the Delaware Valley, and greedy Quakers claim East Jersey because the half-witted widow of Governor Carteret's cousin sold land she never owned. Those rapacious Scottish tradesmen set up a few mud huts on a dung heap and called it Perth Amboy.

SPINOZA: I am presently preparing a report on this very matter.

MARGARETA: Then make note that all the land from the Hackensack River to the Kittatinny Mountains should be leased to us. I, with some of my van Cortlandt cousins, could easily assume his lordship's burden. We would cut down those bothersome forests, remove the remaining red men, and reap a fine harvest of skin and furs.

SPINOZA: But what, dear madam, can *I* do?

MARGARETA: To quote an old Dutch proverb: *"Tookhis oyfn tish."*

SPINOZA: [*With disdain*] I'm familiar with the expression. I value the honesty of your address, madam, but to quote an old Hebrew proverb: "What's in it for me?"

MARGARETA: A goodly portion, Dacosta. As Lord Cornbury's secretary, you stand to influence his thinking. The disposal of crown lands is his decision. The governor has so much land and so many pressing debts—'tis rumored that his last state robe alone cost a month's revenue. [*Walks about the office appraising it. Winningly*] When I was a little girl in Amsterdam we had many friends of

435

the Hebrew faith. We Dutch opened our cities to them. For we too had tasted the bitter yoke of Catholic Spain.

PASTOR: *Verdomde spanjaarden!* (Damned Spaniards!)

MARGARETA: It must not seem strange to you, my dear Dacosta, that we wish to preserve some fine Dutch traditions. Therefore, with open heart we offer you—nay, your people here in New Amsterdam—a final haven: a portion of land from the West Jersey claim to be used by your tribe as a cemetery. [*She folds her arms, satisfied.*]

SPINOZA: Thank you, Madame de Peyster. Dutch hospitality is well known to our people. And your concern for our dead is most touching, but may I be so bold as to press for the rights of those living, namely a fraction of those lands you wish to lease given over to those of us in New York of the Hebrew faith.

PASTOR: *Verdomde joden!* (Damned Jews.)

MARGARETA: Impossible. What do Jews need land for? Can a Jew plant? Can a Jew clear forests? Can a Jew defend himself against a savage horde?

(*Enter* MUNSEE *with the beaver tail.* SPINOZA *is relieved by this interruption.*)

SPINOZA: Ah, Zev, how fares my good wife Leah?

MUNSEE: [*Thrusts package to the* PASTOR *with distaste.*] Take. Wife say thank you. *Tomaque* . . . [*Pointing to package*] Beaver is *matta . . . trayf.*

PASTOR: *Maak je weg komt, wildeman!* (Savage, get out!)

(*Exit* MUNSEE.)

MARGARETA: When we receive the land rights to the West Jersey tracts, you shall receive the deeds to a plot of land sufficient for a fine new synagogue and the right to dwell within its precincts.

SPINOZA: Mistress, you are bidding for territories that are as vast as your mother country. I ask for only one tenth of that. Is that too much to ask?

MARGARETA: [*Outraged*] Now, attend, Jew. Your association with the corrupt governor puts your people in a precarious position. If that debt-ridden monstrosity were to lose favor with the English queen—

PASTOR: *Verdomde engelse hoer!* (Damned English whore!)

SPINOZA: [*Holding up hand*] One eighth!

MARGARETA: Parasite!

SPINOZA: One seventh!

MARGARETA: Christ-killer!

SPINOZA: One sixth!

MARGARETA: Bloodsucker!

SPINOZA: One fifth!

MARGARETA: Vermin! Leech! Accursed race!

PASTOR: Shylock!

MARGARETA: Usurer!

(*The preceding epithets overlap the following scene.* ANNA MARIA BAYARD *and* RIP VAN DAM *are promenading in a pasture on the site of present-day Prince Street near Macdougal.*)

Scene 6

ANNA MARIA: Four, five, six, nay, *seven* children—the Bayard women are blessed with fruitfulness. And we shall have a garden in the back where they may play, right where we stand. And over there . . . [*Pointing*] we'll have a privet hedge to separate us from Father's yard. Such a generous spirit for giving us the land. You don't care for him. Never mind. Enough land to lay out our . . . [*Looking at him shyly*] bed sheets and linen to dry in the sunshine, and yet some room for a little garden of healing herbs. Sage, rosemary, coriander, rue, and cyclamen—for love. You're not listening. Rip, do you hear me?

RIP: [*Peering at the sky*] Look, 'tis an eagle flying over the Hudson. See how it seems to stand in the sky.

ANNA MARIA: [*Looking up*] 'Tis only an osprey.

RIP: An eagle.

ANNA MARIA: Am I your dove?

RIP: What?

ANNA MARIA: Am I your dove? Adriaan Vanderspiegel calls Sarah *his* dove.

RIP: Tame barnyard fowl. I'd rather be an eagle, free to fly, to soar, to plunge, above men's dominion, catching his prey when he will, answerable to no one.

ANNA MARIA: They say they mate for life.

RIP: Damn! Must you put nice boundaries on this world? A garden here, a wall there, a father in that corner, a husband in this.

ANNA MARIA: What is our world but nature subdued, a struggle against anarchic riot? What is man but a beast constrained?

RIP: I would go West, where no man has trod. I grow tired of this parceling of my life: duty to my faith, bounds to family, bonds to you.

ANNA MARIA: These words on the eve of our marriage?

RIP: Forgive me, I rave. I did not mean to hurt you.

ANNA MARIA: You've been ill-humored since your encounter with that beastly Cornbury.

RIP: Since that meeting my sleep has been torn. My dreams follow me past the sentinel of light. They haunt my day.

ANNA MARIA: That man has bewitched you!

RIP: Cornbury is your garden run riot; as if some madman had strewn willy-nilly handfuls of warring seeds. Here roses nod to deadly nightshade, and nettles brush with lilies. There entwine the tulip and the weed. The tendrils of this garden have invaded my thoughts.

ANNA MARIA: An infusion of foxglove and hellebore clears a troubled mind.

RIP: Don't you find it queer that he treats both Jew and black African as intimates, does not disdain the savage, has no animus towards women, but seeks to improve their beauty, and in the martial arts has no equal? Don't you find that queer?

ANNA MARIA: Yes, yes, but still I wouldn't miss his Queen Anne celebration for all the world. Everyone will be there.

RIP: I shan't go.

ANNA MARIA: Oh, come, his apish tricks will lighten your heart. And if *his* humor palls, his magpie wife will amuse us in his stead.

RIP: No.

ANNA MARIA: My dearest Rip, your melancholy will soon depart. In our own nest, under festive quilts, there riot takes its rightful course. You will teach me what all men know, and I shall submit to my sweet master.

RIP: You make my cheeks grow red.

ANNA MARIA: Silly man, you who would destroy all boundaries are scarce willing to mount the frail wall of my defense. [*Pointing*] Look, Rip, there's a little spring, and a soft mossy glade. Shall we sit awhile?

RIP: 'Tis time we returned. Your father will be out of sorts.

ANNA MARIA: I can soothe his ill temper. Come with me.

RIP: Nay.

ANNA MARIA: Let your Dutch stubbornness yield to a softer voice. Come. *Kom met mij? Ja?*

RIP: Nay.

ANNA MARIA: [*Leads him off.*] Yes?

RIP: Nay.

ANNA MARIA: [*Commandingly*] *Yes.*

Scene 7

A chamber in the governor's mansion.

EDWARD, *seated behind a Queen Anne desk in a man's claret-colored suit, is rereading a letter he has just completed. Halfway through the letter he rises and walks about the room.*

EDWARD: "I declare my opinion to be, that all these colonies ought to be kept entirely dependent upon and subservient to England, and that can never be if they are suffered to go on in the notions they have; for the consequence will be that if once they can see they can care for themselves, not only comfortably but handsomely, too, without the help of England, they who are already not very fond of submitting to government would soon think of putting in execution designs they have long harbored in their breasts.

(*Enter his wife,* MARIE, *a woman of fashion wearing a large crucifix. She is of Irish and French extraction. She is a haunted, pale, fading beauty. She has a French accent. She comes in as silently as possible, but every time she moves there is a clank.*)

EDWARD: This will not seem strange when you consider what sort of people this country is inhabited by."* [*Like a psychic in a vaudeville show*] A silver cup, a teapot of fine porcelain make, a garnet brooch, and a pewter chamber pot. Perhaps a—

MARIE: Édouard, *pourquoi tu me persécutes?* May I not go out for a little breath of air?

EDWARD: Marie, whom have we visited today?

MARIE: Madame de Lancey.

EDWARD: Then your harvest has been a poor one. Madame de Lancey is acquainted with your habits.

MARIE: Of what do you accuse your *pauvre petite Marie?*

EDWARD: Of a crime for which a more civilized country would chop off your hand. [*He lifts* MARIE's *skirt, revealing dangling household items and jewelry attached to her petticoat.*]

MARIE: [*Bursting into tears*] You spoil everything. You have your little pleasures, and you allow your poor wife none.

EDWARD: I don't disdain your pleasures, *ma chère,* but for everything you attach yourself to I receive a bill, and those thieving Dutch charge thrice the value of the trifle.

MARIE: I can't help myself. What would you have me do? Oh, Édouard, *mon cher,* forced to leave Versailles at a

---

* "Lord Cornbury to Sec. Hodges," *Documentary History of the State of New York.*

tender age—yes, yes, a virgin— [EDWARD *shrugs*.] —married to a man of such strange tastes, whose own father detests him and lives on only to deprive his son of his title and inheritance; attached against my will to a Protestant court; deprived of the solace of the true faith; [*She starts to detach the objects and place them on the floor after kissing them first. The stolen items are arranged before a curtain.*] —suffering the anguish of a mother who lost four children before a priest could be found to give them the sacrament of holy baptism; torn apart by the cabals of a foreign court; ordered to learn the barbaric English tongue; condemned to eat boiled food and sit on chairs of ungilded woods; to smile when I wanted to weep; to bend my knees to a monarch false —Dutch William—and to mask one's—how you say?— *loyauté,* allegiance, to true majesty, James Stuart; compelled to empty the chamber pots of an heretic princess—

EDWARD: My cousin, Queen Anne—

MARIE: —who exiled us in poverty to send us to the end of the world to do penance for *your* sins. [*She rips open a curtain, behind which is an Italianate statue of the Holy Virgin. She throws herself on her knees before it and recites the "Hail, Mary" in French.*] Je Vous salue, Marie, pleine de grâce, le Seigneur est avec Vous. . . .

EDWARD: [*Rips back the curtain.*] Marie! You go too far! Your extravagant professions of faith will undo us.

MARIE: [*Suddenly practical*] And your extravagant gowns must bring us to ruin. Oh, Édouard, I care not where your fancy leads and am indifferent to the fury your behavior provokes among the *canaille, mais vraiment, mon mari,* you play to an audience of one—*moi.*

EDWARD: *Hélas,* I would play to an audience of none. Does the rose bloom for the gardener? It blooms because it must; it blooms perhaps only for those who would see it. But my talents do not go unperceived. Only yesterday Margareta de Peyster begged my advice on the proper cut of her bodice.

MARIE: *Prend garde,* Édouard, that woman smiles with one cheek and spits with another. Listen carefully. When I entered Madame de Lancey's chamber, unannounced as is my custom, she was reading a letter. She seemed most startled. Was it I, or was it something she was reading? My pulse quickened. Madame de Lancey with a *billet-doux*? A lover? *Quelle folie! Pour un instant* I was back at Versailles. *Une intrigue charmante.* . . . [*She produces the letter from her bosom.*] *Voilà!* [*Hands it to* EDWARD.]

EDWARD: It's in Dutch. I'll call Spinoza.

(*He rings a bell.* AFRICA *enters as he rings. She catches sight of objects filched by* MARIE.)

AFRICA: I see that her ladyship's been visiting.

MARIE: *Salope!*

AFRICA: [*Hexes* MARIE *with an arcane gesture.*] *Dumbaya zamoosh!*

EDWARD: [*Reading letter*] "Privy Council"?

MARIE: [*To* AFRICA] *Merdeuse.*

AFRICA: *Lanash.*

EDWARD: [*Shouting*] Spinoza!

(EDWARD *goes to the door and opens it.* SPINOZA *falls in.*)

SPINOZA: [*From the floor*] My lord?

EDWARD: [*Thrusting the letter to* SPINOZA] I pray you, render this in English.

SPINOZA: [*Places magnifying glass in front of letter*]
   "2 kegs of molasses
    5 capons plucked
    1 barrel of malt vinegar—"

EDWARD: The other side.

SPINOZA: "My dear Mistress de Lancey: The time grows short. It is imperative that action be taken, especially after young van Dam's encounter with the Beast. Pastor van Dam swears that a strange fever has seized his son, causing him to leave his parents' house and breaking the heart of his intended bride."

EDWARD: [*Smiling*] Hmm.

SPINOZA: "If our men are too cowardly to tread the righteous path, we women must undertake the journey. We must cleanse the temple of abomination. It is our duty to persuade our husbands to rise up against this evil tyrant and his Popish wife." Must I continue this slander, your lordship?

AFRICA: In my country we know how to treat such people.

MARIE: [*Disappointed*] I thought it was a love letter.

EDWARD: Pray continue.

SPINOZA: "I understand your fears on embarking on this perilous journey. Your husband may lack understanding, but from what I've heard you will have the support of that strong young footman Dirk to console you."

MARIE: I told you it was about *l'amour*.

EDWARD: Hush.

SPINOZA: "Therefore, do your utmost to convince your husband to support our cause. The next English boat will bring us authority from Her Majesty's own Privy Council. Down with Cornbury! Yours in God's wrath, Margareta de Peyster." There's a postscript. "Act now or ruin your marriage."

MARIE: I shall poison the de Peyster bitch!

AFRICA: [*Taking out snakeskin bag*] I have just the thing.

SPINOZA: God of our father! That Jezebel!

AFRICA: Three drops in her chocolate . . .

MARIE: [*Taking out a vial*] Two drops of this . . . *Une morte affreuse.*

EDWARD: Ladies, ladies, your loyalty is admirable, but to take arms against this woman would be like swatting a fly with a cannon. Dear Margareta, I thought your warmth was true affection. *Hélas*, once again those in high position suffer the spleen and envy of their lessers.

SPINOZA: Your charity is commendable, but do not dismiss Mistress de Peyster so lightly. She will stop at nothing to bring about your ruin. I beg you to take measures in keeping with your office to defend yourself. Take the advice of a survivor of a persecuted race. Curb your extravagances, pay off some of your debtors—a mere token —and, above all, cease your—how shall I say it?—your public demonstration of your similarity to the Queen.

William M. Hoffman and Anthony Holland

EDWARD: Postpone the Queen Anne Birthday Ball? Never!
MARIE: But, Édouard—
AFRICA: When the bees are angry even the hippopotamus lowers his head.
EDWARD: Never! The Queen's governor shall not bow to this Dutch rabble. Besides, it's too late. I've written an entertainment and rehearsed the actors. And I've already sold South Jersey to pay for my robes. You should see them. [*Transfixed*] Exquisite . . . pearl-white satin, with a mass of silver lace, the shoulders covered, and the neckline square. The sleeves are narrow down to the elbows, with wide flounces of lace mixed with *point-de-Venise*. [*The stage darkens as the description continues and the overture to the New World Masque is heard.*] The underskirt is mounted on iron hoops, very wide at the hem. I shall wear a sprig of . . .

Scene 8

The banquet room of the governor's mansion.

It is the night of the Queen Anne Birthday Ball. During the interval between this and the preceding scene a curtain is lowered. It is decorated with a painted portrait of Queen Anne, which bears a strange resemblance to Edward. During the musical overture we hear the sound of last-minute hammerings and such cries, in a thick Irish brogue, as, "Watch out, it's falling! Get out of the way," followed by a huge crash. We hear EDWARD *crying, "I never want to see your face again!" etc. The following New World Masque is performed with enormous but amateurish enthusiasm. The music is in the style of Handel.*

NARRATOR: [*In front of curtain. He is wearing English court costume.*]
In honor of Her Majesty the Queen
His excellence Lord Cornb'ry's set this scene

To celebrate our Lady's day of birth
And bring to you a little joy and mirth.

On New York town the Muses do descend;
We pray our humble play doth not offend.
It pleases us that we please you
By music fair to hear and verses true.

Begin we then anon a New World Masque—
And if we stumble your pardon we do ask.

(*A flourish as the curtain rises. We hear the sound of tomtoms.* MUNSEE, *wearing a loincloth and feathers, stands center stage posed like a cigar store Indian.*)

The red man garbed in Nature's naked glory
Does make a mete commencement for our story.

(MUNSEE *dances standard Indian war dance.*)

He lived in peace and followed his own way
Until the white man brought another day.

(*Enter a* SPANISH SOLDIER *dressed like De Soto.*)

From Catholic Spain came soldiers bold
To save red souls—and steal their gold.

(*The* SPANIARD *does a fifteen-second flamenco dance that ends with an attack on* MUNSEE. *Enter a Frans Hals* DUTCHMAN *wearing wooden shoes.*)

From brave Netherlands tradesmen did arrive
And with the red men did hard bargains drive.

(DUTCHMAN *does a clog dance that ends with an attack on* MUNSEE)

445

And soon to work, to toil, it seemed fitting,
In chains they brought the blacks to do their
bidding.

(*Enter* AFRICA *dressed by Bendel's slave boutique. She
does a specialty number that clearly upstages all previous
efforts.*

AFRICA'*s dance is followed by a brief quadrille that dis-
integrates into a shoving match. The music, at first har-
monious, grows dissonant. Over the music the* NARRATOR
continues.)

It's not man's wont to live in harmony;
The sound of arms makes clear our destiny.
The first to die were red men proud,
Their help rewarded by a Christian shroud.

(*The* SPANIARD *kills* MUNSEE *and quickly makes the sign
of the cross over him.* MUNSEE, *drafted as an actor, refuses to die easily.*)

The next to die in New World anarchy
Were white men caught by clash of monarchy.

(*The* DUTCHMAN *and the* SPANIARD *fight to music.* AFRICA
"*languishes.*" *Before they murder each other there is a
fanfare. They fall to their knees.*)

All seemed ruined in this new land
Until Britannia's firm and justly hand
Subdued her foes and ended wasteful strife,
And brought to all a new and better life.

(*Another and greater fanfare. Enter* EDWARD *dressed in
the gown he described at the end of the preceding scene.
This is his finest costume. He carries an orb and scepter.
The* NARRATOR *addresses* EDWARD.)

Anna, royal mistress of our hearts,
Defender of the faith and all these parts,
We celebrate your birth with pomp and joy—

(*Enter* MARGARETA *from audience. She points a pistol at* EDWARD.)

MARGARETA: Arrest that man!

(*Music stops.*)

EDWARD: By whose authority do you dare interrupt the Queen's celebration?

MARGARETA: [*Brandishing a document*] By order of the Privy Council of Her Majesty and the Civil Court of the colony of New York, which order your arrest on the grounds of dissolute indebtedness. Cornbury, you have defaulted on your last loan!

EDWARD: Madam, you cannot arrest the Queen's governor.

MARGARETA: Sir, it is in her name that we are arresting you.

EDWARD: I am her cousin, madam—and besides, I haven't sung yet. [*He starts singing and the shocked* ORCHESTRA *starts up, at first feebly then with great force. He sings a florid Handelian aria in falsetto.*)

Gracious Queen, thy name resounds
O'er the starry firmament.
Sing, ye flutes, and, trumpets, sound,
Pluck, ye harps, to ornament.
Aquarian-guided Monarch, you,
'Tis with—

(*The* ACTORS *desert* EDWARD. MARGARETA *approaches as* TWO SOLDIERS *enter from the wings. They drag* EDWARD *off singing and screaming as the lights go down. The last note we hear from* EDWARD *is a high one.*)

CURTAIN

ACT II

Scene 1

Debtors' prison. A room with one barred window and a door. It is dimly lit.

EDWARD, MARIE, and AFRICA have been arrested and are suffering from three weeks of incarceration. AFRICA is asleep, in the throes of a nightmare. Sporadically she mumbles incoherently. MARIE is reading Les Fables *of La Fontaine before she retires for the long night. EDWARD paces. He is dressed in dull male attire.*

MARIE: The candle burns low. I have no light to read.

EDWARD: I should think you know that book by heart.

MARIE: *Ah, quelle grande consolation.* Your English writers have written nothing so *sage* as La Fontaine. When the mob carried off all our books I only saved my fables. [*Closing the book. With a sigh*] "*Je plie et ne romps pas.*"

EDWARD: Which you hid under your skirt. 'Tis a pity you did not look to your jewels as well.

MARIE: I did, but they violated me and took them. But their greed made them overlook this book. This volume was given to me by Madame de Sévigné.

EDWARD: That tale again.

MARIE: [*Ignoring* EDWARD] If she knew that her gift and her *petite Marie* would end their life's journey in prison—

EDWARD: Not prison, Marie. We must look on this place of confinement as a sanctuary from debt.

MARIE: *Sanctuaire?* No light to read, bed of straw—

EDWARD: Stripped of my office, I am vulnerable, *ma chère.* Here we must wait until my ancient father finally dies. Then we can be free to leave this—

MARIE: No wine with meals, never allowed to leave to pay my little calls—

EDWARD: To leave and go where? I have nothing fit to put on. Not even a simple *robe de chambre* or a lace cap—

MARIE: No cards to play at whist of an evening—

EDWARD: Or even ombre, or basset. You are right, Marie! It is impossible here! Intolerable! [*Runs to the door and shouts.*] Atticus! Atticus!

(*A lout of thirty-five enters.*)

ATTICUS: *Mister* Rockefeller to your lordship.

EDWARD: *Mister* Rockefeller, may we have some more candles? It is oppressively dark in here.

ATTICUS: Who's to pay for them?

EDWARD: The Civil Court.

ATTICUS: You can't get anything out of them. I don't run no palace for gentlefolk here. You'll get nothing from me. No pretty games at night for you, the devil's games of cards, and the reading of Popish tracts. Honest folk go to bed when the dark comes.

EDWARD: You, sir, are impertinent, and your speech and breath are vile.

MARIE: Dog of a jailer! *Animal! Mon Dieu,* if the eighteenth century begins this way for people of quality, how will it end?

ATTICUS: People of quality, my arse. In this land a humble Rockefeller is a whole lot better than a loony frog-woman and a man that likes to wear skirts instead of gettin' under 'em.

EDWARD: I represent Her Majesty the Queen, you lout.

ATTICUS: From what I hear about her you look a whole lot better in 'em than she.

EDWARD: That is treason. Rockefeller, beware.

MARIE: The cur is right. She was grotesque when I last saw her—covered with stinking bandages.

EDWARD: Go back to your reading, madam. I will hear no slurs on my cousin.

MARIE: [*Blowing out candle*] I'll save what's left for another night. After all, I know what happens in "The Ant and the Grasshopper." [*Closes book and reclines on a straw pallet.*]

ATTICUS: [*Whispering to* EDWARD] Milord, please to come here.

EDWARD: What is it, Rockefeller? [*Approaches the* JAILER.]

ATTICUS: Closer, your lordship.

EDWARD: Faugh, sir, you stink of rum.

ATTICUS: It keeps me warm. Here, your lordship, take your hand and feel this. [*Places* EDWARD's *hand on his crotch.*] I know you like this kind of meat. Big enough?

EDWARD: On the contrary. [*He withdraws his hand.*] Go fuck a beaver. [*He turns away.*]

ATTICUS: You'll come a-begging!

EDWARD: I doubt it.

ATTICUS: Pervert!

(ATTICUS *exits. The lights dim further. In the near-darkness* EDWARD *turns his back to the audience.*

A beat of silence, then an arpeggio on a harpsichord. Enter QUEEN ANNE *on a wheelchair. With one gouty leg up, she is swathed in bandages. She wears a crown. She is ill, fat, and ugly.*)

ANNE: Edward.

(*He turns.*)

EDWARD: Your Majesty!

ANNE: Be not so formal, I pray, but let us use the names we called each other as children. I was Ziphares and—

EDWARD: And I was Semandra.

ANNE: Poor Semandra.

EDWARD: Poor Ziphares.

ANNE: Approach, Semandra. [EDWARD *approaches.*] I know that most cannot stand the smell, but I'm so lonely.

[EDWARD *kneels at her feet. She pats his head.*] I was always ill-starred, but you, Semandra, were to be the center of passions.

EDWARD: No, Ziphares, I only reflected your glory. How they love you, your people.

ANNE: Today. And in the next ballad they wish me dead and call for Hanover to reign. . . . But we did have some silver days. Remember when I loved Sarah, my Mrs. Freeman, and you were William's pet.

EDWARD: Do you remember when you fled London to join your sister?

ANNE: And you left my father's side to run off with Churchill? Oh, those were exciting times. I could walk then.

EDWARD: And dance and hunt. We hunted hares at Winchester, remember?

ANNE: Where to amuse ourselves we exchanged clothes. Was that the beginning of your extravagant folly? Though the Lord knows you never harmed a soul by it.

EDWARD: I thought I looked good in them. In a world of such treachery and madness, it's hardly worth dwelling on it. . . . Was it that rainy summer we sang together?

ANNE: Yes, Semandra, we did sing together. How did it go?

EDWARD: We wrote it together. [*He sings.*]
          Rose, rose, rose, dear rose—

ANNE: Ah, yes.

EDWARD AND ANNE: Will your petals turn to red?
          or shall winter leave you dead?

EDWARD: Ziphares waits thy sweet return—
          For spring Semandra's heart doth
            yearn.

EDWARD AND ANNE: Rose, rose, rose, dear rose.

(*The light gradually dims. The singing overlaps the raucous beginning to the following scene.*)

Scene 2

A chamber in the governor's mansion.

A trio of WOMEN *dressed in black noisily devastate the belongings of Lord Cornbury. Apart from her friends,* MARGARETA *sits at* EDWARD's *desk perusing documents.*

HESTER DE LANCEY: [*Viciously tearing off a dress draped over the shoulders of* SARAH VANDERSPIEGEL] You bitch! 'Tis a color that suits me, not your red, pocked face.

SARAH VANDERSPIEGEL: Your great udders would rip it at the seams.

ANNA MARIA BAYARD: [*Trying on a hat*] How think you it suits me?

HESTER: Like a riband on a prize sow.

ANNA MARIA: Slut!

SARAH: Give it back, Hester!

HESTER: Nay!

(HESTER *and* SARAH *play tug of war and rip the garment in two. They fall to the floor laughing.* ANNA MARIA *opens the curtain, revealing* MARIE's *Virgin. She decks the Virgin in* EDWARD's *clothing as* SARAH *and* HESTER *fight.*)

SARAH: Foul wind!

HESTER: Foul box!

ANNA MARIA: [*Drinking from a crystal decanter and toasting a portrait of Queen Anne*] Grossest box, they say! God save the Queen!

(HESTER *and* SARAH *crawl to gain possession of the decanter.*)

HESTER: [*To* ANNA MARIA] Quaff me, sister. I dearly love porto.

ANNA MARIA: So no one can deny.

SARAH: [*Grabbing the decanter*] To the Queen's governor! May he rot in prison forever!

MARGARETA: [*Aside*] Forever is not long enough.

(HESTER, SARAH, *and* ANNA MARIA *rush behind the screen. A kind of fashion show ensues, in which the three* WOMEN, *dressed in various costumes of* EDWARD, *act out the major events in his rise to power. As the* WOMEN *become more wanton, they become more beautiful.*)

HESTER: [*Appearing first*] " 'Tis a little thing I wore to please Lord Churchill." [*She exits behind screen.*]

ANNA MARIA: "Whose eye once caught and heart once gained passed me on to . . ." [*She exits behind screen.*]

SARAH: "His lord high bugger, Bentinck, called Little Hans in Holland, known in England as Big Henry." [*She exits behind screen.*]

HESTER: [*In a new costume*] "His Grace, the Duke of Portland, who, enflamed by my . . ." [*Slaps her ass.*] " 'charms,' gave me entrée to . . ." [*She exits.*]

ANNA MARIA: [*In a new costume*] "Our own Dutch William." [*She curtsies, presenting her ass to the audience. She lifts up her skirts. Behind the screen someone makes the sound of a fart.* ANNA MARIA *straightens, faces the audience, and says with great seriousness:*] "God bless the House of Orange." [*Exits.*]

SARAH: [*In a new costume*] "King William, in gratitude for such loyal service, gave me as reward . . . [*Enter* ANNA MARIA *and* HESTER] the governship of those rich lands beyond the sea, our own New York and Jer-sey."

(As MARGARETA *applauds,* ANNA MARIA, HESTER, *and* SARAH *attempt a curtain call.*)

MARGARETA: Well done, women. Your ribald games would amuse even our deposed governor. Cornbury would smile at such a recounting of his rise to power. 'Twould lighten his otherwise tedious hours in prison.

SARAH: It cannot be denied that his lordship had the best wardrobe in the colony. In matters of taste he was supreme arbiter. Once he told me, "Sarah, you have a swan's neck. Show it, show it! Let your head rise from a sea of lace!"

HESTER: He admired only your neck, but most positively fell in love with my ear. Once at the governor's mansion he toasted me, saying, "Madame de Lancey's right lobe has no equal. Like the beauty of Helen, it would kindle another Trojan War."

ANNA MARIA: How can you be grateful to the conceits of a madman? If he told you your droppings were precious stones, would you display them?

HESTER: How now, Anna Maria? There is always a little truth in madness. [*Fondling her ear*] Surely if Cornbury had admired some part of you—

ANNA MARIA: I care not for his grotesque flattery. Like an evil demon he has robbed my womb of its promised harvest. He has placed a blight upon my wedding and widowed me before my time.

HESTER: Rip lies in no churchyard. Even yesterday my footman encountered him in Molly's Tavern—sure, that place is hell's own cauldron—and Master Rip seemed filled with life, loudly railing against his father's constraints.

ANNA MARIA: [*In tears*] How seemed he, my poor Rip?

SARAH: [*Comforting* ANNA MARIA] Hush, Hester, his soul is forever damned. The abandonment of a virgin is no cause for amusement. [*To* ANNA MARIA] You shall be avenged. Cornbury and his popish wife and haughty slave—

HESTER: They say she's a princess!

SARAH: She's a black witch. When Cornbury's gone, I'll teach her other ways. That strong back shall pull a plow, and she shall be mated like any other animal to increase my herd.

HESTER: And his wife shall garner the punishments to which she has been so far immune. The Frenchwoman shall be branded a thief and cast out into the wilderness.

ANNA MARIA: That's not punishment enough! Lady Cornbury is a whore married to a whore!

MARGARETA: [Stands.] No worse, no better, ladies, as we should know, who sell our virtue for even less.

HESTER: Indeed?

MARGARETA: Was it for Master de Lancey's fierce ardor that you accepted him as a husband? Do you dream of your husband when you lie with his footman?

SARAH: [Putting a protective arm about the affronted HESTER] You who have no man and whom no man has wanted have not the right to judge.

MARGARETA: Sarah, my dearest child, my knowledge is hard come by. [She sits on edge of desk.] I have not been immune to Cupid's darts, but rather than be the mother of a stinking, sucking brood, seven surviving of twenty painful births, I am the blessed, barren mother of none, husband of my husband, mistress of myself. My girl, even with a man, children, wealth, you envy the trappings of a lunatic.

ANNA MARIA: And you envy his power.

MARGARETA: [Standing] To come and go as he pleases; to couple with whom he chooses, sticking his rod into mate, master, or mistress; to own his family name, obliterating his wife's; to rise and fall according to his own endeavor, oblivious to the efforts of his spouse. Hypocrite! Of course I envy Cornbury's power!

SARAH: [Conciliatory] Margareta, you confuse us.

ANNA MARIA: You own van Cortlandt land in your own right.

HESTER: And you come and go when you please.

SARAH: Even our husbands will agree that you brought down the tyrant. What further can a woman wish for?

MARGARETA: [Relaxing in chair behind desk] I wish to be the governor. After all, ladies, it's no more outrageous than our governor wanting to be the Queen.

(The WOMEN titter. Their laughter is electronically amplified as the lights go down. The sound is like the laughter of Klytemnestra and her servants in the Birgit Nilsson recording of Strauss's Elektra. *This scene overlaps the next one*.)

Scene 3

Debtors' prison.

In the darkness the laughter ebbs. The lights come up, revealing AFRICA *recounting a tale to* EDWARD *and* MARIE. *Brilliant sunshine streams through the barred window, illuminating* AFRICA.

AFRICA: As we left the village the last sound I heard was the laughter of the village maidens. I was only twelve. . . .

MARIE: Go on, *ma chère.* You entrance us.

AFRICA: I was happy and frightened—happy because the *kundala-baku-** were over, the purification rites for a virgin princess. I was frightened because I was leaving home for the first time. . . .

MARIE: A *sentiment* I know well.

AFRICA: I was going to the kingdom of my future husband, whom I had never seen. The women had assured me that he was both handsome and brave.

MARIE: I had no such hopes [*Pointedly looking at* EDWARD] —myself.

EDWARD: *Tais-toi, Marie, je voudrais entendre cette histoire fantastique.*

AFRICA: As they bore me through the forest on a palanquin, I could hear the songs of myriad birds. [*Whistles a lovely but excruciatingly difficult bird call.*] They blended with the ever more distant sounds of the village drums. My fears gave way to imaginings as the land grew foreign. Although the old women had told me what were to be my duties as first wife of a great prince, I was without

---

* "Kundala-baku" is to be followed by Bantu "clicking" sounds.

experience. How would his mother greet me? What would he look like? What would it feel like?

As thus I mused I heard cries of outrage and wailing from the front of the cortège. A slave had stumbled and dropped a tray bearing ceremonial yam cakes, among our people an ill omen. My lady-in-waiting bade me drive it from my mind, for surely would the gods protect me. . . . And surely she was wrong.

For upon arrival at the great river—as grand as the Hudson—we were set upon by Arab traders. Men whom I had seen smiling at my father's court now turned their angry faces toward me. My slaves fled in terror. In vain I cried in protest; I was now a slave myself.

EDWARD: Poor princess.

MARIE: *Pauvre princesse.*

AFRICA: Princess no more, nor bride, nor daughter. I was only a frightened girl enslaved to men who dealt in flesh. [*She shudders.*] The gods have mercifully released me from the memory of the deathly caravan that bore me through the desert to Tangiers. My station recognized, I was destined to be the newest acquisition of Ahmed, the Bey of Tangiers.

My shackles were removed, and I was stripped, bathed, and anointed with precious balms. The spiteful eunuchs brought me to the chambers of their master. I had not long to wait for what they had prepared me. . . . [*Reliving the moment*] He stood before me, handsome were it not for the malevolence of his eyes. He put his fingers on my lips . . . my throat . . . my nipples . . . my— between my thighs. He turned me round. . . . [AFRICA *closes her eyes.*]

EDWARD: Don't stop!

MARIE: *Continue!*

AFRICA: [*Opening her eyes. They are wide with horror.*] I looked up. Suddenly we were not alone. Guttural sounds escaped from the Bey's contorted mouth as he was garroted by two great men. It was horrible! Months later I was to learn that Ahmed Bey was o'erthrown by a younger brother. Such is the custom of those people.

His brother, having little taste for women, gave me
as a gift to a merchant with whom he wished to ingratiate
himself.

(EDWARD *and* MARIE *sigh*.)

Served up again, and this time to a man sickly
pale to my unaccustomed eyes, I was given to a stern
follower of the crucified god. After drenching me with
water, he mumbled some words and set me to work in
his kitchen. Mercifully, Hendrik van Loon had no interest in either sex. At night he counted his gold and left
me alone. The airs of my continent are not kind to people
of your race. Mijnheer van Loon soon expired of a
fever. . . . [*She smiles.*] I found myself on a great ship,
a girl of fourteen alone with forty sailors.

EDWARD: And a virgin still?

AFRICA: A virgin still . . . I was the captain's choice. . . .
Bound hand and foot—

EDWARD: Yes?

AFRICA: Pinioned to his bed—

MARIE: Go on.

AFRICA: Screaming for mercy till they gagged me, I knew
this time no gods would intervene. Closer came the
captain, the unfamiliar odor of his race assailing my
nostrils. He placed his dirty paw under my torn chemise
and hoarsely whispered—

(*Enter* ATTICUS ROCKEFELLER, *leading* RIP, SPINOZA, AND
MUNSEE—*all in chains.*)

ATTICUS: There's room for more in here! 'Tis not been
filled up yet! [*Exit.*]

EDWARD: Visitors! My friends have come to visit. How
thoughtful. Welcome to our quarters. Our dearest Africa
was just relating the story of her perilous life.

MARIE: Cher Maître Spinoza, did you bring some new
books?

SPINOZA: No, my lady. Ruffians descended on us and dragged us here. My lord, we come not as guests.

(MUNSEE *faints*.)

MUNSEE: Ah!

SPINOZA: Look to my brother Zev!

AFRICA: He's bleeding! I shall bind his wounds.

SPINOZA: Zev fought like Samson 'gainst the Philistines when the soldiers led by vengeful Margareta de Peyster came to arrest us at my home.

EDWARD: What now? Her wrath lies heavy even on my friends. My dear Spinoza, I am truly sorry that your loyalty to me has brought about your downfall.

SPINOZA: Precipitous change is my people's lot. [*Bows deeply to* MARIE, *who nods.*] I was instructing Munsee in the oral tradition of my people.

EDWARD: How now, sir?

SPINOZA: Today being Saturday, Leah, my good wife, was about to serve our humble Sabbath meal.

MARIE: Speak not of food, *je vous en prie*.

SPINOZA: I was speaking to our brother Munsee about the faith of the Hebrews, bantering the mysteries of God's creation.

(EDWARD *looks relieved*.)

MUNSEE: [*Coming out of his swoon*] Was it not Rabbi ben Ezra who said in his commentary to the Babylonian Talmud—?

AFRICA: Speak not, brave warrior. Conserve your strength.

MUNSEE: [*Looking at* AFRICA] *Whinne*. Beautiful woman. I am in that paradise my fathers spoke of, where dead heroes are cradled by maidens.

AFRICA: Alas, sir, this is not your paradise but prison, and I fear for our well-being.

EDWARD: [*Finally notices* RIP.] Rip! Rip van Dam! Alas, we never did dance that gavotte. What brings you to this sad place?

RIP: May I have a word with you alone, my lord?

EDWARD: Of course, my young sir. [*He turns to the* GROUP.] I command you not to listen. [*They all stop up their ears and turn their backs. The lights dim except on* RIP *and* EDWARD. *Gradually during the following conversation the others flagrantly eavesdrop.* EDWARD *gushes.*] I must seem a sorry sight to you. As you can see, they allowed me to bring nothing—not even a fan, a handkerchief, my healing lotions, my honey water—excuse me, sir, I rush on.

RIP: You are in grave peril, my lord.

EDWARD: [*Ignoring* RIP] They could have let me pack a portmanteau. How kind of you to visit me. I perceived you were different from the others the very moment we met. There was something finer in your carriage, although your breeding—

RIP: There are plots against your person, my lord.

EDWARD: Why talk about plots? We have so little time. Has no one ever told you that your eyes counterfeit lapus lazuli flecked with gold. Queen Mary had such a precious stone. She would have liked you, Rip. She was fond of Dutchmen and once told me—

RIP: They will kill you, my lord!

EDWARD: [*Dismissing even this*] My life has been threatened in several capitals. My dear Rip, this day was to be as sad as the rest, cheerless and empty, void, nil, null. But I feel much improved. [*He takes* RIP's *hands.*] But what is this? Shackles?

RIP: Yes, my lord.

EDWARD: Insufferable! How dare they?

RIP: They are capable of much more, sir. They intend—

EDWARD: Those scoundrels will forfeit their lives when I send—

MARIE: *Idiot*, let the boy speak!

EDWARD: I have always followed the counsels of my immediate impressions. Speak.

RIP: 'Tis with difficulty that my lips form these words. . . . We Dutch are a brooding lot, given more to venting our spleen than showing our affections.

EDWARD: [*Quizzical*] Indeed?

RIP: You know that my father is a pastor. The living presence of hell is ever with me. [*Reliving the event*] Once as a boy—it was midwinter—the pond at Lispenard Meadows had frozen over. I was skating at dusk—alone. I had always been an indifferent skater, but that late afternoon—was it the early sunset? was it the clarity of the air? or the stillness broken only by the sound of my skating?—

MARIE: [*Aside*] I hate Dutch landscapes.

RIP: I only remember skating with remarkable ease, pirouetting, twirling, jumping. In this state my face must have been suffused with the joy of accomplishments, for such must have been its expression when my father sprang at me. He had come himself to fetch me home for dinner, and had been watching me unawares. He said, "Such exuberance is ungodly. There is no joy on earth, except in serving God!" And then he struck me down—

AFRICA: [*Aside*] The Pastor's zeal is well known to every serving girl in town.

EDWARD: Cruel father.

RIP: Cruel shepherd, cruel flock. As my father did strike me down, so will his people strike at you. They hate you not so much for your corruption as for the prodigality of your nature, the lavish abundance of your spirit. Your very being is a provocation to them.

EDWARD: At the Court of Saint James, my behavior was the cause of no alarms.

RIP: 'Tis not the whole cloth, my lord. There are some, and no small number, who, like me, admire your courageous heart. These people, for the most part of low estate, detest the sanctions imposed upon their liberty in the name of God.

EDWARD: Have they closed Moll's?

RIP: All public entertainments have been forbidden. Even the almshouse that you had erected has been shut. The poor, huddled in the streets, talk of your administration as a golden age. The Jews, my lord, whom you so magnanimously tolerated, are in danger.

SPINOZA: [*Aside*] And I told Leah it couldn't happen here.

RIP: Thus did I form a party, a rabble called by some, of like-minded youths drawn from every station, to thwart the designs of the van Cortlandt faction. Unhappily, we failed, betrayed by a nephew of Margareta de Peyster, who now rules this unfortunate city.

(RIP, *in despair, buries his head in his arms.* EDWARD, *fatherly, comforts him.*)

EDWARD: We are touched.

RIP: You must flee, sir. They will murder you.

EDWARD: I am cousin to the Queen. They wouldn't dare.

(*With the following words the lights change, and the others assail* EDWARD *with their advice. Overlapping*)

MARIE: So said Mary, Queen of Scots.

SPINOZA: So said Charles the First.

AFRICA: So said the Bey of Tangiers.

MUNSEE: We must flee.

SPINOZA: He's right.

AFRICA: For sure.

EDWARD: I'm too old to flee.

RIP: You must.

SPINOZA: I agree with Master van Dam. I fear we all are in danger and must take leave.

MUNSEE: With haste.

EDWARD: I hate being rushed.

(*While the others were trying to convince* EDWARD *to flee,* MARIE *has walked to the cell door. She has primped and now is hiking up her skirts.*)

MARIE: Oh, Monsieur Rockefeller, Monsieur Rockefeller!

EDWARD: What are you doing? Are you mad?

AFRICA: [*To* EDWARD] Hush now, that lady knows what she's about. [*Sidles up to* MARIE.] Sir, sir, my lady has the vapors!

(*Enter* ROCKEFELLER, *drunk.*)

ATTICUS: What's that? Nothing but complaints from that loony.

MARIE: *Cher monsieur*, my bodice is too tight. I swoon!

(*She falls into* AFRICA's *arms, revealing her charms. Those charms she doesn't,* AFRICA *does.*)

AFRICA: You must help my poor mistress. You're so strong and you're the only *man* here.

ATTICUS: [*Aroused*] You think so?

MARIE: [*Faintly*] Only you can do it. [*Pointing to her breasts*] Here, here.

(ATTICUS *thrusts his arms through the bars. They are immediately grasped by* MARIE *and* AFRICA. MUNSEE *rabbit-punches him into unconsciousness. With dexterity* MARIE *emerges from the heap with a key ring.*)

MARIE: So much for endless discussion. Édouard, move it!

(*The entire* GROUP *waits for* MARIE *to open the jail door. In line they join hands and start to leave.* EDWARD *is the last. It looks like the escape from* The Road to Zanzibar. *Enter* MARGARETA *and* PASTOR VAN DAM.)

MARGARETA: Stop where you are! [*The* CORNBURY PARTY *smile and continue on their way.*] I assure you, good people, it's not the hour for a stroll. My musketmen who wait outside are quick-tempered and unruly.

(*The* CORNBURY PARTY *look to* EDWARD *for leadership. With a gesture that starts with "masculine" defiance and ends with "feminine" boredom,* EDWARD *turns around.*)

EDWARD: I really wasn't dressed for walking. [*The others silently seat themselves, defeated.*] Madam, we deem it an honor that you visit us in our sordid lodgings. Pray, can we be of service?

MARGARETA: On the contrary, sir, we come to be of service to you.

PASTOR: The fires of hell are waiting for you!

EDWARD: [*Ignoring the* PASTOR] How so, madam?

MARGARETA: The foment that you have inspired in our young has enraged the public conscience. The town raves openly against you, declaring your presence a pollution. We have tried to calm them, but to no avail. They call for your head.

RIP: [*To* PASTOR] Father, are you party to these lies?

PASTOR: You are no longer my son, sodomite!

MARGARETA: Therefore, for your own safety we have arranged for your removal to more secure quarters in Harlem.

EDWARD: Where at your leave it can be said that I was taken with a fever and so expired, or found at the foot of a stairwell, my neck broken. You will say the former governor was too fond of his port. Or perhaps I might die suddenly of apoplexy after a gluttonous meal of oysters.

MARGARETA: Surely you have more trust in me.

MARIE: *Ma foi*, does one trust a viper?

EDWARD: We would rather not be removed to Harlem. We have grown fond of these four walls. It was only yesterday that I remarked to my wife that fresh paint and gay hangings would make this place tolerable.

MARIE: [*To* MARGARETA] *Baise mon cul royal catholique français!* You have no manners, no heart, no . . . I pity you.

(*Beat.*)

MARGARETA: Candlestick wife! You have been driven mad for lack of a man. You pity me?

MARIE: On our wedding night Édouard took me five times. His conjugal attentions were more than any woman could demand.

MARGARETA: And the fruit of his endeavors, your children?

MARIE: [*Counting on her fingers*] The two oldest are with their grandfather in London, big English *garçons* like their *papa*.

EDWARD: [*Embarrassed*] Oh, Marie.

MARIE: And Charles, James, and Henrietta are with my family at Versailles. And no candlestick has fathered this new life I feel. [*She pats her belly*. AFRICA *shrugs*.]

MARGARETA: If this be true, six times have you cuckolded your . . . husband.

(EDWARD *steps between the two women and takes center stage*.)

EDWARD: It is ignominious to defend ourselves with children. So *New World*. However useful they may be to populate an empty land, in our world they serve mainly to perpetuate a noble line.

Children. The oldest awaits his father's death with a smile, the younger would gladly see the elder in the grave. And the father bitterly measures his years by the height of his offspring. Children are no proof of manhood. [*He is playing for time, desperately looking for a chance to escape*.]

What makes a man? Strength? Naked I would wrestle a bear. I assure you the victor's wreath would be mine. Horsemanship? My seat and endurance caught the eye of even the Spanish ambassador, that master of the horse, Juan Gonzaga Baltasár Carlos María de Santiago Olivares y López. The hunt? One autumn for the pleasure of His Majesty I slew a herd of wild boar. But I've since grown weary of blood and waste. *La chasse* is no proof of manhood. The arts of war? At the battle of the Boyne, Mars himself would have left the couch of Venus to see me worship at his gory altar. Love? A healthy appetite follows no regimen. Here a plum, there a joint of venison, here a melon, there a piquant sauce. Even you, Margareta—don't deny it—could have had a place on my menu. [*He approaches* MARGARETA.]

MARGARETA: Stand back, Cornbury.

EDWARD: Why do you loathe me? I have only admired you.
The sharpness of your mind, the hunger of your curiosity,
encouraged me to believe that you were the unkindled
soul I was to set aflame with the spark of civilization.

MARGARETA: Torch? Soul? Civilization? You are a lunatic.
We gossiped. I was confidante to what secrets you cared
to share. Oh, yes, I was rewarded by a peacock fan one
month, a ruby ring another, and even a fine nightdress
that you grew tired of. I listened well, and sometimes
knew enough to make you laugh. You like to laugh.

In the course of our time together, sipping the
chocolate you so dearly love, I became privy to a world
I knew not of. How else could Margareta van Cortlandt
of rude New York come to meet the great French
monarch, to learn of our English majesties?

You were my tutor, my guide. You taught me that
the powerful answer to none, even God, and are prepared to change allegiance—even their holy faith—as
quick as the wind.

Is that what you call civilization?

EDWARD: The frailties of the mighty are sound lessons for
your own advancement, dear Madam Governor Elect.
In those quiet winter afternoons we spent closeted together you sipped chocolate with Civilization. You talked
with Her yourself. [*Takes center stage.*]

I am Civilization! I am the vessel of the manners that
you do not have. I am the ultimate arbiter of taste
whether it be the hue of a ribbon or the façade of a
palace. Did you know I have plans for a tiny summer
palace in the Hamptons? Civilization is the nurturing
breath of goodwill. I embrace everyone. [*Everyone backs
away in horror.*] In my arms there is room for Jews—a
thousand years of fiscal experience. Room for the
daughters of Ham—handmaidens of the lively arts. Never
cease your seductive melodies. And as for the Red Man,
that powerful body needs no *raison d'être*. Would you,
Margareta de Peyster, destroy civilization, usurp my
governorship, bestowed on me by the Queen, whose
power comes from God?

MARGARETA: Insane hypocrite, your birth is so high that all people beneath you seem the same. If I could be your intimate, so could a black princess, a cultivated Jew, and even a savage.

PASTOR: Cast out these devils!

MARGARETA: [*Delivering an election speech*] Do they know the price of a dry summer? Do they cultivate a frozen ground? Do they fear being flayed alive by heathen devils? To the highborn we are so much shit in the street.

But I say, what need have we of the highborn? Of what use in this land is rank, privilege, and taste? We need no masters but ourselves under a stern God.

(*Meanwhile* EDWARD, *taking advantage of the hypnotic effect of* MARGARETA's *rhetoric on* PASTOR VAN DAM, *steals his sword.* EDWARD *holds the* PASTOR *hostage.*)

EDWARD: Set us free and give us safe conduct through your mob, madam. I hold the pastor as hostage.

MARGARETA: [*Draws a pistol and shoots the* PASTOR *in the arm.*] No hostages. [*Sighs of anguish issue from* EDWARD's *party.*] Now I must insist you depart at once. If you persist in the folly of staying, I shudder to think what evils might befall your family.

EDWARD: [*Admitting defeat*] I see your point, madam. The wiser course would be for me to leave *alone.*

AFRICA: Don't go, my lord!

EDWARD: To ensure that our accommodations will be suitable. I pray you, worry not.

MARIE: *Je vais t'accompagner, mon cher* Édouard.

EDWARD: How thoughtful, my dear, but this brief solitude will do me good.

MARIE: Édouard, they will kill you! Once you are gone I will suffer the same fate.

MARGARETA: Madam, we shall have need of the petty skills of a Frenchwoman. You can teach your courtly language and do some sewing.

MARIE: I'd rather die a martyr to my faith. [*Crosses herself.*]

MARGARETA: And as for this princess—

(*She advances on* AFRICA. MUNSEE *bars the way.*)

MUNSEE: Touch her and you die!

MARGARETA: Savage, I shall have you whipped until you beg for my Christian mercy.

MUNSEE: That you will never hear.

EDWARD: Oh, come, Margareta, 'tis me you despise. I shall do your bidding. Those with power have no need of rage.

RIP: Please, my lord, let me ride with you.

EDWARD: That won't be necessary. . . . Madam de Peyster, you will permit me a few moments to dress. It is not suitable for Lord Cornbury to ride to Harlem *en déshabille.*

MARGARETA: But of course.

EDWARD: Ah, me, I have nothing to wear. [*Beat.*] But shortage puts an artist's mind to test; the very lack becomes a challenge.

(EDWARD *surveys his party. The following is a ritual in which* EDWARD *as celebrant is dressed for a great ceremony.*)

MARIE: Here, take my manto. It was you who chose it. [*She removes her outer dress.*]

AFRICA: This turban, my lord . . . [*She hands him turban.*] . . . only I know its special knot.

SPINOZA: Please accept my handkerchief of Venetian lace.

(*He gives him a lace handkerchief.* MUNSEE *places his beads around* EDWARD'*s neck.*)

RIP: I have nothing to give you—save my admiration. [*He kisses* EDWARD'*s hand.*]

EDWARD: [*Removing himself to a distance from the party.*] How do I look?

MARIE: Never better.

EDWARD: [*To* MARGARETA] We are prepared for the journey, madam.

(*Led by* MARGARETA, EDWARD *and* PASTOR VAN DAM *exit.*
MARIE *falls to her knees and genuflects. The effect is like
a baroque painting of the Magdalen: tears stream down
her face, her hair is in disarray, and she lays bare her
bosom.*)

MARIE: Now I am truly alone. [*She prays in French.*]
SPINOZA: [*A cry from the heart: Psalm 30.*]
      "In you, O Lord, I take refuge.
      Let me never be put to shame.
      In your justice, set me free,
      Hear me and speedily rescue me."

(AFRICA *lowers her head and is comforted by* MUNSEE.)

RIP: He was a great American.
    (*Suddenly a cannon salute shakes the theater, then a
trumpet fanfare and the shouts of a cheering* CROWD.
Enter EDWARD *on the arm of* LORD RICHARD LOVELACE,
followed by the now obsequious DE PEYSTER PARTY.)

LOVELACE: [*He looks like Louis Hayward in full court
costume. His elegance is dazzling.*] . . . and so, my dear
Edward, Sarah Churchill was livid, her husband in dis-
grace again, and she herself supplanted in the Queen's
affection by that drab Abigail Hill.
EDWARD: You must have a million stories. But how are they
doing their hair?
LOVELACE: Oh, Edward, there's not so variable a thing in
nature as a lady's headdress.
EDWARD: My lord Lovelace, you know my wife.
MARIE: [*Curtsies.*] Welcome to New York, my lord.
LOVELACE: I fear, my lord and my lady Cornbury, I am the
bearer of sad news. You are no longer Edward Hyde,
Lord Cornbury, but Edward, Earl of Clarendon. Your
father died four months ago.
MARIE: *Enfin!*
EDWARD: It's into black again.

469

LOVELACE: And you must make haste back to England to settle your vast inheritance.

(*All congratulate* EDWARD.)

MARIE: Who would have thought that the humble Marie Bouvier would one day be the Countess Clarendon?

LOVELACE: And now for the bad news. [*Silence. All look at* LOVELACE.] I'm the new governor, and I order you, my lord Clarendon, to pay all your debts. Her Majesty herself told me, this time you've gone too far.

EDWARD: Her Majesty's wishes shall be obeyed.

MARGARETA: He owes me three thousand pounds! The swindler!

LOVELACE: Silence! Pursue your claims at the proper time. Can't you see his lordship is crushed by grief? Let us proceed to a less cramped abode. [*Everyone leaves except* EDWARD, LOVELACE, *and* RIP.] Three months on that ship —I thought I'd go out of my mind! Now tell me *everything*. [RIP *diplomatically starts to take his leave*.] Who is *he*?

EDWARD: Master van Dam.

RIP: [*Approaches.*] Sir?

EDWARD: Governor Lovelace, allow me to present a most loyal friend and devoted protégé: Rip van Dam.

RIP: [*Bows.*] Your servant, sir.

LOVELACE: A friend of his lordship's should be a friend of mine. Will you do me the honor of attending the banquet this evening at the governor's mansion?

RIP: 'Twill be a service I gladly perform. [*As* LOVELACE *and* RIP *exit arm in arm* . . .]

LOVELACE: [*To* RIP] You ride, of course. I've brought my favorite hunter with me. A roan with a white flame on her forehead. I call her Dawn. . . .

EDWARD: [*Alone on stage. He picks up an hourglass.*]
First a bath, then a rest—
'Tis this new-made earl's request.
Robed in mourning black as night,
Yet my fortune rises bright.

I'll need some rouge to pass this day;
So close to death, yet now I play.
A patch or two would fix my face;
To hide these jowls a bit of lace.

Virtue wins by merest whim;
Life proceeds by margins slim.
Governor Lovelace, wait for me! There's not a word I
want to miss!

(*He exits. Up immediately the end of Korngold's swash-
buckling* Seahawk *music, which continues under the following Epilogue. A blue scrim and netting lower, suggesting a sailing ship. We hear sea bells and gulls and the
sound of waves, also shouts such as* "Draw up the anchor,
mi'lads," "Heave ho, my hearties," *and* "Let her catch
the wind." *We are suddenly catapulted from the prison
to the final scene of Rouben Mamoulian's* Queen Christina—*MGM, 1933.*)

Epilogue

Enter MARIE *and* AFRICA *in identical traveling cloaks.*

MARIE: [*Now friendly to* AFRICA] There are so many sights,
Princesse, that I wish to show you. Your *début* at court
will be *extraordinaire.*
AFRICA: [*Fluently*] *Merci mille fois, ma chère Marie.* But
don't you look forward to the benefits of a sea voyage
after so much excitement? Lord Lovelace was a most
generous host. Last night's banquet proved splendid.
MARIE: Marred only by the news of the untimely death of
Margareta de Peyster.
AFRICA: One must be careful of what one eats.

(*They turn to each other and smile. Enter* SPINOZA *in the
same kind of cloak.*)

471

MARIE AND AFRICA: [*To* SPINOZA] *Bonjour, monsieur.* [*He bows.*]

MARIE: We voyage only to England but you go much farther, to the land holy to both of us. Pray, sir, a request.

SPINOZA: Certainly, madam.

MARIE: That I receive from Jerusalem a piece of the True Cross.

SPINOZA: I shall do my utmost, my dear lady. [*Enter* MUNSEE *in cloak.*] But grant me this wish.

MUNSEE: I wish to see the world.

SPINOZA: Take him under your protection.

MARIE: The glamour attached to such patronage will resound to my credit. An African princess and a Red Indian prince. *Quelle triomphe!*

(*Enter* EDWARD *in cloak with* MOLLY, *who carries a wicker basket.*)

MOLLY: . . . remember, your grace, a lemon a day keeps the scurvy away. Watch out for the swine fever! If the countess feels poorly, these jams will bring her around.

EDWARD: Thank you, my friend.

MOLLY: And don't forget, Your Grace, my sister Henrietta—she lives above the Boar and Rose—they all know her. Tell her *not* to come here. New York is scarce ready for her yet. I best be off, or I shall start to cry. [*She attempts to curtsy and leaves.*]

EDWARD: [*Standing center stage*] Adieu. We're on our way at last! [*The audience becomes the people on shore and the sights of New York harbor. All wave good-bye.*] Look, Marie, the steeple of Trinity Church!

MARIE: There goes City Hall.

AFRICA: The Brooklyn Ferry.

MUNSEE: The East River.

SPINOZA: Wall Street.

EDWARD: [*Like Garbo in* Queen Christina, *the wind ruffling his hair. The music gradually swells.*] You know, my friends, no matter what the vicissitudes that fate will bring—corruption, crowding, the overexuberance of spirits that strangers mistake for rude manners—I believe that someday New York will be great. It will always rise Phoenix-like from disasters. With its great towers it will be the envy of its sister cities, a beacon to the Old World, and a gateway to the New. . . . Pray, do you think History will remember us?

(*A deafening cannon salute.*)

MARIE: Hear, Édouard, how they love us!

CURTAIN

BIBLIOGRAPHY

Invaluable to any research into gay plays and theater are:

Loeffler, Donald L. *The Homosexual Character in Dramas.* New York: Arno Press, 1975.

Parker, William. *Homosexuality: A Selective Bibliography.* Metuchen, N.J.: Scarecrow Press, 1971.

―――. *Homosexuality: Bibliography, Supplement,* 1970–1975. Metuchen, N.J.: Scarecrow Press, 1975.

Young, Ian. *The Male Homosexual in Literature: A Bibliography.* Metuchen, N.J.: Scarecrow Press, 1975.

Articles in newspapers and magazines about gay plays and theater:

Hall, Richard. "Conversations with Eric Bentley." *The Advocate,* March 23, 1977.

―――. "The Elements of Gay Theater." *Gay Sunshine,* Spring/Summer 1978.

―――. "Gay Theater: Notes from a Diary." *Christopher Street,* June 1978.

―――. "Theater of Sex." *Gaysweek,* October 24, 1977.

Helbing, Terry. "Gay Arts: There's No Such Thing but Everybody Loves It." *The Villager,* October 20, 1977.

―――. "Gay Theater Issue: An Introduction." *Christopher Street,* June 1978.

Pierce, Allan. "Homophobia and the Critics." *Christopher Street,* June 1978.

Shewey, Don. "Gay Theater." (Parts 1 and 2) *Blueboy,* June and July 1978.

Whitmore, George. "Towards a Gay Theater." *Gaysweek,* November 7, 1977.

The following list is of plays (originally written in English) with either gay themes or characters, or of plays that are of interest as gay theater. Note that many of the plays have not been published. In that case, place and date of first production are listed.

Albee, Edward. THE AMERICAN DREAM. New York: Coward-McCann, 1966.

———. THE BALLAD OF THE SAD CAFE. Boston: Houghton Mifflin, 1963.

———. MALCOLM. New York: Atheneum, 1966.

———. TINY ALICE. New York: Atheneum, 1965.

———. THE ZOO STORY. New York: Coward-McCann, 1960.

Allen, Seth. SISSY. La Mama, New York, 1976.

Anderson, Maxwell. THE BAD SEED. New York: Dramatists Play Service, 1957.

Anderson, Robert. TEA AND SYMPATHY. New York: Random House, 1953.

Anouilh, Jean. BECKET. New York: Coward-McCann, 1960.

Arzoomanian, Roy S. THE COOP. Actors Playhouse, New York, 1966.

Babe, Thomas. A PRAYER FOR MY DAUGHTER. Public Theater, New York, 1978.

Barry, Julian. LENNY: A PLAY BASED ON THE LIFE AND WORDS OF LENNY BRUCE. New York: Grove Press, 1972.

Barry, Philip. HERE COME THE CLOWNS. New York: Coward-McCann, 1939.

Barton, Lee W. NIGHTRIDE. Van Dam Theater, New York, 1971.

Behan, Brendan. THE HOSTAGE. New York: Grove Press, 1965.

Bentley, Eric. LORD ALFRED'S LOVER. Canadian Theatre Review, 1978.

Birimisa, George. DADDY VIOLET. Caffe Cino, New York, 1967.

———. A DRESS MADE OF DIAMONDS. Matrix Theater, Los Angeles, 1974.

———. GEORGIE PORGIE in *More Plays from Off-Off-Broadway*. Indianapolis: Bobbs-Merrill, 1973.

———. MISTER JELLO. La Mama, New York, 1968.

———. POGEY BAIT. San Francisco: *Drummer* magazine, Nos. 12 & 13, 1977.

Borske, Haal. THE BROWN CLOWN. Caffe Cino, New York, 1967.

Bowen, John. TREVOR. London: Methuen, 1968.

Brooks, Donald. XIRCUS: THE PRIVATE LIFE OF JESUS CHRIST. Performing Garage, New York, 1971.

Brown, Walter Leyden. FIRST DEATH. Extension Theater, New York, 1972.

Carlino, Lewis John. EPIPHANY in *Cages*. New York: Random House, 1964.

Carmines, Al. THE FAGGOT. Judson Poets Theater, New York, 1973.

Causey, Alan. JULIA CAESAR. New York, La Mama, 1970.

Chayefsky, Paddy. THE LATENT HETEROSEXUAL. New York: Random House, 1967.

Christofer, Michael. THE SHADOW BOX. New York: Avon, 1978.

Clark, Ron, and Bobrick, Sam. NORMAN, IS THAT YOU? New York: Samuel French, 1970.

Collinson, Laurence. THINKING STRAIGHT in *Homosexual Acts*. London: Interaction Inprint, 1975.

Combs, Frederick. THE CHILDREN'S MASS. Theater de Lys, New York, 1973.

Comden, Betty, and Green, Adolph. APPLAUSE. New York: Random House, 1971.

Coward, Noel. DESIGN FOR LIVING. New York: Doubleday, 1933.

————. A SONG AT TWILIGHT in *Suite in Three Keys*. London: Heinemann, 1966.

Coxe, Louis O., and Chapman, Robert. BILLY BUDD. New York: Hill & Wang, 1962.

Crowley, Mart. THE BOYS IN THE BAND. New York: Noonday, 1968.

Csontos, David. ONE-LINERS. Glines Theater, New York, 1977.

Curzon, Daniel. SEX SHOW: COMEDY MADNESS. Mabuhay Gardens Theater, San Francisco, 1977.

Delaney, Shelagh. A TASTE OF HONEY. New York: Grove Press, 1959.

del Valle, Peter, and Sterner, Steven. LOVERS. Glines Theater, New York, 1975.

Drexler, Rosalyn. HOME MOVIES in *The Line of Least Existence and Other Plays*. New York: Random House, 1967.

Duberman, Martin. *Male Armor* (includes METAPHORS; THE COLONIAL DUDES; THE GUTTMAN ORDINARY SCALE; THE RECORDER;

THE ELECTRIC MAP; PAYMENTS; ELAGABALUS). New York: Dutton, 1975.

————. THE MEMORY BANK. New York: Dial, 1970.

————. VISIONS OF KEROUAC: A PLAY. Boston: Little, Brown, 1977.

Dyer, Charles. STAIRCASE. New York: Grove Press, 1966.

Eyen, Tom. COURT. La Mama, New York, 1965.

————. THE DIRTIEST SHOW IN TOWN. La Mama, New York, 1970.

————. FRUSTRATA, THE DIRTY LITTLE GIRL WITH THE PAPER ROSE STUCK IN HER HEAD, IS DEMENTED. La Mama, New York, 1964.

————. MISS NEFERTITI REGRETS. La Mama, New York, 1965.

————. THE NEON WOMAN. Hurrah, New York, 1978.

————. *Sarah B. Divine! and Other Plays* (includes THE THREE SISTERS FROM SPRINGFIELD, ILLINOIS: I. WHY HANNAH'S SKIRT WON'T STAY DOWN, II. WHO KILLED MY BALD SISTER SOPHIE?, III. WHAT IS MAKING GILDA SO GREY?; ARETHA IN THE ICE PALACE; THE KAMA SUTRA (AN ORGANIC HAPPENING); MY NEXT HUSBAND WILL BE A BEAUTY; THE DEATH OF OFF-BROADWAY (A STREET PLAY); THE WHITE WHORE AND THE BIT PLAYER; GRAND TENEMENT/NOVEMBER 22ND). New York: Winter House, 1971.

————. WOMEN BEHIND BARS. New York: Samuel French, 1974.

Feiffer, Jules. LITTLE MURDERS. New York: Random House, 1968.

Ferguson, James B. WONDERFUL LIVES! Glines Theater, New York, 1977.

Fierstein, Harvey. CANNIBAL WOMAN TARTARE. Broome St. Theater, Madison, Wis., 1976.

————. FLATBUSH TOSCA. New York Theater Ensemble, New York, 1975.

————. FREAKY PUSSY. New York Theater Ensemble, New York, 1974.

————. IN SEARCH OF THE COBRA JEWELS. Bastiano Studio, New York, 1973.

————. THE INTERNATIONAL STUD. New York: *Gaysweek*, July 10, 1978.

Fornés, María Irene. FEFU AND HER FRIENDS. American Place Theater, New York, 1978.

———. MOLLY'S DREAM in *The Off-Off-Broadway Book*. New York: Bobbs-Merrill, 1972.

Foster, Paul. SATYRICON in *The Off-Off-Broadway Book*. Indianapolis: Bobbs-Merrill, 1972.

Friedman, Bruce Jay. STEAMBATH. New York: Knopf, 1971.

Gaard, David. *And Puppy Dog Tails*. Bouwerie Lane Theater, New York, 1969.

Gazzo, Michael. A HATFUL OF RAIN in *Famous American Plays of the Fifties*. New York: Dell, 1962.

Genet, Jean. THE MAIDS AND DEATHWATCH. New York: Grove Press, 1954.

Gibbs, Wolcott. SEASON IN THE SUN. New York: Random House, 1951.

Goetz, Ruth, and Goetz, Augustus. THE IMMORALIST. New York: Dramatists Play Service, 1954.

Goldman, James. THE LION IN WINTER. New York: Random House, 1966.

Gordone, Charles. NO PLACE TO BE SOMEBODY. Indianapolis: Bobbs-Merrill, 1969.

Gray, Simon. BUTLEY. New York: Viking Press, 1972.

———. OTHERWISE ENGAGED. New York: Penguin, 1976.

———. SPOILED. London: Methuen, 1971.

———. WISE CHILD. London: Faber and Faber, 1968.

Greco, Stephen; Hamilton, J.B.; Kingman, Scott; and Jones, Robin. GULP! Glines Theater, New York, 1977.

Guare, John. LANDSCAPE OF THE BODY. New York: Dramatists Play Service, 1978.

———. RICH AND FAMOUS. New York: Dramatists Play Service, 1977.

Hakim, Eleanor. ELIPHANT AND FLAMINGO VAUDEVILLE. New York, *Scripts*, #10.

———. A LESBIAN PLAY FOR LUCY. Medusa's Revenge Theater, New York, 1978.

Hall, Richard. LOVE MATCH. Glines Theater, New York, 1977.

———. THE PRISONER OF LOVE. Glines Theater, New York, 1977.

Hampton, Christopher. TOTAL ECLIPSE. London: Faber and Faber, 1969.

———. WHEN DID YOU LAST SEE MY MOTHER? London: Faber and Faber, 1967.

Hansberry, Lorraine. THE SIGN IN SIDNEY BRUSTEIN'S WINDOW. New York: Random House, 1965.

Harris, Ted. SILHOUETTES. Actors Playhouse, New York, 1970.

Heide, Bob. AMERICAN HAMBURGER. Theater for the New City, New York, 1977.

———. MOON in *The Best of Off-Off-Broadway*. New York: Dutton, 1969.

Hellman, Lillian. THE CHILDREN'S HOUR. New York: Knopf, 1934.

Herbert, John. FORTUNE AND MEN'S EYES. New York: Grove Press, 1967.

Herlihy, James Leo. STOP, YOU'RE KILLING ME. New York: Simon & Schuster, 1970.

Hester, Hal; Apolinar, Danny; and Driver, Donald. YOUR OWN THING in *Twelfth Night and Your Own Thing*. New York: Dell, 1970.

Hoffman, William M. GILLES DE RAIS. Gate Theater, New York, 1976.

———. GOOD NIGHT, I LOVE YOU. Caffe Cino, New York, 1964.

———. THANK YOU, MISS VICTORIA in *New American Plays, Vol. 3*. New York: Hill & Wang, 1970.

———. A QUICK NUT BREAD TO MAKE YOUR MOUTH WATER in *Spontaneous Combustion*. New York: Winter House, 1972.

———, and Holland, Anthony. SHOE PALACE MURRAY. ACT, San Francisco, 1978.

Holt, Rochelle L. WALKING INTO THE DAWN: A CELEBRATION. Magic Theater, Omaha, Neb., 1975.

Hopkins, John. FIND YOUR WAY HOME. New York: Samuel French, 1975.

Inge, William. THE BOY IN THE BASEMENT in *Summer Brave and Eleven Short Plays*. New York: Random House, 1962.

———. THE DARK AT THE TOP OF THE STAIRS. New York: Random House, 1958.

———. A LOSS OF ROSES. New York: Random House, 1959.

———. NATURAL AFFECTION. New York: Random House, 1962.

————. WHERE'S DADDY? New York: Random House, 1966.

Innaurato, Albert. EARTHWORMS. Playwrights Horizons Theater, 1977.

————. GEMINI AND THE TRANSFIGURATION OF BENNO BLIMPIE. New York: James T. White, 1978.

————. ULYSSES IN TRACTION. Circle Repertory Company, New York, 1978.

Jones, Leroi. THE BAPTISM and THE TOILET. New York: Grove Press, 1966.

Kardish, Larry. BRUSSELS SPROUTS. Toronto: Playwrights Co-op Press, 1972.

Katz, Jonathan. COMING OUT! A DOCUMENTARY PLAY ABOUT GAY LIFE AND LIBERATION IN THE U.S.A. New York: Arno Press, 1975.

Kingsley, Sidney. NIGHT LIFE. New York: Dramatists Play Service, 1966.

Kirkwood, James. P.S. YOUR CAT IS DEAD. New York: Stein & Day 1972.

————, and Dante, Nicholas. A CHORUS LINE. Public Theater, New York, 1975.

Kopit, Arthur. SING TO ME THROUGH OPEN WINDOWS in *The Day The Whores Came Out to Play Tennis*. New York: Hill & Wang, 1965.

Koutoukas, H.M. TIDY PASSIONS in *More Plays from Off-Off-Broadway*. Indianapolis: Bobbs-Merrill, 1972.

Kvares, Donald. MUSHROOMS in *The Best of Off-Off-Broadway*. New York: Dutton, 1969.

Laurents, Arthur. THE ENCLAVE. Theater Four, New York, 1973.

Levin, Meyer. COMPULSION. New York: Simon & Schuster, 1956.

Lind, Jakov. ERGO. New York: Hill & Wang, 1968.

Lotman, Loretta. PEARLS THAT COALESCE. Deja Vu Theater, Los Angeles, 1977.

————. TRANS-LESBIANIC FOLLIES. Gay Academic Union National Conference, Columbia University, 1975.

Lotman, Loretta *et al*. SOMETHING HOPEFUL. Glines Theater, New York, 1975.

Ludlam, Charles. BLUEBEARD in *More Plays from Off-Off-Broadway*. Indianapolis: Bobbs-Merrill, 1972.

481

————. CAMILLE. Thirteenth Street Theater, New York, 1973.

————. CAPRICE. Performing Garage, New York, 1976.

————. CONQUEST OF THE UNIVERSE. Bouwerie Lane Theater, New York, 1967.

————. CORN. Thirteenth Street Theater, New York, 1972.

————. EUNUCHS OF THE FORBIDDEN CITY. New York: *Scripts*, No. 6, April 1972.

————. THE GRAND TAROT. Gotham Art Theater, New York, 1971.

————. STAGE BLOOD. Evergreen Theater, New York, 1974.

————. THE VENTRILOQUIST'S WIFE. Reno Sweeney, New York, 1978.

————, and Bill Vehr. TURDS IN HELL. New York: *The Drama Review*. September 1970.

Magdalany, Philip. SECTION NINE. McCarter Theater, Princeton, N.J., 1974.

Mailer, Norman. THE DEER PARK. Putnam, New York, 1955.

Mandel, Loring. ADVISE AND CONSENT. New York: Samuel French, 1961.

Marcus, Frank. THE WINDOW. New York, Samuel French, 1970.

Marlowe, Christopher. EDWARD II. New York: Avon, 1974.

McNally, Terrence. AND THINGS THAT GO BUMP IN THE NIGHT in *Playwrights for Tomorrow, Vol 1*. Minneapolis: University of Minnesota Press, 1966.

————. BRINGING IT ALL BACK HOME in *Three Plays*. New York: Dramatists Play Service, 1970.

————. NOON in *Morning, Noon and Night*. New York: Random House, 1968.

————. THE RITZ in *The Ritz and Other Plays*. New York: Dodd, Mead, 1976.

————. WHERE HAS TOMMY FLOWERS GONE? New York: Dramatists Play Service, 1972.

Miller, Arthur. A VIEW FROM THE BRIDGE. New York: Viking Press, 1955.

Milligan, Andy. COCTEAU. Players Theater, New York, 1972.

Nash, N. Richard. GIRLS OF SUMMER. New York: Samuel French, 1957.

Nolte, Charles. DO NOT PASS GO in *Minnesota Showcase: Four Plays*. Minneapolis: University of Minnesota Press, 1975.

Orton, Joe. CRIMES OF PASSION in *The Complete Plays of Joe Orton*. New York: Grove Press, 1977.

————. LOOT. New York: Grove Press, 1968.

————. WHAT THE BUTLER SAW. New York: Grove Press, 1970.

Osborne, John. THE BLOOD OF THE BAMBERGS in *Plays for England*. London: Faber and Faber, 1963.

————. THE ENTERTAINER. London: Faber and Faber, 1957.

————. THE HOTEL IN AMSTERDAM in *Time Present and The Hotel in Amsterdam*. London: Faber and Faber, 1968.

————. INADMISSABLE EVIDENCE. London: Faber and Faber, 1965.

————. A PATRIOT FOR ME. New York: Dodd, Mead, 1973.

————. THE PICTURE OF DORIAN GRAY: A MORAL ENTERTAINMENT. London: Faber and Faber, 1973.

Palmer, John. A TOUCH OF GOD IN THE GOLDEN AGE. Toronto: Playrights Co-op Press, 1971.

Parker, Dorothy, and d'Usseau, Arnaud. LADIES OF THE CORRIDOR. New York: Samuel French, 1954.

Patrick, Robert. ABSOLUTE POWER OVER MOVIE STARS. Old Reliable Theater, New York, 1968.

————. ANGEL, HONEY, BABY, DARLING, DEAR. Old Reliable Theater, New York, 1968.

————. DIAGHILEV AND NIJINSKY. Los Angeles: *Era* magazine, Nos. 2, 3, 4, 1974.

————. DYNEL. Old Reliable Theater, New York, 1968.

————. FOG in *Now: Theater der Erfahrung*. Cologne: Verlag M. Dumont Schauberg, 1971.

————. HIPPY AS A LARK. New York: *Stage Lights* magazine, No. 2, 1973.

————. KENNEDY'S CHILDREN. New York: Random House, 1977.

————. LILY OF THE VALLEY OF THE DOLLS. Old Reliable Theater, New York, 1969.

————. LUDWIG AND WAGNER. Los Angeles: *Era* magazine, Nos. 2, 3, 4, 1974.

————. MERCY DROP. W.P.A. Theater, New York, 1973.

————. REPORT TO THE MAYOR. New York, Everyman Theater Company, 1977.

————. ROBERT PATRICK'S CHEEP THEATRICKS! (includes I CAME TO NEW YORK TO WRITE; THE HAUNTED HOST; JOYCE DYNEL; THE ARNOLD BLISS SHOW; ONE PERSON; PREGGIN AND LISS). New York: Samuel French, 1975.

————. THE SLEEPING BAG. Tony Bastiano's Workshop, New York, 1965.

————. UN BEL DI. New York: *Performance* magazine, March–April, 1973.

Perr, Harvey. THE WAR WIDOW. Glines Theater, New York, 1978.

Piñero, Miguel. SHORT EYES. New York: Hill & Wang, 1975.

Pinter, Harold. THE BASEMENT in *Tea Party and Other Plays*. New York: Grove Press, 1967.

————. THE BIRTHDAY PARTY. New York: Grove Press, 1961.

————. THE CARETAKER. New York: Grove Press, 1961.

————. THE COLLECTION in *Three Plays*. New York: Grove Press, 1962.

————. OLD TIMES. New York: Grove Press, 1972.

Rabe, David. IN THE BOOM BOOM ROOM. New York: Knopf, 1975.

————. STREAMERS. New York: Knopf, 1977.

Ragni, Jerome, and Rado, James. HAIR. New York: Pocket Books, 1969.

Rattigan, Terence. MAN AND BOY. New York: Samuel French, 1963.

————. ROSS: A DRAMATIC PORTRAIT. London: Hamish Hamilton, 1960.

Renard, Joseph. A BOY NAMED DOG. W.P.A. Theater, New York, 1974.

Roc, John. FIRE. New York: Atheneum, 1969.

Rochester, John Wilmot, Earl of. SODOM; OR THE QUINTESSENCE OF DEBAUCHERY. North Hollywood, Calif.: Brandon House, 1966.

Ronan, Richard L. HIPPOLYTUS. Iowa: Iowa Theater Lab, 1977.

Schary, Dore. THE DEVIL'S ADVOCATE. New York: Morrow, 1961.

Scoppetone, Sandra. HOME AGAIN, HOME AGAIN, JIGGITY-JIG. TOSOS, New York, 1974.

Shaffer, Peter. BLACK COMEDY, INCLUDING WHITE LIES. New York: Stein & Day, 1976.

———. FIVE FINGER EXERCISE. New York: Samuel French, 1958.

———. THE ROYAL HUNT OF THE SUN. London: Stein & Day, 1965.

Shairp, Mordaunt. THE GREEN BAY TREE. London: Allen and Unwin, 1933.

Sherman, Martin. PASSING BY. Glines Theater, New York, 1975.

Silver, Fred. IN GAY COMPANY. Little Hippodrome, New York, 1974.

Simo, A.M. BAYOU. Medusa's Revenge Theater, New York, 1977.

Sisley, Emily. THE FREDDIE CORVO SHOW. Glines Theater, New York, 1977.

Smith, Michael. COUNTRY MUSIC in *The Off-Off-Broadway Book.* Indianapolis: Bobbs-Merrill, 1972.

Spencer, Colin. SPITTING IMAGE in *Plays and Players.* London: September 1968.

Staten, P.S. A DISTURBANCE OF MIRRORS. Eugene O'Neill Memorial Theater Center, Waterford, Conn., 1976.

Stuart, Sebastian. NIGHT FEVER. Vandam Theater, New York, 1977.

Tavel, Ronald. ARENAS OF LUTETIA in *Experiments in Prose.* Chicago: Swallow Press, 1969.

———. *Bigfoot and Other Plays* (includes BOY ON THE STRAIGHTBACK CHAIR; THE LIFE OF JUANITA CASTRO; INDIRA GANDHI'S DARING DEVICE; KITCHENETTE; SHOWER). New York: Winter House, 1973.

———. CHRISTINA'S WORLD. Chicago: *Chicago Review*, Winter Spring, 1963.

———. GORILLA QUEEN in *The Best of Off-Off Broadway.* New York: Dutton, 1969.

———. THE LIFE OF LADY GODIVA in *The New Underground Theatre.* New York: Bantam, 1968.

———. THE OVENS OF ANITA ORANGEJUICE. Westbeth Theater, New York, 1978.

———. TARZAN OF THE FLICKS. Maplewood, N.J.: *Blacklist*, No. 6, 1965.

————. VINYL in *Clyde* magazine, New York: Vol. II, no. 2, 1966.

————. VINYL VISITS AN FM STATION. New York: *The Drama Review*, September 1970.

Terry, Megan. CALM DOWN, MOTHER in *Eight Plays from Off-Off-Broadway*. New York: Bobbs-Merrill, 1966.

————. SANIBAL AND CAPTIVA in *Spontaneous Combustion*. New York: Winter House, 1972.

————. WILLA-WILLIE-BILL'S DOPE GARDEN (A MEDITATION IN ONE ACT ON WILLA CATHER). New York: *Christopher Street* magazine, June 1978.

Tynan, Kenneth (*et al.*). OH, CALCUTTA! New York: Grove Press, 1969.

Vaccaro, John, and Roth, Bernard. PERSIA, A DESERT CHEAPIE. La Mama, New York, 1972.

Van Itallie, Jean-Claude. WAR. New York: Dramatists Play Service, 1967.

Vidal, Gore. THE BEST MAN. Boston: Little, Brown, 1960.

————. ROMULUS THE GREAT. New York: Dramatists Play Service, 1967.

Wakeman, Alan. SHIPS in *Homosexual Acts*. London: Interaction-Inprint, 1975.

Weiss, Jeff. A FUNNY WALK HOME. Caffe Cino, New York, 1967.

————. THE INTERNATIONAL WRESTLING MATCH. La Mama, New York, 1969.

————. PUSHOVER: AN OLD-FASHIONED HOMOSEXUAL MYSTERY PLAY. LaMama, New York, 1973.

————. THAT'S HOW THE RENT GETS PAID. LaMama, New York, 1966.

Wheeler, Hugh. BIG FISH, LITTLE FISH. New York: Random House, 1961.

————. LOOK WE'VE COME THROUGH in *Broadway's Beautiful Losers*. New York: Simon & Schuster, 1972.

Whitmore, George. THE CASEWORKER. Playwrights Horizons, New York, 1976.

Williams, Tennessee. CAMINO REAL. New York: New Directions, 1953.

————. CAT ON A HOT TIN ROOF. New York: New Directions, 1975.

————. CONFESSIONAL in *Dragon Country*. New York: New New Directions, 1970.

————. KINGDOM OF EARTH—THE SEVEN DESCENDENTS OF MYRTLE. New York: New Directions, 1968.

————. THE MUTILATED in *Dragon Country*. New York: New Directions, 1970.

————. SMALL CRAFT WARNINGS. New York: New Directions, 1972.

————. A STREETCAR NAMED DESIRE. New York: New Directions, 1947.

————. SUDDENLY, LAST SUMMER. New York: New Directions, 1958.

Wilson, Doric. AND NOW SHE DANCES. Caffe Cino, New York, 1961.

————. THE WEST STREET GANG. TOSOS Theater Co. at the Spike Bar, New York, 1977.

Wilson, Earl Jr. LET MY PEOPLE COME. The Village Gate, New York, 1974.

Wilson, Lanford. BALM IN GILEAD in *Balm in Gilead and Other Plays*. New York: Hill & Wang, 1965.

————. THE FIFTH OF JULY. Circle Repertory Co., New York, 1978.

————. THE GREAT NEBULA IN ORION in *The Great Nebula in Orion and Three Other Plays*. New York: Dramatists Play Service, 1972.

————. THE HOT L BALTIMORE. New York: Hill & Wang, 1973.

————. LEMON SKY. New York: Hill & Wang, 1970.

Wouk, Herman. NATURE'S WAY. Garden City, N.Y.: Doubleday, 1958.

ABOUT THE AUTHORS

Robert Patrick, author of *T-Shirts*, was born September 27, 1937, in Kilgore, Texas. During the Depression his family moved constantly through Texas, Arkansas, Louisiana, and Kansas as his father sought manual work in the oil fields. The only cultural constant was the pervasive pop-media web of radio, records, magazines, and films. Childhood dramatics based on films and fantasy employed his sisters and neighborhood children. In 1961 he wandered by accident into the Caffe Cino in Manhattan. There he hung out until 1964, when he wrote his first play, *The Haunted Host*, for Joe Cino. That play and *Camera Obscura* went on to off-Broadway and countless productions all over the world. He saw well over a hundred productions of his plays at the Cino, La Mama, Arts Elast, Playwrights Workshop, Playwrights Horizons, W.P.A., The Old Reliable, and other off-off houses before he left New York in 1973. His subsequent travels have been worldwide. The occasions for much of this wandering were productions of *Kennedy's Children*. Over twenty-five of his plays are published by Samuel French, Inc., and other publishers. Recent works include *Judas, My Cup Runneth Over*, and *Mutual Benefit Life*. He has received the Show Business Award, five Obie nominations from the *Village Voice*, and grants from both the Rockefeller Foundation and the New York State Council on the Arts. He is interested in traveling wherever his plays are done.

Boy Meets Boy is one of seven collaborations of **Bill Solly** and **Donald Ward.** The others include *100 Miles From Nowhere*, a musical about Canada that was produced off-off-Broadway in 1973–74; *Snow Job*, a farcical comedy about a frozen food convention; *Sweet William*, a musical about Shakespeare; and most recently, *The Great American Backstage Musical*, which has enjoyed successful runs in Los Angeles, San Francisco, and London. Solly and Ward are presently at work on a new musical concerning ancient mythology. Independently of Donald Ward, Bill Solly wrote songs for many years in London for various stars including Maurice Chevalier, Petula Clark, George Burns, and Marty Feldman, and the music and lyrics for the hit revue, *Danny La Rue at the Palace*, which ran for two years in the West End. He has also written two musical fairy tales that have been produced in New York and Los Angeles, *The Cat in the Castle* and *The Three Magic Mushrooms*. Bill Solly was born in Hamilton, Ontario, and Donald Ward in Toronto.

Susan Miller, author of *Confessions of a Female Disorder*, is the recipient of a Rockefeller Playwright-in-Residence Grant (1975), and a National Endowment for the Arts creative writing fellowship (1976). Her major theatrical work includes *Cross Country*, produced as a world premiere by the Mark Taper Forum in Los Angeles in 1976 and as a workshop by the Women's Interart Theater in New York, 1977. *Cross Country* was published in the anthology *West Coast Plays*. Another full-length play, *Flux*, first done as a "sideshow" by the Phoenix Repertory Company in New York, was also produced by the American Repertory Company in London. Most recently *Flux* was produced in workshop by Joseph Papp's New York Shakespeare Festival at the Public Theater in New York. Ms. Miller is the author of *Silverstein and Co.*; *Denim Lecture*; *Daddy*; and *A Commotion of Zebras*. Her television work includes the episode "Home Movie" of the ABC series *Family*, and a commissioned script for the PBS series *Visions*, called "Coming Back."

Lanford Wilson has been widely recognized as one of the most important new American playwrights. Born in Lebanon, Missouri, he was educated at San Diego State College and the University of Chicago. In 1963 his first play, *So Long at the Fair*, premiered at the Caffe Cino in New York. His next works were *Home Free!* and *The Madness of Lady Bright*, which set an off-off-Broadway record of 250 performances. In 1965 Wilson produced his first full-length play, *Balm in Gilead* at La Mama, where he also produced *The Rimers of Eldritch*, which received the Vernon Rice-Drama Desk Award for Best Play of 1967. Several of his plays have been first presented in regional theaters, including *The Gingham Dog* and *Lemon Sky*, both later seen on Broadway. He has written the libretto for Lee Hoiby's opera of Tennessee Williams' *Summer and Smoke* and an original film script with Williams for CBS, "The Migrants," that earned Wilson an Emmy nomination and a Christopher Award. Since becoming resident playwright for the Circle Repertory Company in 1970, his work for them has included *The Great Nebula in Orion*; *The Hot l Baltimore*, which premiered in 1973 and won the New York Drama Critics Circle, the Outer Circle Critics, and Obie awards, and moved to the Circle in the Square theater, where it ran for three years; *The Mound Builders*; *Serenading Louie*; *Brontosaurus*; and his latest full-length play, *The Fifth of July* (1978). Hill & Wang/Farrar, Straus & Giroux has published most of Wilson's work.

Joe Orton was born in Leicester, England, in 1933, and was battered to death by a former lover in August, 1967. He left school at sixteen and went to the Royal Academy of Dramatic Arts two years later. In 1962 he spent six months in prison for defacing library books. In 1964 his first play, *The Ruffian on the Stair*, was broadcast on the BBC radio and his first full-length play, *Entertaining Mr. Sloane* was staged in the West End, as was *Loot* two years later. *The Erpingham Camp* was televised in 1966 and staged at the Royal Court Theater in 1967 in a double bill with *Ruffian on the Stair*. His television plays, *The Good and Faithful Servant* and *Funeral Games*, were aired posthumously in 1967 and 1968. His last play, *What the Butler Saw*, was not staged until 1969. It was successfully revived by the Royal Court in 1975 in a season that also included

important revivals of *Loot* and *Entertaining Mr. Sloane.*
Loot and *Mr. Sloane* have been made into movies. Orton
also wrote a screenplay for the Beatles that was never
filmed. A novel, *Head to Toe*, was published in 1971.

Jane Chambers, author of *A Late Snow*, is both a playwright and novelist. She was born in South Carolina and
attended school in Florida and California. She is a graduate
of Goddard College, Plainfield, Vermont, has written for
television, and has had nine plays produced in professional
theaters. She has been the recipient of a Connecticut Public
Television Award for Best Original Religious Drama
(1971), the Rosenthal Poetry Award (1971), and a New
York State CAPS grant (1977). She was appointed a
Eugene O'Neill Playwright (1972), and her play, *Common
Garden Variety*, was produced at the Mark Taper Lab in
Los Angeles under the auspices of the Office for Advanced
Drama Research (1976). Among her other plays are
Mine!; *The Wife*; *Random Violence* (all produced at the
Women's Interart Theater in New York City); *Tales of the
Revolution and Other American Fables* (produced at the
Eugene O'Neill Theater, Waterford, Connecticut); and *One
Short Day at the Jamboree* (produced at Town Hall, New
York City). Her first novel, *The Burning*, was published
in 1978 by Jove Press.

Frank Marcus was born in Breslau, Germany, in 1928
and spent his childhood under the Nazis. In 1939 his family escaped to Britain. He presented his first play, *Minuet
for Stuffed Birds*, in 1950. Aside from *The Killing of Sister
George*, his stage works include *Cleo* (1965); *The Forma-
tion Dancers* (1964); *Studies of the Nude* (1967); *Mrs.
Mouse, Are You Within?* (1968); *Blank Pages* (1972);
Notes on a Love Affair (1972); and *Christmas Carol*
(1973). All his works are marked by a sympathetic understanding of the behavior of women. Marcus is also a distinguished theater critic, whose work appears in *Sunday
Telegraph* (London), *Plays and Players*, *London Magazine*,
and *The Dramatists' Guild Quarterly*.

Cornbury is the first of a trilogy of comedies that **William M. Hoffman** and **Anthony Holland** collaborated on. The second, *Shoe Palace Murray*, set in the theatrical shoe department of I. Miller's, was premiered in 1978 in San Francisco by the American Conservatory Theater (plays in progress series). Their third effort, *Cherry Orchard Part Two*, continues the trials of Mother Russia from 1903 to 2003. After Hoffman spent several years in book publishing—he is editor of three volumes of Hill & Wang's New American Plays series—he began writing for the Caffe Cino. Since that time he has written fifteen plays (four are published). *Thank You, Miss Victoria*, directed by Tom O'Horgan, played off-Broadway. His latest work, *A Book of Etiquette*, opened at La Mama in 1978. He has received a Guggenheim Fellowship and two National Endowment for the Arts grants. Hoffman also writes for television (CBS) and radio (Earplay). In addition to writing and directing plays, Anthony Holland has a reputation for being one of New York's most gifted actors. An original member of Second City, his stage work includes Jules Feiffer's *The White House Murder Case* (for which he won an Obie), Alan Schneider's revival of *Waiting for Godot*, and Joseph Heller's *We Bombed in New Haven*. His television credits include *M*A*S*H*; *The Mary Tyler Moore Show*; and *ABC Comedy News*. In film he has been seen in *Bye Bye Braverman*; *Klute*; *Hearts of the West*; and *House Calls*. Hoffman and Holland take turns typing and will travel anywhere to see their shows.

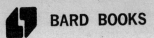 **BARD BOOKS**

distinguished modern fiction

A SELECTION OF RECENT TITLES

ANAIS NIN READER Philip K. Jason (Ed.)	36624	2.50
BETRAYED BY RITA HAYWORTH Manuel Puig	15206	1.65
BILLIARDS AT HALF-PAST NINE Heinrich Böll	32730	1.95
THE CLOWN Heinrich Böll	37523	2.25
DANGLING MAN Saul Bellow	24463	1.65
THE EYE OF THE HEART Barbara Howes, Ed.	20883	2.25
FERTIG Sol Yurick	21477	1.95
FLIGHT TO CANADA Ishmael Reed	35428	2.25
THE GREEN HOUSE Mario Vargas Llosa	15099	1.65
HERMAPHRODEITY Alan Friedman	16865	2.45
HOPSCOTCH Julio Cortázar	36731	2.95
HUNGER Knut Hamsun	26864	1.75
LEAF STORM And Other Stories Gabriel Garcia Márquez	35816	1.95
THE MORNING WATCH James Agee	28316	1.50
ONE HUNDRED YEARS OF SOLITUDE Gabriel Garcia Márquez	34033	2.50
NABOKOV'S DOZEN Vladimir Nabokov	15354	1.65
PRATER VIOLET Christopher Isherwood	36269	1.95
THE RECOGNITIONS William Gaddis	18572	2.65
62: A MODEL KIT Julio Cortázar	17558	1.65
THE VICTIM Saul Bellow	24273	1.75
THE WOMAN OF ANDROS Thornton Wilder	23630	1.65

Where better paperbacks are sold, or directly from the publisher. Include 50¢ per copy for postage and handling; allow 4-6 weeks for delivery.

Avon Books, Mail Order Dept.
224 W. 57th St., New York, N.Y. 10019

BDF 1-79

BARD BOOKS

DISTINGUISHED DRAMA

ARMS AND THE MAN George Bernard Shaw	01628	.60
CANDIDE Lillian Hellman	12211	1.65
THE CHANGING ROOM, HOME, THE CONTRACTOR: THREE PLAYS David Storey	22772	2.45
A HISTORY OF THE AMERICAN FILM Christopher Durang	39271	1.95
EQUUS Peter Shaffer	41996	1.95
THE FANTASTICKS Tom Jones and Harvey Schmidt	41152	1.75
FIVE PLAYS BY RONALD RIBMAN	40006	2.95
GHOSTS Henrik Ibsen	22152	.95
HEDDA GABLER Henrik Ibsen	24620	.95
THE INSPECTOR GENERAL Nikolai Gogol	28878	.95
THE IMPORTANCE OF BEING EARNEST Oscar Wilde	37473	1.25
GREAT SCENES FROM WORLD THEATRE VOLUME I James L. Steffensen, Jr.	42705	2.95
MEMOIR John Murrell	38521	1.95
MISS JULIE August Strindberg	36855	.95
OUR TOWN Thornton Wilder	42054	1.50
THE PLAYBOY OF THE WESTERN WORLD John Millington Synge	22046	.95
THE CHERRY ORCHARD Anton Chekhov	36848	.95
THE SEA GULL Anton Chekhov	24638	.95
THE SHADOW BOX Michael Cristofer	36913	1.95
THREE PLAYS BY THORNTON WILDER Thornton Wilder	27623	2.25
UNCLE VANYA Anton Chekhov	18663	.75
THE WILD DUCK Henrik Ibsen	23093	.95